# Vital Statistics on Congress 1997–1998

# Vital Statistics on Congress 1997–1998

Norman J. Ornstein
*American Enterprise Institute*

Thomas E. Mann
*The Brookings Institution*

Michael J. Malbin
*State University of New York at Albany*

Congressional Quarterly Inc.
Washington, D.C.

Printed in the United States of America.

Library of Congress Catalog No. 87-659232
ISBN 1-56802-298-0; 1-56802-299-9 (pbk.)
ISSN 0896-9469

# Contents

# Tables and Figures

**Tables**

**Figures**

# Preface

The contemporary Congress seems in constant tumult. Members themselves, often unsure of their status at any given moment, regularly shift their legislative focus. And the 1994 Republican takeover of both chambers for the first time since 1952 has brought promises of more fundamental change. But exactly how different is the contemporary Congress from its predecessors in terms of its work product, its membership, its political orientation, or its performance. This ninth edition of *Vital Statistics on Congress, 1997–1998* is your lens through which to observe and evaluate the changing shape of politics and the legislative branch of government.

*Vital Statistics* has been published and regularly updated for eighteen years, beginning in the last year of the Carter administration. A glance at any table shows that a member who left in 1980 and won election again in 1996 would scarcely recognize the place, much less most of the members. Changes in the partisan balance, the characteristics of the members, the number of committees and subcommittees, and the staffs have all been considerable and not all linear.

One change has been in the size of Congress. After an explosive growth of government in the 1970s, there has been a focus on downsizing the federal government—including the legislative branch—coupled with a resurgence of concern over the federal budget deficit. The characteristics of the members themselves have also been changing. Increased retirement and incumbent defeats in the House have resulted in the greatest number in modern times of members in their first three terms. And the 1994 midterm elections witnessed a dramatic shift in the Democratic-Republican ratio within the different regions of the country, not to mention the historic change in party control. Today Congress finds itself responding to an increasingly energized public that is demanding change as well as greater accountability from all its elected officials.

The hostility toward Congress that dominated the landscape before the 1994 election was replaced with more satisfaction and complacency by 1996. In late 1997, for the first time in years, a plurality of Americans approved of the performance of Congress. But most lawmakers saw no magic formula to keep public approval high into the future.

How Congress reacts to public views and moods, and has reacted to it in the past, can teach us a great deal about politics in America. This book is intended for all those who watch Congress for that reason, or who observe it as journalists, political scientists, students, lobbyists, citizens, or even as staff and members of the institution.

A good portion of the data here can be found in various congressional reports or publications. Our intention in *Vital Statistics on Congress* is to bring it all together in one convenient volume. The book would not be possible without its many indirect contributors and those who helped us locate some piece of data or other. They include Congressional Quarterly, the Congressional Research Service, the Federal Election Commission, and the staffs of many House and Senate committees and offices. We are also indebted to Caren Barbara, Andrea Santoriello, Gordon Novod, and Beth E. Gray for their help in counting, compiling, checking, and rechecking data and to Amy S. Mitchell who worked very hard on this volume as she did on previous editions. A special debt is owed to her successor, Jeremy C. Pope, who organized and directed the research efforts, managed the compilation and editing, and added his own insights. And thanks to Dave Tarr, executive editor at CQ Books, and to Ann O'Malley for her accurate and thorough editing.

# 1

# Members of Congress

Chapter One provides data on the regional distribution, partisanship, seniority, and social characteristics of members of Congress. Table 1-1 and Figure 1-1 examine congressional apportionment within eight regions from 1910 (when the U.S. House of Representatives reached its permanent size of 435) through 1990. Between 1910 and 1990 the South and the West consistently gained seats, while the Border, New England, Mid-Atlantic, and Plains regions consistently lost them. In addition, the 1980 census brought a major gain to the Rocky Mountain states. Since 1960 the most notable losses have come in the Mid-Atlantic, the Midwest, and the Plains regions, led by New York (down from a high of forty-five seats in the 1940s to thirty-one in the 1990s) and Pennsylvania (down from thirty-three to twenty-one seats in the same period). The 1990 census revealed that these trends continued unabated, with considerable gains for Florida, Texas, and California, and notable losses for several Northeast and Midwest states. In the 1990s California has by far the largest congressional delegation followed by New York, Texas, and Florida. (In the 1940s New York had the largest congressional delegation, followed by Pennsylvania, Illinois, Ohio, and California.)

Shifts in the number of House seats have been accompanied by changes in the ratio of Democrats to Republicans within all the various regions (see Tables 1-2 and 1-3 and Figure 1-2). In the 1920s, for example, the Democrats completely dominated the South and had a substantial edge in the Border states, while the Republicans were dominant in six other regions, particularly New England, the Midwest, and the Plains states. By the mid-1930s, the Democrats had taken control of every region except New England and the Plains (which together had only 63 of the 435 seats). Although Democratic strength in several of these regions fell during the 1940s and 1950s, they dominated into the 1960s. Only in the sparsely populated Plains states did the Republicans have a marked advantage; they also maintained a sizable majority in the Midwest.

By 1980 the regional map of party strength had changed again, and it continued to change throughout the decade. The Democratic proportion of southern and Border state seats fell from the 90 percent to the 65 percent range, reflecting the increased competitiveness of the parties in these areas. Similarly, Democratic Party strength in the Rocky Mountain states fell from 73.3 percent of the seats in 1960 to 36.8 percent after the 1980 election and to 29.2 percent after 1984, indicating a marked Republican resurgence. But the Democrats rebounded, reaching near parity with Republicans in 1990, with 45.8 percent of the seats and maintaining that level following the 1992 election.

The 1994 elections altered the House map dramatically when Republicans won seats almost across the board and reached an overall majority. The only region where the GOP did not capture at least 50 percent of the House seats was New England, where Democrats gained 3 percentage points to reach 63.6. The most significant GOP advancements came in the Rocky Mountain, Pacific Coast, Border, and southern states. Republicans had slowly been making advancements in the South until, in this election, they handily won a majority of the seats for the first time since Reconstruction. Prior to the election, the only southern state in which Republicans held a majority of House seats was Florida. After 1996 the Republicans held majorities in Alabama, Florida, Georgia, Louisiana, Mississippi, South Carolina, and Tennessee; with the Democrats holding Texas and Virginia; and ties in North Carolina and Arkansas.

While Democrats made overall gains in 1996, the major regional forces that were at work in 1994 remained strong. In the South and Rocky Mountain states Democratic strength fell to 43.2 and 20.8 percent, respectively. Democrats made minor gains in the Mid-Atlantic, Midwest, and Pacific regions, and solidified control over New England, taking over 80 percent of the seats. It was not enough though, as the larger number of total southern seats insured a continuing Republican majority in the 105th Congress.

As Table 1-3 demonstrates, the changes in state apportionments and party strength across regions have important implications for the regional composition of the political parties within Congress. In the 1920s the Democratic Party in the House was dominated by the Deep South. Most Republican members of the House were from the East and the Midwest. By the 1940s representatives from the South no longer constituted a majority of the Democratic Party but a sizable plurality (a majority if one includes Border states), while Republican strength remained concentrated in the East and the Midwest.

By 1990 both parties had changed substantially in regional character. House Democrats still include more members from the South than from any other region, but the proportion has dropped to only 26.1 percent with increased shares from the Mid-Atlantic, the Midwest, and the Pacific Coast regions. Together these three regions made up nearly half of House Democrats. Republicans had gained an increased proportion of members from the South and the Rocky Mountain states, with some decline in the Mid-Atlantic, Plains, and New England regions. In fact, by 1996, Republicans held only four seats in New England, their worst regional showing since the New Deal era in the South. The Republicans remain in the majority on the strength of their superior level of support in the South and the West, with strong representation in the Plains states. It is clear from Table l-3 that in the past several decades there has been a transformation of the South and several other regions that has changed the nature of both parties in Congress.

Tables 1-4 and 1-5 reveal similar trends in the Senate. The tables show the changes in the Senate with the advent of Republican control in 1980, the Democrats' return to power in 1986, and then the Republican takeover in 1994. The shifting party fortunes in the South are particularly noteworthy. The Republican majority in the Senate now rests upon its dominance of the Rocky Mountain and southern states.

A comparison of Table 1-5 with Table 1-3 shows that although broad party trends over time are similar for the House and the Senate, the different bases of elections for the two bodies lead to significant differences in the regional makeup of the House and Senate Democratic and Republican parties. Both Senate parties (but especially the Republicans) show considerably more Plains, Rocky Mountain, and New England influence than their House counterparts do because these three regions, although sparsely populated, elect forty senators.

Conversely, the House Democratic and Republican parties have greater proportions of members from the Mid-Atlantic and Midwest regions than the Senate parties do. The Republican share of the post-1996 Senate from the Midwest and Mid-Atlantic regions was only 7.3 percent each, compared with 16.2 and 13.6 percent for the House Republican Party in the Midwest and Mid-Atlantic regions, respectively. Another interesting element of the Senate party configurations is that Republicans from the southern and Rocky Mountain states make up more than 45 percent of Senate Republicans while Senate Democrats are more evenly divided among the eight regions. Regional differences within parties and across chambers have interesting implications for House-versus-Senate responses to future Sunbelt-Frostbelt or other regional tensions that may flare in the coming decade: energy, economics, and the environment.

Tables 1-6 and 1-7 show the seniority of members of the House and Senate since 1953. Throughout the 1960s there was a steady increase in the proportion of very senior House members—"careerists"—and an intermittent but real decline in the proportion of very junior legislators (see Table 1-6). Both trends peaked at the beginning of the Ninety-second Congress (1971)—the twenty-year club reached 20 percent of the House membership, while the proportion that had served six years or less fell to 34 percent. It was the peak as well in mean terms served.

These trends reversed dramatically during the 1970s. In the Ninety-seventh Congress (1981-1982), junior members made up 47 percent of the House and the careerists only 11 percent. A 1.7-to-1 ratio of juniors to seniors in 1971 had changed to a 4.3-to-1 ratio in only a decade. The record number of retirements after the Vietnam War was the major factor in this decline of seniority in the House. Clearly these changes contributed to the reforms enacted in the House during the same period. However, by 1991 the cycle had nearly come full circle; the ratio was down to 1.8-to-1 (approaching the 1.7-to-1 ratio from 1971) reflecting the low turnover in 1984-1990 House elections. In the 102d Congress, the number of senior members reached its highest level (17 percent of the members having served ten or more terms) since 1973. This trend would not continue, however, as 1992 marked a year of significant change in Congress. A near record number of retirements, as well as a significant number of primary and general election defeats, paved the way for a large influx of new members. The 110-member freshman class of the 103d Congress was the largest of its kind since 1949. The number of senior members decreased somewhat, from 17 percent in the 102d Congress to 15 percent in the 103d, as did the percentage of members serving four to six and seven to nine terms.

The shift toward a more junior House continued in 1994. The members serving their second term leapt from 9 percent in 1992 to 23 percent in 1994. There were eighty-six freshmen in 1994 so that over half of the representatives were serving their first, second, or third term, meaning 52 percent had come to Congress in the 1990s. The trend leveled off in 1996, but the percentage of representatives serving in their first three terms was still high at 56 percent and nearly 62 percent of the House has arrived in the 1990s. The number of members serving four to six terms declined from 25 percent in 1992 to 16 percent in 1996.

Table 1-7 shows years of service in the Senate over the same time span. In contrast to the House, a smaller proportion of the members of the Senate of the 1950s could be considered careerists. Senior senators with three terms or more made up only 6 percent to 10 percent of the Senate. This pattern began to change in the late 1950s and early 1960s, as the number of senators in their third term grew, and in the late 1960s, as the same people swelled the ranks of the most senior group.

At the low end of the seniority scale, other patterns prevail. The number of first-term senators, which averaged about forty in the 1950s and early 1960s, dropped markedly to an average of about thirty in the mid-1960s and reached a low point of twenty-five in 1971. The number of freshmen climbed again in the 1970s and, paralleling the House, hit a post-World War II high of forty-eight in 1979, then jumped to a remarkable fifty-five after the 1980 election. While there was a good size freshman class in 1992 (thirteen), the mean and median years of service in the Senate continued to rise, with the mean reaching its highest level since 1975 and the median surpassing its previous high of eleven years. In 1994 the number of senior senators reached twenty-five members—the highest number since at least 1953 (the earliest year we tabulated). Those senators serving seven to twelve years also increased sharply from seventeen to twenty-six. Conversely, the 1992 junior retirements combined with the 1994 departures and defeats cut the number of members in their second term by twelve, from thirty-two to twenty. In 1996 fourteen senators retired (including Bob Dole), bringing in one of the youngest classes in over a decade, with almost two-thirds of the senators serving in their first two terms.

Tables 1-8 through 1-13 list prior occupations of members of Congress by body and party from the 83d through the 104th Congresses. Overall, it is clear that lawyers, business executives, and bankers continue to dominate both houses of Congress, though in proportions somewhat different from those in earlier times: 39 percent of the current House membership and 54 percent of the senators are lawyers. Although these numbers are high, they do not compare with the Ninetieth Congress, when 56 percent of House members and 68 percent of the senators were lawyers. In fact while the number of lawyers has decreased in the last three congresses, the 1994 elections brought the share of House members with experience in business or banking to 37 percent, up from thirty percent in 1992. In 1996 the percentage of representatives with a business or banking background climbed to 42 percent—even eclipsing lawyers.

Among other significant occupations, the House and Senate have seen the number of farmers decline since the 1950s and 1960s, from an average of 11 or 12 percent in the House to around 5 percent and from 18 to 20 percent in the Senate to 8 percent. The number of educators in the House, which seemed to be on the decline in the 1980s, increased significantly with the election of the 102d Congress and has continued to rise. The figure now stands at 17 percent, up from less than 9 percent in the 100th Congress. Educators make up 13 percent of the current Senate.

There are party differences, though not startling ones, in occupation. More House Republicans than House Democrats come from the world of business and banking. And the gap seems to be widening. Currently, business people and bankers make up more than 55 percent of Republican House members and only 27 percent of Democratic members. More Democrats than Republicans in the House are lawyers and educators, though these disparities seem to be getting less extreme.

Tables 1-14 and 1-15 show the religious affiliations of members of both houses of Congress. Note the increase, since the 1960s, in the number of Catholics and Jews and the decline in the number of Methodists and Presbyterians. Patterns remained stable in the 1980s and 1990s, but with a steady increase in the number of Baptists.

Tables 1-16 through 1-18 show the number of blacks, Hispanics, and women, respectively, in Congress. Of particular interest is the party shift from the nineteenth century to the mid-twentieth for black members, their steep increase in the Ninety-first and Ninety-second Congresses, and the steep increases in the 1980s of Republican women. The 1990 election marked the first time a black Republican had been elected to the House of Representatives in more than a half century. Blacks made significant gains with the 1992 elections, due in large part to redistricting and the creation of new black majority districts mandated by the Voting Rights Act of 1965. They held onto these gains in 1994. Women also made substantial gains with the election of 1992. Although the total number of women in Congress did not increase in 1994, there was a significant shift in the party lines with five new Republican women. Women make up 12 percent of the House in the 105th Congress, compared with 6.4 percent in the 102d. There is a total of nine women in the Senate, an all time high in that chamber.

Table 1-19 traces the shifts in party members and partisan control in the House and Senate since the Thirty-fourth Congress in 1855-1857. The respective eras of Republican and Democratic dominance of Congress are clearly shown in this table. The consistent Democratic majorities in the past few decades make the Republican 1994 takeover of both the House and Senate, and their solidifying victory in 1996, all the more striking.

The Republican gains in recent elections are markedly regional in character. This has significant ramifications for future elections. If the GOP continues to win elections in growing regions like the West and the South, the nation may well see a true political realignment (though it is still too early to tell). This new regional character to politics makes very competitive regions like the Midwest crucial in future elections.

**Table 1-1** Apportionment of Congressional Seats, by Region and State, 1910–1990 (435 seats)

| *Region and state* | *1910* | *1930* | *1940* | *1950* | *1960* | *1970* | *1980* | *1990* |
|---|---|---|---|---|---|---|---|---|
| South | 104 | 102 | 105 | 106 | 106 | 108 | 116 | 125 |
| Alabama | 10 | 9 | 9 | 9 | 8 | 7 | 7 | 7 |
| Arkansas | 7 | 7 | 7 | 6 | 4 | 4 | 4 | 4 |
| Florida | 4 | 5 | 6 | 8 | 12 | 15 | 19 | 23 |
| Georgia | 12 | 10 | 10 | 10 | 10 | 10 | 10 | 11 |
| Louisiana | 8 | 8 | 8 | 8 | 8 | 8 | 8 | 7 |
| Mississippi | 8 | 7 | 7 | 6 | 5 | 5 | 5 | 5 |
| North Carolina | 10 | 11 | 12 | 12 | 11 | 11 | 11 | 12 |
| South Carolina | 7 | 6 | 6 | 6 | 6 | 6 | 6 | 6 |
| Tennessee | 10 | 9 | 10 | 9 | 9 | 8 | 9 | 9 |
| Texas | 18 | 21 | 21 | 22 | 23 | 24 | 27 | 30 |
| Virginia | 10 | 9 | 9 | 10 | 10 | 10 | 10 | 11 |
| Border | 47 | 43 | 42 | 38 | 36 | 35 | 34 | 32 |
| Kentucky | 11 | 9 | 9 | 8 | 7 | 7 | 7 | 6 |
| Maryland | 6 | 6 | 6 | 7 | 8 | 8 | 8 | 8 |
| Missouri | 16 | 13 | 13 | 11 | 10 | 10 | 9 | 9 |
| Oklahoma | 8 | 9 | 8 | 6 | 6 | 6 | 6 | 6 |
| West Virginia | 6 | 6 | 6 | 6 | 5 | 4 | 4 | 3 |
| New England | 32 | 29 | 28 | 28 | 25 | 25 | 24 | 23 |
| Connecticut | 5 | 6 | 6 | 6 | 6 | 6 | 6 | 6 |
| Maine | 4 | 3 | 3 | 3 | 2 | 2 | 2 | 2 |
| Massachusetts | 16 | 15 | 14 | 14 | 12 | 12 | 11 | 10 |
| New Hampshire | 2 | 2 | 2 | 2 | 2 | 2 | 2 | 2 |
| Rhode Island | 3 | 2 | 2 | 2 | 2 | 2 | 2 | 2 |
| Vermont | 2 | 1 | 1 | 1 | 1 | 1 | 1 | 1 |
| Mid-Atlantic | 92 | 94 | 93 | 88 | 84 | 80 | 72 | 66 |
| Delaware | 1 | 1 | 1 | 1 | 1 | 1 | 1 | 1 |
| New Jersey | 12 | 14 | 14 | 14 | 15 | 15 | 14 | 13 |
| New York | 43 | 45 | 45 | 43 | 41 | 39 | 34 | 31 |
| Pennsylvania | 36 | 34 | 33 | 30 | 27 | 25 | 23 | 21 |
| Midwest | 86 | 90 | 87 | 87 | 88 | 86 | 80 | 74 |
| Illinois | 27 | 27 | 26 | 25 | 24 | 24 | 22 | 20 |
| Indiana | 13 | 12 | 11 | 11 | 11 | 11 | 10 | 10 |
| Michigan | 13 | 17 | 17 | 18 | 19 | 19 | 18 | 16 |
| Ohio | 22 | 24 | 23 | 23 | 24 | 23 | 21 | 19 |
| Wisconsin | 11 | 10 | 10 | 10 | 10 | 9 | 9 | 9 |
| Plains | 41 | 34 | 31 | 31 | 27 | 25 | 24 | 22 |
| Iowa | 11 | 9 | 8 | 8 | 7 | 6 | 6 | 5 |
| Kansas | 8 | 7 | 6 | 6 | 5 | 5 | 5 | 4 |
| Minnesota | 10 | 9 | 9 | 9 | 8 | 8 | 8 | 8 |
| Nebraska | 6 | 5 | 4 | 4 | 3 | 3 | 3 | 3 |
| North Dakota | 3 | 2 | 2 | 2 | 2 | 1 | 1 | 1 |
| South Dakota | 3 | 2 | 2 | 2 | 2 | 2 | 1 | 1 |

*(Table continues)*

**Table 1-1** *(Continued)*

| *Region and state* | *1910* | *1930* | *1940* | *1950* | *1960* | *1970* | *1980* | *1990* |
|---|---|---|---|---|---|---|---|---|
| Rocky Mountain | 14 | 14 | 16 | 16 | 17 | 19 | 24 | 24 |
| Arizona | 1 | 1 | 2 | 2 | 3 | 4 | 5 | 6 |
| Colorado | 4 | 4 | 4 | 4 | 4 | 5 | 6 | 6 |
| Idaho | 2 | 2 | 2 | 2 | 2 | 2 | 2 | 2 |
| Montana | 2 | 2 | 2 | 2 | 2 | 2 | 2 | 1 |
| Nevada | 1 | 1 | 1 | 1 | 1 | 1 | 2 | 2 |
| New Mexico | 1[a] | 1 | 2 | 2 | 2 | 2 | 3 | 3 |
| Utah | 2 | 2 | 2 | 2 | 2 | 2 | 3 | 3 |
| Wyoming | 1 | 1 | 1 | 1 | 1 | 1 | 1 | 1 |
| Pacific Coast | 19 | 29 | 33 | 43 | 52 | 57 | 61 | 69 |
| Alaska | — | — | — | 1[b] | 1 | 1 | 1 | 1 |
| California | 11 | 20 | 23 | 30 | 38 | 43 | 45 | 52 |
| Hawaii | — | — | — | 1[b] | 2 | 2 | 2 | 2 |
| Oregon | 3 | 3 | 4 | 4 | 4 | 4 | 5 | 5 |
| Washington | 5 | 6 | 6 | 7 | 7 | 7 | 8 | 9 |

[a] New Mexico became a state in 1912; in 1910 it had a nonvoting delegate in Congress.
[b] Alaska became a state on January 3, 1959, Hawaii on August 21, 1959. In 1950 each had a non-voting delegate in Congress, making the total for that year 437; subsequent reapportionment reduced the total to 435.

*Sources: Congressional Quarterly's Guide to U.S. Elections* (Washington, D.C.: Congressional Quarterly, 1975), 531; *Congressional Quarterly's Guide to U.S. Elections,* 2d ed. (Washington, D.C.: Congressional Quarterly, 1985), 1125; Richard E. Cohen, "House Headed for a Big Reshuffling," *National Journal,* January 7, 1989, 25; *Congressional Quarterly Weekly Report,* December 29, 1990, 4240.

Figure 1-1 Apportionment of Congressional Seats by Region, 1910 and 1990

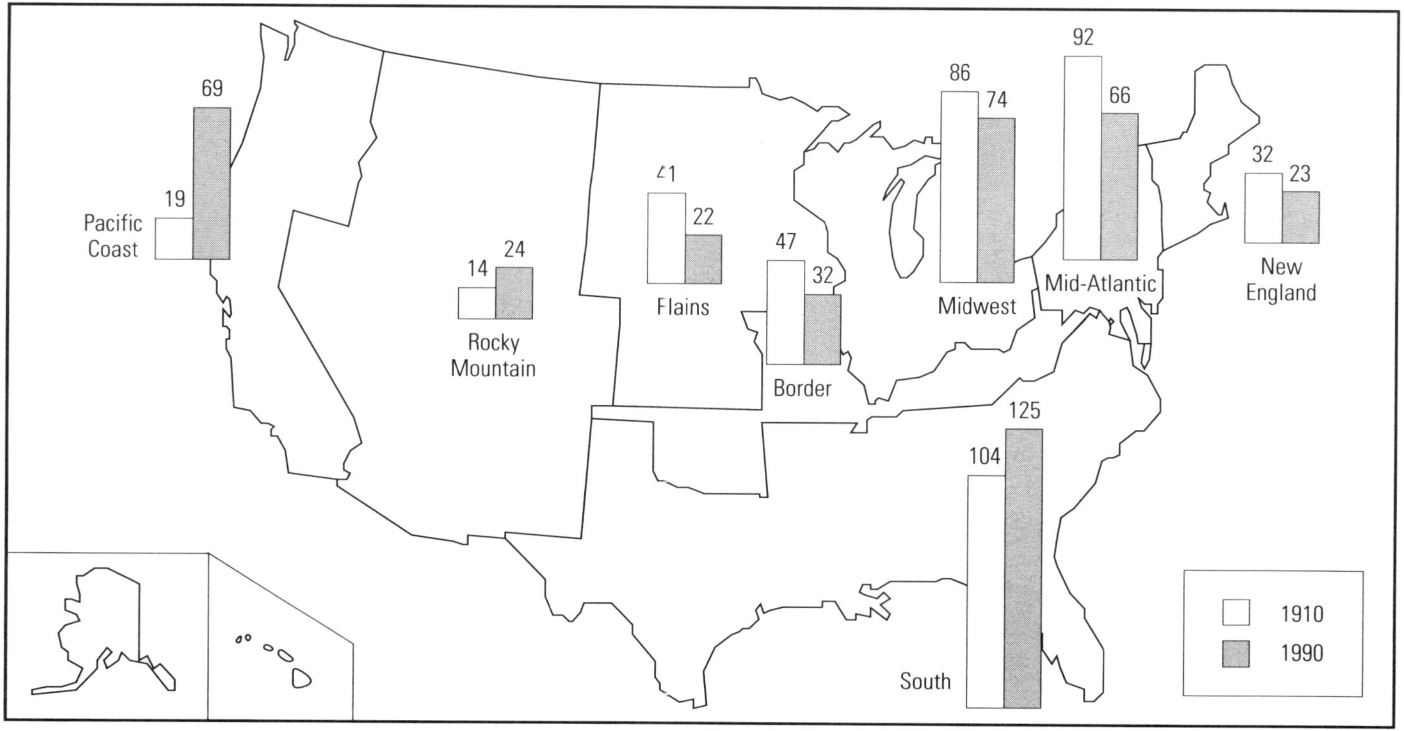


*Source:* Table 1-1.

**Table 1-2** Democratic Party Strength in the House, by Region, 1924–1996

| *Region* | *1924* | *1936* | *1948* | *1960* | *1972* | *1980* | *1982* | *1986* | *1988* | *1990* | *1992* | *1994* | *1996* |
|---|---|---|---|---|---|---|---|---|---|---|---|---|---|
| South | | | | | | | | | | | | | |
| Percent | 97.1 | 98.0 | 98.1 | 94.2 | 68.2 | 64.5 | 71.2 | 66.4 | 66.4 | 66.4 | 61.6 | 48.8 | 43.2 |
| Seats | 104 | 101 | 105 | 104 | 107 | 107 | 116 | 116 | 116 | 116 | 125 | 125 | 125 |
| Border | | | | | | | | | | | | | |
| Percent | 58.7 | 95.2 | 88.1 | 84.2 | 77.1 | 67.6 | 76.4 | 67.6 | 67.6 | 67.6 | 65.6 | 50.0 | 40.6 |
| Seats | 46 | 42 | 42 | 38 | 35 | 34 | 34 | 34 | 34 | 34 | 32 | 32 | 32 |
| New England | | | | | | | | | | | | | |
| Percent | 12.5 | 44.8 | 39.3 | 50.0 | 64.0 | 64.0 | 66.6 | 62.5 | 58.3 | 69.6 | 63.6 | 63.6 | 81.8 |
| Seats | 32 | 29 | 28 | 28 | 25 | 25 | 24 | 24 | 24 | 23[a] | 22[a] | 22[a] | 22[a] |
| Mid-Atlantic | | | | | | | | | | | | | |
| Percent | 26.7 | 68.0 | 48.9 | 49.4 | 53.8 | 53.8 | 58.3 | 56.9 | 58.3 | 56.9 | 54.5 | 50.0 | 53.0 |
| Seats | 90[b] | 94 | 92[c] | 87 | 80 | 80 | 72 | 72 | 72 | 72 | 66 | 66 | 66 |
| Midwest | | | | | | | | | | | | | |
| Percent | 16.9 | 78.3 | 43.7 | 40.7 | 38.4 | 51.2 | 55.0 | 57.5 | 58.8 | 61.2 | 58.1 | 43.2 | 50.0 |
| Seats | 83[d] | 83[e] | 87 | 86 | 86 | 84 | 80 | 80 | 80 | 80 | 74 | 74 | 74 |
| Plains | | | | | | | | | | | | | |
| Percent | 15.4 | 44.8 | 16.1 | 19.4 | 33.3 | 36.0 | 54.2 | 45.8 | 50.0 | 54.2 | 54.5 | 36.4 | 36.4 |
| Seats | 39[f] | 29[g] | 31 | 31 | 24 | 25 | 24 | 24 | 24 | 24 | 22 | 22 | 22 |

| | | | | | | | | | | | | | |
|---|---|---|---|---|---|---|---|---|---|---|---|---|---|
| Rocky Mountain | | | | | | | | | | | | | |
| Percent | 28.6 | 93.3 | 75.0 | 73.3 | 42.1 | 36.8 | 33.3 | 37.5 | 37.5 | 45.8 | 45.8 | 25.0 | 20.8 |
| Seats | 14 | 15 | 16 | 15 | 19 | 19 | 24 | 24 | 24 | 24 | 24 | 24 | 24 |
| Pacific Coast | | | | | | | | | | | | | |
| Percent | 19.0 | 80.0 | 36.3 | 51.2 | 57.9 | 56.1 | 62.3 | 59.0 | 59.0 | 60.6 | 63.8 | 49.3 | 55.1 |
| Seats | 21 | 30[h] | 33 | 43 | 57 | 57 | 61 | 61 | 61 | 61 | 69 | 69 | 69 |

*Note:* Numbers refer to the Congress that followed the election. Number of seats is total for all parties in the region (exceptions noted below). Does not include vacant seats. Discrepancy in the number of regional seats before and after 1980 is caused by post-1980 redistricting.

[a] Excludes one seat held by an Independent from Vermont.
[b] Excludes one seat held by a Socialist from New York.
[c] Excludes one seat occupied by a representative from New York who was a member of the American Labor Party.
[d] Excludes one seat held by a Socialist from Wisconsin.
[e] Excludes seven seats held by Progressives from Wisconsin.
[f] Excludes two seats occupied by representatives from Minnesota who were members of the Farmer Labor Party.
[g] Excludes five seats occupied by representatives from Minnesota who were members of the Farmer Labor Party.
[h] Excludes one seat held by a Progressive from California.

*Sources: Congressional Directory* (Washington, D.C.: U.S. Government Printing Office, 1925, 1937, 1949, 1961, 1973, 1981, 1983, 1985); *Congressional Quarterly Weekly Report,* November 8, 1986, 2843; November 22, 1986, 2958; November 12, 1988, 3269; November 10, 1990, 3802; November 7, 1992, 3571; November 12, 1994, 3236; November 9, 1996, 3226.

**Table 1-3** Democratic and Republican Seats in the House, by Region, 1924–1996

| | *1924* | | *1936* | | *1948* | | *1960* | | *1972* | | *1980* | | *1988* | | *1990* | | *1992* | | *1994* | | *1996* | |
|---|---|---|---|---|---|---|---|---|---|---|---|---|---|---|---|---|---|---|---|---|---|---|
| Region | D | R | D | R | D | R | D | R | D | R | D | R | D | R | D | R | D | R | D | R | D | R |
| South | | | | | | | | | | | | | | | | | | | | | | |
| Percent | 54.9 | 1.2 | 29.8 | 2.2 | 39.2 | 1.2 | 37.5 | 3.5 | 30.3 | 17.7 | 28.5 | 20.1 | 29.6 | 22.2 | 28.9 | 23.3 | 29.8 | 27.2 | 30.0 | 27.7 | 26.1 | 31.3 |
| Seats | 101 | 3 | 99 | 2 | 103 | 2 | 98 | 6 | 73 | 34 | 69 | 38 | 77 | 39 | 77 | 39 | 77 | 48 | 61 | 64 | 54 | 71 |
| Border | | | | | | | | | | | | | | | | | | | | | | |
| Percent | 14.7 | 7.8 | 12.0 | 2.2 | 14.1 | 2.9 | 12.3 | 3.5 | 11.2 | 4.2 | 9.5 | 5.8 | 8.8 | 6.2 | 8.6 | 6.6 | 8.1 | 6.2 | 7.9 | 6.9 | 6.3 | 8.3 |
| Seats | 27 | 19 | 40 | 2 | 37 | 5 | 32 | 6 | 27 | 8 | 23 | 11 | 23 | 11 | 23 | 11 | 21 | 11 | 16 | 16 | 13 | 19 |
| New England | | | | | | | | | | | | | | | | | | | | | | |
| Percent | 2.2 | 11.4 | 3.9 | 17.6 | 4.2 | 9.9 | 5.4 | 8.2 | 6.6 | 4.7 | 6.6 | 4.8 | 5.4 | 5.7 | 6.0 | 4.3 | 5.4 | 4.5 | 6.9 | 3.5 | 8.7 | 1.8 |
| Seats | 4 | 28 | 13 | 16 | 11 | 17 | 14 | 14 | 16 | 9 | 16 | 9 | 14 | 10 | 16 | 7 | 14 | 8 | 14 | 8 | 18 | 4 |
| Mid-Atlantic | | | | | | | | | | | | | | | | | | | | | | |
| Percent | 13.0 | 26.9 | 19.3 | 33.0 | 17.1 | 27.5 | 16.5 | 25.7 | 17.8 | 19.3 | 17.8 | 19.6 | 16.2 | 17.1 | 15.3 | 18.6 | 14.0 | 17.0 | 16.2 | 14.3 | 17.0 | 13.6 |
| Seats | 24 | 66 | 64 | 30 | 45 | 47 | 43 | 44 | 43 | 37 | 43 | 37 | 42 | 30 | 41 | 31 | 36 | 30 | 33 | 33 | 35 | 51 |
| Midwest | | | | | | | | | | | | | | | | | | | | | | |
| Percent | 7.6 | 28.2 | 19.6 | 19.8 | 14.4 | 28.7 | 13.4 | 29.8 | 13.7 | 27.6 | 17.8 | 21.7 | 18.1 | 18.9 | 18.4 | 18.6 | 16.7 | 17.6 | 15.8 | 18.2 | 18.0 | 16.2 |
| Seats | 14 | 69 | 65 | 18 | 38 | 49 | 35 | 51 | 33 | 53 | 43 | 41 | 47 | 33 | 49 | 31 | 43 | 31 | 32 | 42 | 37 | 37 |
| Plains | | | | | | | | | | | | | | | | | | | | | | |
| Percent | 3.3 | 13.5 | 4.0 | 17.6 | 1.9 | 15.2 | 2.3 | 14.6 | 3.3 | 8.3 | 3.7 | 8.5 | 4.6 | 6.9 | 4.9 | 6.6 | 4.6 | 5.7 | 3.9 | 6.1 | 3.4 | 6.1 |
| Seats | 6 | 33 | 13 | 16 | 5 | 26 | 6 | 25 | 8 | 16 | 9 | 16 | 12 | 12 | 13 | 11 | 12 | 10 | 8 | 14 | 8 | 14 |

| | | | | | | | | | | | | | | | | | | | | |
|---|---|---|---|---|---|---|---|---|---|---|---|---|---|---|---|---|---|---|---|---|
| Rocky Mountain | | | | | | | | | | | | | | | | | | | | |
| Percent | 2.2 | 4.1 | 4.2 | 1.1 | 4.6 | 2.3 | 4.2 | 2.3 | 3.3 | 5.7 | 2.9 | 6.3 | 3.5 | 8.6 | 4.1 | 7.8 | 4.3 | 7.4 | 3.0 | 7.8 | 2.4 | 8.3 |
| Seats | 4 | 10 | 14 | 1 | 12 | 4 | 11 | 4 | 8 | 11 | 7 | 12 | 9 | 15 | 11 | 13 | 11 | 13 | 6 | 18 | 5 | 19 |
| Pacific Coast | | | | | | | | | | | | | | | | | | | | |
| Percent | 2.2 | 6.9 | 7.2 | 6.6 | 4.6 | 12.3 | 8.4 | 12.3 | 13.7 | 12.5 | 13.2 | 13.2 | 13.8 | 14.3 | 13.8 | 14.4 | 17.0 | 14.2 | 16.7 | 15.2 | 18.4 | 13.6 |
| Seats | 4 | 17 | 24 | 6 | 12 | 21 | 22 | 21 | 33 | 24 | 32 | 25 | 36 | 25 | 37 | 24 | 44 | 25 | 34 | 35 | 38 | 31 |
| Total seats | 184 | 245 | 332 | 91 | 263 | 171[a] | 261 | 171 | 241 | 192 | 242 | 189 | 260 | 175 | 267 | 167[b] | 258 | 176[b] | 204 | 230[b] | 207 | 227[b] |

*Note:* D indicates Democrats; R indicates Republicans. Third-party members and vacant seats have been excluded. Percentages may not add to 100.0 because of rounding.

[a] There was one Independent elected in 1948.
[b] Bernard Sanders was elected as an Independent from Vermont.

*Sources: Congressional Directory,* 1925, 1937, 1949, 1961, 1973, 1981, 1983, 1985; *Congressional Quarterly Weekly Report,* November 12, 1988, 3269; November 10, 1990, 3802; November 7, 1992, 3571; November 12, 1994, 3236; November 9, 1996, 3226.

**Table 1-4** Democratic Party Strength in the Senate, by Region, 1924–1996

| *Region* | *1924* | *1936* | *1948* | *1960* | *1972* | *1980* | *1982* | *1984* | *1986* | *1988* | *1990* | *1992* | *1994* | *1996* |
|---|---|---|---|---|---|---|---|---|---|---|---|---|---|---|
| South | | | | | | | | | | | | | | |
| Percent | 100.0 | 100.0 | 100.0 | 100.0 | 68.2 | 54.4 | 50.0 | 54.5 | 72.7 | 68.2 | 68.2 | 59.1 | 40.9[a] | 31.8 |
| Seats | 22 | 22 | 22 | 22 | 22 | 22 | 22 | 22 | 22 | 22 | 22 | 22 | 22 | 22 |
| Border | | | | | | | | | | | | | | |
| Percent | 50.0 | 100.0 | 80.0 | 60.0 | 50.0 | 70.0 | 70.0 | 60.0 | 60.0 | 60.0 | 60.0 | 60.0 | 50.0 | 50.0 |
| Seats | 10 | 10 | 10 | 10 | 10 | 10 | 10 | 10 | 10 | 10 | 10 | 10 | 10 | 10 |
| New England | | | | | | | | | | | | | | |
| Percent | 8.3 | 50.0 | 25.0 | 41.7 | 58.3 | 50.0 | 50.0 | 50.0 | 50.0 | 58.3 | 58.3 | 58.3 | 50.0 | 50.0 |
| Seats | 12 | 12 | 12 | 12 | 12 | 12 | 12 | 12 | 12 | 12 | 12 | 12 | 12 | 12 |
| Mid-Atlantic | | | | | | | | | | | | | | |
| Percent | 37.5 | 75.0 | 37.5 | 25.0 | 25.0 | 50.0 | 50.0 | 50.0 | 50.0 | 50.0 | 50.0 | 62.5 | 50.0 | 50.0 |
| Seats | 8 | 8 | 8 | 8 | 8 | 8 | 8 | 8 | 8 | 8 | 8 | 8 | 8 | 8 |
| Midwest | | | | | | | | | | | | | | |
| Percent | 10.0 | 88.9 | 20.0 | 70.0 | 60.0 | 60.0 | 60.0 | 70.0 | 70.0 | 70.0 | 70.0 | 80.0 | 60.0 | 60.0 |
| Seats | 10 | 9[b] | 10 | 10 | 10 | 10 | 10 | 10 | 10 | 10 | 10 | 10 | 10 | 10 |
| Plains | | | | | | | | | | | | | | |
| Percent | 0.0 | 66.7 | 16.7 | 25.0 | 58.3 | 25.0 | 25.0 | 33.3 | 50.0 | 50.0 | 58.3 | 58.3 | 58.3 | 58.3 |
| Seats | 11[c] | 9[d] | 12 | 12 | 12 | 12 | 12 | 12 | 12 | 12 | 12 | 12 | 12 | 12 |

| | | | | | | | | | | | | | | |
|---|---|---|---|---|---|---|---|---|---|---|---|---|---|---|
| Rocky Mountain | | | | | | | | | | | | | | |
| Percent | 50.0 | 93.8 | 75.0 | 75.0 | 56.2 | 31.3 | 31.3 | 31.3 | 37.5 | 37.5 | 37.5 | 37.5 | 31.2[e] | 31.2 |
| Seats | 16 | 16 | 16 | 16 | 16 | 16 | 16 | 16 | 16 | 16 | 16 | 16 | 16 | 16 |
| Pacific Coast | | | | | | | | | | | | | | |
| Percent | 16.7 | 50.0 | 33.3 | 80.0 | 60.0 | 40.0 | 40.0 | 30.0 | 40.0 | 40.0 | 40.0 | 50.0 | 50.0 | 60.0 |
| Seats | 6 | 6 | 6 | 10 | 10 | 10 | 10 | 10 | 10 | 10 | 10 | 10 | 10 | 10 |

*Note:* Number of seats is total for all parties in the region (exceptions noted below).

[a] Includes Sen. Richard Shelby (Ala.) who switched from the Democratic to the Republican Party on the day following the election.
[b] Excludes one Progressive from Wisconsin.
[c] Excludes one senator from Minnesota who was a member of the Farmer Labor Party.
[d] Excludes two senators from Minnesota and one senator from Nebraska who were members of the Farmer Labor Party.
[e] Does not include Sen. Ben Nighthorse Campbell (Colo.) who switched from the Democratic to the Republican Party March 3, 1995.

*Sources: Congressional Directory,* 1925, 1937, 1949, 1961, 1973, 1981, 1983, 1985; *Congressional Quarterly Weekly Report,* November 8, 1986, 2812, 2839; November 12, 1988, 3264; November 10, 1990, 3826; November 7, 1992, 3558; November 12, 1994, 3236; November 9, 1996, 3226.

Figure 1-2 Democratic Party Strength in Congress, by Region, 1924–1996 (percentage of Democratic seats in regional delegation)

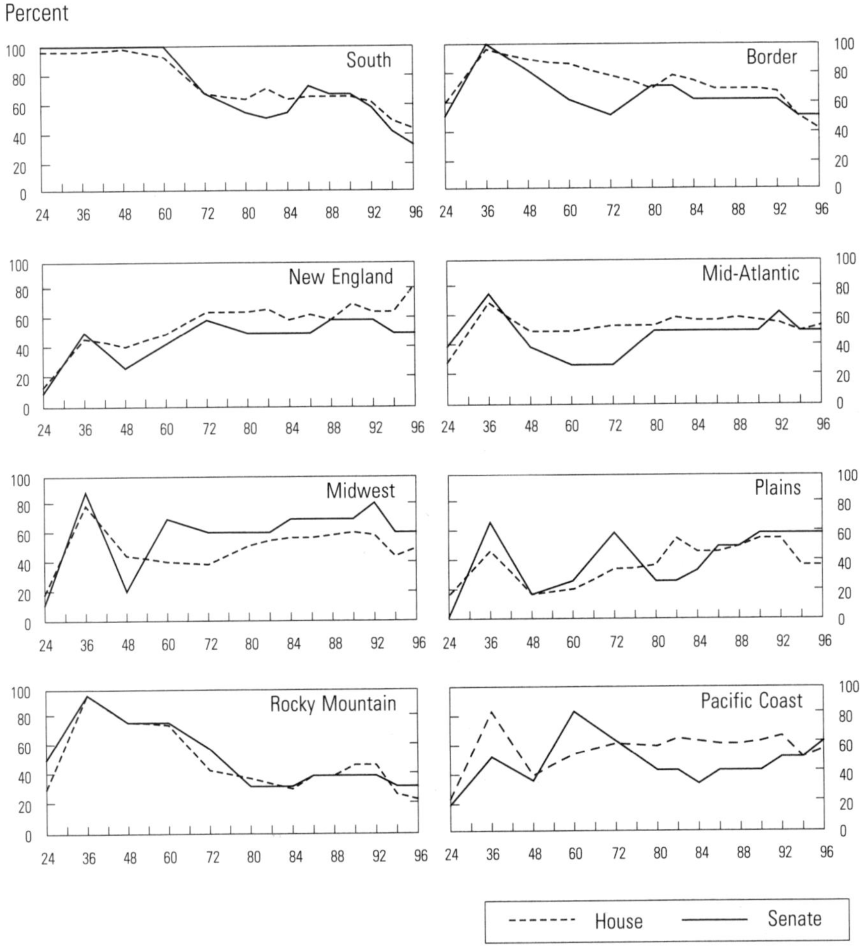


*Sources:* Tables 1-2 and 1-4.

**Table 1-5** Democratic and Republican Seats in the Senate, by Region, 1924–1996

| | *1924* | | *1936* | | *1948* | | *1960* | | *1972* | | *1980* | | *1988* | | *1990* | | *1992* | | *1994* | | *1996* | |
|---|---|---|---|---|---|---|---|---|---|---|---|---|---|---|---|---|---|---|---|---|---|---|
| *Region* | D | R | D | R | D | R | D | R | D | R | D | R | D | R | D | R | D | R | D | R | D | R |
| South | | | | | | | | | | | | | | | | | | | | | | |
| Percent | 53.7 | 0.0 | 28.9 | 0.0 | 40.7 | 0.0 | 33.8 | 0.0 | 26.3 | 16.3 | 25.5 | 18.9 | 27.3 | 15.6 | 26.8 | 15.9 | 22.8 | 20.9 | 19.1 | 24.5[a] | 15.6 | 27.3 |
| Seats | 22 | 0 | 22 | 0 | 22 | 0 | 22 | 0 | 15 | 7 | 12 | 10 | 15 | 7 | 15 | 7 | 13 | 9 | 9 | 13 | 7 | 15 |
| Border | | | | | | | | | | | | | | | | | | | | | | |
| Percent | 12.2 | 9.3 | 13.2 | 0.0 | 14.8 | 4.8 | 9.2 | 11.4 | 8.8 | 11.6 | 14.9 | 5.7 | 10.6 | 8.9 | 10.7 | 9.1 | 10.5 | 7.3 | 10.6 | 9.4 | 11.1 | 9.1 |
| Seats | 5 | 5 | 10 | 0 | 8 | 2 | 6 | 4 | 5 | 5 | 7 | 3 | 6 | 4 | 6 | 4 | 6 | 4 | 5 | 5 | 5 | 5 |
| New England | | | | | | | | | | | | | | | | | | | | | | |
| Percent | 2.4 | 20.4 | 7.9 | 37.5 | 5.6 | 21.4 | 7.7 | 20.0 | 12.3 | 11.6 | 12.8 | 11.3 | 12.7 | 11.1 | 12.5 | 11.4 | 12.3 | 11.6 | 12.8 | 11.3 | 13.3 | 10.9 |
| Seats | 1 | 11 | 6 | 6 | 3 | 9 | 5 | 7 | 7 | 5 | 6 | 6 | 7 | 5 | 7 | 5 | 7 | 5 | 6 | 6 | 6 | 6 |
| Mid-Atlantic | | | | | | | | | | | | | | | | | | | | | | |
| Percent | 7.3 | 9.3 | 7.9 | 12.5 | 5.6 | 11.9 | 3.1 | 17.1 | 3.5 | 13.9 | 8.5 | 7.5 | 7.3 | 8.9 | 7.1 | 9.1 | 8.8 | 7.0 | 8.5 | 7.5 | 8.9 | 7.3 |
| Seats | 3 | 5 | 6 | 2 | 3 | 5 | 2 | 6 | 2 | 6 | 4 | 4 | 4 | 4 | 4 | 4 | 5 | 3 | 4 | 4 | 4 | 4 |
| Midwest | | | | | | | | | | | | | | | | | | | | | | |
| Percent | 2.4 | 16.7 | 10.5 | 6.3 | 3.7 | 19.0 | 10.8 | 8.6 | 10.5 | 9.3 | 12.8 | 7.5 | 12.7 | 6.7 | 12.5 | 6.8 | 14.0 | 4.6 | 12.8 | 7.5 | 13.3 | 7.3 |
| Seats | 1 | 9 | 8 | 1 | 2 | 8 | 7 | 3 | 6 | 4 | 6 | 4 | 7 | 3 | 7 | 3 | 8 | 2 | 6 | 4 | 6 | 4 |
| Plains | | | | | | | | | | | | | | | | | | | | | | |
| Percent | 0.0 | 20.4 | 7.9 | 18.8 | 3.7 | 23.8 | 4.6 | 25.7 | 12.3 | 11.6 | 6.4 | 17.0 | 10.9 | 13.3 | 12.5 | 11.4 | 12.3 | 11.6 | 14.9 | 9.4 | 15.6 | 9.1 |
| Seats | 0 | 11 | 6 | 3 | 2 | 10 | 3 | 9 | 7 | 5 | 3 | 9 | 6 | 6 | 7 | 5 | 7 | 5 | 7 | 5 | 7 | 5 |

*(Table continues)*

**Table 1-5** *(Continued)*

| | | | | | | | | | | | | | | | | | | | | | | |
|---|---|---|---|---|---|---|---|---|---|---|---|---|---|---|---|---|---|---|---|---|---|---|
| Rocky Mountain | | | | | | | | | | | | | | | | | | | | | | |
| Percent | 19.5 | 14.8 | 19.7 | 6.3 | 22.2 | 9.5 | 18.5 | 11.4 | 15.8 | 16.3 | 10.6 | 20.8 | 10.9 | 22.2 | 10.7 | 22.7 | 10.5 | 23.2 | 10.6 | 20.8[b] | 11.1 | 20.0 |
| Seats | 8 | 8 | 15 | 1 | 12 | 4 | 12 | 4 | 9 | 7 | 5 | 11 | 6 | 10 | 6 | 10 | 6 | 10 | 5 | 11 | 5 | 11 |
| Pacific Coast | | | | | | | | | | | | | | | | | | | | | | |
| Percent | 2.4 | 9.3 | 3.9 | 18.8 | 3.7 | 9.5 | 12.3 | 5.7 | 10.5 | 9.3 | 8.5 | 11.3 | 7.3 | 13.3 | 7.1 | 13.6 | 8.8 | 11.6 | 10.6 | 9.4 | 13.3 | 7.3 |
| Seats | 1 | 5 | 3 | 3 | 2 | 4 | 8 | 2 | 6 | 4 | 4 | 6 | 4 | 6 | 4 | 6 | 5 | 5 | 5 | 5 | 6 | 4 |
| Total seats | 41 | 54 | 76 | 16 | 54 | 42 | 65 | 35 | 57 | 43 | 47 | 53 | 55 | 45 | 56 | 44 | 57 | 43 | 47 | 53 | 45 | 55 |

*Note:* D indicates Democrats; R indicates Republicans. Third-party members who did not caucus with either major party have been excluded. Percentages may not add to 100.0 because of rounding.

[a] Includes Sen. Richard Shelby (Ala.) who switched from the Democratic to the Republican Party on the day following the election.
[b] Does not include Sen. Ben Nighthorse Campbell (Colo.) who switched from the Democratic to the Republican Party on March 3, 1995.

*Sources: Congressional Directory,* 1925, 1937, 1949, 1961, 1973, 1981, 1983, 1985; *Congressional Quarterly Weekly Report,* November 12, 1988, 3264; November 10, 1990, 3826; November 7, 1992, 3558; November 12, 1994, 3236; November 9, 1996, 3226.

**Table 1-6** Seniority of Representatives, 1953–1997

| Congress | *Percentage of representatives serving* 1 term | 2 terms | 3 terms | 1–3 terms | 4–6 terms | 7–9 terms | 10 + terms | *Total* | *Mean term* | *Median term* |
|---|---|---|---|---|---|---|---|---|---|---|
| 83d (1953) | | | | | | | | | | |
| Percent | 19 | 17 | 15 | 50 | 27 | 13 | 9 | 100 | 4.5 | 3 |
| Seats | 81 | 73 | 64 | 218 | 117 | 58 | 40 | 433 | | |
| 84th (1955) | | | | | | | | | | |
| Percent | 13 | 17 | 14 | 44 | 27 | 17 | 12 | 100 | 5.0 | 4 |
| Seats | 57 | 73 | 63 | 193 | 119 | 73 | 50 | 435 | | |
| 85th (1957) | | | | | | | | | | |
| Percent | 11 | 12 | 15 | 38 | 33 | 15 | 15 | 100 | 5.4 | 4 |
| Seats | 46 | 50 | 66 | 162 | 142 | 66 | 63 | 433 | | |
| 86th (1959) | | | | | | | | | | |
| Percent | 19 | 10 | 11 | 40 | 31 | 15 | 13 | 100 | 5.2 | 4 |
| Seats | 82 | 45 | 49 | 176 | 136 | 64 | 57 | 436[a] | | |
| 87th (1961) | | | | | | | | | | |
| Percent | 14 | 15 | 8 | 37 | 30 | 17 | 15 | 100 | 5.5 | 5 |
| Seats | 62 | 65 | 36 | 163 | 131 | 76 | 67 | 437[b] | | |
| 88th (1963) | | | | | | | | | | |
| Percent | 15 | 14 | 12 | 42 | 24 | 18 | 16 | 100 | 5.5 | 5 |
| Seats | 67 | 62 | 53 | 182 | 106 | 78 | 68 | 434 | | |
| 89th (1965) | | | | | | | | | | |
| Percent | 21 | 13 | 11 | 46 | 22 | 17 | 15 | 100 | 5.1 | 4 |
| Seats | 91 | 58 | 49 | 198 | 97 | 73 | 67 | 435 | | |
| 90th (1967) | | | | | | | | | | |
| Percent | 17 | 15 | 11 | 42 | 25 | 16 | 17 | 100 | 5.3 | 4 |
| Seats | 73 | 64 | 47 | 184 | 108 | 69 | 74 | 435 | | |
| 91st (1969) | | | | | | | | | | |
| Percent | 9 | 17 | 13 | 39 | 29 | 15 | 17 | 100 | 5.6 | 5 |
| Seats | 40 | 75 | 56 | 171 | 126 | 65 | 73 | 435 | | |
| 92d (1971) | | | | | | | | | | |
| Percent | 13 | 10 | 15 | 37 | 28 | 16 | 19 | 100 | 5.8 | 5 |
| Seats | 56 | 42 | 64 | 162 | 121 | 68 | 83 | 434 | | |
| 93d (1973) | | | | | | | | | | |
| Percent | 16 | 13 | 9 | 38 | 29 | 15 | 17 | 100 | 5.5 | 5 |
| Seats | 69 | 55 | 38 | 162 | 128 | 66 | 76 | 432 | | |
| 94th (1975) | | | | | | | | | | |
| Percent | 21 | 15 | 9 | 45 | 23 | 18 | 14 | 100 | 5.2 | 4 |
| Seats | 92 | 64 | 40 | 196 | 100 | 78 | 61 | 435 | | |
| 95th (1977) | | | | | | | | | | |
| Percent | 15 | 22 | 13 | 50 | 20 | 16 | 14 | 100 | 4.9 | 3 |
| Seats | 67 | 94 | 58 | 219 | 87 | 70 | 59 | 435 | | |

*(Table continues)*

**Table 1-6** *(Continued)*

| | *Percentage of representatives serving* | | | | | | | | | |
|---|---|---|---|---|---|---|---|---|---|---|
| *Congress* | 1 term | 2 terms | 3 terms | 1–3 terms | 4–6 terms | 7–9 terms | 10 + terms | *Total* | *Mean term* | *Median term* |
| 96th (1979) | | | | | | | | | | |
| Percent | 18 | 15 | 18 | 51 | 22 | 15 | 12 | 100 | 4.8 | 3 |
| Seats | 77 | 64 | 78 | 219 | 95 | 65 | 54 | 433 | | |
| 97th (1981) | | | | | | | | | | |
| Percent | 17 | 17 | 14 | 48 | 28 | 13 | 11 | 100 | 4.7 | 4 |
| Seats | 74 | 76 | 59 | 209 | 121 | 56 | 49 | 435 | | |
| 98th (1983) | | | | | | | | | | |
| Percent | 18 | 15 | 15 | 48 | 29 | 10 | 12 | 100 | 4.7 | 4 |
| Seats | 80 | 64 | 66 | 210 | 125 | 45 | 54 | 434 | | |
| 99th (1985) | | | | | | | | | | |
| Percent | 10 | 18 | 14 | 42 | 32 | 13 | 12 | 100 | 5.1 | 4 |
| Seats | 43 | 79 | 62 | 184 | 138 | 58 | 54 | 434 | | |
| 100th (1987) | | | | | | | | | | |
| Percent | 11 | 9 | 17 | 37 | 33 | 15 | 16 | 100 | 5.5 | 5 |
| Seats | 50 | 38 | 75 | 163 | 143 | 64 | 65 | 435 | | |
| 101st (1989) | | | | | | | | | | |
| Percent | 8 | 12 | 8 | 28 | 38 | 20 | 14 | 100 | 5.8 | 5 |
| Seats | 33 | 54 | 33 | 120 | 167 | 86 | 60 | 433 | | |
| 102d (1991) | | | | | | | | | | |
| Percent | 10 | 9 | 11 | 32 | 31 | 21 | 17 | 100 | 6.1 | 5 |
| Seats | 44 | 41 | 48 | 133 | 137 | 91 | 74 | 435 | | |
| 103d (1993) | | | | | | | | | | |
| Percent | 25 | 10 | 9 | 44 | 25 | 16 | 15 | 100 | 5.2 | 4 |
| Seats | 110 | 44 | 38 | 192 | 109 | 69 | 65 | 435 | | |
| 104th (1995) | | | | | | | | | | |
| Percent | 20 | 22 | 9 | 51 | 16 | 18 | 14 | 100 | 4.9 | 3 |
| Seats | 86 | 97 | 37 | 220 | 78 | 78 | 59 | 435 | | |
| 105th (1997) | | | | | | | | | | |
| Percent | 18 | 17 | 20 | 56 | 16 | 15 | 13 | 100 | 4.8 | 3 |
| Seats | 79 | 76 | 88 | 243 | 71 | 65 | 56 | 435 | | |

*Note:* Terms are consecutive. Percentages may not add to totals because of rounding.

[a] Alaska was admitted as a state in 1958. The total figure includes the addition of Alaska's representative.

[b] Alaska was admitted as a state in 1958 and Hawaii in 1959. The total figure includes the addition of Alaska's and Hawaii's representatives. In 1963 the other states absorbed the proportionate loss in representatives necessary to give Alaska and Hawaii permanent representation under the 435-member figure established in 1911.

*Sources: Congressional Quarterly Almanac,* 1953–1994; *Congressional Quarterly Weekly Report,* January 10, 1981; January 8, 1983; December 27, 1986; January 7, 1989; January 12, 1991; January 16, 1993; February 18, 1995; February 22, 1997; *Congressional Directory,* 1962–1993.

**Table 1-7** Seniority of Senators, 1953–1997

| Congress | | *Number of senators serving* 6 years or less | 7–12 years | 13–18 years | 19 years or more | *Total* | *Mean years service* | *Median years service* |
|---|---|---|---|---|---|---|---|---|
| 83d | (1953) | 46 (16) | 29 | 14 | 7 | 96 | 8.5 | 7 |
| 84th | (1955) | 42 (14) | 37 | 8 | 9 | 96 | 8.4 | 7 |
| 85th | (1957) | 37 (10) | 36 | 13 | 10 | 96 | 9.6 | 9 |
| 86th | (1959) | 42 (20) | 30 | 14 | 12 | 98 | 9.4 | 8 |
| 87th | (1961) | 42 (7) | 25 | 22 | 11 | 100 | 9.7 | 9 |
| 88th | (1963) | 42 (12) | 26 | 18 | 14 | 100 | 9.9 | 7 |
| 89th | (1965) | 29 (8) | 36 | 16 | 19 | 100 | 11.1 | 9 |
| 90th | (1967) | 28 (7) | 34 | 19 | 19 | 100 | 11.6 | 9 |
| 91st | (1969) | 32 (14) | 32 | 17 | 19 | 100 | 11.2 | 11 |
| 92d | (1971) | 25 (10) | 24 | 29 | 22 | 100 | 11.5 | 11 |
| 93d | (1973) | 40 (13) | 20 | 20 | 20 | 100 | 11.2 | 9 |
| 94th | (1975) | 35 (11) | 22 | 23 | 19 | 99 | 11.5 | 9 |
| 95th | (1977) | 42 (17) | 25 | 13 | 20 | 100 | 10.6 | 9 |
| 96th | (1979) | 48 (20) | 24 | 10 | 18 | 100 | 9.6 | 7 |
| 97th | (1981) | 55 (18) | 20 | 10 | 15 | 100 | 8.5 | 5 |
| 98th | (1983) | 43 (5) | 28 | 16 | 13 | 100 | 9.6 | 7 |
| 99th | (1985) | 32 (7) | 38 | 18 | 12 | 100 | 10.1 | 9 |
| 100th | (1987) | 26 (13) | 44 | 16 | 14 | 100 | 9.6 | 8 |
| 101st | (1989) | 31 (10) | 26 | 29 | 14 | 100 | 9.8 | 10 |
| 102d | (1991) | 30 (5) | 23 | 28 | 19 | 100 | 11.1 | 11 |
| 103d | (1993) | 30 (13) | 17 | 32 | 21 | 100 | 11.3 | 12 |
| 104th | (1995) | 29 (11) | 26 | 20 | 25 | 100 | 12.3 | 11 |
| 105th | (1997) | 40 (15) | 24 | 13 | 23 | 100 | 11.2 | 9 |

*Note:* Figures in parentheses are the number of freshmen senators. Senators who are currently in their first full term are listed under the "6 years or less" column.

*Sources: Congressional Directory,* 1953 through 1985; *Congressional Quarterly Almanac* (Washington, D.C.: Congressional Quarterly, various years); *Congressional Quarterly Weekly Report,* October 11, 1986; November 8, 1986; November 12, 1988; November 19, 1988; November 10, 1990; *National Journal,* November 7, 1992, 2562; November 12, 1994, 2644; November 9, 1996.

**Table 1-8** Prior Occupations of Representatives, 83d–105th Congresses, 1953–1997

| *Occupation* | *83d* 1953 | *84th* 1955 | *86th* 1959 | *89th* 1965 | *90th* 1967 | *91st* 1969 | *92d* 1971 | *93d* 1973 | *94th* 1975 |
|---|---|---|---|---|---|---|---|---|---|
| Acting/ entertainer | — | — | — | — | — | — | — | — | — |
| Aeronautics | — | — | — | — | — | — | — | — | — |
| Agriculture | 53 | 51 | 45 | 44 | 39 | 34 | 36 | 38 | 31 |
| Business or banking | 131 | 127 | 130 | 156 | 161 | 159 | 145 | 155 | 140 |
| Clergy | — | — | — | 3 | 3 | 2 | 2 | 4 | 5 |
| Congressional aide | — | — | — | — | — | — | — | — | — |
| Education | 46 | 47 | 41 | 68 | 57 | 59 | 61 | 59 | 64 |
| Engineering | 5 | 5 | 3 | 9 | 6 | 6 | 3 | 2 | 3 |
| Journalism | 36 | 33 | 35 | 43 | 39 | 39 | 30 | 23 | 24 |
| Labor leader | — | — | — | 3 | 2 | 3 | 3 | 3 | 3 |
| Law | 247 | 245 | 242 | 247 | 246 | 242 | 236 | 221 | 221 |
| Law en- forcement | — | — | — | — | — | 2 | 1 | 2 | 2 |
| Medicine | 6 | 5 | 4 | 3 | 3 | 5 | 6 | 5 | 5 |
| Military | — | — | — | — | — | — | — | — | — |
| Professional sports | — | — | — | — | — | — | — | — | — |
| Public service/ politics | — | — | — | — | — | — | — | — | — |
| Veteran | 246 | 261 | 261 | 310 | 320 | 320 | 316 | 317 | 307 |

*Note:* Dashes indicate years and occupations for which Congressional Quarterly did not compile data.

[a] Includes Bernard Sanders (I-Vt.).

*Sources: Congressional Quarterly Almanac; Congressional Quarterly Weekly Report,* November 8, 1986, 2862; November 12, 1988, 3295; November 10, 1990, 3837; November 7, 1992, Supplement, 9; November 12, 1994, Supplement, 11; January 4, 1997, 29.

| *95th* | *96th* | *97th* | *98th* | *99th* | *100th* | *101st* | *102d* | *103d* | *104th* | *105th* |
|---|---|---|---|---|---|---|---|---|---|---|
| 1977 | 1979 | 1981 | 1983 | 1985 | 1987 | 1989 | 1991 | 1993 | 1995 | 1997 |
| — | — | — | — | — | 1 | 2 | 2 | 1 | 1 | 1 |
| — | — | — | 3 | 4 | 3 | 3 | 1 | 2 | 1 | 1 |
| 16 | 19 | 28 | 26 | 29 | 20 | 19 | 20 | 19 | 20 | 22 |
| 118 | 127 | 134 | 138 | 147 | 142 | 138 | 157 | 131 | 162 | 181 |
| 6 | 6 | 3 | 2 | 2 | 2 | 2 | 2 | 2 | 2 | 1 |
| 5 | 10 | 11 | 16 | 16 | — | — | — | — | — | — |
| 70 | 57 | 59 | 43 | 37 | 38 | 42 | 57[a] | 66[a] | 75[a] | 74[a] |
| 2 | 2 | 5 | 5 | 6 | 4 | 4 | 7 | 5 | 6 | 8 |
| 27 | 11 | 21 | 22 | 20 | 20 | 17 | 25[a] | 24[a] | 15[a] | 12[a] |
| 6 | 4 | 5 | 2 | 2 | 2 | 2 | 3 | 2 | 2 | 1 |
| 222 | 205 | 194 | 200 | 190 | 184 | 184 | 183 | 181 | 171 | 172 |
| 7 | 5 | 5 | 5 | 8 | 7 | 8 | 5 | 10 | 11 | 10 |
| 2 | 6 | 6 | 6 | 5 | 3 | 4 | 5 | 6 | 10 | 12 |
| — | — | — | 1 | 1 | 0 | 0 | 1 | 0 | 0 | 1 |
| — | — | — | 3 | 3 | 5 | 4 | 3 | 1 | 2 | 3 |
| — | — | — | — | — | 94 | 94 | 61 | 87 | 102 | 100 |
| — | — | — | — | — | — | — | — | — | — | — |

**Table 1-9** Prior Occupations of Democratic Representatives, 83d–105th Congresses, 1953–1997

| *Occupation* | *83d* 1953 | *84th* 1955 | *86th* 1959 | *89th* 1965 | *90th* 1967 | *91st* 1969 | *92d* 1971 | *93d* 1973 | *94th* 1975 |
|---|---|---|---|---|---|---|---|---|---|
| Acting/ entertainer | — | — | — | — | — | — | — | — | — |
| Aeronautics | — | — | — | — | — | — | — | — | — |
| Agriculture | 21 | 22 | 28 | 26 | 17 | 14 | 19 | 14 | 13 |
| Business or banking | 55 | 59 | 71 | 98 | 82 | 76 | 70 | 72 | 84 |
| Clergy | — | — | — | 2 | 1 | 1 | 1 | 2 | 4 |
| Congressional aide | — | — | — | — | — | — | — | — | — |
| Education | 18 | 26 | 30 | 54 | 43 | 40 | 39 | 41 | 51 |
| Engineering | 3 | 3 | 2 | 6 | 4 | 3 | 2 | 1 | 1 |
| Journalism | 18 | 16 | 21 | 27 | 22 | 22 | 17 | 16 | 19 |
| Labor leader | — | — | — | 3 | 2 | 3 | 3 | 3 | 3 |
| Law | 130 | 136 | 168 | 171 | 150 | 150 | 150 | 137 | 158 |
| Law enforcement | — | — | — | — | — | 1 | 1 | 1 | 2 |
| Medicine | 2 | 2 | 2 | 1 | 1 | 2 | 4 | 3 | 3 |
| Military | — | — | — | — | — | — | — | — | — |
| Professional sports | — | — | — | — | — | — | — | — | — |
| Public service/ politics | — | — | — | — | — | — | — | — | — |
| Veteran | 118 | 131 | 175 | 210 | 183 | 181 | 185 | 175 | 198 |
| Total number of Democratic members | 213 | 232 | 283 | 295 | 248 | 243 | 255 | 243 | 291 |

*Note:* Dashes indicate years and occupations for which Congressional Quarterly did not compile data.

*Sources: Congressional Quarterly Almanac,* various years; *Congressional Quarterly Weekly Report,* November 8, 1986, 2862; November 12, 1988, 3295; November 10, 1990, 3837; November 7, 1992, Supplement, 9; November 12, 1994, Supplement, 11; January 4, 1997, 29.

| *95th* 1977 | *96th* 1979 | *97th* 1981 | *98th* 1983 | *99th* 1985 | *100th* 1987 | *101st* 1989 | *102d* 1991 | *103d* 1993 | *104th* 1995 | *105th* 1997 |
|---|---|---|---|---|---|---|---|---|---|---|
| — | — | — | — | — | 0 | 1 | 1 | 0 | 0 | 0 |
| — | — | — | 0 | 1 | 0 | 0 | 0 | 0 | 0 | 0 |
| 6 | 10 | 11 | 13 | 13 | 10 | 8 | 11 | 7 | 6 | 8 |
| 69 | 71 | 58 | 73 | 72 | 66 | 66 | 77 | 56 | 46 | 55 |
| 4 | 4 | 2 | 2 | 2 | 2 | 2 | 2 | 1 | 1 | 1 |
| 3 | 7 | 9 | 10 | 10 | — | — | — | — | — | — |
| 56 | 44 | 39 | 29 | 24 | 24 | 25 | 37 | 45 | 39 | 40 |
| 0 | 0 | 2 | 2 | 2 | 2 | 2 | 4 | 2 | 1 | 1 |
| 15 | 6 | 9 | 13 | 10 | 11 | 9 | 14 | 11 | 4 | 4 |
| 6 | 3 | 4 | 2 | 2 | 2 | 2 | 3 | 2 | 1 | 1 |
| 154 | 135 | 121 | 132 | 122 | 122 | 122 | 126 | 122 | 93 | 87 |
| 7 | 4 | 4 | 2 | 6 | 6 | 6 | 4 | 8 | 7 | 8 |
| 1 | 1 | 2 | 2 | 3 | 1 | 2 | 3 | 4 | 2 | 3 |
| — | — | — | 0 | 0 | 0 | 0 | 0 | 0 | 0 | 0 |
| — | — | — | 2 | 2 | 3 | 3 | 2 | 0 | 0 | 0 |
| — | — | — | — | — | 59 | 58 | 41 | 51 | 53 | 54 |
| — | — | — | — | — | — | — | — | — | — | — |
| 292 | 277 | 243 | 267 | 253 | 258 | 260 | 267 | 258 | 204 | 207 |

**Table 1-10** Prior Occupations of Republican Representatives, 83d–105th Congresses, 1953–1997

| *Occupation* | *83d* 1953 | *84th* 1955 | *86th* 1959 | *89th* 1965 | *90th* 1967 | *91st* 1969 | *92d* 1971 | *93d* 1973 | *94th* 1975 |
|---|---|---|---|---|---|---|---|---|---|
| Acting/ entertainer | — | — | — | — | — | — | — | — | — |
| Aeronautics | — | — | — | — | — | — | — | — | — |
| Agriculture | 32 | 29 | 17 | 18 | 22 | 20 | 17 | 24 | 18 |
| Business or banking | 76 | 68 | 59 | 58 | 79 | 83 | 75 | 83 | 56 |
| Clergy | — | — | — | 1 | 2 | 1 | 1 | 2 | 1 |
| Congressional aide | — | — | — | — | — | — | — | — | — |
| Education | 28 | 21 | 11 | 14 | 14 | 19 | 22 | 18 | 13 |
| Engineering | 2 | 2 | 1 | 3 | 2 | 3 | 1 | 1 | 2 |
| Journalism | 18 | 17 | 14 | 16 | 17 | 17 | 13 | 7 | 5 |
| Labor leader | — | — | — | 0 | 0 | 0 | 0 | 0 | 0 |
| Law | 117 | 109 | 74 | 76 | 96 | 92 | 86 | 84 | 63 |
| Law en-forcement | — | — | — | — | — | 1 | 0 | 1 | 0 |
| Medicine | 4 | 3 | 2 | 2 | 2 | 3 | 2 | 2 | 2 |
| Military | — | — | — | — | — | — | — | — | — |
| Professional sports | — | — | — | — | — | — | — | — | — |
| Public service/ politics | — | — | — | — | — | — | — | — | — |
| Veteran | 128 | 130 | 86 | 100 | 137 | 139 | 131 | 142 | 109 |
| Total number of Republican members | 221 | 203 | 153 | 140 | 187 | 192 | 180 | 192 | 144 |

*Note:* Dashes indicate years and occupations for which Congressional Quarterly did not compile data.

*Sources: Congressional Quarterly Almanac,* various years; *Congressional Quarterly Weekly Report,* November 8, 1986, 2862; November 12, 1988, 3295; November 10, 1990, 3837; November 7, 1992, Supplement, 9; November 12, 1994, Supplement, 11; January 4, 1997, 29.

| *95th* 1977 | *96th* 1979 | *97th* 1981 | *98th* 1983 | *99th* 1985 | *100th* 1987 | *101st* 1989 | *102d* 1991 | *103d* 1993 | *104th* 1995 | *105th* 1997 |
|---|---|---|---|---|---|---|---|---|---|---|
| — | — | — | — | — | 1 | 1 | 1 | 1 | 1 | 1 |
| — | — | — | 3 | 3 | 3 | 3 | 1 | 2 | 1 | 1 |
| 10 | 9 | 17 | 13 | 16 | 10 | 11 | 9 | 12 | 14 | 14 |
| 49 | 56 | 76 | 65 | 75 | 76 | 72 | 80 | 75 | 116 | 126 |
| 2 | 2 | 1 | 0 | 0 | 0 | 0 | 0 | 1 | 1 | 0 |
| 2 | 3 | 2 | 6 | 6 | — | — | — | — | — | — |
| 14 | 13 | 20 | 14 | 13 | 14 | 17 | 19 | 20 | 35 | 33 |
| 2 | 2 | 3 | 3 | 4 | 2 | 2 | 3 | 3 | 5 | 7 |
| 12 | 5 | 12 | 9 | 10 | 9 | 8 | 10 | 12 | 10 | 7 |
| 0 | 1 | 1 | 0 | 0 | 0 | 0 | 0 | 0 | 1 | 0 |
| 68 | 70 | 73 | 68 | 68 | 62 | 62 | 57 | 59 | 78 | 85 |
| 0 | 1 | 1 | 3 | 2 | 1 | 2 | 1 | 2 | 4 | 2 |
| 1 | 5 | 4 | 4 | 2 | 2 | 2 | 2 | 2 | 8 | 9 |
| — | | | 1 | 1 | 0 | 0 | 1 | 0 | 0 | 1 |
| — | — | — | 1 | 1 | 2 | 1 | 1 | 1 | 2 | 3 |
| — | — | — | — | — | 35 | 36 | 20 | 36 | 49 | 46 |
| — | — | — | — | — | — | — | — | — | — | — |
| 143 | 158 | 192 | 167 | 182 | 177 | 175 | 167 | 176 | 230 | 227 |

**Table 1-11** Prior Occupations of Senators, 83d–105th Congresses, 1953–1997

| *Occupation* | *83d* 1953 | *84th* 1955 | *86th* 1959 | *89th* 1965 | *90th* 1967 | *91st* 1969 | *92d* 1971 | *93d* 1973 | *94th* 1975 |
|---|---|---|---|---|---|---|---|---|---|
| Acting/ entertainer | — | — | — | — | — | — | — | — | — |
| Aeronautics | — | — | — | — | — | — | — | — | — |
| Agriculture | 22 | 21 | 17 | 18 | 18 | 16 | 13 | 11 | 10 |
| Business or banking | 28 | 28 | 28 | 25 | 23 | 25 | 27 | 22 | 22 |
| Clergy | — | — | — | 0 | 0 | 0 | 0 | 0 | 0 |
| Congressional aide | — | — | — | — | — | — | — | — | — |
| Education | 17 | 17 | 16 | 16 | 15 | 14 | 11 | 10 | 8 |
| Engineering | 5 | 2 | 2 | 2 | 2 | 2 | 2 | 2 | 2 |
| Journalism | 10 | 10 | 13 | 10 | 10 | 8 | 7 | 5 | 5 |
| Labor leader | — | — | — | 1 | 0 | 0 | 0 | 0 | 0 |
| Law | 59 | 60 | 61 | 67 | 68 | 68 | 65 | 68 | 67 |
| Law en-forcement | — | — | — | — | — | 0 | 0 | 0 | 0 |
| Medicine | 1 | 2 | 1 | 1 | 1 | 0 | 1 | 1 | 1 |
| Military | — | — | — | — | — | — | — | — | — |
| Professional sports | — | — | — | — | — | — | — | — | — |
| Public service/ politics | — | — | — | — | — | — | — | — | — |
| Veteran | 63 | 62 | 61 | 63 | 65 | 69 | 73 | 73 | 73 |

*Note:* Dashes indicate years and occupations for which Congressional Quarterly did not compile data.

*Sources: Congressional Quarterly Almanac,* various years; *Congressional Quarterly Weekly Report,* November 8, 1986, 2862; November 12, 1988, 3295; November 10, 1990, 3837; November 7, 1992, Supplement, 9; November 12, 1994, Supplement, 11; January 4, 1997, 29.

| *95th* 1975 | *96th* 1977 | *97th* 1981 | *98th* 1983 | *99th* 1985 | *100th* 1987 | *101st* 19989 | *102d* 1991 | *103d* 1993 | *104th* 1995 | *105th* 1997 |
|---|---|---|---|---|---|---|---|---|---|---|
| — | — | — | — | — | 0 | 0 | 0 | 0 | 1 | 1 |
| — | — | — | 2 | 2 | 2 | 2 | 1 | 1 | 1 | 1 |
| 9 | 6 | 9 | 9 | 10 | 5 | 4 | 8 | 8 | 9 | 8 |
| 24 | 29 | 28 | 29 | 31 | 28 | 28 | 32 | 24 | 24 | 33 |
| 1 | 1 | 1 | 1 | 1 | 1 | 1 | 1 | 1 | 0 | 1 |
| 0 | 0 | 0 | 0 | 0 | — | — | — | — | — | — |
| 13 | 7 | 10 | 12 | 12 | 12 | 11 | 10 | 11 | 10 | 13 |
| 0 | 0 | 2 | 0 | 1 | 1 | 0 | 0 | 0 | 0 | 0 |
| 6 | 2 | 7 | 7 | 8 | 8 | 8 | 10 | 9 | 8 | 9 |
| 0 | 0 | 0 | 0 | 0 | 0 | 0 | 0 | 0 | 0 | 0 |
| 68 | 65 | 59 | 61 | 61 | 62 | 63 | 61 | 58 | 54 | 53 |
| 0 | 0 | 0 | 0 | 0 | 0 | 0 | 0 | 0 | 0 | 0 |
| 1 | 1 | 1 | 1 | 1 | 1 | 0 | 0 | 0 | 1 | 2 |
| — | — | — | 1 | 1 | 1 | 1 | 1 | 1 | 1 | 1 |
| — | — | — | 1 | 1 | 1 | 1 | 1 | 1 | 1 | 0 |
| — | — | — | — | — | 20 | 20 | 5 | 10 | 12 | 26 |
| — | — | — | — | — | — | — | — | — | — | — |

**Table 1-12** Prior Occupations of Democratic Senators, 83d–105th Congresses, 1953–1997

| *Occupation* | *83d* 1953 | *84th* 1955 | *86th* 1959 | *89th* 1965 | *90th* 1967 | *91st* 1969 | *92d* 1971 | *93d* 1973 | *94th* 1975 |
|---|---|---|---|---|---|---|---|---|---|
| Acting/ entertainer | — | — | — | — | — | — | — | — | — |
| Aeronautics | — | — | — | — | — | — | — | — | — |
| Agriculture | 8 | 7 | 7 | 10 | 9 | 7 | 5 | 4 | 5 |
| Business or banking | 11 | 10 | 14 | 14 | 12 | 12 | 15 | 12 | 12 |
| Clergy | — | — | — | 0 | 0 | 0 | 0 | 0 | 0 |
| Congressional aide | — | — | — | — | — | — | — | — | — |
| Education | 11 | 11 | 13 | 12 | 10 | 9 | 6 | 7 | 6 |
| Engineering | 2 | 0 | 2 | 2 | 2 | 2 | 2 | 2 | 2 |
| Journalism | 5 | 6 | 10 | 7 | 7 | 5 | 5 | 4 | 4 |
| Labor leader | — | — | — | 1 | 0 | 0 | 0 | 0 | 0 |
| Law | 34 | 27 | 43 | 48 | 48 | 42 | 41 | 42 | 45 |
| Law en- forcement | — | — | — | — | — | — | 0 | 0 | 0 |
| Medicine | 1 | 2 | 1 | 1 | 1 | 0 | 1 | 1 | 1 |
| Military | — | — | — | — | — | — | — | — | — |
| Professional sports | — | — | — | — | — | — | — | — | — |
| Public service/ politics | — | — | — | — | — | — | — | — | — |
| Veteran | 31 | 32 | 40 | 44 | 43 | 41 | 41 | 42 | 45 |
| Total number of Democratic members | 46 | 48 | 64 | 68 | 64 | 58 | 54 | 56 | 60 |

*Note:* Dashes indicate years and occupations for which Congressional Quarterly did not compile data.

*Sources: Congressional Quarterly Almanac,* various years, *Congressional Quarterly Weekly Report,* November 8, 1986, 2862; November 12, 1988, 3295; November 10, 1990, 3837; November 7, 1992, Supplement, 9; November 12, 1994, Supplement, 11; January 4, 1997, 29.

| *95th* 1977 | *96th* 1979 | *97th* 1981 | *98th* 1983 | *99th* 1985 | *100th* 1987 | *101st* 1989 | *102d* 1991 | *103d* 1993 | *104th* 1995 | *105th* 1997 |
|---|---|---|---|---|---|---|---|---|---|---|
| — | — | — | — | — | 0 | 0 | 0 | 0 | 0 | 0 |
| — | — | — | 1 | 1 | 1 | 1 | 1 | 1 | 1 | 1 |
| 3 | 2 | 2 | 2 | 3 | 2 | 1 | 3 | 3 | 4 | 2 |
| 14 | 15 | 13 | 14 | 12 | 13 | 13 | 15 | 12 | 11 | 8 |
| 0 | 0 | 0 | 0 | 0 | 0 | 0 | 0 | 0 | 0 | 0 |
| 0 | 0 | 0 | 0 | 0 | — | — | — | — | — | — |
| 8 | 4 | 5 | 5 | 4 | 6 | 6 | 6 | 6 | 5 | 5 |
| 0 | 0 | 1 | 0 | 0 | 0 | 0 | 0 | 0 | 0 | 0 |
| 4 | 2 | 4 | 5 | 6 | 6 | 5 | 8 | 7 | 5 | 2 |
| 0 | 0 | 0 | 0 | 0 | 0 | 0 | 0 | 0 | 0 | 0 |
| 46 | 43 | 33 | 32 | 32 | 35 | 36 | 35 | 33 | 26 | 26 |
| 0 | 0 | 0 | 0 | 0 | 0 | 0 | 0 | 0 | 0 | 0 |
| 1 | 1 | 1 | 1 | 1 | 1 | 0 | 0 | 0 | 0 | 0 |
| — | — | — | 0 | 1 | 0 | 0 | 0 | 0 | 0 | 0 |
| — | — | — | 1 | 0 | 1 | 1 | 1 | 1 | 1 | 0 |
| — | — | — | — | — | 13 | 14 | 4 | 8 | 7 | 9 |
| — | — | — | — | — | — | — | — | — | — | — |
| 61 | 58 | 46 | 46 | 47 | 55 | 55 | 56 | 57 | 47 | 45 |

**Table 1-13** Prior Occupations of Republican Senators, 83d–105th Congresses, 1953–1997

| *Occupation* | *83d* 1953 | *84th* 1955 | *86th* 1959 | *89th* 1965 | *90th* 1967 | *91st* 1969 | *92d* 1971 | *93d* 1973 | *94th* 1975 |
|---|---|---|---|---|---|---|---|---|---|
| Acting/ entertainer | — | — | — | — | — | — | — | — | — |
| Aeronautics | — | — | — | — | — | — | — | — | — |
| Agriculture | 14 | 14 | 10 | 8 | 9 | 9 | 8 | 7 | 5 |
| Business or banking | 17 | 18 | 14 | 11 | 11 | 13 | 12 | 10 | 10 |
| Clergy | — | — | — | 0 | 0 | 0 | 0 | 0 | 0 |
| Congressional aide | — | — | — | — | — | — | — | — | — |
| Education | 6 | 6 | 3 | 4 | 5 | 5 | 5 | 3 | 2 |
| Engineering | 3 | 2 | 0 | 0 | 0 | 0 | 0 | 0 | 0 |
| Journalism | 5 | 4 | 3 | 3 | 3 | 3 | 2 | 1 | 1 |
| Labor leader | — | — | — | 0 | 0 | 0 | 0 | 0 | 0 |
| Law | 25 | 33 | 18 | 19 | 20 | 26 | 24 | 26 | 22 |
| Law en-forcement | — | — | — | — | 0 | 0 | 0 | 0 | 0 |
| Medicine | 0 | 0 | 0 | 0 | 0 | 0 | 0 | 0 | 0 |
| Military | — | — | — | — | — | — | — | — | — |
| Professional sports | — | — | — | — | — | — | — | — | — |
| Public service/ politics | — | — | — | — | — | — | — | — | — |
| Veteran | 32 | 30 | 21 | 19 | 22 | 28 | 32 | 31 | 28 |
| Total number of Republican members | 48 | 47 | 34 | 32 | 36 | 42 | 44 | 42 | 37 |

*Note:* Dashes indicate years and occupations for which Congressional Quarterly did not compile data.

*Sources: Congressional Quarterly Almanac,* various years; *Congressional Quarterly Weekly Report,* November 8, 1986, 2862; November 12, 1988, 3295; November 10, 1990, 3837; November 7, 1992, Supplement, 9; November 12, 1994, Supplement, 11; January 4, 1997, 29.

| *95th* 1977 | *96th* 1979 | *97th* 1981 | *98th* 1983 | *99th* 1985 | *100th* 1987 | *101st* 1989 | *102d* 1991 | *103d* 1993 | *104th* 1995 | *105th* 1997 |
|---|---|---|---|---|---|---|---|---|---|---|
| — | — | — | — | — | 0 | 0 | 0 | 0 | 1 | 1 |
| — | — | — | 1 | 1 | 1 | 1 | 0 | 0 | 0 | 0 |
| 6 | 4 | 7 | 7 | 7 | 3 | 3 | 5 | 5 | 5 | 6 |
| 10 | 14 | 15 | 15 | 19 | 15 | 15 | 17 | 12 | 13 | 25 |
| 1 | 1 | 1 | 1 | 1 | 1 | 1 | 1 | 1 | 0 | 1 |
| 0 | 0 | 0 | 0 | 0 | — | — | — | — | — | — |
| 5 | 3 | 5 | 7 | 8 | 6 | 5 | 4 | 5 | 5 | 8 |
| 0 | 0 | 1 | 0 | 1 | 1 | 0 | 0 | 0 | 0 | 0 |
| 2 | 0 | 3 | 2 | 2 | 2 | 3 | 2 | 2 | 3 | 7 |
| 0 | 0 | 0 | 0 | 0 | 0 | 0 | 0 | 0 | 0 | 0 |
| 22 | 22 | 26 | 29 | 29 | 27 | 27 | 26 | 25 | 28 | 27 |
| 0 | 0 | 0 | 0 | 0 | 0 | 0 | 0 | 0 | 0 | 0 |
| 0 | 0 | 0 | 0 | 0 | 0 | 0 | 0 | 0 | 1 | 2 |
| — | — | — | 1 | 1 | 1 | 1 | 1 | 1 | 1 | 1 |
| — | — | — | 0 | 0 | 0 | 0 | 0 | 0 | 0 | 0 |
| — | — | — | — | — | 7 | 6 | 1 | 2 | 5 | 17 |
| — | — | — | — | — | — | — | — | — | — | — |
| 38 | 41 | 53 | 54 | 53 | 45 | 45 | 44 | 43 | 53 | 55 |

**Table 1-14** Religious Affiliations of Representatives, 89th–105th Congresses, 1965–1997

| | *89th (1965)* | | | *90th (1967)* | | | *91st (1969)* | | | *92d (1971)* | | | *93d (1973)* | | | *94th (1975)* | | | *96th (1979)* | | |
|---|---|---|---|---|---|---|---|---|---|---|---|---|---|---|---|---|---|---|---|---|---|
| | D | R | Total | D | R | Total | D | R | Total | D | R | Total | D | R | Total | D | R | Total | D | R | Total |
| Catholic | 81 | 13 | 94 | 73 | 22 | 95 | 72 | 24 | 96 | 77 | 24 | 101 | 69 | 30 | 99 | 88 | 22 | 110 | 93 | 23 | 116 |
| Jewish | 14 | 1 | 15 | 14 | 2 | 16 | 15 | 2 | 17 | 10 | 2 | 12 | 10 | 2 | 12 | 17 | 3 | 20 | 18 | 5 | 23 |
| Protestant | | | | | | | | | | | | | | | | | | | | | |
| Baptist | 33 | 9 | 42 | 30 | 12 | 42 | 30 | 13 | 43 | 32 | 10 | 42 | 33 | 12 | 45 | 37 | 10 | 47 | 33 | 10 | 43 |
| Episcopalian | 29 | 25 | 54 | 25 | 25 | 50 | 22 | 27 | 49 | 27 | 22 | 49 | 25 | 25 | 50 | 29 | 21 | 50 | 29 | 22 | 51 |
| Methodist | 46 | 23 | 69 | 37 | 32 | 69 | 34 | 32 | 66 | 33 | 32 | 65 | 30 | 33 | 63 | 40 | 23 | 63 | 32 | 26 | 58 |
| Presbyterian | 30 | 26 | 56 | 27 | 37 | 64 | 26 | 38 | 64 | 26 | 41 | 67 | 25 | 35 | 60 | 25 | 25 | 50 | 25 | 27 | 52 |
| All other | 62 | 43 | 105 | 43 | 54 | 97 | 44 | 56 | 100 | 49 | 49 | 98 | 50 | 55 | 105 | 55 | 40 | 95 | 47 | 45 | 92 |
| Total | 295 | 140 | 435 | 249 | 184 | 433 | 243 | 192 | 435 | 254 | 180 | 434 | 242 | 192 | 434 | 291 | 144 | 435 | 277 | 158 | 435 |

*(Table continues)*

**Table 1-14** *(Continued)*

| | *97th (1981)* | | | *99th (1985)* | | | *101st (1989)* | | | *102d (1991)* | | | *103d (1993)* | | | *104th (1995)* | | | *105th (1997)* | | |
|---|---|---|---|---|---|---|---|---|---|---|---|---|---|---|---|---|---|---|---|---|---|
| | D | R | Total | D | R | Total | D | R | Total | D | R | Total | D | R | Total | D | R | Total | D | R | Total |
| Catholic | 81 | 38 | 119 | 82 | 43 | 125 | 81 | 39 | 120 | 85 | 37 | 122 | 77 | 41 | 118 | 71 | 54 | 125 | 76 | 51 | 127 |
| Jewish | 21 | 6 | 27 | 24 | 6 | 30 | 26 | 5 | 31 | 26 | 6 | 33[a] | 26 | 5 | 32[a] | 20 | 4 | 25[a] | 21 | 3 | 25[a] |
| Protestant | | | | | | | | | | | | | | | | | | | | | |
| Baptist | 28 | 13 | 41 | 27 | 9 | 36 | 33 | 10 | 43 | 35 | 12 | 47 | 38 | 13 | 51 | 30 | 27 | 57 | 31 | 27 | 58 |
| Episcopalian | 25 | 27 | 52 | 22 | 22 | 44 | 22 | 21 | 43 | 24 | 17 | 41 | 18 | 17 | 35 | 13 | 21 | 34 | 10 | 21 | 31 |
| Methodist | 26 | 30 | 56 | 35 | 27 | 62 | 38 | 25 | 63 | 38 | 24 | 62 | 31 | 23 | 54 | 21 | 29 | 50 | 17 | 29 | 46 |
| Presbyterian | 18 | 28 | 46 | 22 | 25 | 47 | 16 | 26 | 42 | 15 | 27 | 42 | 20 | 26 | 46 | 17 | 30 | 47 | 15 | 28 | 43 |
| All other | 4 | 50 | 94 | 41 | 50 | 91 | 44 | 49 | 93 | 44 | 44 | 88 | 49 | 50 | 99 | 32 | 65 | 97 | 37 | 68 | 105 |
| Total | 243 | 192 | 435 | 253 | 182 | 435 | 260 | 175 | 435 | 267 | 167 | 435[a] | 258 | 176 | 435[a] | 204 | 230 | 435[a] | 207 | 227 | 435[a] |

*Note:* D indicates Democrats; R indicates Republicans.

[a] Totals include Bernard Sanders (I-Vt.).

*Sources: Congressional Quarterly Almanac,* various years; *Congressional Quarterly Weekly Report,* November 10, 1984, 2922; November 12, 1988, 3295; November 10, 1990, 3837; November 7, 1992, Supplement, 9; November 12, 1994, Supplement, 11; January 4, 1997, 29.

**Table 1-15** Religious Affiliations of Senators, 89th–105th Congresses, 1965–1997

| | *89th (1965)* | | | *90th (1967)* | | | *91st (1969)* | | | *92d (1971)* | | | *93d (1973)* | | | *94th (1975)* | | | *96th (1979)* | | |
|---|---|---|---|---|---|---|---|---|---|---|---|---|---|---|---|---|---|---|---|---|---|
| | D | R | Total | D | R | Total | D | R | Total | D | R | Total | D | R | Total | D | R | Total | D | R | Total |
| Catholic | 12 | 2 | 14 | 11 | 2 | 13 | 10 | 3 | 13 | 9 | 3 | 12 | 10 | 4 | 14 | 11 | 4 | 15 | 9 | 4 | 13 |
| Jewish | 1 | 1 | 2 | 1 | 1 | 2 | 1 | 1 | 2 | 1 | 1 | 2 | 1 | 1 | 2 | 2 | 1 | 3 | 5 | 2 | 7 |
| Protestant | | | | | | | | | | | | | | | | | | | | | |
| Baptist | 9 | 3 | 12 | 7 | 4 | 11 | 6 | 3 | 9 | 5 | 3 | 8 | 5 | 3 | 8 | 6 | 3 | 9 | 6 | 5 | 11 |
| Episcopalian | 8 | 7 | 15 | 8 | 7 | 15 | 5 | 10 | 15 | 4 | 13 | 17 | 6 | 11 | 17 | 6 | 9 | 15 | 5 | 12 | 17 |
| Methodist | 15 | 7 | 22 | 15 | 8 | 23 | 14 | 8 | 22 | 13 | 7 | 20 | 13 | 5 | 18 | 11 | 5 | 16 | 13 | 6 | 19 |
| Presbyterian | 8 | 3 | 11 | 8 | 4 | 12 | 8 | 5 | 13 | 10 | 6 | 16 | 8 | 6 | 14 | 10 | 7 | 17 | 10 | 2 | 12 |
| All other | 15 | 9 | 24 | 14 | 10 | 24 | 14 | 12 | 26 | 13 | 12 | 25 | 15 | 12 | 27 | 15 | 9 | 24 | 11 | 10 | 21 |
| Total | 68 | 32 | 100 | 64 | 36 | 100 | 58 | 42 | 100 | 55 | 45 | 100 | 58 | 42 | 100 | 61 | 38 | 99 | 59 | 41 | 100 |

*(Table continues)*

**Table 1-15** *(Continued)*

| | 97th (1981) | | | 99th (1985) | | | 101st (1989) | | | 102d (1991) | | | 103d (1993) | | | 104th (1995) | | | 105th (1997) | | |
|---|---|---|---|---|---|---|---|---|---|---|---|---|---|---|---|---|---|---|---|---|---|
| | D | R | Total | D | R | Total | D | R | Total | D | R | Total | D | R | Total | D | R | Total | D | R | Total |
| Catholic | 9 | 8 | 17 | 11 | 8 | 19 | 12 | 7 | 19 | 12 | 8 | 20 | 15 | 8 | 23 | 12 | 8 | 20 | 15 | 9 | 24 |
| Jewish | 3 | 3 | 6 | 4 | 4 | 8 | 5 | 3 | 8 | 6 | 2 | 8 | 9 | 1 | 10 | 8 | 1 | 9 | 9 | 1 | 10 |
| Protestant | | | | | | | | | | | | | | | | | | | | | |
| Baptist | 3 | 6 | 9 | 4 | 7 | 11 | 4 | 8 | 12 | 4 | 8 | 12 | 4 | 7 | 11 | 3 | 7 | 10 | 2 | 7 | 9 |
| Episcopalian | 5 | 15 | 20 | 4 | 17 | 21 | 7 | 13 | 20 | 6 | 12 | 18 | 4 | 11 | 15 | 4 | 10 | 14 | 2 | 9 | 11 |
| Methodist | 9 | 9 | 18 | 9 | 7 | 16 | 9 | 4 | 13 | 9 | 4 | 13 | 7 | 5 | 12 | 5 | 6 | 11 | 5 | 8 | 13 |
| Presbyterian | 8 | 2 | 10 | 8 | 1 | 9 | 7 | 2 | 9 | 7 | 2 | 9 | 5 | 3 | 8 | 4 | 4 | 8 | 2 | 8 | 10 |
| All other | 10 | 10 | 20 | 7 | 9 | 16 | 11 | 8 | 19 | 11 | 9 | 20 | 13 | 8 | 21 | 11 | 17 | 28 | 10 | 13 | 23 |
| Total | 47 | 53 | 100 | 47 | 53 | 100 | 55 | 45 | 100 | 55 | 45 | 100 | 57 | 43 | 100 | 47 | 53 | 100 | 45 | 55 | 100 |

*Note:* D indicates Democrats; R indicates Republicans.

*Sources: Congressional Quarterly Almanac,* various years; *Congressional Quarterly Weekly Report,* November 10, 1984, 2922; November 12, 1988, 3295; November 10, 1990, 3837; November 7, 1992, Supplement, 9; November 12, 1994, Supplement, 11; January 4, 1997, 29.

**Table 1-16** Blacks in Congress, 41st–105th Congresses, 1869–1997

| | *House* | | *Senate* | | | *House* | | *Senate* | |
|---|---|---|---|---|---|---|---|---|---|
| *Congress* | D | R | D | R | *Congress* | D | R | D | R |
| 41st (1869) | — | 2 | — | 1 | 81st (1949) | 2 | — | — | — |
| 42d (1871) | — | 5 | — | — | 82d (1951) | 2 | — | — | — |
| 43d (1873) | — | 7 | — | — | 83d (1953) | 2 | — | — | — |
| 44th (1875) | — | 7 | — | 1 | 84th (1955) | 3 | — | — | — |
| 45th (1877) | — | 3 | — | 1 | 85th (1957) | 3 | — | — | — |
| 46th (1879) | — | — | — | 1 | 86th (1959) | 3 | — | — | — |
| 47th (1881) | — | 2 | — | — | 87th (1961) | 3 | — | — | — |
| 48th (1883) | — | 2 | — | — | 88th (1963) | 4 | — | — | — |
| 49th (1885) | — | 2 | — | — | 89th (1965) | 5 | — | — | — |
| 50th (1887) | — | — | — | — | 90th (1967) | 5 | — | — | 1 |
| 51st (1889) | — | 3 | — | — | 91st (1969) | 9 | — | — | 1 |
| 52d (1891) | — | 1 | — | — | 92d (1971) | 13 | — | — | 1 |
| 53d (1893) | — | 1 | — | — | 93d (1973) | 16 | — | — | 1 |
| 54th (1895) | — | 1 | — | — | 94th (1975) | 16 | — | — | 1 |
| 55th (1897) | — | 1 | — | — | 95th (1977) | 15 | — | — | 1 |
| 56th (1899)[a] | — | 1 | — | — | 96th (1979) | 15 | — | — | — |
| 71st (1929) | — | 1 | — | — | 97th (1981) | 17 | — | — | — |
| 72d (1931) | — | 1 | — | — | 98th (1983) | 20 | — | — | — |
| 73d (1933) | — | 1 | — | — | 99th (1985) | 20 | — | — | — |
| 74th (1935) | 1 | — | — | — | 100th (1987) | 22 | — | — | — |
| 75th (1937) | 1 | — | — | — | 101st (1989) | 23 | — | — | — |
| 76th (1939) | 1 | — | — | — | 102d (1991) | 25 | 1 | — | — |
| 77th (1941) | 1 | — | — | — | 103d (1993) | 38 | 1 | 1 | — |
| 78th (1943) | 1 | — | — | — | 104th (1995) | 37 | 2 | 1 | — |
| 79th (1945) | 2 | — | — | — | 105th (1997) | 36 | 1 | 1 | — |
| 80th (1947) | 2 | — | — | — | | | | | |

*Note:* Does not include Eleanor Holmes Norton, a nonvoting delegate who represents Washington, D.C.

[a] After the Fifty-sixth Congress, there were no black members in either the House or Senate until the Seventy-first Congress.

*Sources: Black Americans in Congress, 1870-1977,* H.Doc. 95-258, 95th Cong., 1st sess., 1977; *Congressional Quarterly Almanac,* various years; *Congressional Quarterly Weekly Report,* November 10, 1984, 2921; November 8, 1986, 2863; November 12, 1988, 3294; November 10, 1990, 3836; November 7, 1992, Supplement, 8; November 12, 1994, Supplement, 10; January 4, 1997, 28.

**Table 1-17** Hispanic Americans in Congress, 45th–105th Congresses, 1877–1997

| | *House* | | *Senate* | | | *House* | | *Senate* | |
|---|---|---|---|---|---|---|---|---|---|
| *Congress* | D | R | D | R | *Congress* | D | R | D | R |
| 45th (1877) | — | 1 | — | — | 76th (1939) | 1 | — | 1 | — |
| 46th (1879) | — | 1 | — | — | 77th (1941) | — | — | 1 | — |
| 47th (1881) | — | 1 | — | — | 78th (1943) | 1 | — | 1 | — |
| 48th (1883) | — | — | — | — | 79th (1945) | 1 | — | 1 | — |
| 49th (1885) | — | — | — | — | 80th (1947) | 1 | — | 1 | — |
| 50th (1887) | — | — | — | — | 81st (1949) | 1 | — | 1 | — |
| 51st (1889) | — | — | — | — | 82d (1951) | 1 | — | 1 | — |
| 52d (1891) | — | — | — | — | 83d (1953) | 1 | — | 1 | — |
| 53d (1893) | — | — | — | — | 84th (1955) | 1 | — | 1 | — |
| 54th (1895) | — | — | — | — | 85th (1957) | 1 | — | 1 | — |
| 55th (1897) | — | — | — | — | 86th (1959) | 1 | — | 1 | — |
| 56th (1899) | — | — | — | — | 87th (1961) | 2 | — | 1 | — |
| 57th (1901) | — | — | — | — | 88th (1963) | 3 | — | 1 | — |
| 58th (1903) | — | — | — | — | 89th (1965) | 3 | — | 1 | — |
| 59th (1905) | — | — | — | — | 90th (1967) | 3 | — | 1 | — |
| 60th (1907) | — | — | — | — | 91st (1969) | 3 | 1 | 1 | — |
| 61st (1909) | — | — | — | — | 92d (1971) | 4 | 1 | 1 | — |
| 62d (1911) | — | — | — | — | 93d (1973) | 4 | 1 | 1 | — |
| 63d (1913) | 1 | — | — | — | 94th (1975) | 4 | 1 | 1 | — |
| 64th (1915) | 1 | 1 | — | — | 95th (1977) | 4 | 1 | — | — |
| 65th (1917) | 1 | — | — | — | 96th (1979) | 5 | 1 | — | — |
| 66th (1919) | 1 | 1 | — | — | 97th (1981) | 6 | 1 | — | — |
| 67th (1921) | 1 | 1 | — | — | 98th (1983) | 9 | 1 | — | — |
| 68th (1923) | 1 | — | — | — | 99th (1985) | 10 | 1 | — | — |
| 69th (1925) | 1 | — | — | — | 100th (1987) | 10 | 1 | — | — |
| 70th (1927) | 1 | — | — | 1 | 101st (1989) | 9 | 1 | — | — |
| 71st (1929) | — | — | — | — | 102d (1991) | 10 | 1 | — | — |
| 72d (1931) | 2 | — | — | — | 103d (1993) | 14 | 3 | — | — |
| 73d (1933) | 2 | — | — | — | 104th (1995) | 14 | 3 | — | — |
| 74th (1935) | 1 | — | 1 | — | 105th (1997) | 14 | 3 | — | — |
| 75th (1937) | 1 | — | 1 | — | | | | | |

*Note:* Statistics do not include delegates or commissioners. Since the 17th Congress, there have been three Democrats and five Republicans who have served in the House of Representatives as delegates for territories that would later become states. In addition, Joseph Marion Hernandez (W-Fla.) served as a delegate to the U.S. House of Representatives during the 17th Congress. There have also been nineteen Hispanic Americans who have served as delegates to the House of Representatives representing the territories of Puerto Rico, Guam, and the Virgin Islands since 1901.

*Sources: Biographical Directory of the United States Congress 1774–1989; Congressional Quarterly Almanac,* various years.

**Table 1-18** Women in Congress, 65th–105th Congresses, 1917–1997

| | House | | Senate | | | House | | Senate | |
|---|---|---|---|---|---|---|---|---|---|
| *Congress* | D | R | D | R | *Congress* | D | R | D | R |
| 65th (1917) | — | 1 | — | — | 86th (1959) | 9 | 8 | — | 1 |
| 66th (1919) | — | — | — | — | 87th (1961) | 11 | 7 | 1 | 1 |
| 67th (1921) | — | 2 | — | 1 | 88th (1963) | 6 | 6 | 1 | 1 |
| 68th (1923) | — | 1 | — | — | 89th (1965) | 7 | 4 | 1 | 1 |
| 69th (1925) | 1 | 2 | — | — | 90th (1967) | 5 | 5 | — | 1 |
| 70th (1927) | 2 | 3 | — | — | 91st (1969) | 6 | 4 | — | 1 |
| 71st (1929) | 4 | 5 | — | — | 92d (1971) | 10 | 3 | — | 1 |
| 72d (1931) | 4 | 3 | 1 | — | 93d (1973) | 14 | 2 | 1 | — |
| 73d (1933) | 4 | 3 | 1 | — | 94th (1975) | 14 | 5 | — | — |
| 74th (1935) | 4 | 2 | 2 | — | 95th (1977) | 13 | 5 | — | — |
| 75th (1937) | 4 | 1 | 2 | — | 96th (1979) | 11 | 5 | 1 | 1 |
| 76th (1939) | 4 | 4 | 1 | — | 97th (1981) | 10 | 9 | — | 2 |
| 77th (1941) | 4 | 5 | 1 | — | 98th (1983) | 13 | 9 | — | 2 |
| 78th (1943) | 2 | 6 | 1 | — | 99th (1985) | 13 | 9 | — | 2 |
| 79th (1945) | 6 | 5 | — | — | 100th (1987) | 12[a] | 11 | 1 | 1 |
| 80th (1947) | 3 | 4 | — | 1 | 101st (1989) | 14 | 11 | 1 | 1 |
| 81st (1949) | 5 | 4 | — | 1 | 102d (1991) | 19 | 9 | 1 | 1 |
| 82d (1951) | 4 | 6 | — | 1 | 103d (1993) | 36 | 12 | 5 | 1 |
| 83d (1953) | 5 | 7 | — | 1 | 104th (1995) | 31 | 17 | 5 | 3[b] |
| 84th (1955) | 10 | 7 | — | 1 | 105th (1997) | 35 | 16 | 6 | 3 |
| 85th (1957) | 9 | 6 | — | 1 | | | | | |

*Note:* Includes only women who were sworn in as members and served more than one day.

[a] Includes the late Sala Burton, who died after being sworn into the 100th Congress, and who was replaced by another Democratic woman, Nancy Pelosi.

[b] Sheila Frahm (R-Kan.) was appointed to fill the vacancy left by Sen. Robert Dole (R-Kan.) bringing the total to four Republican woman senators. Frahm ran for the open Senate seat but lost in the Kansas Republican primary.

Sources: *Women in Congress,* H. Rept. 94-1732, 94th Cong., 2d sess., 1976; *Congressional Quarterly Almanac,* various years; *Congressional Quarterly Weekly Report,* November 10, 1984, 2921; November 8, 1986, 2863; November 12, 1988, 3294; November 10, 1990, 3836; November 7, 1992, Supplement, 8; November 12, 1994, Supplement, 10; January 4, 1997, 28.

**Table 1–19** Political Parties of Senators and Representatives, 34th–105th Congresses, 1855–1997

| *Congress* | | *Senate* | | | | | *House of Representatives* | | | | |
|---|---|---|---|---|---|---|---|---|---|---|---|
| | | Number of senators | Demo-crats | Repub-licans | Other parties | Vacant | Number of repre-sentatives | Demo-crats | Repub-licans | Other parties | Vacant |
| 34th | (1855–1857) | 62 | 42 | 15 | 5 | — | 234 | 83 | 108 | 43 | |
| 35th | (1857–1859) | 64 | 39 | 20 | 5 | — | 237 | 131 | 92 | 14 | — |
| 36th | (1859–1861) | 66 | 38 | 26 | 2 | — | 237 | 101 | 113 | 23 | — |
| 37th | (1861–1863) | 50 | 11 | 31 | 7 | 1 | 178 | 42 | 106 | 28 | 2 |
| 38th | (1863–1865) | 51 | 12 | 39 | — | — | 183 | 80 | 103 | — | — |
| 39th | (1865–1867) | 52 | 10 | 42 | — | — | 191 | 46 | 145 | — | — |
| 40th | (1867–1869) | 53 | 11 | 42 | — | — | 193 | 49 | 143 | — | 1 |
| 41st | (1869–1871) | 74 | 11 | 61 | — | 2 | 243 | 73 | 170 | — | — |
| 42d | (1871–1873) | 74 | 17 | 57 | — | — | 243 | 104 | 139 | — | — |
| 43d | (1873–1875) | 74 | 19 | 54 | — | 1 | 293 | 88 | 203 | — | 2 |
| 44th | (1875–1877) | 76 | 29 | 46 | — | 1 | 293 | 181 | 107 | 3 | 2 |
| 45th | (1877–1879) | 76 | 36 | 39 | 1 | — | 293 | 156 | 137 | — | — |
| 46th | (1879–1881) | 76 | 43 | 33 | — | — | 293 | 150 | 128 | 14 | 1 |
| 47th | (1881–1883) | 76 | 37 | 37 | 2 | — | 293 | 130 | 152 | 11 | — |
| 48th | (1883–1885) | 76 | 36 | 40 | — | — | 325 | 200 | 119 | 6 | — |
| 49th | (1885–1887) | 76 | 34 | 41 | — | 1 | 325 | 182 | 140 | 2 | 1 |
| 50th | (1887–1889) | 76 | 37 | 39 | — | — | 325 | 170 | 151 | 4 | — |
| 51st | (1889–1891) | 84 | 37 | 47 | — | — | 330 | 156 | 173 | 1 | — |
| 52d | (1891–1893) | 88 | 39 | 47 | 2 | — | 333 | 231 | 88 | 14 | — |
| 53d | (1893–1895) | 88 | 44 | 38 | 3 | 3 | 356 | 220 | 126 | 10 | — |
| 54th | (1895–1897) | 88 | 39 | 44 | 5 | — | 357 | 104 | 246 | 7 | — |
| 55th | (1897–1899) | 90 | 34 | 46 | 10 | — | 357 | 134 | 206 | 16 | 1 |
| 56th | (1899–1901) | 90 | 26 | 53 | 11 | — | 357 | 163 | 185 | 9 | — |
| 57th | (1901–1903) | 90 | 29 | 56 | 3 | 2 | 357 | 153 | 198 | 5 | 1 |

*(Table continues)*

**Table 1–19** *(Continued)*

| *Congress* | | Senate: Number of senators | Senate: Demo-crats | Senate: Repub-licans | Senate: Other parties | Senate: Vacant | House of Representatives: Number of repre-sentatives | House: Demo-crats | House: Repub-licans | House: Other parties | House: Vacant |
|---|---|---|---|---|---|---|---|---|---|---|---|
| 58th | (1903–1905) | 90 | 32 | 58 | — | — | 386 | 178 | 207 | — | 1 |
| 59th | (1905–1907) | 90 | 32 | 58 | — | — | 386 | 136 | 250 | — | — |
| 60th | (1907–1909) | 92 | 29 | 61 | — | 2 | 386 | 164 | 222 | — | — |
| 61st | (1909–1911) | 92 | 32 | 59 | — | 1 | 391 | 172 | 219 | — | — |
| 62d | (1911–1913) | 92 | 42 | 49 | — | 1 | 391 | 228 | 162 | 1 | — |
| 63d | (1913–1915) | 96 | 51 | 44 | 1 | — | 435 | 290 | 127 | 18 | — |
| 64th | (1915–1917) | 96 | 56 | 39 | 1 | — | 435 | 231 | 193 | 8 | 3 |
| 65th | (1917–1919) | 96 | 53 | 42 | 1 | — | 435 | 210[a] | 216 | 9 | — |
| 66th | (1919–1921) | 96 | 47 | 48 | 1 | — | 435 | 191 | 237 | 7 | — |
| 67th | (1921–1923) | 96 | 37 | 59 | — | — | 435 | 132 | 300 | 1 | 2 |
| 68th | (1923–1925) | 96 | 43 | 51 | 2 | — | 435 | 207 | 225 | 3 | — |
| 69th | (1925–1927) | 96 | 40 | 54 | 1 | 1 | 435 | 183 | 247 | 5 | — |
| 70th | (1927–1929) | 96 | 47 | 48 | 1 | — | 435 | 195 | 237 | 3 | — |
| 71st | (1929–1931) | 96 | 39 | 56 | 1 | — | 435 | 163 | 267 | 1 | 4 |
| 72d | (1931–1933) | 96 | 47 | 48 | 1 | — | 435 | 216[b] | 218 | 1 | — |
| 73d | (1933–1935) | 96 | 59 | 36 | 1 | — | 435 | 313 | 117 | 5 | — |
| 74th | (1935–1937) | 96 | 69 | 25 | 2 | — | 435 | 322 | 103 | 10 | — |
| 75th | (1937–1939) | 96 | 75 | 17 | 4 | — | 435 | 333 | 89 | 13 | — |
| 76th | (1939–1941) | 96 | 69 | 23 | 4 | — | 435 | 262 | 169 | 4 | — |
| 77th | (1941–1943) | 96 | 66 | 28 | 2 | — | 435 | 267 | 162 | 6 | — |
| 78th | (1943–1945) | 96 | 57 | 38 | 1 | — | 435 | 222 | 209 | 4 | — |
| 79th | (1945–1947) | 96 | 57 | 38 | 1 | — | 435 | 243 | 190 | 2 | — |
| 80th | (1947–1949) | 96 | 45 | 51 | — | — | 435 | 188 | 246 | 1 | — |
| 81st | (1949–1951) | 96 | 54 | 42 | — | — | 435 | 263 | 171 | 1 | — |
| 82d | (1951–1953) | 96 | 48 | 47 | 1 | — | 435 | 234 | 199 | 2 | — |
| 83d | (1953–1955) | 96 | 46 | 48 | 2 | — | 435 | 213 | 221 | 1 | — |

| | | | | | | | | | | | |
|---|---|---|---|---|---|---|---|---|---|---|---|
| 84th | (1955–1957) | 96 | 48 | 47 | 1 | — | 435 | 232 | 203 | — | — |
| 85th | (1957–1959) | 96 | 49 | 47 | — | — | 435 | 234 | 201 | — | — |
| 86th | (1959–1961) | 98 | 64 | 34 | — | — | 436[c] | 283 | 153 | — | — |
| 87th | (1961–1963) | 100 | 64 | 36 | — | — | 437[d] | 262 | 175 | — | — |
| 88th | (1963–1965) | 100 | 67 | 33 | — | — | 435 | 258 | 176 | — | 1 |
| 89th | (1965–1967) | 100 | 68 | 32 | — | — | 435 | 295 | 140 | — | — |
| 90th | (1967–1969) | 100 | 64 | 36 | — | — | 435 | 248 | 187 | — | — |
| 91st | (1969–1971) | 100 | 58 | 42 | — | — | 435 | 243 | 192 | — | — |
| 92d | (1971–1973) | 100 | 54 | 44 | 2 | — | 435 | 255 | 180 | — | — |
| 93d | (1973–1975) | 100 | 56 | 42 | 2 | — | 435 | 242 | 192 | 1 | — |
| 94th | (1975–1977) | 100 | 61 | 37 | 2 | — | 435 | 291 | 144 | — | — |
| 95th | (1977–1979) | 100 | 61 | 38 | 1 | — | 435 | 292 | 143 | — | — |
| 96th | (1979–1981) | 100 | 58 | 41 | 1 | — | 435 | 277 | 158 | — | — |
| 97th | (1981–1983) | 100 | 46 | 53 | 1 | — | 435 | 243 | 192 | — | — |
| 98th | (1983–1985) | 100 | 46 | 54 | — | — | 435 | 268 | 167 | — | — |
| 99th | (1985–1987) | 100 | 47 | 53 | — | — | 435 | 253 | 182 | — | — |
| 100th | (1987–1989) | 100 | 55[e] | 45 | — | — | 435 | 258 | 177[f] | — | — |
| 101st | (1989–1991) | 100 | 55 | 45 | — | — | 435 | 260 | 175 | — | — |
| 102d | (1991–1993) | 100 | 56 | 44 | — | — | 435 | 267 | 167 | 1 | — |
| 103d | (1993–1995) | 100 | 57 | 43 | — | — | 435 | 258 | 176 | 1 | — |
| 104th | (1995–1997) | 100 | 47[g] | 53 | — | — | 435 | 204 | 230 | 1 | — |
| 105th | (1997–1998) | 100 | 45 | 55 | — | — | 435 | 207 | 227 | 1 | — |

*Note:* All figures reflect immediate election results.

[a] Democrats organized House with help of other parties.

[b] Democrats organized House because of Republican deaths.

[c] Proclamation declaring Alaska a state issued January 3, 1959.

[d] Proclamation declaring Hawaii a state issued August 21, 1959.

[e] Includes the late Sen. Edward Zorinsky (D-Nev.), who was replaced by Sen. David Karnes, a Republican, thus changing the ratio when he was sworn in on March 11, 1987, to 54 Democrats and 46 Republicans.

[f] Includes the late Stewart McKinney (R-Conn.).

[g] Sen. Ben Nighthorse Campbell (Colo.) switched from the Democratic to Republican Party March 3, 1995, making the ratio 46-54.

*Sources: Statistics of the Presidential and Congressional Elections of November 4, 1980,* compiled from official sources by Thomas E. Ladd, under direction of Edmund L. Henshaw, Jr., clerk of the House of Representatives (Washington, D.C., 1981); *Congressional Directory* (1983, 1985); *Congressional Quarterly Weekly Report,* November 8, 1986, 2812, 2839, 2843, 2856–2857; November 22, 1986; March 14, 1987, 483; November 12, 1988; November 10, 1990; November 7, 1992; November 12, 1994; January 4, 1997, 3.

# 2

# Elections

For the members of the House and Senate, there are no more vital statistics than those on congressional elections. Whatever their personal goals within Congress, members must first win reelection. Yet, as the dramatic change in party control of the Senate in the 1980 elections and both chambers in the 1994 elections made clear, individual electoral success is not enough—the fate of party colleagues is extraordinarily important in shaping the internal character of Congress and therefore the ability of individual members to accomplish their legislative and political goals.

The data in Table 2-1 document the steady decline in turnout in presidential and congressional elections since 1960. Turnout has decreased in each presidential election, with the only reversal coming in 1992 when a three-candidate election probably helped turnout increase 5 percentage points. The trend returned to normal in 1996, however, when less than half of the country voted in the presidential election.

Table 2-2 relates the party's popular vote to the percentage of seats in the House of Representatives actually won over the past five decades. The long-term Democratic control of Congress is evident in this table, although Democratic support appears slightly less robust when looking at the national popular vote for the parties rather than the seats won. In the mid-1960s and again in 1980, the Republicans came within striking distance of the Democrats in national popular vote; yet they never won more than 44 percent of the seats in those years. This malapportionment, in which the majority party enjoys seat margins much more favorable than its vote margins—shown clearly by the figures in the last column of Table 2-2—is common to electoral systems with single-member districts. A gain of a certain percentage in a party's popular vote usually allows it to pick up two or three times that percentage in seats. Republican successes in the 1980 House elections cut the Democratic majority party seat bonus to half what it had been in 1976 and 1978. In 1982 an impressive effort by the national Republican Party held the Democratic seat pick-up to twenty-six (or 5.9 percent) in spite of a 5.2 percent increase in votes. In 1984, however, the Republicans failed to convert a sizable vote gain into seats, and in 1988 they actually lost seats while gaining votes, a malady typical of minority parties in this form of electoral system. In 1990 the Democrats managed to pick up a few seats without winning any additional popular votes.

In 1992 Republicans made gains in both the percentage of major party vote and in the number of seats won over their 1990 margins. Democrats, on the other hand, drew their lowest share of the aggregate nationwide vote since 1980. These numbers provided only a modest foreshadowing of what was to come in 1994. The Republican increase in votes and seats was the most sizable gain by either party since 1948. The Republican sweep almost eliminated the seat bonus, producing for the first time in four decades a rough parity between both parties' votes and seats. In 1996 the majority Republicans took advantage of the seat/vote bonus; their percentage of congressional seats declined only 0.7 percent even as their share of votes dropped nearly 3.5 percentage points.

Net seats picked up by each party as a result of House and Senate general and special elections are shown in Table 2-3. The election of 1958 was especially important to Senate Democrats in maintaining their majority during the subsequent two decades, a majority that ended abruptly with the surprising pickup of twelve seats by the Republicans in the 1980 elections. The Republican majority proved much less durable, ending after only six years with the Democratic sweep of the 1986 Senate elections. House Democrats, however, saw their strength wax and wane in pairs of elections until the Watergate year of 1974, which gave them a margin sufficient to protect their majority in the face of Republican gains in 1978 and 1980. The 1992 election marked the first net gain by House Republicans since 1984. After displaying the potential for substantial gains after the 1993 special elections, Republicans shocked the political community by gaining fifty-two House and eight Senate seats in the 1994 general election. This was the largest gain in House seats by either party since the Democrats gained seventy-five seats in 1948, and it ended a forty-year reign by the Democrats. In 1996 the Republicans saw some of their seats slip back to the Democrats, but still managed to hold onto a slim majority in the House.

Table 2-4 presents the number of seats lost or gained by the president's party in midterm elections, data that have long fascinated analysts of U.S. politics. In every midterm election but one since the Civil War, the party of the president has lost ground in the House of Representatives. The exception was 1934, which signaled the last major realignment in the party system. The number of seats changing party hands has varied widely over time, but in recent midterms prior to 1994, a trend of smaller losses had been established. In the previous five midterm elections occurring in the first term of a president, the average loss was only thirteen seats. Then in 1994 this pattern ended with a presidential party loss of fifty-two seats in the House, the greatest midterm loss in more than five decades.

The 1994 elections were even more surprising to analysts because the magnitude of the loss is generally determined by the previous presidential election: smaller numbers of candidates elected on the coattails of the president result in more modest midterm losses. But in 1992, the Democrats had actually lost ten seats—making their huge loss in 1994 a much bigger shock.

The midterm pattern of Senate elections is different from that of the House, chiefly because only a third of the Senate is up for reelection at a time, with tremendous variation in the proportion of those seats held by the president's party. In the thirty-three midterm elections since the Civil War, the president's party gained seats in ten of them.

Table 2-5 and Figure 2-1 demonstrate that although more seats change party control than the net shifts in Table 2-3 suggest, the stabilizing impact of House elections remains impressive: in no election since 1954 have more than 14 percent of the 435 seats changed party hands. Nevertheless, recent elections reflect an increased trend in seats switching party control. The election of 1988 had fewer seats (nine) change hands than at any time in American history. But in 1990, twenty-one seats switched party control and in 1992 forty-three—roughly 10 percent of the House membership. The 1994 elections had an even larger shift, sixty seats or 13.8 percent of the House. Though this percentage is still small, it is the largest shift recorded in this table—even greater than the watershed year of 1974. Further, much of this turnover was inspired by a growing public dissatisfaction with government, which made incumbents very nervous in 1996. Thirty-five seats changing hands was a significant number, but it was not on par with the previous two election cycles. The Republicans lost a few vulnerable members, but won a number of open seats. There the Republicans were the clear winners, taking ten of fourteen contests, many of these in southern districts that appear to be drifting increasingly Republican.

The numbers in this table also confirm that the 1994 election was not a vote against the status quo, regardless of party. It was aimed directly at the Democrats. Fifty-six of the sixty seats that switched party hands went from Democratic to Republican control; not one Republican-held incumbent seat went Democratic.

In contrast to the small percentage of change in the House, as many as one-third of the Senate seats up for election in any one year have changed party control. However, change is not always the rule; in 1992 a mere four seats changed hands (see Table 2-6 and Figure 2-2). In addition, despite the impressive advantages of incumbency, parties have, in most cases, picked up more of their gains not in open seats but in races against incumbents. But 1994 and 1996 bucked this trend, with six open seats changing hands in 1994 and three open seats changing in 1996. All went to Republicans.

Finally, one is struck again by the importance of particular elections for long-term party control. In 1958 for the Senate and in 1974 for the House, the Democrats posted impressive gains that were maintained in subsequent elections. The Republicans striking victory in 1994 was followed by another victory in 1996, but their overall margin of victory was not convincing enough to point to any enduring realignment (despite the regional evidence presented in chapter one). We must wait and see whether 1994 will truly lead to long-term Republican control in either one or both of the chambers.

Tables 2-7 and 2-8 chronicle the fate of House and Senate incumbents. In most years of the modern Congress, the bulk of House incumbents who sought reelection usually succeeded. Even landslides in the general election ordinarily led to the defeat of only 10 percent of the incumbents seeking reelection. A substantial increase in retirements in the 1970s was largely responsible for the relatively high turnover during that period. As presented in Table 2-7, reelection rates in 1986 and 1988 were extraordinarily high—only six incumbents defeated in each general election—generating outcries from groups who believed that campaigns and election rules unfairly favored incumbents. But recent elections have shown a reversed trend with relatively high numbers of incumbents losing elections. Elections in 1996 did not see as much attrition, but the number of defeated incumbents was still much higher than in the mid- to late-1980s.

Election year 1992 saw the largest number of voluntary retirements (sixty-five) from the House in the post-war era. And another forty-three incumbents were defeated (nineteen in primaries, the highest in more than fifty years), producing the most turnover in a single election since 1948. The 1994 elections, though not having as many retirements or primary defeats as in 1992, had the most members defeated in the general election since the 1974 post-Watergate upsurge. The 1996 elections saw 21 incumbents defeated in the general election, a relatively high number for recent years, but a clear leveling in the trend.

Senate incumbents usually have not fared as well as their House counterparts because the level of competition in statewide races is generally higher. That pattern held true in 1992, when 82.1 percent of those senators seeking reelection were reelected, compared with 88.3 percent of House members. The contrast was stark in 1986: 7 of 28 senators seeking reelection were defeated in the general election, while only 6 of 391 representatives met the same fate. The 1994 elections upset this trend as Senate incumbents fared better than their House counterparts. Senators had a reelection rate of 92.3 percent. The 1996 elections returned to the norm with a slightly higher percentage of representatives being reelected, though both were above 90 percent.

Still, both renomination and reelection have proven to be more difficult hurdles for senators than for representatives. Table 2-9 provides a party breakdown of House and Senate retirements. The 1994 elections tied a record set in 1978 for most Senate retirements: nine. This was quickly overshadowed, however, by an unprecedented thirteen retirements, along with Bob Dole's early, voluntary departure to run for president in 1996.

Tables 2-10 and 2-11 examine the number of terms served by incumbents defeated in primary and general elections of the House and Senate, respectively. Table 2-10 shows that in the early years most defeated House incumbents were in their first term. Fifty-four percent of those defeated in 1946, 55 percent of those defeated in 1948, and 60 percent of those defeated in 1966 were in their first terms. Then the pattern changed, and from 1974 through 1992 the number of years members had served was spread much more evenly, especially within the first to fourth terms. In 1992 the largest number of defeated incumbents were in their fifth term. But in 1994 voters again ousted more first termers, seventeen of the thirty-eight defeated incumbents. While a handful of highly visible, senior members lost in 1994, including Dan Rostenkowski and Jack Brooks, the number of "old bulls" defeated was actually far less than in 1992. In 1996 the Republicans lost a number of freshmen bringing the average terms of the defeated incumbents down to 1.8, the lowest since 1986 when only a handful were defeated. Democratic incumbents lost only three seats, one of their best showings in recent elections.

Table 2-11 shows a slightly different pattern in the Senate. While the total number of defeated incumbents varied over time, the members were consistently in their first or second terms. Of the thirteen incumbents who lost in 1946, more than 50 percent (seven) were in their first term. Nine of the ten defeated incumbents in 1948 were first-termers, as were six of the ten in 1958 and 1978. The defeated incumbents in 1980 fell across a wider range of service years—five in their first term and three in their third and fourth terms. But then in 1992 all five of the defeated were in their first or second term.

In terms of the margin of victory rather than the rate of reelection, some change has occurred in the electoral standing of House and Senate incumbents. The proportion of House incumbents who have won reelection with at least 60 percent of the major party vote increased from about three-fifths in the 1950s and early 1960s to three-fourths in the 1970s, and to almost nine-tenths in the late 1980s (see Table 2-12). This trend began to change in 1990, however, when the percentage of incumbents reelected with at least 60 percent of the major party vote dropped from 88.5 to 76.4. The 1992 elections saw even fewer incumbents, 65.6 percent reelected by a so-called "safe" margin. And in 1994 that number dropped another percentage point to 64.5 percent, the lowest percentage since 1964. Most experts attribute the increased competitiveness to a combination of factors including redistricting, anti-incumbent sentiment, fewer uncontested seats, and the growing number of voters who call themselves Independent.[1] The anti-incumbency feeling seemed to recede in 1996. Citizens began to feel somewhat less pessimistic about the country and this is reflected in the House where 73.6 percent of the incumbents reached the "safe" margin.

Table 2-13 demonstrates fluctuation in the Senate margins of victory as well, highlighting the different patterns in the South and the North. From the 1940s through the mid 1970s, the percentage of incumbents in the South with 60 percent or more of the major party vote fell from 100 to 57.1 percent while those in the rest of the country increased about fifteen percentage points. From

1980-1990 there was a significant increase nationwide. Then in 1992 and 1994 the percentage of those within the "safe margin" stabilized in the South but sharply declined in the rest of the country, back to the levels of the 1960s.

Viewed from the perspective of congressional careers, elections still pose a significant challenge to incumbents. Table 2-14 reveals that more than two-thirds of the senators and over half of the representatives serving in the 104th Congress received less than 55 percent of the vote, and even more of them less than 60 percent, in at least one election. Moreover, when the conditions of initial election to Congress are examined (Table 2-15), it is apparent that many representatives and a majority of senators have themselves either defeated incumbents or replaced retiring incumbents of the other party.

Tables 2-16 and 2-17 point to the substantial divergence between presidential and congressional voting. Since 1956, when the Democrats in the House and Senate withstood Dwight D. Eisenhower's sweeping victory in the presidential election, more than one-fourth of all congressional districts have supported a presidential candidate of one party and a House candidate of the other (Table 2-16). The proportion of districts with split results reached a peak in 1972 when Richard Nixon received 60.8 percent of the presidential vote while his party's candidates won only 46.4 percent of the congressional vote leaving the Democrats with a solid majority in the House. In 1992 the percentage of districts with split ticket results fell to its lowest level since 1952.

A president's ability to claim long coattails depends on both the size of his victory and the number of seats his party gains in Congress. Presidents John F. Kennedy and Jimmy Carter lost on both counts: the Republicans actually gained twenty-two House seats in 1960 and held their ground in 1976, while both victorious Democratic presidents ran ahead of Democratic representatives in only twenty-two districts (Table 2-17). In 1972 Richard Nixon ran ahead of a majority of the Republicans elected to the House, but this was small consolation in view of his failure to pull a sizable bloc of new Republicans into the House. In contrast, Lyndon Johnson could claim credit for dramatically increasing his party's margin in Congress. His reward was the Great Society legislation of 1965 and 1966.

In 1980 Ronald Reagan's presidential victory was accompanied by impressive Republican gains in the House, but fell short of the number needed to take control. Moreover, Reagan ran behind most of his party colleagues in the House. The more important manifestation of a Reagan tide was thought to be in the Senate, where a total of 50,000 votes accounted for seven Republican victories and, as a consequence, majority status. Reagan's 1984 landslide in the presidential sweepstakes, however, left barely a trace in the Senate and House elections. In 1988 George Bush saw his party lose seats in the House, underscoring the absence of presidential coattails. The Democrats suffered a similar fate in 1992, losing seats in the House while winning back the presidency after twelve years of Republican rule. President Clinton fared somewhat better in

1996, although Democrats failed to win enough seats to reclaim a House majority.

The past two decades have witnessed a substantial increase in the impact of local forces in congressional elections. Although the United States has never had a uniform swing across constituencies as Britain has, the figures in Table 2-18 illustrate how difficult it is to make national interpretations of the results of U.S. congressional elections. Election returns at the district level increasingly diverge from the national returns. These figures suggest an electoral base for the increasingly individualized behavior in the House of Representatives. The range in the swing across districts has increased markedly since the 1950s, and the variance, which measures the extent to which changes in local returns differ from the change in national returns, has more than doubled. Even the dramatic 1994 midterm elections, widely considered the most nationalized elections in decades, featured divergent swings across districts. In 1996 district variation receded in the face of a highly partisan national contest.

Table 2-19 presents data that confirm the basis in individual voting behavior for many of the electoral patterns reported in this chapter. The decline in the proportion of party-line voters in House elections during the late 1960s and 1970s is consistent with the view that voting became increasingly candidate centered. Yet the resurgence of party-line voting in recent midterm elections suggests that the electorate retains the capacity to respond to national political events in highly partisan ways.

## NOTE

1. The growing number of and support for third party candidates has led to a gap between the number of members who captured 60 percent of the major party vote (recorded in Table 2-12) and 60 percent of the total vote. The 1994 difference was just under two percentage points.

**Table 2-1** Turnout in Presidential and House Elections, 1930–1996 (percentage of voting age population)

| *Year* | *Presidential elections* | *House elections* |
|---|---|---|
| 1930 | — | 33.7 |
| 1932 | 52.4 | 49.7 |
| 1934 | — | 41.4 |
| 1936 | 56.9 | 53.5 |
| 1938 | — | 44.0 |
| 1940 | 58.9 | 55.4 |
| 1942 | — | 32.5 |
| 1944 | 56.0 | 52.7 |
| 1946 | — | 37.1 |
| 1948 | 51.1 | 48.1 |
| 1950 | — | 41.1 |
| 1952 | 61.6 | 57.6 |
| 1954 | — | 41.7 |
| 1956 | 59.3 | 55.9 |
| 1958 | — | 43.0 |
| 1960 | 62.6 | 58.5 |
| 1962 | — | 45.4 |
| 1964 | 61.9 | 57.8 |
| 1966 | — | 45.4 |
| 1968 | 60.9 | 55.1 |
| 1970 | — | 43.5 |
| 1972 | 55.4 | 50.9 |
| 1974 | — | 36.1 |
| 1976 | 54.4 | 49.5 |
| 1978 | — | 35.1 |
| 1980 | 53.4 | 48.1 |
| 1982 | — | 37.7 |
| 1984 | 53.3 | 47.4 |
| 1986 | — | 33.4 |
| 1988 | 50.1 | 44.7 |
| 1990 | — | 33.0 |
| 1992 | 55.2 | 50.8 |
| 1994 | — | 36.0 |
| 1996 | 49.0 | 47.0 |

*Sources:* U.S. Bureau of the Census, *Statistical Abstract of the United States* (Washington, D.C.: U.S. Government Printing Office, 1930 through 1976); U.S. Bureau of the Census, *Current Population Reports,* ser. P-25, no. 948 (Washington, D.C.: U.S. Government Printing Office); Clerk of the House of Representatives, *Statistics of the Presidential and Congressional Elections of November 6, 1984* (Washington, D.C.: U.S. Government Printing Office, 1985); *Congressional Quarterly Weekly Report,* March 31, 1979, 571; April 25, 1981, 716; February 17, 1983, 389; March 14, 1987, 485; January 21, 1989, 135; February 23, 1991, 484; April 17, 1993, 965-968; April 15, 1995, 1078; January 18, 1997.

**Table 2-2** Popular Vote and House Seats Won by Party, 1946–1996

| | *Democratic candidates* | | *Republican candidates* | | *Change from last election*[a] | | *Difference between Democratic percentage of seats and votes won* |
|---|---|---|---|---|---|---|---|
| *Year* | Percentage of all votes[b] | Percentage of seats won | Percentage of all votes[b] | Percentage of seats won | Percentage of major party votes | Percentage of seats won | |
| 1946 | 44.3 | 43.3 | 53.5 | 56.7 | 6.4R | 12.8R | –1.0 |
| 1948 | 51.6 | 60.6 | 45.4 | 39.4 | 7.9D | 17.3D | 9.0 |
| 1950 | 48.9 | 54.0 | 48.9 | 46.0 | 3.2R | 6.6R | 5.1 |
| 1952 | 49.2 | 49.1 | 49.3 | 50.9 | 0.1R | 4.9R | –0.1 |
| 1954 | 52.1 | 53.3 | 47.0 | 46.7 | 2.6D | 4.2D | 1.2 |
| 1956 | 50.7 | 53.8 | 48.7 | 46.2 | 1.5R | 0.5D | 3.1 |
| 1958 | 55.5 | 64.9 | 43.6 | 35.1 | 5.0D | 11.1D | 9.4 |
| 1960 | 54.4 | 60.0 | 44.8 | 40.0 | 1.2R | 4.9R | 5.6 |
| 1962 | 52.1 | 59.4 | 47.1 | 40.6 | 2.3R | 0.6R | 7.3 |
| 1964 | 56.9 | 67.8 | 42.4 | 32.2 | 4.8D | 8.4D | 10.9 |
| 1966 | 50.5 | 57.0 | 48.0 | 43.0 | 6.0R | 10.8R | 6.5 |
| 1968 | 50.0 | 55.9 | 48.2 | 44.1 | 0.3R | 1.1R | 5.9 |
| 1970 | 53.0 | 58.6 | 44.5 | 41.4 | 3.4D | 2.7D | 5.6 |
| 1972 | 51.7 | 55.8 | 46.4 | 44.2 | 1.7R | 2.8R | 4.1 |
| 1974 | 57.1 | 66.9 | 40.5 | 33.1 | 5.8D | 11.1D | 9.8 |
| 1976 | 56.2 | 67.1 | 42.1 | 32.9 | 1.3R | 0.2D | 10.9 |
| 1978 | 53.4 | 63.7 | 44.7 | 36.3 | 2.8R | 3.4R | 10.3 |
| 1980 | 50.4 | 55.9 | 48.0 | 44.1 | 3.2R | 7.8R | 5.5 |
| 1982 | 55.2 | 61.8 | 43.3 | 38.2 | 5.2D | 5.9D | 6.6 |
| 1984 | 52.1 | 58.2 | 47.0 | 41.8 | 4.1R | 3.6R | 6.1 |

| | | | | | | | |
|---|---|---|---|---|---|---|---|
| 1986 | 54.5 | 59.3 | 44.6 | 40.7 | 2.4D | 1.2D | 4.8 |
| 1988 | 53.3 | 59.8 | 45.5 | 40.2 | 1.1R | 0.5D | 6.5 |
| 1990 | 52.9 | 61.4 | 45.0 | 38.4[c] | 0.1D | 1.6D | 8.5 |
| 1992 | 50.8 | 59.3 | 45.6 | 40.5[c] | 1.4R | 2.1R | 8.5 |
| 1994 | 45.4 | 46.9 | 52.4 | 52.9[c] | 6.3R | 12.4R | –1.5 |
| 1996 | 48.5 | 47.6 | 48.9 | 52.2[c] | 3.4D | 0.7D | –0.9 |

[a] Data show percentage-point increase over previous election in votes or seats won by Republicans (R) or Democrats (D).

[b] Republican and Democratic percentages of all votes excludes districts in which candidates ran unopposed and no vote was recorded: for 1978, 8 districts from Arkansas, Florida, and Oklahoma; for 1980, 12 districts from Arkansas, Florida, Louisiana, and Oklahoma; for 1982, 11 districts from Florida and Louisiana; for 1984, 16 districts from Arkansas, Florida, and Louisiana; for 1986, 14 districts from Florida, Louisiana, and Oklahoma; for 1988, 16 districts from Florida and Louisiana; for 1990, 12 districts from Florida and Louisiana; for 1994, 13 districts from Florida and Louisiana; for 1996, 12 districts from Florida, Louisiana, Kentucky, West Virginia, and Georgia.

[c] For 1990–1996, total percentage of seats won—Democratic and Republican—does not equal one hundred due to the election of Bernard Sanders (I-Vt.).

*Sources: Congressional Quarterly Weekly Report,* June 11, 1977, 1141; March 31, 1979, 571; April 25, 1981, 713; November 11, 1982, 2817–2825; February 19, 1983, 387; April 15, 1985, 687; March 14, 1987, 484; May 6, 1989, 1063; February 23, 1991, 487; April 17, 1993, 965–968; April 15, 1995, 1076–1079; February 15, 1997, 444. Thomas E. Mann and Norman J. Ornstein, eds., *The American Elections of 1982* (Washington, D.C.: American Enterprise Institute, 1983).

**Table 2-3** Net Party Gains in House and Senate Seats, General and Special Elections, 1946–1996

| | *General elections*[a] | | *Special elections*[b] | |
|---|---|---|---|---|
| *Year* | House | Senate | House | Senate |
| | | | 2R (13) | 3R (8) |
| 1946 | 56R | 13R | | |
| | | | 0 (16) | 0 (3) |
| 1948 | 75D | 9D | | |
| | | | 0 (10) | 2R (6) |
| 1950 | 28R | 5R | | |
| | | | 3R (13) | 2R (4) |
| 1952 | 22R | 1R | | |
| | | | 2D (8) | 0 (9) |
| 1954 | 19D | 2D | | |
| | | | 0 (2) | 2R (3) |
| 1956 | 2D | 1D | | |
| | | | 0 (10) | 1D (4) |
| 1958 | 49D | 15D | | |
| | | | 1R (7) | 1D (3) |
| 1960 | 22R | 2R | | |
| | | | 0 (12) | 0 (6) |
| 1962 | 1R | 3D | | |
| | | | 2R (9) | 0 (2) |
| 1964 | 37D | 1D | | |
| | | | 0 (8) | 1R (3) |
| 1966 | 47R | 4R | | |
| | | | 1R (5) | 0 (0) |
| 1968 | 5R | 6R | | |
| | | | 3D (9) | 0 (2) |
| 1970 | 12D | 2R | | |
| | | | 0 (9) | 0 (2) |
| 1972 | 12R | 2D | | |
| | | | 4D (10) | 0 (0) |
| 1974 | 49D | 4D | | |
| | | | 0 (6) | 1D (1) |
| 1976 | 1D | 0 | | |
| | | | 4R (6) | 1R (2) |
| 1978 | 15R | 3R | | |
| | | | 1R (6) | 0 (0) |
| 1980 | 34R | 12R | | |
| | | | 1D (8) | 0 (0) |
| 1982 | 26D | 1R | | |
| | | | 1R (7) | 1R (1) |
| 1984 | 14R | 2D | | |
| | | | 0 (4) | 1D (1) |
| 1986 | 5D | 8D | | |
| | | | 1R (6) | 0 (0) |

| Year | *General elections*[a] | | *Special elections*[b] | |
|---|---|---|---|---|
| | House | Senate | House | Senate |
| 1988 | 2D | 0 | | |
| | | | 1D (11) | 0 (1) |
| 1990 | 9D | 1D | | |
| | | | 1D (6) | 2D (3)[c] |
| 1992 | 10R | 0 | | |
| | | | 2R (7) | 1R (2) |
| 1994 | 52R | 8R[d] | | |
| | | | 1R (5) | 1D (1) |
| 1996 | 9D | 2R | | |

*Note:* D indicates Democrats; R indicates Republicans.

[a] The general election figure is the difference between the number of seats won by the party gaining seats in that election and the number of seats won by that party in the preceding general election.

[b] The special election figure is the net shift in seats held by the major parties as a result of special elections held between the two general elections. The figure does not include special elections held on the day of the general election. The number of special elections is given in parentheses.

[c] The total number of special elections (3) includes the special election of Dianne Feinstein (D-Calif.) to fill the seat to which John Seymour was temporarily appointed. The special election was held at the same time as the general election (November 3, 1992).

[d] Sen. Richard Shelby (Ala.) switched from the Democratic to the Republican Party the day after the election, bringing the total Republican gain to nine.

*Sources: Statistics of the Congressional Election of November 7, 1978* (Washington, D.C.: U.S. Government Printing Office, 1979), 45; *Congressional Quarterly Almanac,* vols. 2-50 (Washington, D.C.: Congressional Quarterly, 1946-1994); *Congressional Quarterly's Guide to U.S. Elections* (Washington, D.C.: Congressional Quarterly, 1975); *Congressional Quarterly Weekly Report,* November 8, 1986; November 12, 1988; and conversations with the Federal Election Commission. For 1992: *National Journal,* November 7, 1992, 2555; *Congressional Quarterly Almanac* 1991. For 1993-1994: *Congressional Quarterly Almanac* 1993; *Congressional Quarterly Weekly Report,* various issues, 1994. Congressional Quarterly Research Service. For 1995–1996: *Congressional Quarterly Weekly Report,* various issues.

**Table 2-4** Losses by President's Party in Midterm Elections, 1862–1994

| *Year* | *Party holding presidency* | *President's party gain/loss of seats in House* | *President's party gain/loss of seats in Senate* |
|---|---|---|---|
| 1862 | R | –3 | 8 |
| 1866 | R | –2 | 0 |
| 1870 | R | –31 | –4 |
| 1874 | R | –96 | –8 |
| 1878 | R | –9 | –6 |
| 1882 | R | –33 | 3 |
| 1886 | D | –12 | 3 |
| 1890 | R | –85 | 0 |
| 1894 | D | –116 | –5 |
| 1898 | R | –21 | 7 |
| 1902 | R | 9[a] | 2 |
| 1906 | R | –28 | 3 |
| 1910 | R | –57 | –10 |
| 1914 | D | –59 | 5 |
| 1918 | D | –19 | –6 |
| 1922 | R | –75 | –8 |
| 1926 | R | –10 | –6 |
| 1930 | R | –49 | –8 |
| 1934 | D | 9 | 10 |
| 1938 | D | –71 | –6 |
| 1942 | D | –55 | –9 |
| 1946 | D | –45 | –12 |
| 1950 | D | –29 | –6 |
| 1954 | R | –18 | –1 |
| 1958 | R | –48 | –13 |
| 1962 | D | –4 | 3 |
| 1966 | D | –47 | –4 |
| 1970 | R | –12 | 2 |
| 1974 | R | –48 | –5 |
| 1978 | D | –15 | –3 |
| 1982 | R | –26 | 1 |
| 1986 | R | –5 | –8 |
| 1990 | R | –8 | –1 |
| 1994 | D | –52 | –8[b] |

*Note:* Each entry is the difference between the number of seats won by the president's party in that midterm election and the number of seats won by that party in the preceding general election. Because of changes in the overall number of seats in the Senate and House, in the number of seats won by third parties, and in the number of vacancies, a Republican loss is not always matched precisely by a Democratic gain, or vice versa.

[a] Although the Republicans gained nine seats in the 1902 elections, they actually lost ground to the Democrats, who gained twenty-five seats after the increase in the overall number of representatives after the 1900 census.

[b] Sen. Richard Shelby (Ala.) switched from the Democratic to the Republican Party the day following the election for a total loss of nine seats.

*Sources: Statistics of the Congressional Election of November 7, 1978,* 44-45; Thomas Mann and Norman Ornstein, "The 1982 Election: What Will It Mean?" *Public Opinion,* June/July 1981, 49; *Congressional Quarterly Almanac,* vols. 10-40; *Congressional Quarterly Weekly Report,* November 8, 1986; November 10, 1990; *National Journal,* November 12, 1994.

**Table 2-5** House Seats That Changed Party, 1954–1996

| | | *Incumbent defeated* | | *Open seat* | |
|---|---|---|---|---|---|
| *Year* | *Total changes* | D→R | R→D | D→R | R→D |
| 1954 | 26 | 3 | 18 | 2 | 3 |
| 1956 | 20 | 7 | 7 | 2 | 4 |
| 1958 | 50 | 1 | 35 | 0 | 14 |
| 1960 | 37 | 23 | 2 | 6 | 6 |
| 1962 | 19 | 9 | 5 | 2 | 3 |
| 1964 | 57 | 5 | 39 | 5 | 8 |
| 1966 | 47 | 39 | 1 | 4 | 3 |
| 1968 | 11 | 5 | 0 | 2 | 4 |
| 1970 | 25 | 2 | 9 | 6 | 8 |
| 1972 | 23 | 6 | 3 | 9 | 5 |
| 1974 | 55 | 4 | 36 | 2 | 13 |
| 1976 | 22 | 7 | 5 | 3 | 7 |
| 1978 | 33 | 14 | 5 | 8 | 6 |
| 1980 | 41 | 27 | 3 | 10 | 1 |
| 1982 | 31 | 1 | 22 | 3 | 5 |
| 1984 | 22 | 13 | 3 | 5 | 1 |
| 1986 | 21 | 1 | 5 | 7 | 8 |
| 1988 | 9 | 2 | 4 | 1 | 2 |
| 1990 | 21 | 6 | 9 | 0 | 6 |
| 1992 | 43 | 16 | 8 | 11 | 8 |
| 1994 | 60 | 34 | 0 | 22 | 4 |
| 1996 | 35 | 3 | 18 | 10 | 4 |

*Note:* D indicates Democrat; R indicates Republican. This table reflects shifts in party control of seats from immediately before to immediately after the November elections. It does not include party gains resulting from the creation of new districts and does not account for situations in which two districts were reduced to one, thus forcing incumbents to run against each other.

*Sources: Congressional Quarterly Almanac,* vols. 10-40; *Congressional Quarterly Weekly Report,* November 10, 1984, 2900; November 8, 1986, 2844; November 12, 1988, 3270; November 10, 1990, 3801; *National Journal,* November 7, 1992, 2555; November 12, 1994, 2652; November 9, 1996.

Figure 2-1 House Seats that Changed Party, 1954–1996

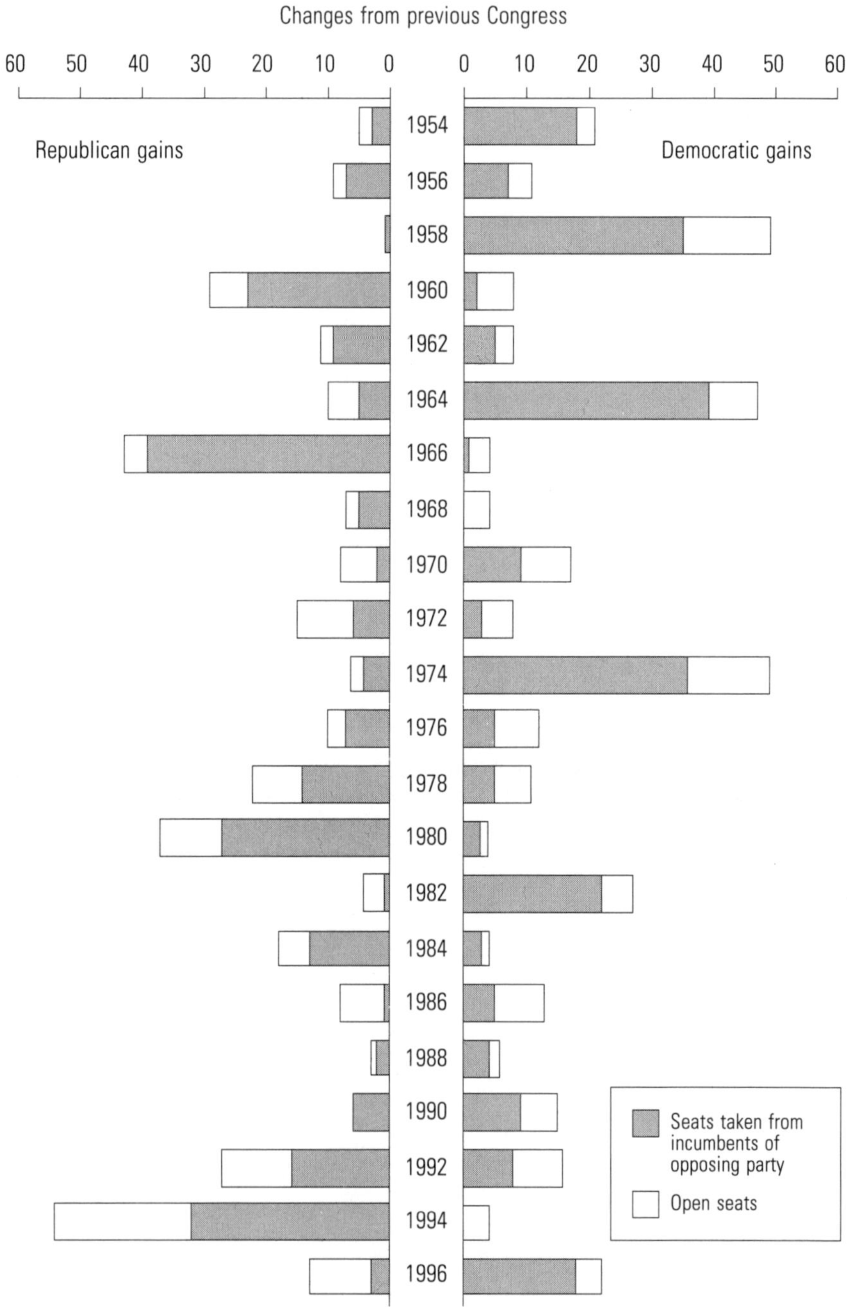


*Source:* Table 2-5.

**Table 2-6** Senate Seats That Changed Party, 1954–1996

| | | *Incumbent defeated* | | *Open seat* | |
|---|---|---|---|---|---|
| *Year* | *changes* | D→R | R→D | D→R | R→D |
| 1954 | 8 | 2 | 4 | 1 | 1 |
| 1956 | 8 | 1 | 3 | 3 | 1 |
| 1958 | 13 | 0 | 11 | 0 | 2 |
| 1960 | 2 | 1 | 0 | 1 | 0 |
| 1962 | 8 | 2 | 3 | 0 | 3 |
| 1964 | 4 | 1 | 3 | 0 | 0 |
| 1966 | 3 | 1 | 0 | 2 | 0 |
| 1968 | 9 | 4 | 0 | 3 | 2 |
| 1970 | 6 | 3 | 2 | 1 | 0 |
| 1972 | 10 | 1 | 4 | 3 | 2 |
| 1974 | 6 | 0 | 2 | 1 | 3 |
| 1976 | 14 | 5 | 4 | 2 | 3 |
| 1978 | 13 | 5 | 2 | 3 | 3 |
| 1980 | 12 | 9 | 0 | 3 | 0 |
| 1982 | 4 | 1 | 1 | 1 | 1 |
| 1984 | 4 | 1 | 2 | 0 | 1 |
| 1986 | 10 | 0 | 7 | 1 | 2 |
| 1988 | 7 | 1 | 3 | 2 | 1 |
| 1990 | 1 | 0 | 1 | 0 | 0 |
| 1992 | 4 | 2 | 2 | 0 | 0 |
| 1994 | 8[a] | 2 | 0 | 6 | 0 |
| 1996 | 4 | 0 | 1 | 3 | 0 |

*Note:* D indicates Democrat; R indicates Republican. This table reflects shifts in party control of seats from immediately before to immediately after the November election.

[a] Sen. Richard Shelby (Ala.) switched from the Democratic to the Republican Party the day after the election, bringing the total change to nine.

*Sources: Congressional Quarterly Almanac,* vols. 10-40; *National Journal,* November 10, 1984, 2137, 2147; *Congressional Quarterly Weekly Report,* November 8, 1986, 2813; November 12, 1988, 3264; November 10, 1990, 3825; *National Journal,* November 7, 1992, 2555; November 12, 1994, 2635; November 9, 1996.

Figure 2-2 Senate Seats that Changed Party, 1954–1996

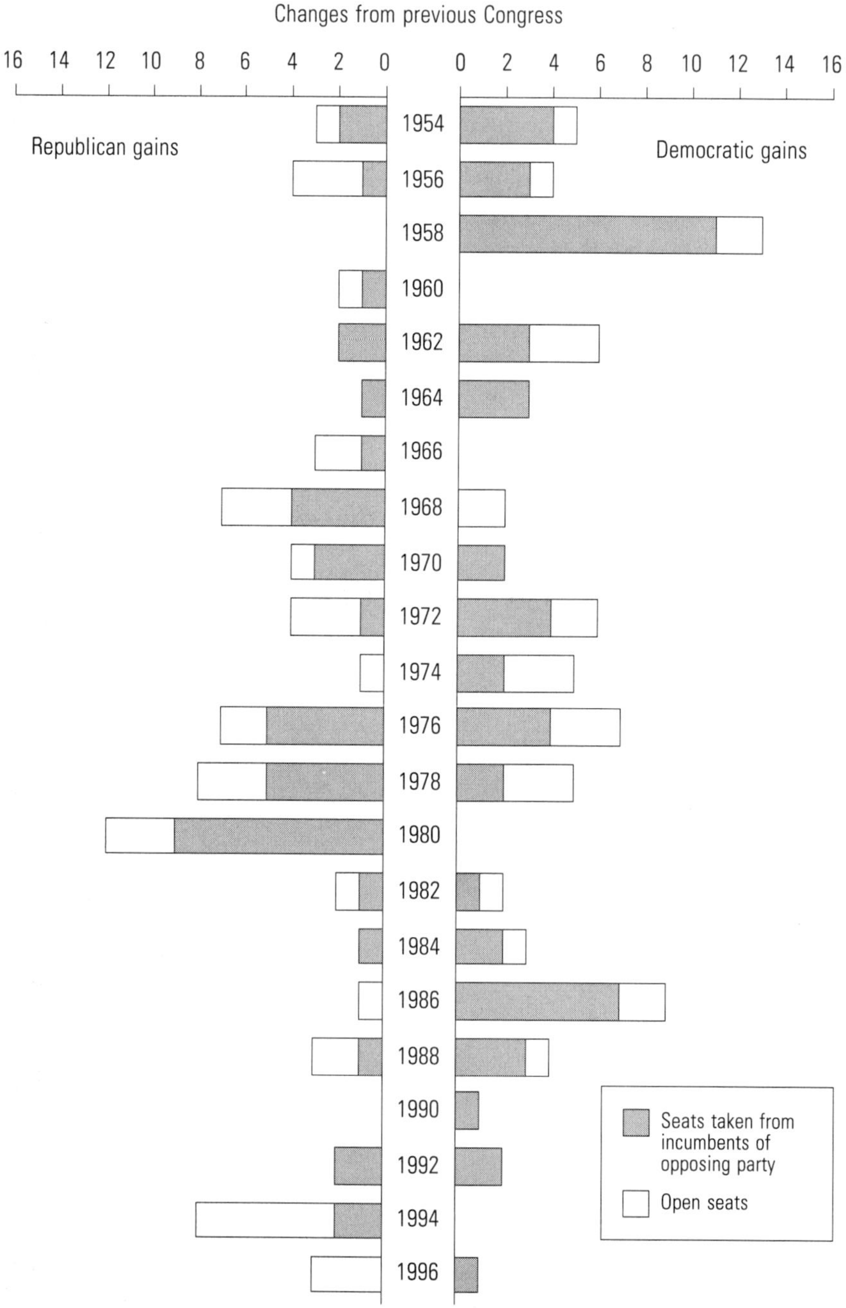


*Source:* Table 2-6.

**Table 2-7** House Incumbents Retired, Defeated, or Reelected, 1946–1996

| *Year* | *Retired*[a] | *Total seeking reelection* | *Defeated in primaries* | *Defeated in general election* | *Total reelected* | *Percentage of those seeking reelection* | *Reelected as percentage of House membership* |
|---|---|---|---|---|---|---|---|
| 1946 | 32 | 398 | 18 | 52 | 328 | 82.4 | 75.4 |
| 1948 | 29 | 400 | 15 | 68 | 317 | 79.3 | 72.9 |
| 1950 | 29 | 400 | 6 | 32 | 362 | 90.5 | 83.2 |
| 1952 | 42 | 389 | 9 | 26 | 354 | 91.0 | 81.4 |
| 1954 | 24 | 407 | 6 | 22 | 379 | 93.1 | 87.1 |
| 1956 | 21 | 411 | 6 | 16 | 389 | 94.6 | 89.4 |
| 1958 | 33 | 396 | 3 | 37 | 356 | 89.9 | 81.8 |
| 1960 | 26 | 405 | 5 | 25 | 375 | 92.6 | 86.2 |
| 1962 | 24 | 402 | 12 | 22 | 368 | 91.5 | 84.6 |
| 1964 | 33 | 397 | 8 | 45 | 344 | 86.6 | 79.1 |
| 1966 | 22 | 411 | 8 | 41 | 362 | 88.1 | 83.2 |
| 1968 | 23 | 409 | 4 | 9 | 396 | 96.8 | 91.0 |
| 1970 | 29 | 401 | 10 | 12 | 379 | 94.5 | 87.1 |
| 1972 | 40 | 393 | 11 | 13 | 365 | 93.6 | 83.9 |
| 1974 | 43 | 391 | 8 | 40 | 343 | 87.7 | 78.9 |
| 1976 | 47 | 384 | 3 | 13 | 368 | 95.8 | 84.6 |
| 1978 | 49 | 3B2 | 5 | 19 | 358 | 93.7 | 82.3 |
| 1980 | 34 | 398 | 6 | 31 | 361 | 90.7 | 83.0 |
| 1982 | 40 | 393 | 10 | 29 | 354 | 90.1 | 81.4 |
| 1984 | 22 | 411 | 3 | 16 | 392 | 95.4 | 90.1 |
| 1986 | 40 | 394 | 3 | 6 | 385 | 97.7 | 88.5 |
| 1988 | 23 | 409 | 1 | 6 | 402 | 98.3 | 92.4 |
| 1990 | 27 | 406 | 1 | 15 | 390 | 96.0 | 89.7 |
| 1992 | 65 | 368 | 19 | 24 | 325 | 88.3 | 74.7 |
| 1994 | 48 | 387 | 4 | 34 | 349 | 90.2 | 80.0 |
| 1996 | 49 | 384 | 2 | 21 | 361 | 94.0 | 83.0 |

[a] Does not include persons who died or resigned before the election.

*Sources: Congressional Quarterly Weekly Report,* January 12, 1980, 81; April 5, 1980, 908; November 8, 1980, 3320–3321; November 10, 1984, 2900; October 11, 1986, 2398; November 8, 1986, 2844; November 12, 1988, 3270; November 7, 1992, 3579; *National Journal,* November 6, 1982, 1881; November 10, 1984, 2147; November 10, 1990, 2719; November 12, 1994, 2650–2651; November 9, 1997.

**Table 2-8** Senate Incumbents Retired, Defeated, or Reelected, 1946–1996

| *Year* | *Retired*[a] | *Total seeking reelection* | *Defeated in primaries* | *Defeated in general election* | *Total reelected* | *Reelected as percentage of those seeking reelection* |
|---|---|---|---|---|---|---|
| 1946 | 9 | 30 | 6 | 7 | 17 | 56.7 |
| 1948 | 8 | 25 | 2 | 8 | 15 | 60.0 |
| 1950 | 4 | 32 | 5 | 5 | 22 | 68.8 |
| 1952 | 4 | 31 | 2 | 9 | 20 | 64.5 |
| 1954 | 6 | 32 | 2 | 6 | 24 | 75.0 |
| 1956 | 6 | 29 | 0 | 4 | 25 | 86.2 |
| 1958 | 6 | 28 | 0 | 10 | 18 | 64.3 |
| 1960 | 5 | 29 | 0 | 1 | 28 | 96.6 |
| 1962 | 4 | 35 | 1 | 5 | 29 | 82.9 |
| 1964 | 2 | 33 | 1 | 4 | 28 | 84.8 |
| 1966 | 3 | 32 | 3 | 1 | 28 | 87.5 |
| 1968 | 6 | 28 | 4 | 4 | 20 | 71.4 |
| 1970 | 4 | 31 | 1 | 6 | 24 | 77.4 |
| 1972 | 6 | 27 | 2 | 5 | 20 | 74.1 |
| 1974 | 7 | 27 | 2 | 2 | 23 | 85.2 |
| 1976 | 8 | 25 | 0 | 9 | 16 | 64.0 |
| 1978 | 10 | 25 | 3 | 7 | 15 | 60.0 |
| 1980 | 5 | 29 | 4 | 9 | 16 | 55.2 |
| 1982 | 3 | 30 | 0 | 2 | 28 | 93.3 |
| 1984 | 4 | 29 | 0 | 3 | 26 | 89.6 |
| 1986 | 6 | 28 | 0 | 7 | 21 | 75.0 |
| 1988 | 6 | 27 | 0 | 4 | 23 | 85.2 |
| 1990 | 3 | 32 | 0 | 1 | 31 | 96.9 |
| 1992 | 7 | 28 | 1 | 4 | 23 | 82.1 |
| 1994 | 9 | 26 | 0 | 2 | 24 | 92.3 |
| 1996 | 13 | 21 | 1[b] | 1 | 19 | 90.5 |

[a] Does not include persons who died or resigned before the election.
[b] Sheila Frahm, appointed to fill Robert Dole's term, is counted as an incumbent in Kansas's "B" seat.

*Sources: Congressional Quarterly Weekly Report,* January 12, 1980, 81; April 5, 1980, 908; November 8, 1980, 3302; November 6, 1982, 2791; November 10, 1984, 2905; October 11, 1986, 2398; November 8, 1986, 2813; November 12, 1988; November 10, 1990; November 7, 1992, 3557; *National Journal,* November 12, 1994; November 9, 1996.

**Table 2-9** House and Senate Retirements by Party, 1930–1996

| | *House* | | *Senate* | |
|---|---|---|---|---|
| *Year* | D | R | D | R |
| 1930 | 8 | 15 | 2 | 5 |
| 1932 | 16 | 23 | 1 | 1 |
| 1934 | 29 | 9 | 3 | 1 |
| 1936 | 29 | 3 | 4 | 2 |
| 1938 | 21 | 5 | 3 | 1 |
| 1940 | 16 | 6 | 1 | 2 |
| 1942 | 20 | 12 | 0 | 0 |
| 1944 | 17 | 5 | 3 | 2 |
| 1946 | 17 | 15 | 4 | 3 |
| 1948 | 17 | 12 | 3 | 4 |
| 1950 | 12 | 17 | 3 | 1 |
| 1952 | 25 | 17 | 2 | 1 |
| 1954 | 11 | 13 | 1 | 1 |
| 1956 | 7 | 13 | 4 | 1 |
| 1958 | 6 | 27 | 0 | 6 |
| 1960 | 11 | 15 | 3 | 1 |
| 1962 | 10 | 14 | 2 | 2 |
| 1964 | 17 | 16 | 1 | 1 |
| 1966 | 14 | 8 | 1 | 2 |
| 1968 | 13 | 10 | 4 | 3 |
| 1970 | 11 | 19 | 3 | 1 |
| 1972 | 20 | 20 | 3 | 3 |
| 1974 | 23 | 21 | 3 | 4 |
| 1976 | 31 | 16 | 4 | 4 |
| 1978 | 31 | 18 | 4 | 5 |
| 1980 | 21 | 13 | 2 | 3 |
| 1982 | 19 | 21 | 1 | 2 |
| 1984 | 9 | 13 | 2 | 2 |
| 1986 | 20 | 20 | 3 | 3 |
| 1988 | 10 | 13 | 3 | 3 |
| 1990 | 10 | 17 | 0 | 3 |
| 1992 | 41 | 24 | 4 | 3 |
| 1994 | 28 | 20 | 6 | 3 |
| 1996 | 28 | 21 | 8 | 5 |

*Note:* These figures include members who did not run again for the office they held and members who sought other offices; they do not include members who died or resigned before the end of the Congress.

*Sources:* Mildred L. Amer, "Information on the Number of House Retirees, 1930-1992," Congressional Research Service, Staff Report, Washington, D.C., May 19, 1992. *Congressional Quarterly Weekly Report,* November 8, 1980, 3320-3321; October 11, 1986, 2398; November 12, 1988; November 10, 1990; *National Journal,* November 6, 1982, 1881; November 11, 1984, 2147; November 10, 1990; November 7, 1992; November 12, 1994; November 9, 1996.

**Table 2-10** Defeated House Incumbents, 1946-1996

| *Election* | *Party* | *Incumbents lost* | *Average terms* | *Consecutive terms served* | | | | | | |
|---|---|---|---|---|---|---|---|---|---|---|
| | | | | 1 | 2 | 3 | 1–3 | 4–6 | 7–9 | 10+ |
| 1946 | Democrat | 62 | 2.7 | 35 | 5 | 4 | 44 | 11 | 5 | 2 |
| | Republican | 7 | 3.6 | 2 | 0 | 1 | 3 | 3 | 1 | 0 |
| | Total | 69 | 2.8 | 37 | 5 | 5 | 47 | 14 | 6 | 2 |
| 1948 | Democrat[a] | 9 | 2.7 | 4 | 1 | 1 | 6 | 3 | 0 | 0 |
| | Republican | 73 | 2.2 | 41 | 3 | 12 | 56 | 14 | 2 | 1 |
| | Total | 82 | 2.2 | 45 | 4 | 13 | 62 | 17 | 2 | 1 |
| 1958 | Democrat[b] | 6 | 5.0 | 1 | 1 | 0 | 2 | 2 | 1 | 1 |
| | Republican | 34 | 4.3 | 9 | 0 | 4 | 13 | 14 | 6 | 1 |
| | Total | 40 | 4.4 | 10 | 1 | 4 | 15 | 16 | 7 | 2 |
| 1966 | Democrat | 43 | 3.3 | 26 | 6 | 0 | 32 | 4 | 1 | 6 |
| | Republican | 2 | 11.0 | 1 | 0 | 0 | 1 | 0 | 0 | 1 |
| | Total | 45 | 3.7 | 27 | 6 | 0 | 33 | 4 | 1 | 7 |
| 1974 | Democrat | 9 | 4.7 | 1 | 1 | 1 | 3 | 3 | 2 | 1 |
| | Republican | 39 | 3.8 | 11 | 2 | 6 | 19 | 15 | 2 | 3 |
| | Total | 48 | 3.9 | 12 | 3 | 7 | 22 | 18 | 4 | 4 |
| 1978 | Democrat | 19 | 4.0 | 3 | 8 | 2 | 13 | 2 | 1 | 3 |
| | Republican | 5 | 5.4 | 2 | 0 | 0 | 2 | 2 | 0 | 1 |
| | Total | 24 | 4.2 | 5 | 8 | 2 | 15 | 4 | 1 | 4 |
| 1980 | Democrat | 32 | 5.2 | 5 | 2 | 10 | 17 | 5 | 4 | 6 |
| | Republican | 5 | 5.3 | 1 | 0 | 1 | 2 | 1 | 1 | 1 |
| | Total | 37 | 5.2 | 6 | 2 | 11 | 19 | 6 | 5 | 7 |
| 1982 | Democrat | 4 | 2.9 | 1 | 0 | 1 | 2 | 2 | 0 | 0 |
| | Republican[c] | 23 | 3.0 | 12 | 3 | 2 | 17 | 2 | 2 | 2 |
| | Total | 27 | 3.0 | 13 | 3 | 3 | 19 | 4 | 2 | 2 |

| | | | | | | | | | | |
|---|---|---|---|---|---|---|---|---|---|---|
| 1984 | Democrat | 16 | 4.1 | 6 | 1 | 2 | 9 | 4 | 1 | 2 |
| | Republican | 3 | 3.7 | 0 | 0 | 2 | 2 | 1 | 0 | 0 |
| | Total | 19 | 4.1 | 6 | 1 | 4 | 11 | 5 | 1 | 2 |
| 1986 | Democrat | 3 | 1.8 | 2 | 0 | 0 | 2 | 1 | 0 | 0 |
| | Republican | 6 | 1.5 | 4 | 1 | 1 | 6 | 0 | 0 | 0 |
| | Total | 9 | 1.6 | 6 | 1 | 1 | 8 | 1 | 0 | 0 |
| 1988 | Democrat | 2 | 12.0 | 0 | 0 | 0 | 0 | 0 | 0 | 2 |
| | Republican | 5 | 1.6 | 2 | 3 | 0 | 5 | 0 | 0 | 0 |
| | Total | 7 | 4.6 | 2 | 3 | 0 | 5 | 0 | 0 | 2 |
| 1990 | Democrat | 6 | 6.3 | 0 | 1 | 0 | 1 | 3 | 1 | 1 |
| | Republican[d] | 10 | 3.6 | 2 | 3 | 0 | 5 | 4 | 1 | 0 |
| | Total | 16 | 4.6 | 2 | 4 | 0 | 6 | 7 | 2 | 1 |
| 1992 | Democrat | 30 | 5.6 | 2 | 1 | 4 | 7 | 12 | 10 | 1 |
| | Republican | 13 | 6.8 | 2 | 0 | 2 | 4 | 1 | 6 | 2 |
| | Total | 43 | 6.0 | 4 | 1 | 6 | 11 | 13 | 16 | 3 |
| 1994 | Democrat | 37 | 4.2 | 16 | 3 | 5 | 24 | 7 | 2 | 4 |
| | Republican | 1 | 1.0 | 1 | 0 | 0 | 1 | 0 | 0 | 0 |
| | Total | 38 | 4.1 | 17 | 3 | 5 | 25 | 7 | 2 | 4 |
| 1996 | Democrat[e] | 3 | 4.7 | 1 | 0 | 1 | 2 | 0 | 0 | 1 |
| | Republican | 18 | 1.8 | 12 | 4 | 1 | 17 | 0 | 1 | 0 |
| | Total | 21 | 2.1 | 13 | 4 | 2 | 19 | 0 | 1 | 1 |

*Note:* The 1966 and 1982 numbers do not include races where incumbents ran against incumbents due to redistricting. And, incumbents who lost in the primary as their party's incumbent but then ran in the general election as a write-in or third party candidate were counted as an incumbent loss.

[a] Includes Leo Isacson (N.Y.) who was a member of the American Labor Party.
[b] Includes Vincent Dellay (N.J.) who was elected as a Republican but switched to a Democrat. He ran for reelection as an Independent.
[c] Includes Eugene Atkinson (Pa.) who began his House service January 3, 1979, as a Democrat. He became a Republican on October 14, 1981.
[d] Includes Bill Grant (Fla.) who began his House service January 6, 1987, as a Democrat, but later switched parties. The Republican Conference let his seniority count from 1987, and includes Donald Lukens (Ohio) who was defeated in the primary, then resigned October 24, 1990.
[e] One Democratic incumbent who served more than ten terms in office was defeated.

*Sources:* 1946, 1948, 1958, 1966, 1974, 1977–1993, *Congressional Quarterly Almanac; National Journal,* November 12, 1994 and November 9, 1996; *Biographical Directory of the United States Congress 1774–1989.*

**Table 2-11** Defeated Senate Incumbents, 1946–1996

| | | | | *Consecutive terms served* | | | | | |
|---|---|---|---|---|---|---|---|---|---|
| *Election* | *Party* | *Incumbents lost* | *Average terms* | 1 | 2 | 3 | 4 | 5 | 6+ |
| 1946 | Democrat | 11 | 1.6 | 7 | 2 | 1 | 1 | 0 | 0 |
| | Republican | 2 | 4.0 | 0 | 0 | 0 | 2 | 0 | 0 |
| | Total | 13 | 2.0 | 7 | 2 | 1 | 3 | 0 | 0 |
| 1948 | Democrat | 2 | 1.5 | 1 | 1 | 0 | 0 | 0 | 0 |
| | Republican | 8 | 1.0 | 8 | 0 | 0 | 0 | 0 | 0 |
| | Total | 10 | 1.1 | 9 | 1 | 0 | 0 | 0 | 0 |
| 1958 | Republican | 10 | 1.4 | 6 | 4 | 0 | 0 | 0 | 0 |
| | Total | 10 | 1.4 | 6 | 4 | 0 | 0 | 0 | 0 |
| 1966 | Democrat | 4 | 2.0 | 2 | 0 | 2 | 0 | 0 | 0 |
| | Total | 4 | 2.0 | 2 | 0 | 2 | 0 | 0 | 0 |
| 1974 | Democrat | 2 | 3.0 | 1 | 0 | 0 | 0 | 1 | 0 |
| | Republican | 2 | 1.5 | 1 | 1 | 0 | 0 | 0 | 0 |
| | Total | 4 | 2.2 | 2 | 1 | 0 | 0 | 1 | 0 |
| 1978 | Democrat | 7 | 0.9 | 6 | 0 | 1 | 0 | 0 | 0 |
| | Republican | 3 | 2.7 | 0 | 2 | 0 | 1 | 0 | 0 |
| | Total | 10 | 1.4 | 6 | 2 | 1 | 1 | 0 | 0 |
| 1980 | Democrat | 12 | 2.4 | 5 | 1 | 3 | 2 | 0 | 1 |
| | Republican | 1 | 4.0 | 0 | 0 | 0 | 1 | 0 | 0 |
| | Total | 13 | 2.6 | 5 | 1 | 3 | 3 | 0 | 1 |
| 1982 | Democrat | 1 | 4.0 | 0 | 0 | 0 | 1 | 0 | 0 |
| | Republican | 1 | 1.0 | 1 | 0 | 0 | 0 | 0 | 0 |
| | Total | 2 | 2.5 | 1 | 0 | 0 | 1 | 0 | 0 |

| | | | | | | | | | |
|---|---|---|---|---|---|---|---|---|---|
| 1984 | Democrat | 1 | 2.0 | 0 | 1 | 0 | 0 | 0 | 0 |
| | Republican | 2 | 2.0 | 1 | 0 | 1 | 0 | 0 | 0 |
| | Total | 3 | 2.0 | 1 | 1 | 1 | 0 | 0 | 0 |
| 1986 | Republican[a] | 7 | 0.9 | 7 | 0 | 0 | 0 | 0 | 0 |
| | Total | 7 | 0.9 | 7 | 0 | 0 | 0 | 0 | 0 |
| 1988 | Democrat | 1 | 2.0 | 0 | 1 | 0 | 0 | 0 | 0 |
| | Republican | 3 | 1.4 | 2 | 0 | 1 | 0 | 0 | 0 |
| | Total | 4 | 1.6 | 2 | 1 | 1 | 0 | 0 | 0 |
| 1990 | Republican | 1 | 2.0 | 0 | 1 | 0 | 0 | 0 | 0 |
| | Total | 1 | 2.0 | 0 | 1 | 0 | 0 | 0 | 0 |
| 1992 | Democrat | 3 | 1.3 | 2 | 1 | 0 | 0 | 0 | 0 |
| | Republican | 2 | 1.2 | 1 | 1 | 0 | 0 | 0 | 0 |
| | Total | 5 | 1.3 | 3 | 2 | 0 | 0 | 0 | 0 |
| 1994 | Democrat | 2 | 1.8 | 1 | 0 | 1 | 0 | 0 | 0 |
| | Total | 2 | 1.8 | 1 | 0 | 1 | 0 | 0 | 0 |
| 1996 | Republican | 2 | 2.0 | 1 | 0 | 1 | 0 | 0 | 0 |
| | Total | 2 | 2.0 | 1 | 0 | 1 | 0 | 0 | 0 |

[a] Includes James Broyhill (N.C.) who was appointed July 14, 1986, until November 4, 1986. He lost to Terry Sanford who took over the seat on November 5, 1986.

*Sources:* 1946, 1948, 1958, 1966, 1974, 1977-1993, *Congressional Quarterly Almanac; National Journal,* November 12, 1994, November 9, 1996; *Biographical Directory of the United States Congress 1774–1989.*

**Table 2-12** House Elections Won with 60 Percent of Major Party Vote, 1956–1996

| *Year* | *Number of incumbents running in general election* | *Percentage of incumbents reelected with at least 60 percent of the major party vote* |
|---|---|---|
| 1956 | 403 | 59.1 |
| 1958 | 390 | 63.1 |
| 1960 | 400 | 58.9 |
| 1962 | 376 | 63.6 |
| 1964 | 388 | 58.5 |
| 1966 | 401 | 67.7 |
| 1968 | 397 | 72.2 |
| 1970 | 389 | 77.3 |
| 1972 | 373 | 77.8 |
| 1974 | 383 | 66.4 |
| 1976 | 381 | 71.9 |
| 1978 | 377 | 78.0 |
| 1980 | 392 | 72.9 |
| 1982 | 383 | 68.9 |
| 1984 | 406 | 74.6 |
| 1986 | 391 | 86.4 |
| 1988 | 407 | 88.5 |
| 1990 | 406 | 76.4 |
| 1992 | 349 | 65.6 |
| 1994 | 383 | 64.5 |
| 1996 | 383 | 73.6 |

*Sources:* Albert D. Cover and David R. Mayhew, "Congressional Dynamics and the Decline of Competitive Congressional Elections," in *Congress Reconsidered,* 2d ed., ed. Lawrence C. Dodd and Bruce I. Oppenheimer (Washington, D.C.: CQ Press, 1981); *Congressional Quarterly Weekly Report,* April 25, 1981, 717–725; February 19, 1983, 386–394; April 13, 1985, 689–695; March 14, 1987, 486–493; November 12, 1988; February 23, 1991, 493–500; Mann and Ornstein, *The American Elections of 1982; Congressional Quarterly Weekly Report,* April 17, 1993, 973–980; April 15, 1995, 1090–1097; February 15, 1997, 447–455.

**Table 2-13** Senate Elections Won with 60 Percent of Major Party Vote, 1944–1996

| *Election period* | *Number of incumbents running in general election* | *Percentage of incumbents reelected with at least 60 percent of the major party vote*[a] | | |
|---|---|---|---|---|
| | | South | North | Total U.S. |
| 1944–1948 | 61 | 100.0 | 22.9 | 39.3 |
| 1950–1954 | 76 | 100.0 | 18.3 | 35.5 |
| 1956–1960 | 84 | 95.5 | 24.2 | 42.9 |
| 1962–1966 | 86 | 70.0 | 36.4 | 44.2 |
| 1968–1972 | 74 | 71.4 | 38.3 | 44.6 |
| 1974–1978 | 70 | 57.1 | 37.5 | 41.4 |
| 1980–1984[b] | 84 | 63.3 | 51.9 | 54.1 |
| 1986–1990 | 87 | 68.2 | 53.9 | 57.5 |
| 1992–1994 | 53 | 66.7 | 34.2 | 43.4 |
| 1994–1996 | 19 | 33.3 | 0 | 31.6 |

[a] For the purposes of this table, senators appointed to the Senate are not considered incumbents in the elections just after appointment.

[b] Includes two Democratic incumbents from Louisiana, who, by winning more than 50 percent of the vote in that state's all-party primary, avoided a general election contest. In 1980 Russell Long won 59.8 percent of the vote, and in 1984 J. Bennett Johnston won 86 percent of the vote.

*Sources:* Cover and Mayhew, "Congressional Dynamics"; *Congressional Quarterly Weekly Report,* April 25, 1981, 717–725; February 19, 1983, 386–394; April 13, 1985, 689–695; March 14, 1987, 484–493; November 12, 1988; February 23, 1991, 493–500; April 17, 1993, 973–980; April 15, 1995, 1090–1097; *National Journal,* November 9, 1996.

**Table 2-14** Marginal Races Among Members of the 105th Congress, 1996

| *Chamber* | *Members who ever won a congressional election by 60 percent or less* | | *Members who ever won a congressional election by 55 percent or less* | |
|---|---|---|---|---|
| | Number | Percentage | Number | Percentage |
| House | 324 | 74.5 | 233 | 53.6 |
| Senate | 93 | 93.0 | 75 | 75.0 |

*Source: Congressional Quarterly Weekly Report,* February 15, 1997, 447–455.

**Table 2-15** Conditions of Initial Election for Members of the 105th Congress, 1997

| | *House* | | | | *Senate* | | |
|---|---|---|---|---|---|---|---|
| *Condition* | Democrats | Republicans | Total | Percentage of entire house | Democrats | Republicans | Total |
| Defeated incumbent | | | | | | | |
| In primary | 15 | 5 | 20 | 4.6 | 5 | 1 | 6 |
| In general election | 41 | 57 | 98 | 22.5 | 19 | 11 | 30 |
| Succeeded retiring incumbent | | | | | | | |
| Of same party | 99 | 77 | 176 | 40.6 | 16 | 22 | 38 |
| Of other party | 19 | 55 | 74 | 17.0 | 5 | 17 | 22 |
| Succeeded deceased incumbent | | | | | | | |
| Of same party | 9 | 12 | 21 | 4.8 | 0 | 1 | 1 |
| Of other party | 3 | 14 | 7 | 1.6 | 0 | 1 | 1 |
| Defeated candidate in general election who had earlier defeated incumbent in primary | 1 | 5 | 6 | 1.4 | 0 | 2 | 2 |
| New districts | 20 | 12 | 32 | 7.4 | 0 | 0 | 0 |
| Total | 207 | 227 | 434[a] | 100.0 | 45 | 55 | 100 |

*Note:* Percentages do not add to 100.0 because of rounding.

[a] Total does not include Bernard Sanders (I-Vt.).

*Sources: Congressional Quarterly Almanac,* vols. 11-39; *Congressional Directory* (Washington, D.C.: U.S. Government Printing Office, 1981, 1983, 1985); Alan Ehrenhalt, ed., *Politics in America* (Washington, D.C.: Congressional Quarterly, various years); Michael Barone and Grant Ujifusa, *The Almanac of American Politics* (Washington, D.C.: National Journal, various years); *Congressional Quarterly Weekly Report,* various issues.

**Table 2-16** Ticket Splitting between Presidential and House Candidates, 1900-1996

| | | *Districts with split results*[b] | |
|---|---|---|---|
| *Year* | *Districts*[a] | Number | Percentage |
| 1900 | 295 | 10 | 3.4 |
| 1904 | 310 | 5 | 1.6 |
| 1908 | 314 | 21 | 6.7 |
| 1912 | 333 | 84 | 25.2 |
| 1916 | 333 | 35 | 10.5 |
| 1920 | 344 | 11 | 3.2 |
| 1924 | 356 | 42 | 11.8 |
| 1928 | 359 | 68 | 18.9 |
| 1932 | 355 | 50 | 14.1 |
| 1936 | 361 | 51 | 14.1 |
| 1940 | 362 | 53 | 14.6 |
| 1944 | 367 | 41 | 11.2 |
| 1948 | 422 | 90 | 21.3 |
| 1952 | 435 | 84 | 19.3 |
| 1956 | 435 | 130 | 29.9 |
| 1960 | 437 | 114 | 26.1 |
| 1964 | 435 | 145 | 33.3 |
| 1968 | 435 | 139 | 32.0 |
| 1972 | 435 | 192 | 44.1 |
| 1976 | 435 | 124 | 28.5 |
| 1980 | 435 | 143 | 32.8 |
| 1984 | 435 | 190 | 43.7 |
| 1988 | 435 | 148 | 34.0 |
| 1992 | 435 | 100 | 23.0 |
| 1996 | 435 | 110 | 25.5 |

[a] Before 1952 complete data are not available on every congressional district.
[b] Congressional districts carried by a presidential candidate of one party and a House candidate of another party.

*Sources: Congressional Quarterly Weekly Report,* April 22, 1978, 972, April 12, 1997, 862; Walter Dean Burnham, *Critical Elections* (New York: Norton, 1970), 109; Michael Barone and Grant Ujifusa, *The Almanac of American Politics 1982* (Washington: Barone and Co., 1981); Barone and Ujifusa, *The Almanac of American Politics 1985; National Journal,* April 29, 1989, 1048-1054; May 29, 1993, 1285-1291.

**Table 2-17** District Voting for President and Representative, 1952–1996

| | | *President's vote compared with vote for his party's successful House candidates* | |
|---|---|---|---|
| *Year* | *Number of districts carried by president*[a] | President ran ahead | President ran behind |
| 1952 | 297 | n.a. | n.a. |
| 1956 | 329 | 155 | 43 |
| 1960 | 204 | 22 | 243 |
| 1964 | 375 | 134[b] | 158[b] |
| 1972 | 377 | 104 | 88 |
| 1976 | 220 | 22 | 270 |
| 1980 | 309 | 38[c] | 150[c] |
| 1984 | 372 | 59 | 123 |
| 1988 | 299 | 26 | 149 |
| 1992 | 257 | 4[b,d] | 247[b,d] |
| 1996 | 280 | 27[e] | 174[e] |

n.a. = not available

[a] Refers to the winning presidential candidate in each election.

[b] Does not include districts where the percentage of the total district vote won by House members equaled the percentage of the total district vote won by the president.

[c] Computed on the basis of the actual presidential vote with John Anderson and others included. If recomputed on the basis of Reagan's percentage of the major party vote, the president ran ahead in 59 districts and behind in 129 districts.

[d] Computed on the basis of the actual presidential vote with Ross Perot included. If recomputed on the basis of Clinton's percentage of the major party vote, the president ran ahead in 72 districts and behind in 179 districts.

[e] Computed on the basis of the actual presidential vote with Ross Perot included. If recomputed on the basis of Clinton's percentage of the major party vote, the president ran ahead in 98 districts and behind in 97 districts.

*Sources:* Compiled from information in the *Congressional Quarterly Weekly Report,* April 22, 1978, 972, April 12, 1997, 860; *Congressional Quarterly Almanac,* vol. 22; Barone and Ujifusa, *Almanac of American Politics 1982* and *Almanac of American Politics 1986; National Journal,* April 29, 1989, 1048-1054; May 29, 1993, 1285-1291.

**Table 2-18** Shifts in Democratic Major Party Vote in Congressional Districts, 1956-1996

| *Period* | *Change in democratic percentage nationally* | *Change in Democratic percentage in congressional districts* Greatest loss | Greatest gain | Variance[a] |
|---|---|---|---|---|
| 1956–1958 | 5.0 | –9.5 | 27.3 | 30.3 |
| 1958–1960 | –1.2 | –22.1 | 14.4 | 31.4 |
| 1972–1974 | 5.8 | –18.8 | 36.2 | 92.2 |
| 1974–1976 | –1.3 | –30.7 | 31.6 | 81.0 |
| 1976–1978 | –2.8 | –37.6 | 39.6 | 106.1 |
| 1978–1980 | –3.2 | –27.8 | 37.0 | 85.0 |
| 1982–1984 | –4.1 | –40.6 | 16.5 | 68.8 |
| 1984–1986 | 2.4 | –46.1 | 22.5 | 63.6 |
| 1986–1988 | –1.1 | –23.5 | 36.1 | 65.9 |
| 1988–1990 | 0.1 | –29.1 | 36.4 | 92.6 |
| 1992–1994 | –6.3 | –38.0 | 28.0 | 67.2 |
| 1994–1996 | 3.4 | –31.2 | 21.5 | 51.1 |

*Note:* Includes only those districts in which two major party candidates competed in both elections and in which the boundaries remained unchanged for both elections. Because of massive redrawing of district lines after each decennial census, no figures are computed for 1970–1972, 1980–1982, and 1990–1992.

[a] Variance, the square of the standard deviation, measures the extent to which the changes in local returns differ from the change in national returns.

*Sources:* Information for 1956-1976 from Thomas E. Mann, *Unsafe at Any Margin* (Washington, D.C.: American Enterprise Institute, 1978); for 1978-1980, computed by Larry Bartels, University of California, Berkeley; for 1982-1996, computed from official election returns.

**Table 2-19** Party-Line Voting in Presidential and Congressional Elections, 1956-1996 (as a percentage of all voters)

| | *Presidential election* | | | *Senate elections* | | | *House elections* | | |
|---|---|---|---|---|---|---|---|---|---|
| *Year* | Party-line voters[a] | Defectors[b] | Pure independents[c] | Party-line voters[a] | Defectors[b] | Pure independents[c] | Party-line voters[a] | Defectors[b] | Pure independents[c] |
| 1956 | 76 | 15 | 9 | 79 | 12 | 9 | 82 | 9 | 9 |
| 1958 | | | | 85 | 9 | 5 | 84 | 11 | 5 |
| 1960 | 79 | 13 | 8 | 77 | 15 | 8 | 80 | 12 | 8 |
| 1962 | | | | n.a. | n.a. | n.a. | 83 | 12 | 6 |
| 1964 | 79 | 15 | 5 | 78 | 16 | 6 | 79 | 15 | 5 |
| 1966 | | | | n.a. | n.a. | n.a. | 76 | 16 | 8 |
| 1968 | 69 | 23 | 9 | 74 | 19 | 7 | 74 | 19 | 7 |
| 1970 | | | | 78 | 12 | 10 | 76 | 16 | 8 |
| 1972 | 67 | 25 | 8 | 69 | 22 | 9 | 75 | 17 | 8 |
| 1974 | | | | 73 | 19 | 8 | 74 | 18 | 8 |
| 1976 | 74 | 15 | 11 | 70 | 19 | 11 | 72 | 19 | 9 |
| 1978 | | | | 71 | 20 | 9 | 69 | 22 | 9 |
| 1980 | 70 | 22 | 8 | 71 | 21 | 8 | 69 | 23 | 8 |
| 1982 | | | | 77 | 17 | 6 | 76 | 17 | 6 |
| 1984 | 81 | 12 | 7 | 72 | 19 | 8 | 70 | 23 | 7 |

| | | | | | | | | | |
|---|---|---|---|---|---|---|---|---|---|
| 1986 | | | | 76 | 20 | 4 | 72 | 22 | 6 |
| 1988 | 81 | 12 | 7 | 72 | 20 | 7 | 74 | 20 | 7 |
| 1990 | | | | 75 | 20 | 5 | 72 | 22 | 5 |
| 1992 | 68 | 24 | 9 | 73 | 20 | 7 | 70 | 22 | 8 |
| 1994 | | | | 76 | 18 | 5 | 77 | 17 | 6 |
| 1996 | 80 | 15 | 5 | 77 | 16 | 7 | 77 | 17 | 6 |

n.a. = not available.

*Note:* Percentages may not add to 100 because of rounding.

[a] Party identifiers who vote for the candidate of their party.
[b] Party identifiers who vote for the candidate of the other party.
[c] The SRC/CPS National Election Surveys use a seven-point scale to define party identification, including three categories of Independents—those who "lean" to one or the other party and those who are "pure" Independents. The "leaners" are included here among the party-line voters. Party identification heire means self-identification as determined by surveys.

*Sources:* SRC/CPS *National Election Studies, 1956–1996;* calculations for 1956-1978 from Thomas E. Mann and Raymond E. Wolfinger, "Candidates and Parties in Congressional Elections," *American Political Science Review* (September 1980); calculations for 1980, Gary C. Jacobson, *The Politics of Congressional Elections* (Boston: Little, Brown, 1982); calculations for 1982-1986, Peverill Squire and Michael Hagen, University of California State Data Program; calculations for 1988, Jon Krasno, The Brookings Institution; calculations for 1990 by Benjamin Highton, University of California State Data Program; calculations for 1992 by Herb Asher, Ohio State University; calculations for 1994 and 1996 by Thomas Mann and Sarah Binder, The Brookings Institution.

# 3

# Campaign Finance

From the moment the Republicans won majority control over both chambers of Congress in 1994, political experts were predicting a pitched battle for the majority in 1996, especially for the House. The campaign finance data for 1996 are consistent with these political expectations. Some of the most important news about the 1996 role of money in politics was about activity that took place *outside* the normal channels controlled by federal campaigns laws and disclosed to the general public. As a result, the tables in this chapter give a smaller piece of the full picture than they have done in past years. Nevertheless, they still reveal a great deal about contemporary congressional elections.

The cost of congressional election campaigns continues to increase, but the increase is not uniform across all kinds of candidates. The Senate elections of 1996 actually cost *less* than the elections of 1994, but the staggering of Senate election terms makes two-year comparisons misleading. It is more useful to compare 1996 with 1990 and 1984. Senate candidates spent, on average, about one-third more in 1996 than in 1990. Over the twelve years between 1984 and 1996, the increase was slightly more than 50 percent (Table 3-3)—much smaller than the rate of increase for House candidates. In 1996 the average House candidate spent 21 percent more than in 1994, 59 percent more than in 1990, and 114 percent more than in 1984 (Table 3-1).

It is not hard to understand why House costs have been going up more quickly. Senate elections have been relatively competitive over the whole period, with control of the Senate shifting three times (1980, 1986, and 1994). Even more important for our comparative point is that Senate incumbents were at significantly greater risk than their House counterparts for most of the years between 1978 and 1988. Since 1988, however, Senate incumbents seem to have become stronger (perhaps because the Senate class of 1980 contained an unusually large number of political "amateurs"). At roughly the same time, the risk to House incumbents was going up. The percentage of incumbents defeated in the general election are shown on the next page.

| *Year* | *Senate* | *House* |
|---|---|---|
| 1978 | 32 | 5 |
| 1980 | 36 | 8 |
| 1982 | 7 | 8 |
| 1984 | 11 | 4 |
| 1986 | 25 | 2 |
| 1988 | 13 | 1 |
| 1990 | 3 | 4 |
| 1992 | 15 | 7 |
| 1994 | 8 | 9 |
| 1996 | 5 | 5 |

In financial terms, this means that Senate challengers were relatively well-funded in the early 1980s, and the rate of growth of the 1990s began from a comparatively high base. In contrast, most House challengers of the middle to late 1980s were not credible political professionals, most were underfunded (see challenger-incumbent spending ratios in Table 3-4), and most had almost no chance of winning. When the political climate for the House became unsettled—with the anti-incumbent mood of 1990, redistricting in 1992, the GOP victory in 1994, and the threat to the Republican majority in 1996—better challengers began looking seriously at running, the candidates on both sides raised more money, and more districts became competitive. Thus, the more rapid growth in House costs reflects a more basic change in the underlying politics of House elections between 1988 and 1996. This explanation is supported by the subsets of House candidates in Table 3-1. Open seats were always competitive; the average open seat candidate raised and spent 20 percent more in 1996 than in 1990. Incumbent funds went up 60 percent over the same six years. But the biggest increase was among challengers, who raised and spent, on average, more than twice as much in 1996 than in 1990.

When we break the challengers down even further, some remarkable patterns emerge. For one thing, the "hopeless" challengers—those who receive 40 percent or less of the vote—actually raised *less* money on average in 1996 than in 1994: $101,792 versus $114,198. (See Table 3-5). In nominal dollars, without correcting for inflation, these challengers raised about the same amount as the same group of challengers did a full decade earlier, in 1986 ($92,436). In fact, if we include the 52 incumbents who had no major party opponents filing a disclosure report, more than half (53 percent) of all House incumbents in 1996 faced challengers who raised less than $100,000; almost two-thirds (64 percent) faced challengers who raised less than $200,000. As has always been true, the single most important financial fact that predicts whether a race will be competitive is not the amount raised or spent by the incumbent—most incumbents can raise money at will—but the amount raised by the challenger. Challengers who earned at least 40 percent of the two-party vote in 1996 spent more than $500,000—five times as much as the hopeless group. This was an impressive 57 percent increase over the amount raised by similar challengers in 1994.

Even more remarkable, however, were the numbers for the races incumbents lost. Incumbents who won close contests (50 to 60 percent of the vote) raised about the same amounts as incumbents who lost (roughly $1 million per candidate on average). In other words, the amount raised by the *incumbent* did not make for a decisive difference between success and failure. In contrast, *the average successful challenger of 1996 spent more than $1 million to win.* Fully 101 House candidates spent $1 million or more in 1996—double the number from two years before. Seventy-two of these were incumbents, sixteen were challengers, and thirteen were open-seat candidates (Table 3-2). This was the first time since 1986 that successful challengers have spent as much money as the incumbents they beat (Table 3-5). It was also a robust 56 percent increase over the amount spent by the successful challengers in 1994, and more than double the amount raised and spent by the unsuccessful 1996 challengers who received 40 to 49 percent of the vote.

In Table 3-9 through Table 3-14 we turn our attention away from candidates' spending and margins of victory, toward candidates' receipts, sources of funds, and the activities of organized contributors. In Table 3-9 we see that despite all of the publicity given to political action committees (PACs), House Republicans, Senate Republicans, and Senate Democrats continue to raise most of their money from individual contributors. Only House Democrats raised less than half of their money from individuals, and House Democratic incumbents raised almost the same amount from PACs (41 percent of their money) as from individuals (42 percent). Nevertheless, this represents a significant *decrease* in PAC support for Democratic incumbents, who raised fully half of a larger pie in 1994 from PACs. In 1994, 226 Democratic incumbents raised $71.2 million from PACs, or about $315,000 each. In 1996, 171 Democratic incumbents raised $44.6 million or about $260,000 each. The $55,000 drop can be attributed largely to PACs—especially business PACs—that had been giving to Democrats primarily because of their majority status. House Republicans raised only 29 percent of their money from PACs, compared with 39 percent in 1994, but that smaller percentage came from a larger pie. In raw dollars, House Republicans raised about $190,000 from PACs in 1994 and $237,000 in 1996. In other words, Republicans and Democrats, for the first time, were raising about the same amount of money from PACs (Table 3-9).

The shift is clear when we look at contributions from the PACs' perspectives. In the first few elections under the post–1974 disclosure system, labor PAC money went overwhelmingly to Democrats, business money (corporations and associations) went to Republicans by a 3 to 2 ratio, and non-connected PACs were overwhelmingly Republican and conservative. This began shifting in 1982 and 1984. By 1990 and 1992, two-thirds of the House money and three-fifths of the Senate money from non-connected PACs was going to Democrats. Meanwhile, corporate PACs were giving 54 percent of their House contributions to Democrats and associations were giving the Democrats 59 percent.

But the partisan shift for business in the middle to late 1980s was merely a reflection of a business decision to support incumbents. Twenty-one percent of all corporate PAC contributions to House candidates in 1980 went to challengers; by 1986, the challengers' share had gone down to 4 percent, and has stayed in that range ever since. For all PACs combined (corporate, labor, association, and non-connected), the percentage of House and Senate contributions going to nonincumbents dropped from about 40 percent from 1978 to 1982 to about 25 percent from 1986 to 1994. Two things changed in 1996. Businesses (corporations and associations) remained overwhelmingly pro-incumbent (71 percent of association and 77 percent of corporate PAC contributions), but being pro-incumbent was consistent this time with supporting Republicans. After favoring House and Senate Democrats for more than a decade, 72 percent of corporate PAC and 65 percent of association PAC contributions went to Republicans in 1996. That helped push the Republicans for the first time since disclosure, to a slightly better than even break (52 to 48 percent) on all PAC contributions. (The previous GOP high point was 49 percent in 1980 and 1982.) At the same time as business stayed pro-incumbent but became more Republican, organized labor and some non-connected ideological PACs were keeping their Democratic stripes but concentrating on challengers. (Labor gave a full quarter of its 1996 congressional campaign contributions to House Democratic challengers.) These groups helped non-incumbents receive 35 percent of all PAC contributions in 1996, far more than they had received over the previous ten years.

Even this understates the importance of pro-Democratic organizations to challengers in 1996. In past years, organizations used independent expenditures if they wanted to get around contribution limits to focus their help on a few races. In contrast, the most significant increase in interest group activity during the 1996 elections took place outside the framework of the Federal Election Campaign Act. Advertising can be treated legally as "issue advocacy" as opposed to campaign communication, even if it praises or criticizes a candidate, as long as the communication does not *explicitly* advocate the candidate's defeat or election by using words like "vote for" or "defeat." Organized labor contributed about $47 million to congressional candidates in 1996, about $12 million of which went to House Democratic challengers. In addition to this $12 million, however, labor said during the campaign that it was spending another $35 million on issue advertising to help challengers defeat targeted GOP incumbents. Other organizations on both sides of the partisan aisle spent well over 100 million additional dollars on issue advertising in 1996, and these efforts are likely to grow. As they grow, there will be a corresponding decline in the proportion of electorally relevant activity covered by disclosure requirements, unless the laws about disclosure change.

Table 3-14, on independent expenditures, masks an irony. Electorally relevant activities by interest groups went up, but these activities were barely reflected in our data. Independent spending on congressional elections by everyone *other* than the political parties increased from $4.6 million in 1994 to $8.6 million in 1996. The real source of the growth in independent expenditures between 1994 and 1996 results from a new kind of "independent expenditure" committee—political party committees sponsored by the one set of organizations, political parties, that never before had been thought of as being "independent" of their own party's nominees. This odd kind of committee resulted from the Supreme Court's decision in the case of *Colorado Republican Federal Campaign Committee* v. *Federal Election Commission* (June 1996), in which the Court held that parties, like PACs, had a constitutionally protected right to unlimited independent expenditures. As a direct result of this decision, the two national party committees went from zero independent spending on congressional elections in 1994 to $11.7 million in 1996. Interestingly, this happened at a time when direct political party contributions to, and coordinated expenditures for, congressional candidates actually went down between 1994 and 1996 (Table 3-10). As with the rapidly escalating phenomenon of political party soft-money in presidential politics, political party activity relevant to congressional politics has been taking place, increasingly, outside of traditional, and reasonably well-disclosed, channels. Thus, even though our tables can still help us understand congressional elections, we will have to monitor just how useful they will remain if these kinds of activities continue to grow.

NOTE: Except where specifically indicated, the data in this chapter come from the Federal Election Commission. The entries for the recent years in several tables (3-1 through 3-8) are based on computer data downloaded from the FEC's Direct Access Program. The numbers in Tables 3-9 through 3-14 are either available in, or can be calculated from, the FEC's published *Reports on Financial Activity* or related press releases. These reports are published about a year after each election. For the most recent cycle, we have relied on FEC press releases based on year-end reports. All of the numbers in this chapter for the most recent cycle are subject to revision in the FEC's final reports.

Finally, we need to clarify a difference between our definition of the word "challenger" and "open seat candidate" and the FEC's. If an incumbent runs and is defeated in a primary election, the FEC will treat all of the non-incumbent candidates in the congressional district as challengers. Because our own candidate-centered tables (3-1 through 3-8) only include candidates who run in the general election, we have defined a candidate as a challenger only if that person is running against an incumbent in the general election. If the incumbent was defeated in a primary, the general election candidates are treated as if they are running for an open seat. For the tables we calculated directly from computer data, our definitions apply. For Tables 3-9 through 3-13 that are based on FEC press releases, the FEC's calculations are based on the FEC's definitions.

**Table 3-1** House Campaign Expenditures, 1980–1996 (net dollars)

| | *1980* | *1982* | *1984* | *1986* | *1988* | *1990* | *1992* | *1994* | *1996* |
|---|---|---|---|---|---|---|---|---|---|
| All candidates | | | | | | | | | |
| Total expenditures | 115,222,222 | 174,921,844 | 176,882,849 | 217,562,967 | 222,258,024 | 237,680,795[a] | 331,899,054 | 347,364,273 | 421,750,905 |
| Mean expenditure | 153,221 (*N* = 752) | 228,060 (*N* = 767) | 241,313 (*N* = 733) | 295,602 (*N* = 736) | 273,380 (*N* = 813) | 325,145[a] (*N* = 731) | 408,240[a] (*N* = 813) | 441,378 (*N* = 787)[a] | 516,852 (*N* = 816)[a] |
| Mean, Democrats | 143,277 (*N* = 396) | 213,369 (*N* = 411) | 237,732 (*N* = 399) | 301,955 (*N* = 397) | 286,851 (*N* = 429) | 355,862 (*N* = 381) | 462,897 (*N* = 409) | 487,493 (*N* = 386) | 472,313 (*N* = 412) |
| Mean, Republicans | 164,282 (*N* = 356) | 245,020 (*N* = 356) | 245,591 (*N* = 334) | 290,092 (*N* = 340) | 258,330 (*N* = 384) | 290,910 (*N* = 349) | 352,351 (*N* = 403) | 396,411 (*N* = 400) | 561,304 (*N* = 403) |
| Incumbents | | | | | | | | | |
| Mean, all incumbents | 165,081 (*N* = 391) | 265,001 (*N* = 383) | 279,044 (*N* = 408) | 362,103 (*N* = 389) | 378,544 (*N* = 412) | 422,124 (*N* = 405) | 594,699[a] (*N* = 349) | 561,441 (*N* = 382)[a] | 678,556 (*N* = 382)[a] |
| Mean, Democrats | 158,010 (*N* = 248) | 247,573 (*N* = 216) | 279,203 (*N* = 254) | 349,918 (*N* = 231) | 358,260 (*N* = 248) | 427,178 (*N* = 247) | 621,890 (*N* = 211) | 622,937 (*N* = 225) | 590,814 (*N* = 168) |
| Mean, Republicans | 177,345 (*N* = 143) | 287,543 (*N* = 167) | 278,781 (*N* = 154) | 379,917 (*N* = 158) | 409,217 (*N* = 164) | 414,222 (*N* = 158) | 552,952 (*N* = 137) | 473,281 (*N* = 157) | 746,434 (*N* = 213) |
| Challengers | | | | | | | | | |
| Mean, all challengers | 121,751 (*N* = 277) | 151,717 (*N* = 270) | 161,994 (*N* = 273) | 155,607 (*N* = 262) | 119,621 (*N* = 348) | 134,465[a] (*N* = 270) | 167,411 (*N* = 290) | 240,188 (*N* = 302) | 286,582 (*N* = 330) |
| Mean, Democrats | 93,313 (*N* = 105) | 141,390 (*N* = 137) | 124,508 (*N* = 119) | 170,562 (*N* = 123) | 143,785 (*N* = 154) | 131,194 (*N* = 104) | 143,935 (*N* = 110) | 177,136 (*N* = 110) | 319,472 (*N* = 191) |

*(Table continues)*

**Table 3-1** *(Continued)*

| | *1980* | *1982* | *1984* | *1986* | *1988* | *1990* | *1992* | *1994* | *1996* |
|---|---|---|---|---|---|---|---|---|---|
| Mean, Republicans | 139,111<br>($N = 172$) | 162,354<br>($N = 133$) | 190,960<br>($N = 154$) | 141,356<br>($N = 139$) | 100,440<br>($N = 194$) | 133,889<br>($N = 165$) | 181,757<br>($N = 180$) | 276,312<br>($N = 192$) | 241,389<br>($N = 139$) |
| Open seats | | | | | | | | | |
| Mean, all open-seat candidates | 201,790<br>($N = 84$) | 284,476<br>($N = 114$) | 361,696<br>($N = 52$) | 430,484<br>($N = 86$) | 465,466<br>($N = 53$) | 543,129<br>($N = 56$) | 435,631<br>($N = 174$) | 585,991<br>($N = 103$) | 653,561<br>($N = 104$) |
| Mean, Democrats | 180,312<br>($N = 43$) | 256,004<br>($N = 58$) | 350,804<br>($N = 26$) | 420,138<br>($N = 43$) | 446,959<br>($N = 27$) | 547,541<br>($N = 30$) | 480,375<br>($N = 88$) | 561,569<br>($N = 52$) | 647,490<br>($N = 53$) |
| Mean, Republicans | 224,116<br>($N = 41$) | 314,547<br>($N = 56$) | 372,589<br>($N = 26$) | 440,830<br>($N = 43$) | 484,684<br>($N = 26$) | 538,037<br>($N = 26$) | 389,847<br>($N = 86$) | 611,911<br>($N = 51$) | 659,869<br>($N = 51$) |

*Note:* Includes primary and general election expenditures for general election candidates who filed reports with the Federal Election Commission. The 1979 amendments to the Federal Election Campaign Act exempted low-budget (under $5,000) campaigns from reporting requirements. Low-budget candidates who did file reports are included in the table.

[a] Includes Bernard Sanders (I-Vt.).

**Table 3-2** House Incumbents, Challengers, and Open-Seat Candidates Who Spent $500,000 or $1 Million, 1988–1996

| | *Incumbents* | | *Challengers* | | *Open Seat* | | |
|---|---|---|---|---|---|---|---|
| | D | R | D | R | D | R | Total |
| 1988 | | | | | | | |
| $500,000 + | 65 | 43 | 10 | 7 | 12 | 12 | 149 |
| $1 million + | 9 | 7 | 2 | 0 | 1 | 3 | 22 |
| 1990 | | | | | | | |
| $500,000 + | 76 | 48 | 5 | 12 | 15 | 13 | 170[a] |
| $1 million + | 10 | 4 | 1 | 0 | 1 | 1 | 17 |
| 1992 | | | | | | | |
| $500,000 + | 116 | 65 | 4 | 11 | 32 | 21 | 250[a] |
| $1 million + | 33 | 10 | 0 | 2 | 5 | 2 | 52 |
| 1994 | | | | | | | |
| $500,000 + | 117 | 61 | 8 | 37 | 27 | 32 | 283[a] |
| $1 million + | 34 | 4 | 1 | 8 | 3 | 1 | 51 |
| 1996 | | | | | | | |
| $500,000 + | 84 | 138 | 46 | 21 | 34 | 32 | 356[a] |
| $1 million + | 23 | 49 | 12 | 4 | 5 | 8 | 101 |

[a] Includes Bernard Sanders (I-Vt.).

**Table 3-3** Senate Campaign Expenditures, 1980–1996 (net dollars)

| | *1980* | *1982* | *1984* | *1986* | *1988* | *1990* | *1992* | *1994* | *1996* |
|---|---|---|---|---|---|---|---|---|---|
| All candidates | | | | | | | | | |
| Total expenditures | 74,163,669 | 114,036,379 | 141,962,276 | 183,432,489 | 184,977,565 | 173,674,925 | 198,487,310 | 280,019,203 | 230,806,273 |
| Mean expenditure | 1,106,920 ($N = 67$) | 1,781,815 ($N = 64$) | 2,327,250 ($N = 61$) | 2,737,798 ($N = 67$) | 2,802,690 ($N = 66$) | 2,592,163 ($N = 67$) | 2,876,627 ($N = 69$) | 4,000,274 ($N = 70$) | 3,550,866 ($N = 76$) |
| Mean, Democrats | 1,170,580 ($N = 34$) | 1,881,379 ($N = 32$) | 2,160,637 ($N = 31$) | 2,260,415 ($N = 33$) | 2,938,533 ($N = 33$) | 2,468,527 ($N = 34$) | 2,815,826 ($N = 35$) | 3,395,629 ($N = 35$) | 3,402,098 ($N = 32$) |
| Mean, Republicans | 1,041,332 ($N = 33$) | 1,682,252 ($N = 32$) | 2,499,417 ($N = 30$) | 3,201,141 ($N = 34$) | 2,666,848 ($N = 33$) | 2,719,546 ($N = 33$) | 2,939,218 ($N = 34$) | 4,604,919 ($N = 35$) | 3,695,126 ($N = 33$) |
| Incumbents | | | | | | | | | |
| Mean, all incumbents | 1,301,692 ($N = 25$) | 1,858,140 ($N = 29$) | 2,539,929 ($N = 28$) | 3,374,602 ($N = 28$) | 3,748,126 ($N = 27$) | 3,582,136 ($N = 32$) | 3,852,428 ($N = 27$) | 4,691,617 ($N = 26$) | 4,236,694 ($N = 20$) |
| Mean, Democrats | 1,355,660 ($N = 19$) | 1,696,226 ($N = 18$) | 1,755,004 ($N = 12$) | 2,712,796 ($N = 9$) | 3,457,145 ($N = 15$) | 3,618,244 ($N = 17$) | 2,851,102 ($N = 15$) | 5,154,744 ($N = 16$) | 5,205,263 ($N = 7$) |
| Mean, Republicans | 1,130,792 ($N = 6$) | 2,123,089 ($N = 11$) | 3,128,622 ($N = 16$) | 3,688,089 ($N = 19$) | 4,111,852 ($N = 12$) | 3,541,212 ($N = 15$) | 5,104,086 ($N = 12$) | 3,950,616 ($N = 10$) | 3,715,156 ($N = 13$) |
| Challengers | | | | | | | | | |
| Mean, all challengers | 842,547 ($N = 24$) | 1,217,034 ($N = 29$) | 1,241,434 ($N = 25$) | 1,899,417 ($N = 27$) | 1,820,058 ($N = 17$) | 1,705,098 ($N = 29$) | 1,824,993 ($N = 26$) | 3,997,104 ($N = 26$) | 3,139,479 ($N = 17$) |
| Mean, Democrats | 557,006 ($N = 6$) | 1,516,015 ($N = 11$) | 1,515,412 ($N = 15$) | 1,911,693 ($N = 18$) | 2,160,770 ($N = 12$) | 1,401,259 ($N = 14$) | 2,551,654 ($N = 12$) | 1,266,445 ($N = 10$) | 2,958,889 ($N = 11$) |
| Mean, Republicans | 937,727 ($N = 18$) | 1,034,324 ($N = 18$) | 830,466 ($N = 10$) | 1,874,864 ($N = 9$) | 1,547,489 ($N = 15$) | 1,988,680 ($N = 15$) | 1,202,141 ($N = 14$) | 5,703,766 ($N = 16$) | 3,470,562 ($N = 6$) |

| | | | | | | | | | |
|---|---|---|---|---|---|---|---|---|---|
| Open seats | | | | | | | | | |
| Mean, all open-seat candidates | 1,132,560 ($N = 18$) | 4,142,687 ($N = 6$) | 4,976,051 ($N = 8$) | 3,138,282 ($N = 12$) | 2,886,383 ($N = 12$) | 1,599,792 ($N = 6$) | 2,938,871 ($N = 16$) | 3,006,247 ($N = 18$) | 3,310,759 ($N = 28$) |
| Mean, Democrats | 1,188,903 ($N = 9$) | 4,331,959 ($N = 3$) | 5,797,131 ($N = 4$) | 2,628,009 ($N = 6$) | 3,197,528 ($N = 6$) | 934,046 ($N = 3$) | 3,145,940 ($N = 8$) | 2,634,075 ($N = 9$) | 2,848,759 ($N = 14$) |
| Mean, Republicans | 1,076,218 ($N = 9$) | 3,953,415 ($N = 3$) | 4,154,971 ($N = 4$) | 3,648,555 ($N = 6$) | 2,575,237 ($N = 6$) | 2,265,538 ($N = 3$) | 2,731,801 ($N = 8$) | 3,378,419 ($N = 9$) | 3,772,767 ($N = 14$) |

*Note:* Includes primary and general election expenditures for general election candidates only.

Figure 3-1 Expenditures of House Challengers Who Beat Incumbents, 1976–1996

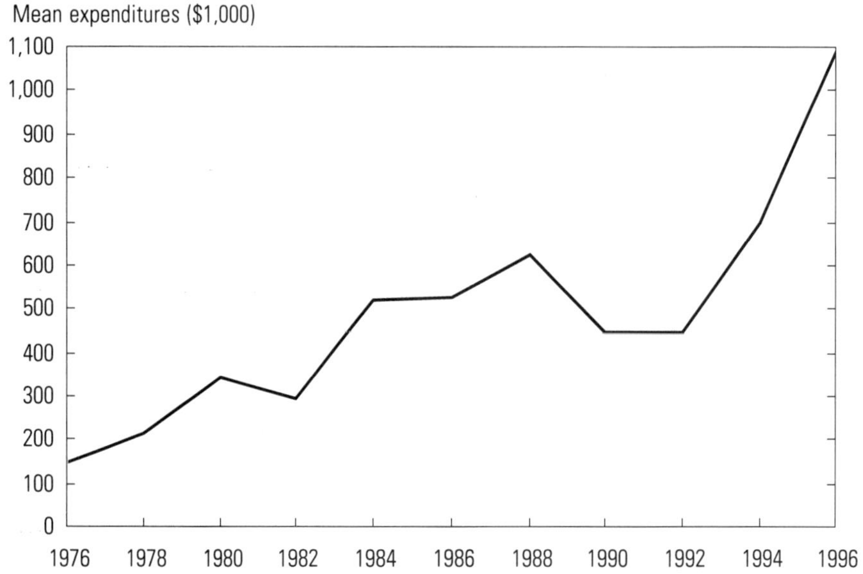


*Source:* Table 3-6.

**Table 3-4** Challenger-Incumbent Spending Ratios, 1976–1996 (in percentages)

| | *'76* | *'78* | *'80* | *'82* | *'84* | *'86* | *'88* | *'90* | *'92* | *'94* | *'96* |
|---|---|---|---|---|---|---|---|---|---|---|---|
| House | 64 | 67 | 74 | 57 | 48 | 43 | 32 | 32 | 28 | 43 | 42 |
| Senate | 73 | 52 | 65 | 65 | 49 | 56 | 49 | 48 | 47 | 85 | 74 |

*Note:* The above figures were obtained by dividing expenditures made by the average challenger who filed reports with the FEC by the expenditures made by the average incumbent.

*Sources:* Tables 3-1 and 3-3.

Figure 3-2 Percentage of Incumbents' Campaign Funds that Came from PACs, House and Senate, 1984–1996

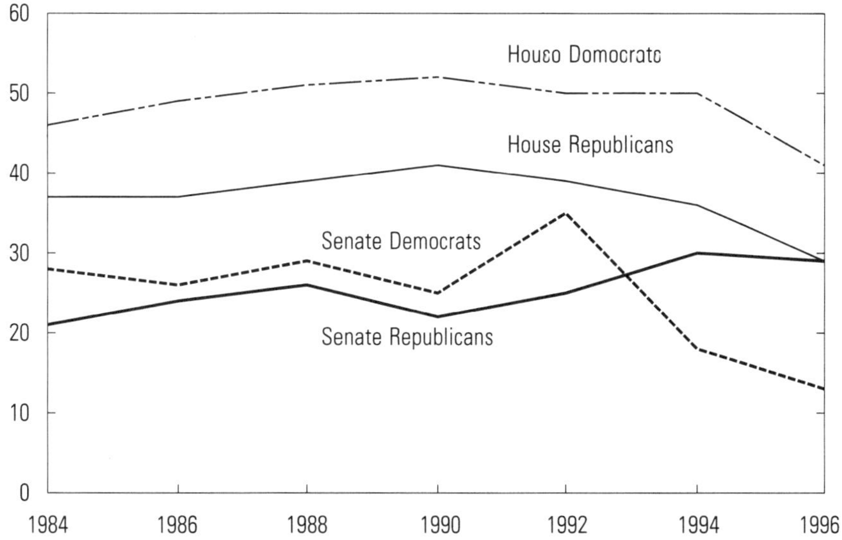


*Source:* Table 3-9.

**Table 3-5** Expenditures of House Incumbents and Challengers, by Election Outcome, 1980–1996 (mean net dollars)

| | *1980* | *1982* | *1984* | *1986* | *1988* | *1990* | *1992* | *1994* | *1996* |
|---|---|---|---|---|---|---|---|---|---|
| Incumbent won with 60% or more[a] | | | | | | | | | |
| Incumbents | 125,912<br>(*N* = 284) | 200,170<br>(*N* = 264) | 232,853<br>(*N* = 318) | 291,876<br>(*N* = 330) | 349,380<br>(*N* = 359) | 362,563<br>(*N* = 313) | 491,345<br>(*N* = 234) | 454,126<br>(*N* = 263) | 522,735<br>(*N* = 261) |
| Democrats | 117,773<br>(*N* = 170) | 206,670<br>(*N* = 178) | 219,506<br>(*N* = 183) | 293,484<br>(*N* = 209) | 342,862<br>(*N* = 220) | 374,552<br>(*N* = 197) | 496,288<br>(*N* = 138) | 454,317<br>(*N* = 120) | 477,204<br>(*N* = 124) |
| Republicans | 138,050<br>(*N* = 114) | 186,717<br>(*N* = 86) | 250,945<br>(*N* = 135) | 289,099<br>(*N* = 121) | 359,697<br>(*N* = 139) | 342,200<br>(*N* = 116) | 483,265<br>(*N* = 95) | 453,965<br>(*N* = 143) | 583,946<br>(*N* = 137) |
| Challengers | 47,525<br>(*N* = 170) | 82,373<br>(*N* = 163) | 71,922<br>(*N* = 184) | 92,436<br>(*N* = 202) | 78,774<br>(*N* = 235) | 60,352<br>(*N* = 180) | 87,728<br>(*N* = 187) | 114,198<br>(*N* = 183) | 101,792<br>(*N* = 211) |
| Democrats | 44,120<br>(*N* = 75) | 36,628<br>(*N* = 62) | 73,835<br>(*N* = 99) | 72,769<br>(*N* = 85) | 87,597<br>(*N* = 102) | 43,088<br>(*N* = 65) | 76,024<br>(*N* = 74) | 133,025<br>(*N* = 96) | 96,758<br>(*N* = 115) |
| Republicans | 50,213<br>(*N* = 95) | 110,454<br>(*N* = 101) | 69,693<br>(*N* = 85) | 106,724<br>(*N* = 117) | 72,007<br>(*N* = 133) | 70,109<br>(*N* = 115) | 94,055<br>(*N* = 111) | 93,423<br>(*N* = 87) | 107,822<br>(*N* = 96) |
| Incumbent won with less than 60% | | | | | | | | | |
| Incumbents | 261,901<br>(*N* = 76) | 394,447<br>(*N* = 90) | 437,752<br>(*N* = 74) | 785,493<br>(*N* = 52) | 701,406<br>(*N* = 44) | 614,856<br>(*N* = 77) | 782,328<br>(*N* = 91) | 721,252<br>(*N* = 85) | 995,561<br>(*N* = 100) |
| Democrats | 223,345<br>(*N* = 50) | 446,542<br>(*N* = 35) | 421,834<br>(*N* = 58) | 938,374<br>(*N* = 20) | 691,035<br>(*N* = 23) | 640,623<br>(*N* = 44) | 833,388<br>(*N* = 57) | 732,729<br>(*N* = 70) | 975,666<br>(*N* = 41) |
| Republicans | 336,046<br>(*N* = 26) | 361,295[b]<br>(*N* = 55) | 495,455<br>(*N* = 16) | 689,943<br>(*N* = 32) | 712,765<br>(*N* = 21) | 580,499<br>(*N* = 33) | 696,727<br>(*N* = 34) | 670,582<br>(*N* = 14) | 1,045,710<br>(*N* = 58) |
| Challengers | 197,499<br>(*N* = 76) | 234,790<br>(*N* = 84) | 307,938<br>(*N* = 72) | 334,946<br>(*N* = 46) | 391,549<br>(*N* = 44) | 248,714<br>(*N* = 75) | 281,211<br>(*N* = 84) | 329,073<br>(*N* = 84) | 515,375<br>(*N* = 97) |

| | | | | | | | | | |
|---|---|---|---|---|---|---|---|---|---|
| Democrats | 195,135 (N = 26) | 182,232[b] (N = 53) | 386,819 (N = 16) | 353,939 (N = 28) | 445,871 (N = 21) | 213,907 (N = 31) | 274,047 (N = 29) | 479,611 (N = 14) | 534,809 (N = 57) |
| Republicans | 198,728 (N = 50) | 324,647 (N = 31) | 285,401 (N = 56) | 305,401 (N = 18) | 341,951 (N = 23) | 273,237 (N = 44) | 283,801 (N = 56) | 298,966 (N = 70) | 487,682 (N = 40) |
| Incumbent was defeated | | | | | | | | | |
| Incumbents | 286,559 (N = 31) | 453,459 (N = 29) | 463,070 (N = 16) | 582,647 (N = 6) | 956,081 (N = 5) | 675,605 (N = 15) | 890,975 (N = 24) | 992,023 (N = 34) | 1,105,641 (N = 21) |
| Democrats | 285,636 (N = 28) | 353,201[b] (N = 3) | 483,204 (N = 13) | 528,101 (N = 1) | 935,494 (N = 2) | 589,795 (N = 6) | 951,743 (N = 16) | 992,023 (N = 34) | 710,406 (N = 3) |
| Republicans | 295,170 (N = 3) | 465,027 (N = 26) | 375,824 (N = 3) | 593,556 (N = 5) | 969,806 (N = 3) | 732,812[c] (N = 9) | 796,437 (N = 8) | 0 0 | 1,171,514 (N = 18) |
| Challengers | 343,093 (N = 31) | 296,273 (N = 23) | 515,622 (N = 16) | 455,071 (N = 11) | 625,120 (N = 5) | 452,582 (N = 15) | 447,076 (N = 19) | 698,668 (N = 34) | 1,087,122 (N = 21) |
| Democrats | 353,855 (N = 4) | 292,781 (N = 22) | 249,462[d] (N = 3) | 504,673 (N = 9) | 808,908 (N = 3) | 526,537 (N = 8) | 351,847 (N = 6) | 0 0 | 1,063,039 (N = 18) |
| Republicans | 341,499 (N = 27) | 373,093 (N = 1) | 577,044 (N = 13) | 231,864 (N = 2) | 349,438 (N = 2) | 334,444 (N = 6) | 491,028 (N = 13) | 698,668 (N = 34) | 1,231,615 (N = 3) |

*Note:* Includes primary and general election expenditures for general election candidates only.

[a] Percentage of the vote received by the two leading candidates.

[b] The number of challengers does not equal that of incumbents because of six incumbent-incumbent races in 1982 due to redistricting. The mean expenditure for Democrats in these races was $585,205; for Republicans, $592,080. The mean expenditure for winners (four Democrats, two Republicans) was $600,337; for losers, $583,824.

[c] One Republican incumbent was defeated by Bernard Sanders (I-Vt.), who spent $569,772.

[d] Includes Albert G. Bustamante who defeated Democratic incumbent Abraham Kazen, Jr. (33-Texas) in a primary.

**Table 3-6** Expenditures for Open House Seats, by Election Outcome, 1984–1996 (mean net dollars)

| | *1984* | *1986* | *1988* | *1990* | *1992* | *1994* | *1996* |
|---|---|---|---|---|---|---|---|
| All winners | 440,912<br>(*N* = 26) | 523,759<br>(*N* = 46) | 615,339<br>(*N* = 27) | 625,760<br>(*N* = 30) | 538,959<br>(*N* = 91) | 602,073<br>(*N* = 52) | 755,872<br>(*N* = 53) |
| Democrats | 428,416<br>(*N* = 8) | 515,570<br>(*N* = 22) | 554,500<br>(*N* = 13) | 593,699<br>(*N* = 18) | 508,167<br>(*N* = 57) | 676,437<br>(*N* = 14) | 747,775<br>(*N* = 24) |
| Republicans | 446,467<br>(*N* = 18) | 531,266<br>(*N* = 24) | 671,832<br>(*N* = 14) | 673,851<br>(*N* = 12) | 590,581<br>(*N* = 34) | 574,676<br>(*N* = 38) | 762,573<br>(*N* = 29) |
| Winners with 60% or more | 372,989<br>(*N* = 8) | 543,382<br>(*N* = 19) | 555,759<br>(*N* = 11) | 632,189<br>(*N* = 14) | 517,909<br>(*N* = 44) | 618,153<br>(*N* = 21) | 611,115<br>(*N* = 18) |
| Democrats | 290,693<br>(*N* = 3) | 537,552<br>(*N* = 7) | 397,458<br>(*N* = 7) | 534,671<br>(*N* = 9) | 397,636<br>(*N* = 33) | 587,314<br>(*N* = 3) | 588,832<br>(*N* = 8) |
| Republicans | 422,366<br>(*N* = 5) | 546,783<br>(*N* = 12) | 832,787<br>(*N* = 4) | 807,721<br>(*N* = 5) | 878,725<br>(*N* = 11) | 623,293<br>(*N* = 18) | 628,942<br>(*N* = 10) |
| Winners with ‹ 60% | 471,100<br>(*N* = 18) | 509,950<br>(*N* = 27) | 656,299<br>(*N* = 16) | 620,135<br>(*N* = 16) | 558,666<br>(*N* = 47) | 591,180<br>(*N* = 31) | 830,318<br>(*N* = 35) |
| Democrats | 511,049<br>(*N* = 5) | 505,312<br>(*N* = 15) | 737,714<br>(*N* = 6) | 652,727<br>(*N* = 9) | 660,147<br>(*N* = 24) | 700,743<br>(*N* = 11) | 827,246<br>(*N* = 16) |
| Republicans | 455,736<br>(*N* = 13) | 515,749<br>(*N* = 12) | 607,450<br>(*N* = 10) | 578,230<br>(*N* = 7) | 452,773<br>(*N* = 23) | 530,921<br>(*N* = 20) | 832,905<br>(*N* = 19) |

| | | | | | | | |
|---|---|---|---|---|---|---|---|
| All losers | 282,480 | 323,718 | 439,980 | 447,785 | 322,344 | 569,593 | 536,703 |
| | ($N = 26$) | ($N = 40$) | ($N = 24$) | ($N = 26$) | ($N = 83$) | ($N = 51$) | ($N = 52$) |
| Democrats | 316,309 | 320,161 | 436,127 | 290,911 | 429,273 | 517,881 | 564,496 |
| | ($N = 18$) | ($N = 21$) | ($N = 13$) | ($N = 12$) | ($N = 31$) | ($N = 38$) | ($N = 29$) |
| Republicans | 206,363 | 326,596 | 455,860 | 421,625 | 258,597 | 720,753 | 501,683 |
| | ($N = 8$) | ($N = 19$) | ($N = 10$) | ($N = 14$) | ($N = 52$) | ($N = 13$) | ($N = 23$) |
| Losers with › 40% | 352,961 | 360,978 | 565,561 | 472,178 | 451,892 | 683,257 | 652,687 |
| | ($N = 18$) | ($N = 23$) | ($N = 16$) | ($N = 16$) | ($N = 47$) | ($N = 31$) | ($N = 35$) |
| Democrats | 393,262 | 294,362 | 506,283 | 436,366 | 476,578 | 596,359 | 659,450 |
| | ($N = 13$) | ($N = 10$) | ($N = 9$) | ($N = 8$) | ($N = 23$) | ($N = 20$) | ($N = 19$) |
| Republicans | 248,180 | 412,220 | 693,525 | 507,989 | 428,234 | 841,253 | 644,657 |
| | ($N = 5$) | ($N = 13$) | ($N = 6$) | ($N = 8$) | ($N = 24$) | ($N = 11$) | ($N = 16$) |
| Losers with 40% or less | 123,896 | 193,794 | 188,819 | 408,756 | 153,212 | 393,415 | 297,943 |
| | ($N = 8$) | ($N = 15$) | ($N = 8$) | ($N = 10$) | ($N = 36$) | ($N = 20$) | ($N = 17$) |
| Democrats | 116,232 | 228,939 | 278,276 | 562,183 | 293,272 | 430,683 | 384,085 |
| | ($N = 5$) | ($N = 9$) | ($N = 4$) | ($N = 4$) | ($N = 8$) | ($N = 18$) | ($N = 10$) |
| Republicans | 136,668 | 141,077 | 99,363 | 306,472 | 113,194 | 58,005 | 174,885 |
| | ($N = 3$) | ($N = 6$) | ($N = 4$) | ($N = 6$) | ($N = 28$) | ($N = 2$) | ($N = 7$) |

**Table 3-7** Expenditures of Senate Incumbents and Challengers, by Election Outcome, 1980–1996 (mean net dollars)

| | *1980* | *1982* | *1984* | *1986* | *1988* | *1990* | *1992* | *1994* | *1996* |
|---|---|---|---|---|---|---|---|---|---|
| Incumbent won with 60% or more[a] | | | | | | | | | |
| Incumbents | 1,162,385 (*N* = 10) | 1,494,578 (*N* = 13) | 1,612,152 (*N* = 18) | 1,963,140 (*N* = 14) | 2,777,202 (*N* = 15) | 2,318,076 (*N* = 19) | 2,698,728 (*N* = 13) | 3,657,063 (*N* = 10) | 2,427,254 (*N* = 6) |
| Democrats | 1,220,616 (*N* = 6) | 1,401,794 (*N* = 12) | 1,620,869 (*N* = 7) | 1,672,182 (*N* = 8) | 2,355,863 (*N* = 10) | 2,441,681 (*N* = 10) | 2,661,953 (*N* = 9) | 1,736,702 (*N* = 3) | 2,252,393 (*N* = 2) |
| Republicans | 1,075,038 (*N* = 4) | 2,607,983 (*N* = 1) | 1,606,604 (*N* = 11) | 2,351,083 (*N* = 6) | 3,619,881 (*N* = 5) | 2,180,738 (*N* = 9) | 2,781,472 (*N* = 4) | 4,480,074 (*N* = 7) | 2,514,685 (*N* = 4) |
| Challengers | 302,812 (*N* = 9) | 777,830 (*N* = 13) | 384,263 (*N* = 15) | 451,671 (*N* = 13) | 591,566 (*N* = 15) | 853,376 (*N* = 16) | 701,442 (*N* = 12) | 1,002,523 (*N* = 10) | 762,003 (*N* = 3) |
| Democrats | 265,822 (*N* = 4) | 424,507 (*N* = 1) | 322,263 (*N* = 10) | 155,853 (*N* = 5) | 835,294 (*N* = 5) | 449,666 (*N* = 8) | 595,192 (*N* = 4) | 1,365,961 (*N* = 7) | 479,791 (*N* = 2) |
| Republicans | 332,404 (*N* = 5) | 807,276 (*N* = 12) | 508,264 (*N* = 5) | 636,557 (*N* = 8) | 469,702 (*N* = 10) | 1,253,086 (*N* = 8) | 754,568 (*N* = 8) | 54,500 (*N* = 3) | 1,326,427 (*N* = 1) |
| Incumbent won with less than 60% | | | | | | | | | |
| Incumbents | 945,423 (*N* = 6) | 2,224,235 (*N* = 14) | 4,505,574 (*N* = 7) | 5,213,789 (*N* = 7) | 6,235,410 (*N* = 8) | 5,279,645 (*N* = 12) | 4,922,413 (*N* = 10) | 5,313,837 (*N* = 14) | 5,054,639 (*N* = 13) |
| Democrats | 796,984 (*N* = 4) | 2,417,100 (*N* = 5) | 1,833,432 (*N* = 4) | 11,037,707 (*N* = 1) | 6,829,055 (*N* = 4) | 5,299,049 (*N* = 7) | 2,844,490 (*N* = 4) | 6,022,553 (*N* = 11) | 6,386,412 (*N* = 5) |
| Republicans | 1,242,300 (*N* = 2) | 2,117,088 (*N* = 9) | 8,068,429 (*N* = 3) | 4,243,136 (*N* = 6) | 5,641,766 (*N* = 4) | 5,252,478 (*N* = 5) | 6,307,696 (*N* = 6) | 2,715,212 (*N* = 3) | 4,222,282 (*N* = 8) |

| | | | | | | | | | |
|---|---|---|---|---|---|---|---|---|---|
| Challengers | 864,870 | 1,615,338 | 2,296,194 | 3,389,477 | 3,784,772 | 2,870,438 | 2,283,708 | 5,546,361 | 3,699,583 |
| | (*N* = 6) | (*N* = 14) | (*N* = 7) | (*N* = 7) | (*N* = 8) | (*N* = 12) | (*N* = 10) | (*N* = 14) | (*N* = 13) |
| Democrats | 1,139,376 | 1,629,490 | 4,028,715 | 1,990,836 | 3,209,075 | 2,927,948 | 3,032,533 | 1,034,241 | 3,574,705 |
| | (*N* = 2) | (*N* = 9) | (*N* = 3) | (*N* = 6) | (*N* = 4) | (*N* = 5) | (*N* = 6) | (*N* = 3) | (*N* = 8) |
| Republicans | 727,617 | 1,589,864 | 996,804 | 11,781,316 | 4,360,469 | 2,829,360 | 1,160,471 | 6,776,953 | 3,899,388 |
| | (*N* = 4) | (*N* = 5) | (*N* = 4) | (*N* = 1) | (*N* = 4) | (*N* = 7) | (*N* = 4) | (*N* = 11) | (*N* = 5) |
| Incumbent was defeated | | | | | | | | | |
| Incumbents | 1,693,991 | 1,658,623 | 3,520,088 | 4,358,340 | 2,579,437 | 7,229,154 | 4,926,992 | 5,508,854 | 4,460,035 |
| | (*N* = 9) | (*N* = 2) | (*N* = 3) | (*N* = 7) | (*N* = 4) | (*N* = 1) | (*N* = 4) | (*N* = 2) | (*N* = 1) |
| Democrats | 1,693,991 | 1,625,042 | 2,380,239 | 0 | 1,338,622 | 0 | 3,751,500 | 5,508,854 | 0 |
| | (*N* = 9) | (*N* = 1) | (*N* = 1) | 0 | (*N* = 1) | 0 | (*N* = 2) | (*N* = 2) | 0 |
| Republicans | 0 | 1,692,204 | 4,090,013 | 4,358,340 | 2,993,042 | 7,229,154 | 6,138,484 | 0 | 4,460,035 |
| | 0 | (*N* = 1) | (*N* = 2) | (*N* = 7) | (*N* = 3) | (*N* = 1) | (*N* = 2) | 0 | (*N* = 1) |
| Challengers | 1,367,400 | 793,123 | 3,066,175 | 3,098,027 | 2,516,337 | 1,380,560 | 4,048,857 | 8,125,137 | 2,990,554 |
| | (*N* = 9) | (*N* = 2) | (*N* = 3) | (*N* = 7) | (*N* = 4) | (*N* = 1) | (*N* = 4) | (*N* = 2) | (*N* = 1) |
| Democrats | 0 | 1,586,245 | 3,711,199 | 3,098,027 | 2,996,572 | 1,380,560 | 5,021,938 | 0 | 2,990,554 |
| | 0 | (*N* = 1) | (*N* = 2) | (*N* = 7) | (*N* = 3) | (*N* = 1) | (*N* = 2) | 0 | (*N* = 1) |
| Republicans | 1,367,400 | 981,197 | 1,776,128 | 0 | 1,075,631 | 0 | 3,075,776 | 8,125,137 | 0 |
| | (*N* = 9) | (*N* = 1) | (*N* = 1) | 0 | (*N* = 1) | 0 | (*N* = 2) | (*N* = 2) | 0 |

*Note:* The Federal Election Commission included the following disclaimer along with its 1986 data, and *Vital Statistics* considers it appropriate for all years: "The small *N*'s and unique nature of some Senate campaigns make all measures of central tendency like averages or medians problematic and, as a result, the Commission would not include tables such as these in its regular release of information."

[a] Percentage of the vote received by the two leading candidates.

**Table 3-8** Expenditures for Open Senate Seats, by Election Outcome, 1986–1996 (mean net dollars)

| | *1986* | *1988* | *1990* | *1992* | *1994* | *1996* |
|---|---|---|---|---|---|---|
| All winners | 3,827,158 ($N = 7$) | 3,781,436 ($N = 6$) | 2,265,538 ($N = 3$) | 3,371,677 ($N = 8$) | 3,378,419 ($N = 9$) | 3,589,381 ($N = 14$) |
| Democrats | 2,714,673 ($N = 4$) | 5,186,633 ($N = 2$) | 0 0 | 4,186,216 ($N = 5$) | 0 0 | 4,495,047 ($N = 5$) |
| Republicans | 5,310,471 ($N = 3$) | 3,078,837 ($N = 4$) | 2,265,538 ($N = 3$) | 2,014,111 ($N = 3$) | 3,378,419 ($N = 9$) | 3,086,234 ($N = 9$) |
| Winners with 60% or more | 2,216,412 ($N = 2$) | 1,879,272 ($N = 2$) | 1,536,352 ($N = 2$) | 1,191,005 ($N = 1$) | 2,754,664 ($N = 4$) | 2,518,754 ($N = 2$) |
| Democrats | 2,057,422 ($N = 1$) | 2,881,666 ($N = 1$) | 0 0 | 1,191,005 ($N = 1$) | 0 0 | 2,732,011 ($N = 1$) |
| Republicans | 2,375,402 ($N = 1$) | 876,877 ($N = 1$) | 1,536,352 ($N = 2$) | 0 0 | 2,754,664 ($N = 4$) | 2,305,496 ($N = 1$) |
| Winners with $<$ 60% | 4,471,457 ($N = 5$) | 4,732,518 ($N = 4$) | 3,723,911 ($N = 1$) | 3,683,201 ($N = 7$) | 3,877,423 ($N = 5$) | 3,767,819 ($N = 12$) |
| Democrats | 2,933,757 ($N = 3$) | 7,491,600 ($N = 1$) | 0 0 | 4,935,019 ($N = 4$) | 0 0 | 4,935,806 ($N = 4$) |
| Republicans | 6,778,006 ($N = 2$) | 3,812,824 ($N = 3$) | 3,723,911 ($N = 1$) | 2,014,111 ($N = 3$) | 3,877,423 ($N = 5$) | 3,183,826 ($N = 8$) |

| | | | | | | |
|---|---|---|---|---|---|---|
| All losers | 2,952,009 (*N* = 7) | 2,000,372 (*N* = 6) | 934,046 (*N* = 3) | 2,506,064 (*N* = 8) | 2,634,075 (*N* = 9) | 3,032,137 (*N* = 14) |
| Democrats | 2,181,463 (*N* = 3) | 2,202,976 (*N* = 4) | 934,046 (*N* = 3) | 1,412,146 (*N* = 3) | 2,634,075 (*N* = 9) | 1,934,142 (*N* = 9) |
| Republicans | 3,529,919 (*N* = 4) | 1,595,165 (*N* = 2) | 0 0 | 3,162,415 (*N* = 5) | 0 0 | 5,008,528 (*N* = 5) |
| Losers with › 40% | 3,686,638 (*N* = 5) | 2,792,524 (*N* = 4) | 1,936,914 (*N* = 1) | 2,792,915 (*N* = 7) | 2,802,500 (*N* = 5) | 3,417,755 (*N* = 12) |
| Democrats | 3,006,346 (*N* = 2) | 2,753,999 (*N* = 3) | 1,936,914 (*N* = 1) | 1,412,146 (*N* = 3) | 2,802,500 (*N* = 5) | 2,093,026 (*N* = 8) |
| Republicans | 4,140,166 (*N* = 3) | 2,908,101 (*N* = 1) | 0 0 | 3,828,492 (*N* = 4) | 0 0 | 6,067,213 (*N* = 4) |
| Losers with 40% or less | 1,115,437 (*N* = 2) | 416,069 (*N* = 2) | 432,612 (*N* = 2) | 498,107 (*N* = 1) | 2,423,544 (*N* = 4) | 718,428 (*N* = 2) |
| Democrats | 531,698 (*N* = 1) | 549,908 (*N* = 1) | 432,613 (*N* = 2) | 0 0 | 2,423,544 (*N* = 4) | 663,066 (*N* = 1) |
| Republicans | 1,699,175 (*N* = 1) | 282,229 (*N* = 1) | 0 0 | 498,107 (*N* = 1) | 0 0 | 773,789 (*N* = 1) |

*Note:* The Federal Election Commission included the following disclaimer along with its 1986 data, and *Vital Statistics* considers it appropriate for all years: "The small *N*'s and unique nature of some Senate campaigns make all measures of central tendency like averages or medians problematic and, as a result, the Commission would not include tables such as these in its regular release of information."

Figure 3-3 Percentage of Nonincumbents' Campaign Funds that Came from Political Parties, House and Senate, 1984–1996

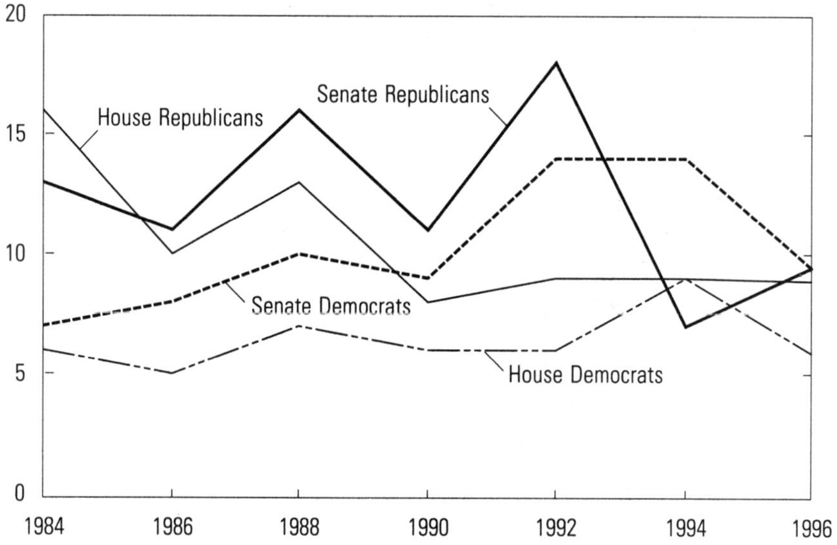


*Note:* Nonincumbents include challengers and open-seat candidates who ran in the general election.
*Source:* Table 3-9.

**Table 3-9** Campaign Funding Sources for House and Senate Candidates, 1984–1996

| *Party and candidate status* | *Number of candidates* | *Contributions plus party expenditures on behalf of candidates ($ millions)* | *Percentage coming from:* Individuals | PACs | Party (contributions plus expenditures) | Candidate to self (contributions plus loans) | Other |
|---|---|---|---|---|---|---|---|
| | | | | *House, 1984* | | | |
| All candidates[a] | 816 | $203.8 | 47 | 36 | 7 | 6 | 5 |
| Democrats | 434 | 107.2 | 44 | 41 | 3 | 6 | 6 |
| Incumbents | 258 | 81.8 | 39 | 46 | 2 | 2 | 11 |
| Challengers | 152 | 16.3 | 43 | 29 | 6 | 18 | 5 |
| Open seats | 24 | 9.1 | 45 | 22 | 6 | 24 | 3 |
| Republicans | 382 | 96.6 | 49 | 30 | 11 | 6 | 5 |
| Incumbents | 154 | 52.1 | 51 | 37 | 6 | 1 | 5 |
| Challengers | 204 | 33.8 | 48 | 18 | 17 | 13 | 4 |
| Open seats | 24 | 10.7 | 47 | 31 | 13 | 7 | 2 |
| | | | | *Senate, 1984* | | | |
| All candidates[a] | 68 | $157.7 | 61 | 18 | 6 | 10 | 4 |
| Democrats | 33 | 73.1 | 56 | 18 | 6 | 16 | 4 |
| Incumbents | 12 | 22.8 | 61 | 28 | 3 | < 1 | 8 |

*(Table continues)*

**Table 3-9** *(Continued)*

| *Party and candidate status* | *Number of candidates* | *Contributions plus party expenditures on behalf of candidates ($ millions)* | *Percentage coming from:* Individuals | PACs | Party (contributions plus expenditures) | Candidate to self (contributions plus loans) | Other |
|---|---|---|---|---|---|---|---|
| Challengers | 17 | 25.5 | 69 | 17 | 9 | 2 | 3 |
| Open seats | 4 | 24.8 | 39 | 9 | 6 | 44 | 2 |
| Republicans | 35 | 84.6 | 65 | 18 | 6 | 5 | 4 |
| Incumbents | 17 | 55.7 | 68 | 21 | 6 | 1 | 5 |
| Challengers | 13 | 10.0 | 55 | 15 | 20 | 8 | 2 |
| Open seats | 5 | 19.0 | 60 | 10 | 9 | 17 | 8 |
| | | | | *House, 1986* | | | |
| All candidates[a] | 810 | $234.2 | 48 | 36 | 4 | 6 | 6 |
| Democrats | 427 | 125.7 | 44 | 42 | 2 | 6 | 6 |
| Incumbents | 235 | 84.1 | 42 | 49 | 1 | 2 | 6 |
| Challengers | 147 | 22.1 | 49 | 29 | 6 | 13 | 3 |
| Open seats | 45 | 19.5 | 47 | 31 | 3 | 15 | 4 |
| Republicans | 383 | 108.5 | 53 | 29 | 6 | 7 | 5 |
| Incumbents | 160 | 67.3 | 53 | 37 | 4 | 1 | 5 |
| Challengers | 182 | 21.4 | 54 | 11 | 10 | 22 | 3 |
| Open seats | 41 | 19.8 | 53 | 24 | 10 | 10 | 3 |

| | | | | | | | |
|---|---|---|---|---|---|---|---|
| | | | | *Senate, 1986* | | | |
| All candidates[a] | 68 | 208.6 | 60 | 21 | 9 | 6 | 4 |
| Democrats | 34 | 90.2 | 56 | 22 | 8 | 9 | 5 |
| Incumbents | 9 | 28.2 | 62 | 26 | 7 | 2 | 3 |
| Challengers | 18 | 40.3 | 51 | 19 | 9 | 16 | 5 |
| Open seats | 7 | 21.7 | 60 | 22 | 8 | 5 | 5 |
| Republicans | 34 | 118.5 | 63 | 21 | 9 | 2 | 5 |
| Incumbents | 18 | 68.9 | 63 | 24 | 8 | < 1 | 5 |
| Challengers | 9 | 20.4 | 64 | 9 | 18 | 6 | 3 |
| Open seats | 7 | 29.1 | 61 | 22 | 6 | 2 | 9 |
| | | | | *House, 1988* | | | |
| All candidates[a] | 813 | $249.0 | 46 | 40 | 4 | 5 | 5 |
| Democrats | 429 | 140.0 | 40 | 47 | 3 | 5 | 5 |
| Incumbents | 238 | 103.8 | 39 | 51 | 2 | 1 | 7 |
| Challengers | 154 | 23.5 | 46 | 31 | 7 | 13 | 3 |
| Open seats | 27 | 12.7 | 39 | 36 | 7 | 14 | 4 |
| Republicans | 384 | 109.0 | 52 | 31 | 6 | 6 | 5 |
| Incumbents | 164 | 73.7 | 51 | 39 | 3 | 1 | 6 |
| Challengers | 194 | 21.6 | 55 | 10 | 13 | 19 | 3 |
| Open seats | 26 | 13.7 | 54 | 21 | 13 | 12 | < 1 |

*(Table continues)*

**Table 3-9** *(Continued)*

| *Party and candidate status* | *Number of candidates* | *Contributions plus party expenditures on behalf of candidates ($ millions)* | *Percentage coming from:* Individuals | PACs | Party (contributions plus expenditures) | Candidate to self (contributions plus loans) | Other |
|---|---|---|---|---|---|---|---|
| | | | | *Senate, 1988* | | | |
| All candidates[a] | 66 | 199.4 | 59 | 22 | 9 | 5 | 5 |
| Democrats | 33 | 103.0 | 58 | 23 | 7 | 8 | 4 |
| Incumbents | 15 | 53.0 | 61 | 29 | 4 | 1 | 5 |
| Challengers | 12 | 29.1 | 66 | 16 | 11 | 3 | 4 |
| Open seats | 6 | 20.9 | 37 | 16 | 8 | 35 | 4 |
| Republicans | 33 | 96.3 | 61 | 22 | 11 | 2 | 4 |
| Incumbents | 12 | 50.8 | 62 | 26 | 8 | <1 | 4 |
| Challengers | 15 | 27.7 | 63 | 11 | 18 | 6 | 2 |
| Open seats | 6 | 17.8 | 54 | 26 | 13 | 1 | 6 |
| | | | | *House, 1990* | | | |
| All candidates[a] | 807 | $257.5 | 44 | 40 | 3 | 6 | 7 |
| Democrats | 413 | 146.5 | 39 | 47 | 3 | 5 | 6 |
| Incumbents | 249 | 113.2 | 37 | 52 | 1 | 2 | 8 |

| | | | | | | | |
|---|---|---|---|---|---|---|---|
| Challengers | 132 | 16.0 | 44 | 27 | 9 | 16 | 4 |
| Open seats | 32 | 17.3 | 42 | 33 | 4 | 17 | 4 |
| Republicans | 394 | 108.8 | 51 | 32 | 4 | 7 | 6 |
| Incumbents | 159 | 70.7 | 50 | 41 | 2 | 1 | 6 |
| Challengers | 206 | 23.9 | 54 | 10 | 7 | 24 | 5 |
| Open seats | 29 | 14.1 | 50 | 24 | 10 | 12 | 4 |
| | | | | *Senate, 1990* | | | |
| All candidates[a] | 67 | $191.0 | 61 | 21 | 7 | 5 | 6 |
| Democrats | 34 | 90.8 | 63 | 22 | 6 | 4 | 5 |
| Incumbents | 17 | 66.7 | 65 | 25 | 5 | 0 | 5 |
| Challengers | 14 | 21.0 | 58 | 12 | 9 | 15 | 6 |
| Open seats | 3 | 3.1 | 50 | 18 | 11 | 21 | ‹ 1 |
| Republicans | 33 | 100.2 | 59 | 21 | 9 | 5 | 6 |
| Incumbents | 15 | 58.9 | 65 | 22 | 7 | 0 | 6 |
| Challengers | 15 | 33.4 | 51 | 16 | 12 | 15 | 6 |
| Open seats | 3 | 7.9 | 43 | 36 | 7 | 0 | 14 |
| | | | | *House, 1992* | | | |
| All candidates[a] | 851 | $331.5 | 47 | 36 | 5 | 9 | 3 |
| Democrats | 427 | 184.7 | 43 | 43 | 4 | 6 | 4 |
| Incumbents | 213 | 122.1 | 40 | 50 | 2 | 1 | 7 |
| Challengers | 140 | 25.1 | 48 | 26 | 10 | 13 | 3 |
| Open seats | 74 | 37.5 | 49 | 30 | 4 | 17 | ‹ 1 |

*(Table continues)*

**Table 3-9** *(Continued)*

| *Party and candidate status* | *Number of candidates* | *Contributions plus party expenditures on behalf of candidates ($ millions)* | *Percentage coming from:* Individuals | PACs | Party (contributions plus expenditures) | Candidate to self (contributions plus loans) | Other |
|---|---|---|---|---|---|---|---|
| Republicans | 424 | 146.9 | 51 | 26 | 6 | 13 | 4 |
| Incumbents | 138 | 74.8 | 52 | 39 | 3 | 1 | 5 |
| Challengers | 216 | 44.5 | 47 | 9 | 10 | 22 | 12 |
| Open seats | 70 | 27.5 | 57 | 21 | 7 | 14 | 1 |
| | | | | *Senate, 1992* | | | |
| All candidates[a] | 71 | $214.2 | 58 | 21 | 13 | 5 | 3 |
| Democrats | 35 | 108.5 | 60 | 23 | 11 | 2 | 4 |
| Incumbents | 15 | 43.9 | 52 | 35 | 6 | 2 | 5 |
| Challengers | 13 | 43.1 | 68 | 12 | 14 | 3 | 3 |
| Open seats | 7 | 21.5 | 61 | 19 | 13 | 3 | 4 |
| Republicans | 36 | 106.9 | 55 | 19 | 15 | 7 | 4 |
| Incumbents | 12 | 59.4 | 58 | 25 | 13 | <1 | 4 |
| Challengers | 17 | 24.0 | 55 | 9 | 20 | 14 | 2 |
| Open seats | 7 | 23.5 | 48 | 16 | 16 | 18 | 2 |

| | | | | | | | |
|---|---|---|---|---|---|---|---|
| | *House, 1994* | | | | | | |
| All candidates[a] | 824 | $371.3 | 49 | 34 | 5 | 8 | 4 |
| Democrats | 403 | 196.7 | 43 | 43 | 5 | 5 | 4 |
| Incumbents | 226 | 142.4 | 34 | 50 | 3 | 1 | 12 |
| Challengers | 130 | 23.6 | 45 | 23 | 11 | 17 | 4 |
| Open seats | 47 | 30.7 | 47 | 27 | 8 | 15 | 3 |
| Republicans | 421 | 174.6 | 56 | 24 | 6 | 11 | 3 |
| Incumbents | 157 | 82.9 | 58 | 36 | 2 | 1 | 3 |
| Challengers | 217 | 58.6 | 56 | 10 | 10 | 20 | 4 |
| Open seats | 47 | 33.1 | 50 | 19 | 8 | 19 | 4 |
| | *Senate, 1994* | | | | | | |
| All candidates[a] | 70 | $291.7 | 54 | 15 | 8 | 19 | 4 |
| Democrats | 35 | 124.9 | 55 | 18 | 10 | 12 | 5 |
| Incumbents | 16 | 86.4 | 54 | 18 | 8 | 14 | 6 |
| Challengers | 10 | 11.7 | 46 | 16 | 13 | 21 | 4 |
| Open seats | 9 | 26.9 | 60 | 16 | 14 | 3 | 7 |
| Republicans | 35 | 166.7 | 53 | 13 | 6 | 24 | 4 |
| Incumbents | 10 | 35.4 | 60 | 30 | 6 | < 1 | 4 |
| Challengers | 16 | 96.1 | 47 | 3 | 5 | 41 | 4 |
| Open seats | 9 | 35.2 | 61 | 21 | 11 | 1 | 6 |
| | *House, 1996* | | | | | | |
| All candidates[a] | 873 | $460.7 | 52 | 25 | 5 | 10 | 8 |
| Democrats | 435 | 211.5 | 44 | 29 | 4 | 12 | 11 |
| Incumbents | 171 | 108.8 | 42 | 41 | 2 | 1 | 14 |

*(Table continues)*

**Table 3-9** *(Continued)*

| *Party and candidate status* | *Number of candidates* | *Contributions plus party expenditures on behalf of candidates ($ millions)* | *Percentage coming from:* | | | | |
|---|---|---|---|---|---|---|---|
| | | | Individuals | PACs | Party (contributions plus expenditures) | Candidate to self (contributions plus loans) | Other |
| Challengers | 211 | 67.2 | 43 | 20 | 6 | 16 | 15 |
| Open seats | 53 | 35.5 | 48 | 26 | 5 | 18 | 3 |
| Republicans | 438 | 249.2 | 58 | 21 | 6 | 9 | 6 |
| Incumbents | 213 | 174.2 | 57 | 29 | 2 | 1 | 11 |
| Challengers | 174 | 40.0 | 64 | 11 | 9 | 13 | 3 |
| Open seats | 51 | 35.0 | 53 | 23 | 8 | 12 | 4 |
| | | | *Senate, 1996* | | | | |
| All candidates[a] | 68 | $242.0 | 59 | 16 | 9 | 8 | 5 |
| Democrats | 34 | 116.2 | 59 | 12 | 8 | 16 | 5 |
| Incumbents | 7 | 36.5 | 73 | 13 | 4 | 5 | 5 |
| Challengers | 14 | 36.5 | 50 | 6 | 8 | 34 | 2 |
| Open seats | 13 | 43.2 | 55 | 18 | 11 | 9 | 7 |
| Republicans | 34 | 125.8 | 59 | 20 | 9 | 8 | 4 |
| Incumbents | 13 | 49.9 | 57 | 29 | 9 | 2 | 3 |
| Challengers | 8 | 25.6 | 70 | 14 | 10 | 3 | 3 |
| Open seats | 13 | 50.3 | 50 | 18 | 9 | 18 | 5 |

[a] Excludes minor-party candidates.

*Source*: Federal Election Commission.

Figure 3-4 Political Party Contributions and Coordinated Expenditures for Congress, 1976–1996

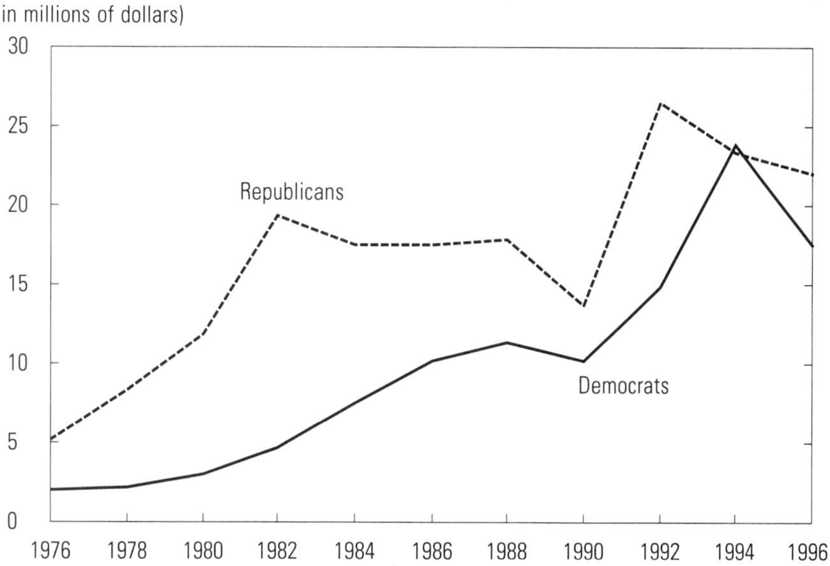


*Source:* Table 3-10.

Figure 3-5 Percentage of PAC Support for Nonincumbents, 1978–1996

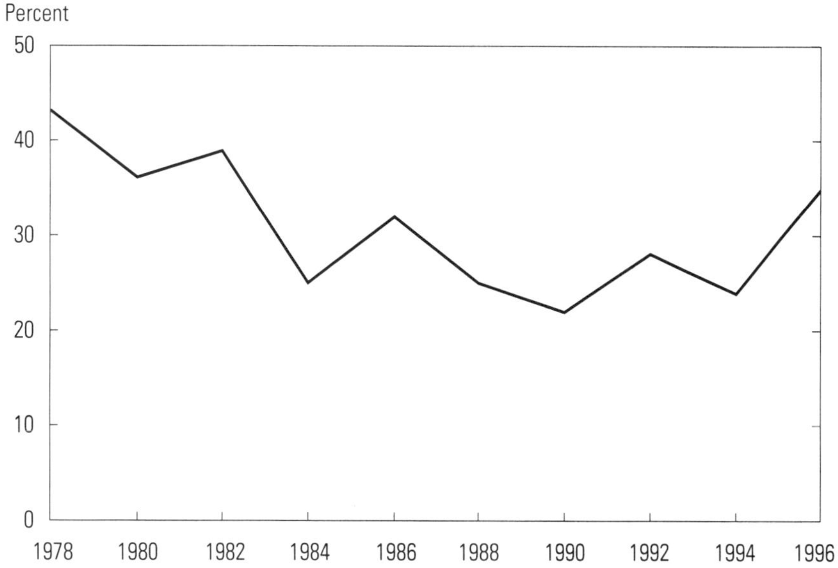


*Note:* Nonincumbents are challengers and open-seat candidates.

*Source:* Table 3-13.

**Table 3-10** Political Party Contributions and Coordinated Expenditures for Congressional Candidates, 1976–1996 (in dollars)

| | *Senate* | | *House* | | |
|---|---|---|---|---|---|
| | Contributions | Expenditures | Contributions | Expenditures | *Total* |
| 1976 | | | | | |
| Democrats | 468,795 | 4,359 | 1,465,629 | 500 | 1,939,283 |
| Republicans | 930,034 | 113,976 | 3,658,310 | 329,583 | 5,031,903 |
| 1978 | | | | | |
| Democrats | 466,683 | 229,218 | 1,262,298 | 72,892 | 2,031,091 |
| Republicans | 703,204 | 2,723,880 | 3,621,104 | 1,297,079 | 8,345,267 |
| 1980 | | | | | |
| Democrats | 480,464 | 1,132,912 | 1,025,989 | 256,346 | 2,895,711 |
| Republicans | 677,004 | 5,434,758 | 3,498,323 | 2,203,748 | 11,813,833 |
| 1982 | | | | | |
| Democrats | 579,337 | 2,265,197 | 1,052,286 | 694,321 | 4,591,141 |
| Republicans | 600,221 | 8,715,761 | 4,720,959 | 5,293,260 | 19,330,201 |
| 1984 | | | | | |
| Democrats | 441,467 | 3,947,731 | 1,280,672 | 1,774,452 | 7,444,322 |
| Republicans | 590,922 | 6,518,415 | 4,060,120 | 6,190,309 | 17,359,766 |
| 1986 | | | | | |
| Democrats | 620,832 | 6,656,286 | 968,913 | 1,836,213 | 10,082,244 |
| Republicans | 729,522 | 10,077,902 | 2,520,278 | 4,111,474 | 17,439,176 |
| 1988 | | | | | |
| Democrats | 501,777 | 6,592,264 | 1,258,952 | 2,891,152 | 11,244,145 |
| Republicans | 719,006 | 10,260,600 | 2,657,069 | 4,162,207 | 17,798,882 |

| | | | | | |
|---|---|---|---|---|---|
| 1990 | | | | | |
| Democrats | 515,332 | 5,210,002 | 943,135 | 3,401,579 | 10,070,048 |
| Republicans | 862,621 | 7,725,853 | 2,019,279 | 3,012,313 | 13,620,066 |
| 1992 | | | | | |
| Democrats | 689,953 | 11,915,873 | 1,234,553 | 5,883,678 | 19,724,102 |
| Republicans | 807,397 | 16,509,940 | 2,197,611 | 6,906,729 | 26,421,677 |
| 1994 | | | | | |
| Democrats | 638,618 | 13,204,309 | 1,501,220 | 8,455,070 | 23,799,217 |
| Republicans | 748,011 | 11,561,865 | 2,036,712 | 8,851,871 | 23,198,460 |
| 1996 | | | | | |
| Democrats | 637,734 | 8,611,897 | 1,387,952 | 6,786,959 | 17,424,542 |
| Republicans | 772,244 | 10,751,093 | 2,462,999 | 7,998,844 | 21,985,180 |

*Note:* The table includes direct contributions made by party committees to congressional candidates and coordinated expenditures made on their behalf, known as 441a(d) expenditures because the legal spending limits are contained in U S. Code, Title 2, sec. 441a(d). Under this provision, party committees are allowed to spend money on behalf of federal candidates, in addition to the money they may contribute directly.

House candidates may receive in direct contributions up to $10,000 each ($5,000 in the primary and $5,000 in the general election) from the national party, congressional campaign committee, Senate campaign committee, and state party. Senate candidates may receive in direct contributions a total of $17,500 from the national party and senatorial campaign committee and another $10,000 each from the congressional and state party.

The limits on 441a(d) expenditures are as follows: (a) for Senate candidates, two cents times the voting age population, or $20,000 in 1974 dollars adjusted for inflation, whichever is greater; (b) for House candidates from states with only one House district, $20,000 in 1974 dollars adjusted for inflation; and (c) for all other House candidates, $10,000 in 1974 dollars adjusted for inflation. State parties are allowed to spend equal amounts on behalf of congressional candidates, and court decisions permit state and local parties to designate a national party committee as its agent for these expenditures.

Combining the maximum national party contributions, home state party contributions, and 441a(d) expenditure limits would have given House candidates $101,820 in 1996. Senate limits ranged from a low of $161,140 in small states to a high of $2,855,998 in California.

**Table 3-11** Number of Registered Political Action Committees, 1974–1996

| *Committee type* | *1974* | *1976* | *1978* | *1980* | *1984* | *1988* | *1990* | *1992* | *1994* | *1996* |
|---|---|---|---|---|---|---|---|---|---|---|
| Corporate | 89 | 433 | 784 | 1,204 | 1,682 | 1,816 | 1,795 | 1,735 | 1,660 | 1,642 |
| Labor | 201 | 224 | 217 | 297 | 394 | 354 | 346 | 347 | 333 | 332 |
| Trade/membership/ health[a] | 318 | 489 | 451 | 574 | 698 | 786 | 774 | 770 | 792 | 838 |
| Nonconnected | — | — | 165 | 378 | 1,053 | 1,115 | 1,062 | 1,145 | 980 | 1,103 |
| Cooperative | — | — | 12 | 42 | 52 | 59 | 59 | 56 | 53 | 41 |
| Corporation without stock | — | — | 24 | 56 | 130 | 138 | 136 | 142 | 136 | 123 |
| Total | 608 | 1,146 | 1,653 | 2,551 | 4,009 | 4,268 | 4,172 | 4,195 | 3,954 | 4,079 |

*Note:* Data as of December 31 for every year.

[a] Includes all noncorporate and nonlabor PACs through December 31, 1976.

*Source:* Federal Election Commission PAC count press release, issued annually.

**Table 3-12** PAC Contributions to Congressional Candidates, 1978–1996 (in millions of dollars)[a]

| *Type of PAC* | *1978* | *1980* | *1982* | *1984* | *1986* | *1988* | *1990* | *1992* | *1994* | *1996* |
|---|---|---|---|---|---|---|---|---|---|---|
| Labor | 9.9 | 13.2 | 20.3 | 24.8 | 29.9 | 33.9 | 33.6 | 39.7 | 40.7 | 46.5 |
| Corporate | 9.5 | 19.2 | 27.5 | 35.5 | 46.2 | 50.4 | 53.5 | 64.3 | 64.1 | 69.7 |
| Trade/member- ship/health | 11.2 | 15.9 | 21.9 | 26.7 | 32.9 | 38.9 | 42.5 | 51.4 | 50.1 | 56.2 |
| Nonconnected | 2.5 | 4.9 | 10.7 | 14.5 | 18.8 | 19.2 | 14.3 | 17.5 | 17.3 | 22.0 |
| Other[b] | 1.0 | 2.0 | 3.2 | 3.8 | 4.9 | 5.4 | 5.9 | 6.6 | 6.6 | 6.8 |
| Total | 34.1 | 55.2 | 83.6 | 105.3 | 132.7 | 147.8 | 149.7 | 179.4 | 178.8 | 201.2 |

[a] Contributions to all candidates for election in the year indicated made during the two-year election cycle.
[b] Cooperatives and corporations without stock.

**Table 3-13** How PACs Distributed Their Contributions to Congressional Candidates, 1978–1996

| | *Percentage distribution* | | | | | | | | *Percentage distribution* | | | | | | | | | |
|---|---|---|---|---|---|---|---|---|---|---|---|---|---|---|---|---|---|---|
| | Incum-bent | | Chal-lenger | | Open seat | | | | Incum-bent | | Chal-lenger | | Open seat | | | | | |
| | D | R | D | R | D | R | *Percent to chamber* | *Dollars to chamber (in millions)* | D | R | D | R | D | R | *Percent to chamber* | *Dollars to chamber (in millions)* | *Total percent* | *Total dollars (in millions)* |
| | *House, 1978* | | | | | | | | *Senate, 1978* | | | | | | | | | |
| Corporate | 22 | 18 | 1 | 10 | 4 | 8 | 63 | 6.2 | 6 | 14 | 2 | 7 | 3 | 6 | 37 | 3.6 | 100 | 9.8 |
| Association | 27 | 20 | 2 | 11 | 7 | 9 | 76 | 8.6 | 5 | 8 | 2 | 4 | 2 | 3 | 24 | 2.8 | 100 | 11.3 |
| Labor | 43 | 2 | 12 | ‹1 | 14 | ‹1 | 72 | 7.5 | 10 | 2 | 9 | ‹1 | 5 | ‹1 | 28 | 2.8 | 100 | 10.3 |
| Nonconnected | 9 | 10 | 3 | 29 | 4 | 18 | 74 | 2.1 | 3 | 5 | 3 | 10 | 1 | 5 | 26 | 0.7 | 100 | 2.8 |
| Other PACs | 49 | 12 | 2 | 1 | 8 | 5 | 77 | 0.8 | 5 | 5 | 3 | 2 | 4 | 3 | 23 | 0.2 | 100 | 1.0 |
| All PACs | 30 | 14 | 5 | 9 | 8 | 7 | 71 | 25.0 | 6 | 8 | 4 | 4 | 3 | 3 | 29 | 10.2 | 100 | 35.2 |
| | *House, 1980* | | | | | | | | *Senate, 1980* | | | | | | | | | |
| Corporate | 23 | 21 | 1 | 13 | 1 | 6 | 64 | 11.7 | 9 | 5 | ‹1 | 17 | 1 | 4 | 36 | 6.4 | 100 | 18.1 |
| Association | 29 | 24 | 1 | 13 | 2 | 6 | 75 | 11.2 | 9 | 4 | 1 | 8 | 1 | 2 | 25 | 3.8 | 100 | 15.0 |
| Labor | 50 | 3 | 12 | ‹1 | 7 | ‹1 | 72 | 8.9 | 18 | 3 | 4 | ‹1 | 3 | ‹1 | 28 | 3.4 | 100 | 12.3 |
| Nonconnected | 13 | 9 | 3 | 26 | 2 | 8 | 62 | 2.8 | 8 | 2 | ‹1 | 20 | ‹1 | 5 | 37 | 1.7 | 100 | 4.5 |
| Other PACs | 40 | 19 | 2 | 2 | 3 | 4 | 72 | 1.4 | 16 | 4 | 1 | 5 | 2 | 2 | 28 | 0.5 | 100 | 1.9 |
| All PACs | 31 | 17 | 3 | 10 | 3 | 5 | 69 | 36.0 | 11 | 4 | 1 | 10 | 2 | 2 | 31 | 15.9 | 100 | 51.9 |
| | *House, 1982* | | | | | | | | *Senate, 1982* | | | | | | | | | |
| Corporate | 22 | 31 | 1 | 6 | 2 | 6 | 69 | 18.1 | 8 | 13 | ‹1 | 5 | ‹1 | 4 | 31 | 8.3 | 100 | 26.4 |
| Association | 26 | 32 | 3 | 6 | 3 | 6 | 77 | 15.9 | 9 | 9 | 1 | 2 | ‹1 | 2 | 23 | 4.9 | 100 | 20.8 |
| Labor | 40 | 3 | 21 | ‹1 | 11 | 1 | 75 | 14.6 | 14 | 2 | 7 | ‹1 | 2 | ‹1 | 25 | 4.8 | 100 | 19.4 |

*(Table continues)*

**Table 3-13** *(Continued)*

| | *Percentage distribution* | | | | | | | | *Percentage distribution* | | | | | | | | | |
|---|---|---|---|---|---|---|---|---|---|---|---|---|---|---|---|---|---|---|
| | Incum-bent | | Chal-lenger | | Open seat | | | | Incum-bent | | Chal-lenger | | Open seat | | | | | |
| | D | R | D | R | D | R | *Percent to chamber* | *Dollars to chamber (in millions)* | D | R | D | R | D | R | *Percent to chamber* | *Dollars to chamber (in millions)* | *Total percent* | *Total dollars (in millions)* |
| Nonconnected | 20 | 13 | 11 | 12 | 5 | 7 | 69 | 6.9 | 9 | 6 | 5 | 7 | 2 | 2 | 31 | 3.2 | 100 | 10.0 |
| Other PACs | 40 | 25 | 3 | 1 | 4 | 3 | 78 | 2.4 | 11 | 5 | 2 | <1 | <1 | 3 | 22 | 0.7 | 100 | 3.1 |
| All PACs | 28 | 22 | 8 | 5 | 5 | 5 | 73 | 57.9 | 9 | 6 | 5 | 7 | 2 | 2 | 27 | 21.8 | 100 | 79.7 |
| | *House, 1984* | | | | | | | | *Senate, 1984* | | | | | | | | | |
| Corporate | 29 | 26 | <1 | 7 | <1 | 4 | 67 | 22.9 | 7 | 19 | 1 | 2 | 1 | 4 | 33 | 11.4 | 100 | 34.3 |
| Association | 36 | 28 | 2 | 5 | 2 | 4 | 77 | 19.8 | 6 | 11 | 2 | 1 | 1 | 1 | 23 | 6.0 | 100 | 25.8 |
| Labor | 57 | 4 | 14 | <1 | 5 | <1 | 80 | 18.7 | 6 | 1 | 9 | <1 | 4 | <1 | 20 | 4.6 | 100 | 23.3 |
| Nonconnected | 26 | 9 | 5 | 15 | 3 | 6 | 63 | 8.6 | 7 | 10 | 10 | 4 | 3 | 2 | 37 | 5.1 | 100 | 13.7 |
| Other PACs | 48 | 23 | 2 | 2 | 1 | 2 | 78 | 2.9 | 7 | 10 | 2 | 1 | 2 | 1 | 22 | 0.8 | 100 | 3.7 |
| All PACs | 38 | 18 | 4 | 6 | 2 | 3 | 72 | 72.9 | 6 | 11 | 4 | 2 | 2 | 2 | 28 | 27.9 | 100 | 100.8 |
| | *House, 1986* | | | | | | | | *Senate, 1986* | | | | | | | | | |
| Corporate | 26 | 24 | 1 | 2 | 1 | 4 | 58 | 26.4 | 5 | 20 | 3 | 3 | 2 | 9 | 42 | 19.0 | 100 | 45.3 |
| Association | 33 | 27 | 2 | 2 | 3 | 5 | 71 | 23.0 | 6 | 12 | 4 | 1 | 2 | 4 | 29 | 9.4 | 100 | 32.4 |
| Labor | 45 | 5 | 14 | <1 | 10 | <1 | 75 | 21.9 | 6 | 2 | 11 | <1 | 6 | <1 | 25 | 7.1 | 100 | 29.1 |
| Nonconnected | 21 | 12 | 8 | 5 | 7 | 6 | 59 | 10.7 | 6 | 11 | 10 | 2 | 7 | 5 | 41 | 7.5 | 100 | 18.2 |
| Other PACs | 36 | 23 | 1 | 2 | 2 | 2 | 67 | 3.2 | 6 | 15 | 6 | 1 | 2 | 3 | 33 | 1.6 | 100 | 4.8 |
| All PACs | 32 | 19 | 5 | 2 | 5 | 4 | 66 | 85.2 | 5 | 13 | 6 | 1 | 4 | 5 | 34 | 44.6 | 100 | 129.8 |
| | *House, 1988* | | | | | | | | *Senate, 1988* | | | | | | | | | |
| Corporate | 31 | 26 | 1 | 2 | 1 | 3 | 63 | 31.6 | 11 | 14 | 1 | 4 | 3 | 5 | 37 | 18.8 | 100 | 50.4 |
| Association | 37 | 26 | 2 | 1 | 3 | 4 | 73 | 28.6 | 9 | 9 | 1 | 2 | 2 | 3 | 27 | 10.4 | 100 | 38.9 |

| | | | | | | | | | | | | | | | | | | |
|---|---|---|---|---|---|---|---|---|---|---|---|---|---|---|---|---|---|---|
| Labor | 50 | 6 | 15 | <1 | 9 | <1 | 79 | 26.8 | 9 | 1 | 6 | <1 | 4 | <1 | 21 | 7.1 | 100 | 33.9 |
| Nonconnected | 25 | 12 | 8 | 4 | 6 | 4 | 59 | 11.4 | 13 | 9 | 7 | 3 | 4 | 4 | 41 | 7.8 | 100 | 19.2 |
| Other PACs | 41 | 23 | 1 | 2 | 2 | 2 | 72 | 3.8 | 12 | 9 | 2 | 1 | 2 | 2 | 28 | 1.5 | 100 | 5.3 |
| All PACs | 36 | 19 | 6 | 1 | 4 | 3 | 69 | 102.2 | 10 | 9 | 3 | 2 | 3 | 3 | 31 | 45.7 | 100 | 147.8 |
| | *House, 1990* | | | | | | | | *Senate, 1990* | | | | | | | | | |
| Corporate | 32 | 25 | 1 | 2 | 2 | 4 | 66 | 35.4 | 13 | 11 | <1 | 6 | <1 | 3 | 34 | 18.0 | 100 | 53.5 |
| Association | 40 | 25 | 2 | 2 | 5 | 5 | 77 | 32.5 | 9 | 8 | 1 | 3 | <1 | 2 | 33 | 10.0 | 100 | 42.5 |
| Labor | 54 | 5 | 9 | <1 | 13 | <1 | 82 | 27.6 | 11 | 1 | 5 | <1 | 1 | <1 | 18 | 6.0 | 100 | 33.6 |
| Nonconnected | 26 | 13 | 4 | 4 | 8 | 5 | 60 | 8.5 | 20 | 10 | 2 | 5 | 1 | 2 | 40 | 5.7 | 100 | 14.3 |
| Other PACs | 46 | 21 | 1 | 2 | 2 | 2 | 74 | 4.3 | 13 | 8 | 1 | 2 | <1 | 2 | 26 | 1.5 | 100 | 5.8 |
| All PACs | 39 | 19 | 3 | 1 | 6 | 4 | 72 | 108.5 | 11 | 9 | 2 | 3 | 1 | 2 | 28 | 41.2 | 100 | 149.7 |
| | *House, 1992* | | | | | | | | *Senate, 1992* | | | | | | | | | |
| Corporate | 32 | 23 | 1 | 3 | 1 | 5 | 67 | 42.9 | 10 | 13 | 2 | 2 | 2 | 5 | 33 | 21.2 | 100 | 64.1 |
| Association | 35 | 22 | 3 | 3 | 7 | 6 | 76 | 38.7 | 8 | 8 | 2 | 1 | 2 | 2 | 24 | 12.4 | 100 | 51.1 |
| Labor | 48 | 3 | 11 | <1 | 16 | 1 | 78 | 30.5 | 9 | 1 | 7 | <1 | 5 | <1 | 22 | 8.6 | 100 | 39.1 |
| Nonconnected | 25 | 11 | 5 | 5 | 9 | 1 | 60 | 10.3 | 12 | 10 | 6 | 2 | 6 | 3 | 40 | 6.9 | 100 | 17.2 |
| Other PACs | 43 | 19 | 1 | 2 | 4 | 3 | 72 | 4.2 | 11 | 9 | 2 | <1 | 4 | 1 | 28 | 1.6 | 100 | 5.7 |
| All PACs | 36 | 17 | 4 | 2 | 8 | 4 | 71 | 127.0 | 9 | 8 | 3 | 1 | 3 | 3 | 29 | 51.1 | 100 | 178.1 |
| | *House, 1994* | | | | | | | | *Senate, 1994* | | | | | | | | | |
| Corporate | 34 | 22 | 1 | 4 | 2 | 5 | 68 | 43.4 | 9 | 9 | <1 | 3 | 2 | 9 | 32 | 20.6 | 100 | 64.1 |
| Association | 37 | 22 | 2 | 5 | 5 | 6 | 77 | 38.6 | 7 | 6 | 1 | 2 | 2 | 5 | 23 | 11.3 | 100 | 50.0 |
| Labor | 55 | 3 | 10 | <1 | 14 | <1 | 82 | 33.3 | 9 | <1 | 4 | <1 | 5 | <1 | 18 | 7.2 | 100 | 40.4 |

*(Table continues)*

**Table 3-13** *(Continued)*

| | *Percentage distribution* | | | | | | | | *Percentage distribution* | | | | | | | | | |
|---|---|---|---|---|---|---|---|---|---|---|---|---|---|---|---|---|---|---|
| | Incum-bent | | Chal-lenger | | Open seat | | | | Incum-bent | | Chal-lenger | | Open seat | | | | | |
| | D | R | D | R | D | R | *Percent to chamber* | *Dollars to chamber (in millions)* | D | R | D | R | D | R | *Percent to chamber* | *Dollars to chamber (in millions)* | *Total percent* | *Total dollars (in millions)* |
| Nonconnected | 31 | 11 | 4 | 7 | 7 | 6 | 66 | 11.6 | 11 | 7 | 1 | 3 | 5 | 5 | 33 | 5.6 | 100 | 17.3 |
| Other PACs | 43 | 18 | 2 | 4 | 4 | 4 | 74 | 4.0 | 11 | 5 | 1 | 1 | 3 | 4 | 26 | 1.8 | 100 | 6.6 |
| All PACs | 40 | 15 | 4 | 4 | 6 | 4 | 74 | 138.8 | 9 | 5 | 1 | 2 | 3 | 5 | 26 | 46.5 | 100 | 178.4 |
| | *House, 1996* | | | | | | | | *Senate, 1996* | | | | | | | | | |
| Corporate | 20 | 44 | <1 | 2 | 2 | 5 | 74 | 51.3 | 2 | 11 | <1 | 3 | 3 | 7 | 26 | 18.3 | 100 | 69.6 |
| Association | 21 | 40 | 3 | 3 | 4 | 6 | 79 | 44.0 | 2 | 8 | 1 | 2 | 3 | 6 | 22 | 12.0 | 100 | 56.0 |
| Labor | 41 | 5 | 25 | <1 | 13 | <1 | 85 | 39.4 | 3 | 1 | 3 | <1 | 8 | <1 | 15 | 6.9 | 100 | 46.3 |
| Nonconnected | 16 | 26 | 10 | 6 | 4 | 7 | 69 | 15.1 | 4 | 9 | 2 | 4 | 5 | 7 | 31 | 6.9 | 100 | 22.0 |
| Other PACs | 27 | 36 | 3 | 3 | 3 | 5 | 76 | 5.2 | 3 | 7 | 2 | 3 | 4 | 5 | 24 | 1.5 | 100 | 6.7 |
| All PACs | 25 | 30 | 8 | 3 | 5 | 5 | 76 | 155.0 | 3 | 7 | 2 | 2 | 5 | 5 | 24 | 45.6 | 100 | 200.6 |

*Note:* General election candidates only. D indicates Democrat; R indicates Republican. Percentages may not add to 100 because of rounding.

*Source:* Federal Election Commission.

Figure 3-6 Independent Expenditures in Senate and House Elections, 1978–1996

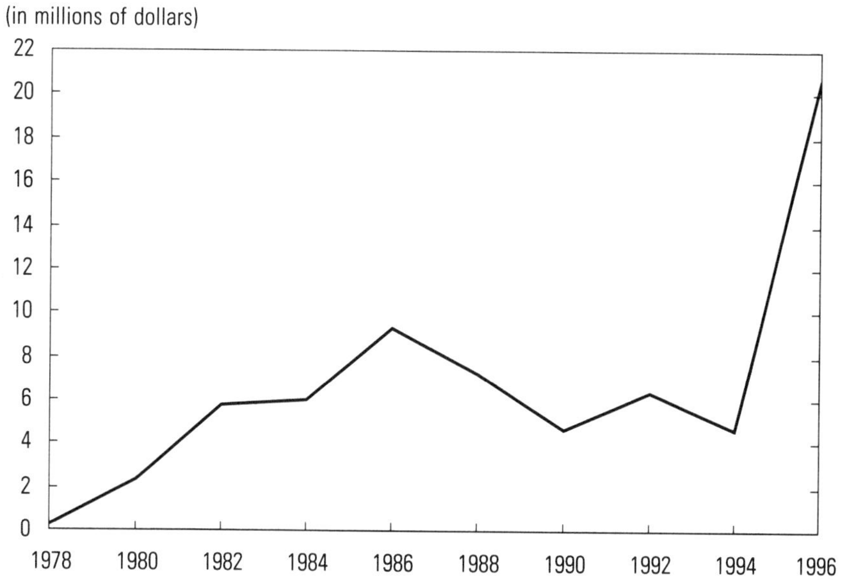


*Source:* Table 3-14.

**Table 3-14** Independent Expenditures in House and Senate Elections, 1978–1996 (in dollars)

| | *For Democrats* | *Against Democrats* | *For Republicans* | *Against Republicans* | *Total* |
|---|---|---|---|---|---|
| 1978 | | | | | |
| House | 28,725 | 31,034 | 70,701 | 5,298 | 135,758 |
| Senate | 102,508 | 36,717 | 26,065 | 1,985 | 167,275 |
| 1980 | | | | | |
| House | 190,615 | 38,023 | 410,478 | 45,132 | 684,248 |
| Senate | 127,381 | 1,282,613 | 261,678 | 12,430 | 1,684,102 |
| 1982 | | | | | |
| House | 241,442 | 862,654 | 492,404 | 66,296 | 1,662,796 |
| Senate | 127,451 | 3,182,986 | 298,410 | 483,750 | 4,092,597 |
| 1984 | | | | | |
| House | 560,727 | 118,171 | 633,646 | 26,847 | 1,339,391 |
| Senate | 326,031 | 410,428 | 1,807,981 | 2,082,207 | 4,626,647 |
| 1986 | | | | | |
| House | 2,385,685 | 227,286 | 1,313,578 | 120,032 | 4,046,581 |
| Senate | 988,382 | 632,412 | 3,342,790 | 348,006 | 5,311,590 |
| 1988 | | | | | |
| House | 1,465,554 | 278,723 | 919,929 | 148,705 | 2,812,911 |
| Senate | 831,064 | 617,066 | 2,809,517 | 143,441 | 4,401,088 |
| 1990 | | | | | |
| House | 709,292 | 130,695 | 669,726 | 74,444 | 1,584,157 |
| Senate | 780,832 | 266,230 | 1,436,553 | 584,429 | 3,068,044 |
| 1992 | | | | | |
| House | 1,485,768 | 430,902 | 1,586,017 | 452,942 | 3,955,629 |
| Senate | 1,137,321 | 164,358 | 864,493 | 210,490 | 2,376,662 |
| 1994 | | | | | |
| House | 502,621 | 488,479 | 1,088,356 | 50,815 | 2,130,271 |
| Senate | 204,212 | 433,947 | 1,309,572 | 537,531 | 2,485,262 |
| 1996 | | | | | |
| House | 711,226 | 158,132 | 2,630,273 | 1,401,101 | 4,900,732 |
| Senate | 337,594 | 5,575,164 | 7,567,653 | 2,239,230 | 15,719,641 |

*Note:* An independent expenditure is defined as an "expenditure by a person for a communication expressly advocating the election or defeat of a clearly identified candidate that is not made with the cooperation or with the prior consent of, or in consultation with, or at the request or suggestion of, a candidate or any agent or authorized committee of such candidate" (11 C.F.R. 109.1[a]).

# 4

# Committees

This chapter provides information on House and Senate committees and chairmanships from 1955 to 1997. Tables 4-1, 4-2, and 4-3 chart the ebb and flow in the number of committees and subcommittees in the House and Senate. It should be noted that the number of subcommittees in a given Congress is a particularly nebulous figure. During any Congress, subcommittees are added or dropped, and some ad hoc or special units may be listed or omitted from the various directories. At least two sources were consulted for each Congress to obtain the number of subcommittees.

Tables 4-1 and 4-2 show an erratic but persistent growth in the number of House panels from the 1950s through the Ninety-fourth Congress (1975–1976), with some stabilization and decline evident in the Ninety-sixth and Ninety-eighth Congresses. The numbers remained relatively stable until the 103d Congress, which saw a significant drop in the overall number of panels in the House. This decrease was due in large part to rules changes that tightened restrictions on the number of subcommittees allowed each standing committee, as well as the elimination of the House's four select committees.

But these reforms were not considered substantial enough. The Joint Committee on the Organization of Congress was created to study the institution and introduce a comprehensive package of reforms. Unfortunately, when the particular recommendations for committee reforms were put before the full chamber, strong opposition and bickering among affected members prevented any significant reforms from being adopted. But at the outset of the 104th Congress, the new Republican majority approved a series of committee changes as part of its agenda to reform the way the House operates. The total number of House panels dropped by 25 percent. In addition to eliminating three committees—the first decline in the number of full committees since 1955—the new rules stipulated that, with three exceptions, no committee could have more than five subcommittees. This lowered the total number of subcommittees to just above the 1955 level. The 105th Congress has retained the same basic structure, with little change in the number of size or committees.

A very different recent pattern for the Senate is revealed in Tables 4-1 and 4-3. As a result of that body's successful committee reorganization in 1977, the number of panels, particularly subcommittees, was cut dramatically—from an overall 205 in 1975–1976 to 130 in 1979–1980. Whereas the House and Senate had an equivalent number of panels in 1975, the House in 1980 had a clear numerical superiority. In the Ninety-seventh Senate—controlled by Republicans—the number of panels rose from its previous base, but quickly declined again. Similar to the House, the number of Senate committees for the 103d and 104th Congresses dropped, but not to the same extent.

Tables 4-4 and 4-5 display the average number of committee assignments of representatives and senators from 1955 to 1996. House committee and subcommittee assignments more than doubled from 1955, when representatives had an average of three assignments each to 1991, when that average had reached 6.8 assignments. The 1995 restructuring, including a limitation to two standing committee and four subcommittee assignments for most members, brought that average back down to under five assignments each. Senate assignments were cut back considerably with the 1977 reorganization, from an average of 17.6 in 1975 to 10.4 in 1980. The average rose slowly until hitting 11.8 in 1993 and then dropped slightly in 1995. But assignment inflation is a persistent phenomenon in the Senate; note that even with the dramatic decrease since 1975, senators are averaging more than twice as many assignments as their House counterparts.

Tables 4-6 and 4-7 examine chairmanships of committees and subcommittees in Congress. Table 4-6 shows that the proportions of majority party House members with chairmanships of one sort or another rose steadily in the 1960s and 1970s. This figure stabilized at about 50 percent in the 1980s and has fallen some since then. The rise in the 1960s was a direct result of the increase in the number of committees and subcommittees (see Table 4-1). Even though the number of panels declined between 1967 and 1971, the number and proportion of Democrats chairing them increased. This was the result of a 1971 Democratic reform that limited members to the chairmanship of only one subcommittee. The number of members with multiple chairmanships declined accordingly, and for the first time more than half of the majority party members held chairmanships of one kind or another.

The number holding multiple chairmanships of any sort fell somewhat through 1982, then rose substantially in 1983 and jumped again in 1985 and 1987. The norm against "stockpiling" chairmanships had apparently been relaxed, but in 1995 the direction shifted again. The total number of majority members serving as chairs decreased, though the smaller majority margin kept the percentage of majority members chairing panels from falling much at all. The impact of the new restriction on the number of subcommittees per committee may be best seen in this table with the sizable drop in the number of members chairing two or more committees. Only one member currently chairs more than two standing committees and subcommittees, versus twenty-five in 1991 and thirty-two in 1967.

The Senate has always been a different story when it comes to chairmanships (see Table 4-7). With the ratio of members to panels much smaller than in the House, few majority party senators have been denied a gavel of one sort or another since the 1950s; indeed, most majority senators have had at least two chairmanships. The average number of chairmanships rose to 2.9 in the mid-1970s, and then declined with the reorganization to 2.1 in 1979–1980.

Rather than diminishing leadership opportunities for junior senators, however, the reorganization expanded them by limiting the number of chairmanships each senator could hold. In 1979 every Democratic senator save one chaired at least one subcommittee or committee. The stunning arrival of a Republican majority did not change this pattern—every Republican senator except Majority Leader Howard Baker chaired at least one subcommittee in the 97th Congress, and all except Baker and one other held chairmanships in the 98th. Since the 100th Congress, the proportion of majority party senators holding chairmanships has remained below 90 percent. A Republican takeover in 1994 did not change the pattern.

Table 4-8 provides insights into the causes and consequences of seniority reforms of the 1970s, in the House of Representatives in particular. In the 1950s and early 1960s, Democrats from the Deep South constituted a near majority of their party (see Table 1-2 for a more detailed regional breakdown), and they held an even greater share of committee chairmanships. Their overall strength in numbers, however, discouraged any challenge to the system of selecting chairmen by nonsoutherners who opposed the system's unrepresentative results. By the late 1960s, the South's share of the Democratic Party in Congress was on the wane, but its hold on chairmanships of committees, especially the most powerful committees, was more tenacious. The declining number of southern members facilitated a change in the seniority pattern for the selection of chairmen in 1971. After this reform and the dramatic ouster of three southern chairmen in December 1974, the figures changed markedly. By 1979 southerners were underrepresented in committee chairmanships, and while they regained some power in the 1980s, southerners failed to regain the disproportionate share of House chairmanships they held in the 1950s and 1960s. One of the most significant results of the 1994 elections was the Republican takeover of the South. For the first time since Reconstruction, Republicans captured a majority of southern seats in the House and the Senate. Still, southerners now make up a smaller percentage of the majority and hold a smaller share of committee chairmanships than in the Democratic majority. The region is still powerful though, as two of the three exclusive committees in the House are chaired by southerners. If Republicans continue to gain seats in the South while holding onto their majority party status, southern Republicans will see their seniority strength rise. But newly approved term limits on committee chairs will limit the ability of senior members to cash in.

Similar changes have occurred in the Senate. Through the departure from the Senate of senior southerners and their replacement at the top rungs of committee seniority by nonsouthern Democrats, a broader and more equal regional distribution of power and subcommittee chairmanships, indicated in Table 4-8, was achieved by the mid-1970s. This meant that few senators felt so shortchanged of power that they would seek to accelerate these trends by a dramatic ouster of chairmen comparable to that in the House in 1974. The South was not disfranchised by the Republican takeover of the Senate in 1981; enough Republicans from the region had accumulated seniority, and enough southerners had been elected as Republicans, that the Senate numbers for 1981 were not dramatically different from those in the preceding Congress, when the Democrats were in the majority. In the meantime, a newer generation of southern Democrats has, almost unnoticed, moved up the seniority ladder. When the Democrats regained the majority in 1986, they were ready: Southerners, once again, had a disproportionately large share of committee chairmanships.

Their seniority strength remained fairly level for the next few years, but then in 1994 they were disfranchised by the Republican takeover. While their percentage of the majority party dropped only 1 percentage point, this was due mostly to a large number of freshman gains. Their seniority strength suffered, leaving them with only 12 percent of the chairmanships. The 105th Congress saw the southerners recoup some of those losses quicker than expected; they held 24 percent of the chairmanships in 1997.

**Table 4-1** Number of Committees in House and Senate, 84th–105th Congresses, 1955–1997

| *Congress* | | *Senate* | *House* | *Total*[a] |
|---|---|---|---|---|
| 84th | (1955–56) | 133 | 130 | 242 |
| 90th | (1967–68) | 155 | 185 | 315 |
| 92d | (1971–72) | 181 | 175 | 333 |
| 94th | (1975–76) | 205 | 204 | 385 |
| 96th | (1979–80) | 130 | 193 | 314 |
| 97th | (1981–82) | 136 | 174 | 300 |
| 98th | (1983–84) | 137 | 172 | 299 |
| 99th | (1985–86) | 120 | 191 | 301 |
| 100th | (1987–88) | 118 | 192 | 298 |
| 101st | (1989–90) | 118 | 189 | 295 |
| 102d | (1991–92) | 119 | 185 | 284 |
| 103d | (1993–94) | 111 | 146 | 252 |
| 104th | (1995–96) | 92 | 110 | 198 |
| 105th | (1997–98) | 92 | 112 | 200 |

*Note:* "Committees" include standing committees, subcommittees of standing committees, select and special committees, subcommittees of select and special committees, joint committees, and subcommittees of joint committees.

[a] Total is less than Senate and House combined because joint panels are counted only once.

*Sources:* Charles B. Brownson, *Congressional Staff Directory* (Washington, D.C.: Congressional Staff Directory, various years); *Congressional Quarterly Almanac* (Washington, D.C.: Congressional Quarterly, various years); *Congressional Yellow Book* (Washington, D.C.: Monitor Publishing Co., quarterly editions); *List of Standing Committees and Subcommittees and Select and Special Committees of the U.S. Senate,* Secretary of the Senate, March 25, 1991; *List of Standing Committees and Select Committees and Their Subcommittees of the House of Representatives,* Clerk of the House of Representatives, March 25, 1991; *Congressional Quarterly Committee Guide,* May 1, 1993; March 25, 1995; March 22, 1997.

**Table 4-2** Number and Type of House Committees, 84th-105th Congresses, 1955-1997

| *Congress* | | *Standing committees* | *Subcommittees of standing committees* | *Select and special committees* | *Subcommittees of select and special committees* | *Joint committees* | *Subcommittees of joint committees* |
|---|---|---|---|---|---|---|---|
| 84th | (1955–56) | 19 | 83 | 2 | 5 | 10 | 11 |
| 90th | (1967–68) | 20 | 133 | 1 | 6 | 10 | 15 |
| 92d | (1971–72) | 21 | 120 | 3 | 8 | 8 | 15 |
| 94th | (1975–76) | 22 | 151 | 3 | 4 | 7 | 17 |
| 96th | (1979–80) | 22 | 149[a] | 5 | 8 | 4 | 5 |
| 97th | (1981–82) | 22 | 132 | 3 | 7 | 4 | 6 |
| 98th | (1983–84) | 22 | 130 | 3 | 7 | 4 | 6 |
| 99th | (1985–86) | 22 | 142 | 5 | 12 | 4 | 6 |
| 100th | (1987–88) | 22 | 140[b] | 6 | 12 | 4 | 8 |
| 101st | (1989–90) | 22 | 138[b] | 5 | 12 | 4 | 8 |
| 102d | (1991–92) | 22 | 135[b] | 5 | 11 | 4 | 8 |
| 103d | (1993–94) | 22 | 115 | 1 | 3 | 5 | 0 |
| 104th | (1995–96) | 19 | 84 | 1 | 2 | 4 | 0 |
| 105th | (1997–98) | 19 | 86 | 1 | 2 | 4 | 0 |

[a] Includes nine budget task forces and the Welfare and Pension Plans Task Force (of the Subcommittee on Labor Management Relations of the Education and Labor Committee).

[b] Includes panels and task forces only if committee has no subcommittees.

*Sources:* Brownson, *Congressional Staff Directory; Congressional Quarterly Almanac; Congressional Yellow Book;* Clerk of the House of Representatives; *Congressional Quarterly Committee Guide,* May 1, 1993; March 25, 1995; March 22, 1997.

**Table 4-3** Number and Type of Senate Committees, 84th–105th Congresses, 1955–1997

| *Congress* | | *Standing committees* | *Subcommittees of standing committees* | *Select and special committees* | *Subcommittees of select and special committees* | *Joint committees* | *Subcommittees of joint committees* |
|---|---|---|---|---|---|---|---|
| 84th | (1955–56) | 15 | 88 | 3 | 6 | 10 | 11 |
| 90th | (1967–68) | 16 | 99 | 3 | 12 | 10 | 15 |
| 92d | (1971–72) | 17 | 123 | 5 | 13 | 8 | 15 |
| 94th | (1975–76) | 18 | 140 | 6 | 17 | 7 | 17 |
| 96th | (1979–80) | 15 | 91 | 5 | 10 | 4 | 5 |
| 97th | (1981–82) | 15 | 94 | 5 | 12 | 4 | 6 |
| 98th | (1983–84) | 16 | 103 | 4 | 4 | 4 | 6 |
| 99th | (1985–86) | 16 | 90 | 4 | 0 | 4 | 6 |
| 100th | (1987–88) | 16 | 85 | 5 | 0 | 4 | 8 |
| 101st | (1989–90) | 16 | 86 | 4 | 0 | 4 | 8 |
| 102d | (1991–92) | 16 | 87 | 4 | 0 | 4 | 8 |
| 103d | (1993–94) | 17 | 86 | 3 | 0 | 5 | 0 |
| 104th | (1995–96) | 17 | 68 | 3 | 0 | 4 | 0 |
| 105th | (1997–98) | 17 | 68 | 3 | 0 | 4 | 0 |

*Sources:* Brownson, *Congressional Staff Directory; Congressional Quarterly Almanac;* Walter Oleszek, "Overview of the Senate Committee System" (Paper prepared for the Commission on the Operation of the Senate, 1977); *Congressional Yellow Book;* Secretary of the Senate; *Congressional Quarterly Committee Guide,* May 1, 1993; March 25, 1995; March 22, 1997.

**Table 4-4** Committee Assignments for Representatives, 84th–105th Congresses, 1955–1997

| *Congress* | | *Mean no. of standing committee assignments* | *Mean no. of subcommittees of standing committee assignments* | *Mean no. of other committee assignments*[a] | *Total* |
|---|---|---|---|---|---|
| 84th | (1955–56) | 1.2 | 1.6 | 0.2 | 3.0 |
| 92d | (1971–72) | 1.5 | 3.2 | 0.4 | 5.1 |
| 94th | (1975–76) | 1.8 | 4.0 | 0.4 | 6.2 |
| 96th | (1979–80) | 1.7 | 3.6 | 0.5 | 5.8 |
| 97th | (1981–82) | 1.7 | 3.4 | 0.4 | 5.5 |
| 98th | (1983–84) | 1.7 | 3.6 | 0.5 | 5.8 |
| 99th | (1985–86) | 1.8 | 4.0 | 0.8 | 6.6 |
| 100th | (1987–88) | 1.7 | 3.8 | 1.0[b] | 6.5 |
| 101st | (1989–90) | 1.8 | 3.9 | 1.1[b] | 6.8 |
| 102d | (1991–92) | 1.9 | 4.0 | 0.9[b] | 6.8 |
| 103d | (1993–94) | 2.0 | 3.7 | 0.2 | 5.9 |
| 104th | (1995–96) | 1.8 | 2.9 | 0.1 | 4.8 |
| 105th | (1997–98) | 1.8 | 3.2 | 0.1 | 4.8 |

[a] "Other" committees include select and special committees, subcommittees of select and special committees, joint committees, and subcommittees of joint committees.

[b] Includes task forces when committee has no other subcommittees.

*Sources:* Brownson, *Congressional Staff Directory; Congressional Quarterly Almanac; Congressional Yellow Book;* Clerk of the House of Representatives; *Congressional Quarterly Committee Guide,* May 1, 1993; March 25, 1995; March 22, 1997.

**Table 4-5** Committee Assignments for Senators, 84th–105th Congresses, 1955–1997

| *Congress* | | *Mean no. of standing committee assignments* | *Mean no. of subcommittees of standing committee assignments* | *Mean no. of other committee assignments*[a] | *Total* |
|---|---|---|---|---|---|
| 84th | (1955–56) | 2.2 | 4.8 | 0.9 | 7.9 |
| 92d | (1971–72) | 2.5 | 9.5 | 3.3 | 15.3 |
| 94th | (1975–76) | 2.5 | 11.0 | 4.1 | 17.6 |
| 96th | (1979–80) | 2.3 | 6.6 | 1.5 | 10.4 |
| 97th | (1981–82) | 2.5 | 6.7 | 1.5 | 10.7 |
| 98th | (1983–84) | 2.9 | 7.5 | 1.2 | 11.6 |
| 99th | (1985–86) | 2.8 | 6.9 | 0.9 | 10.6 |
| 100th | (1987–88) | 2.9 | 7.0 | 1.2 | 11.1 |
| 101st | (1989–90) | 3.0 | 7.0 | 1.1 | 11.1 |
| 102d | (1991–92) | 2.9 | 7.4 | 1.1 | 11.0 |
| 103d | (1993–94) | 3.2 | 7.8 | 0.8 | 11.8 |
| 104th | (1995–96) | 3.1 | 6.2 | 0.7 | 10.8 |
| 105th | (1997–98) | 3.1 | 6.5 | 0.7 | 10.3 |

[a] "Other" committees include select and special committees, subcommittees of select and special committees, joint committees, and subcommittees of joint committees.

*Sources:* Brownson, *Congressional Staff Directory; Congressional Quarterly Almanac; Congressional Yellow Book;* Secretary of the Senate; *Congressional Quarterly Committee Guide,* May 1, 1993; March 25, 1995; March 22, 1997.

**Table 4-6** Majority Party Chairmanships of House Committees and Subcommittees, 84th–105th Congresses, 1955–1997

| *Congress* | | *Party in majority* | *No. of majority party members in House* | *No. chairing standing committees and subcommittees* | *No. with two or more chairmanships* | *% chairing standing committees and subcommittees* | *No. chairing all committees and subcommittees*[a] | *No. with two or more chairmanships* | *% chairing all committees and subcommittees*[a] |
|---|---|---|---|---|---|---|---|---|---|
| 84th | (1955–56) | D | 232 | 63 | 18 | 27.2 | 75 | 22 | 32.3 |
| 90th | (1967–68) | D | 247 | 111 | 32 | 44.9 | 117 | 38 | 47.4 |
| 92d | (1971–72) | D | 254 | 120 | 25 | 47.2 | 131 | 31 | 51.6 |
| 94th | (1975–76) | D | 289 | 142 | 24 | 49.1 | 150 | 28 | 51.9 |
| 96th | (1979–80) | D | 276 | 144 | 19 | 52.2 | 149 | 28 | 54.0 |
| 97th | (1981–82) | D | 243 | 121 | 16 | 49.8 | 125 | 26 | 51.4 |
| 98th | (1983–84) | D | 267 | 124 | 23 | 46.4 | 127 | 33 | 47.6 |
| 99th | (1985–86) | D | 253 | 129 | 27 | 51.0 | 131 | 37 | 51.8 |
| 100th | (1987–88) | D | 258 | 128 | 28 | 49.6 | 132[b] | 42 | 51.2 |
| 101st | (1989–90) | D | 260 | 134 | 26 | 51.5 | 137 | 38 | 52.7 |
| 102d | (1991–92) | D | 267 | 130 | 25 | 48.7 | 135[b] | 37 | 50.6 |
| 103d | (1993–94) | D | 258 | 113 | 19 | 43.8 | 116 | 22 | 45.0 |
| 104th | (1995–96) | R | 230 | 102 | 1 | 44.3 | 103 | 4 | 44.8 |
| 105th | (1997–98) | R | 227 | 101 | 4 | 44.5 | 102 | 9 | 44.9 |

[a] Includes standing committees, subcommittees of standing committees, select and special committees, subcommittees of select and special committees, joint committees, and subcommittees of joint committees.

[b] Includes task forces when committee has no other subcommittees.

*Sources:* Brownson, *Congressional Staff Directory; Congressional Quarterly Almanac;* Clerk of the House of Representatives; *Congressional Quarterly Committee Guide,* May 1, 1993; March 25, 1995; March 22, 1997.

**Table 4-7** Majority Party Chairmanships of Senate Committees and Subcommittees, 84th–105th Congresses, 1955–1997

| *Congress* | | *Party in majority* | *No. of majority party in Senate* | *No. chairing standing committees and sub-committees* | *% chairing standing committees and sub-committees* | *Average no. of standing committees and sub-committees chaired by majority members* | *No. chairing all committees and sub-committees*[a] | *% chairing all committees and sub-committees*[a] | *Average no. of all committees and sub-committees chaired by majority members* |
|---|---|---|---|---|---|---|---|---|---|
| 84th | (1955–56) | D | 48 | 42 | 87.5 | 1.8 | 42 | 87.5 | 2.0 |
| 90th | (1967–68) | D | 64 | 55 | 85.9 | 1.8 | 58 | 90.6 | 2.1 |
| 92d | (1971–72) | D | 55[b] | 51 | 92.7 | 2.6 | 52 | 94.5 | 2.9 |
| 94th | (1975–76) | D | 62[b] | 57 | 91.9 | 2.4 | 57 | 91.9 | 2.9 |
| 96th | (1979–80) | D | 59[b] | 58 | 98.3 | 1.8 | 58 | 98.3 | 2.1 |
| 97th | (1981–82) | R | 53 | 51 | 96.2 | 1.9 | 52 | 98.1 | 2.3 |
| 98th | (1983–84) | R | 54 | 52 | 96.3 | 1.9 | 52 | 96.3 | 2.5 |
| 99th | (1985–86) | R | 53 | 49 | 92.4 | 1.9 | 49 | 92.4 | 2.0 |
| 100th | (1987–88)[c] | D | 54 | 47 | 87.0 | 1.8 | 47 | 87.0 | 2.0 |
| 101st | (1989–90) | D | 55 | 46 | 83.6 | 1.9 | 46 | 83.6 | 1.9 |
| 102d | (1991–92) | D | 56 | 50 | 89.3 | 1.8 | 50 | 89.3 | 2.0 |
| 103d | (1993–94) | D | 57 | 46 | 80.7 | 1.8 | 46 | 80.7 | 1.9 |
| 104th | (1995–96) | R | 54 | 44 | 81.5 | 1.8 | 44 | 81.5 | 1.9 |
| 105th | (1997–98) | R | 55 | 48 | 87.3 | 1.7 | 48 | 87.3 | 1.9 |

[a] Includes standing committees, subcommittees of standing committees, select and special committees, subcommittees of select and special committees, joint committees, and subcommittees of joint committees.

[b] Includes Harry Byrd, Jr., elected as an Independent.

[c] Figures for the 100th Congress were compiled after the death of Sen. Edward Zorinsky (D-Neb.) but before the appointment of his successor and the redistribution of his chairmanships.

*Sources:* Brownson, *Congressional Staff Directory; Congressional Quarterly Almanac;* Secretary of the Senate; *Congressional Quarterly Committee Guide,* May 1, 1993; March 25, 1995; March 22, 1997.

**Table 4-8** Southern Chairmanships of House and Senate Standing Committees, 1955–1997

| | *House* | | | | *Senate* | | | |
|---|---|---|---|---|---|---|---|---|
| *Year* | Number of southern chairmen | % of chair-manships held by southerners | % of exclusive committees[a] chaired by southerners | % of majority party[b] from the South | Number of southern chairmen | % of chair-manships held by southerners | % of exclusive committees[a] chaired by southerners | % of majority party[b] from the South |
| 1955 | 12 | 63 | 67 | 43 | 8 | 53 | 50 | 46 |
| 1967 | 10 | 50 | 100 | 35 | 9 | 56 | 100 | 28 |
| 1971 | 8 | 38 | 100 | 31 | 9 | 53 | 100 | 30 |
| 1975 | 9 | 41 | 33 | 28 | 6 | 33 | 100 | 27 |
| 1979 | 5 | 23 | 33 | 28 | 4 | 27 | 50 | 28 |
| 1981 | 6 | 27 | 33 | 29 | 3 | 20 | 25 | 19 |
| 1983 | 7 | 32 | 67 | 30 | 3 | 19 | 25 | 20 |
| 1985 | 8 | 36 | 67 | 29 | 2 | 13 | 0 | 19 |
| 1987 | 7 | 31 | 67 | 29 | 7 | 44 | 75 | 30 |
| 1989 | 8 | 36 | 67 | 29 | 6 | 38 | 50 | 27 |
| 1991 | 8 | 36 | 33 | 29 | 6 | 38 | 50 | 27 |
| 1993 | 6 | 27 | 33 | 33 | 6 | 35 | 25 | 26 |
| 1995 | 4 | 21 | 67 | 25 | 2 | 12 | 50 | 25 |
| 1997 | 3 | 17 | 67 | 31 | 4 | 24 | 50 | 29 |

[a] In the House: Ways and Means, Rules, and Appropriations; in the Senate: Appropriations, Finance, Foreign Relations, and Armed Services.

[b] In 1981, 1983, 1985, and 1995, the Republicans were the majority party in the Senate; in 1995, they were also the majority party in the House. For all other years in the table, Democrats were the majority party in both the Senate and the House.

*Sources: Congressional Directory* (Washington, D.C.: U.S. Government Printing Office, various years); *Congressional Yellow Book; Congressional Quarterly Committee Guide,* May 1, 1993; March 25, 1995; March 22, 1997.

**Table 4-9** Closed Committee Meetings, 1953–1975

| *Year* | *Total meetings* | *Number closed* | *% closed* |
|---|---|---|---|
| 1953 | 2,640 | 892 | 34 |
| 1954 | 3,002 | 1,243 | 41 |
| 1955 | 2,940 | 1,055 | 36 |
| 1956 | 3,120 | 1,130 | 36 |
| 1957 | 2,517 | 854 | 34 |
| 1958 | 3,472 | 1,167 | 34 |
| 1959 | 3,152 | 940 | 30 |
| 1960 | 2,424 | 840 | 35 |
| 1961 | 3,159 | 1,109 | 35 |
| 1962 | 2,929 | 991 | 34 |
| 1963 | 3,868 | 1,463 | 38 |
| 1964 | 2,393 | 763 | 32 |
| 1965 | 3,903 | 1,537 | 39 |
| 1966 | 3,869 | 1,626 | 42 |
| 1967 | 4,412 | 1,716 | 39 |
| 1968 | 3,080 | 1,328 | 43 |
| 1969 | 4,029 | 1,470 | 36 |
| 1970 | 4,506 | 1,865 | 41 |
| 1971 | 4,816 | 1,731 | 36 |
| 1972 | 4,073 | 1,648 | 40 |
| 1973 | 5,520 | 887 | 16 |
| 1974 | 4,731 | 707 | 15 |
| 1975[a] | 6,325 | 449 | 7 |
| Total | 84,880 | 27,411 | 32 |

*Note:* Subcommittee meetings were included in the totals along with full committee sessions. Open meetings followed by closed meetings were counted twice, once in each category. Joint meetings of separate committees or subcommittees were counted as one meeting for each. The tabulations exclude meetings held when Congress was not in regular session, meetings held outside Washington, D.C., informal meetings without official status, and meetings of the House Rules Committee to consider sending legislation to the floor. Meetings of the House Appropriations Committee, all reported closed until 1971, were not included in the study until 1965.

[a] Figures have not been computed after 1975 because virtually all committee meetings have been open. At the start of the 104th Congress, House Republicans passed a rule that all committee and subcommittee meetings must be open unless it would pose a threat to national security.

*Source: Congressional Quarterly's Guide to Congress,* 2d ed. (Washington, D.C.: Congressional Quarterly, 1976), 370.

# 5

# Congressional Staff and Operating Expenses

Congress is made up of a great deal more than elected senators and representatives. With over 24,000 employees in 1997 (Table 5-1 and Figure 5-1), the legislative branch is larger than the departments of State, Labor, or Housing and Urban Development, making Congress by far the most heavily staffed legislative branch in the world.

In addition to the personal and committee staffs of representatives and senators, Congress also employs major research agencies, such as the Congressional Research Service (CRS) of the Library of Congress, and support personnel, such as mail carriers, police officers, television technicians, computer specialists, printers, carpenters, parking attendants, photographers, and laborers.

The development of this large congressional establishment is a twentieth-century phenomenon. At the turn of the century, representatives had no personal staff, and senators had a total of only thirty-nine personal assistants (see Table 5-2 and Figure 5-1). By contrast, over 11,000 persons served on the personal staffs of representatives and senators in 1995, and almost 2,000 people were employed by congressional committees. The latter figure is significantly lower than previous years because the Republican-controlled Congress reduced committee staff levels by more than 1,000 people.

The long-term enlargement of Congress's support staff reflects both the expanding role of the government in the United States and the changing role of the individual legislator. As government has done more, the congressional workload, in terms of both legislation and constituency service, has increased, and the staffing needs of Congress have expanded accordingly. The most dramatic staff growth took place in the years after World War II. The personal staffs of the House and Senate have increased more than fivefold and sixfold, respectively, since 1947. One reflection of the increased demands on legislators for constituency services and the members' encouragement of those demands for reelection purposes is the dramatic expansion of congressional staff working in constituency offices. More than 44 percent of the personal staffs of representatives and 31 percent of those of senators now work in district or state offices—a dramatic increase since the early 1970s (see Tables 5-3 and 5-4).

The explosion in congressional staffing is also evident on the standing committees: House committee staffs increased nearly twelvefold and Senate committee staffs more than fourfold between 1947 and 1989 (see Table 5-5). Committee staffing has grown steadily since the turn of the century, but the most dramatic increases occurred in the 1970s. House committee staffs were two and three-quarters times as large in 1979 as they were in 1970, and Senate committee staffs doubled over the same period. Staffs of both the House and the Senate declined slightly in 1993. Though Republicans opened the 104th Congress with a rule to cut committee staffs by one-third, the cuts have not been nearly that deep.

The enlargement of House committee staffs after 1970 was to a significant degree a result of the reform movement that swept the chamber. The sentiment for diluting the powers of committee chairmen extended to their nearly exclusive authority to hire and fire committee staff. Reforms allowed a much larger number of subcommittee chairmen and ranking members to hire their own staffs. The 1975 surge in committee staffing in the Senate reflects the passage of Senate Resolution 60, which authorized each senator to have a personal legislative assistant for each committee assignment.

The modest reductions in Senate committee staffs in 1977 were caused by the committee reorganization that went into effect that year, which among other things reduced the number of Senate subcommittees and shifted employees hired under Senate Resolution 60 to personal staff payrolls.

Today congressional staffs have become the target for a good deal of the criticism aimed at Congress. Critics have portrayed congressional staffs as bloated and wasteful. While it is true that staffs have grown sharply since World War II, and particularly in the past quarter century, the majority of that growth occurred from the late 1960s through the mid-1970s. This growth coincided with the decentralization of Congress, noted above, as well as the growth of White House and executive branch staff. Staff growth has actually leveled off since the late 1970s. Today personal congressional staff sizes are at approximately the same level they were twenty years ago, with recent declines. Though the Republican Congress reduced committee staff by about a third, the overall staff levels remain relatively constant.

Tables 5-6 and 5-7 rank the standing committees according to their current staff size. Most committees employ well over fifty persons, a far cry from the post-World War II era of small, intimate, informal committee staffs. Still, reflecting the current negative attitude toward congressional staffs and the cost of employing them, all but six House committees saw their staffs decrease in 1993. In 1995 most committees saw their staffs trimmed to between forty and seventy persons, with only a few powerful committees retaining relatively large staffs. The size of a committee staff does not appear to be related uniformly to the reported power or desirability of an assignment to that committee. The powerful Senate Finance Committee, for example, is modestly staffed compared with the less influential Labor and Human Resources and Governmental Affairs committees. Of course, some committees that are generally considered less desirable assignments may well have expanded their staffs to attract new members.

A significant part of the congressional staff works for Congress's four major research agencies (see Table 5-8). Two of these, the Congressional Budget Office (CBO) and the Office of Technology Assessment (OTA) (which Congress abolished in 1995, appropriating only enough money for it to shut the agency down), were created in the mid-1970s, reflecting a basic factor underlying the growth of congressional staff. The expanded role of the government in domestic and international affairs had made Congress increasingly dependent on the executive branch for information. A growing distrust of the executive branch, which festered during the Johnson and Nixon administrations, convinced Congress of the necessity for congressionally controlled sources of information. Congress thus authorized these new agencies and simultaneously expanded the roles of the Congressional Research Service and the General Accounting Office (GAO). The GAO has multiple functions; its primary job is to review federal spending and management for Congress. In addition, the office offers legal opinions to government agencies, settles disputed claims by or against the United States, and prescribes accounting standards for government-wide use. While a majority of GAO's resources was devoted to these other functions during the 1970s, the balance has since shifted and today roughly 80 percent of GAO's work is directly related to Congress. GAO staff has been cut by about 10 percent in the past few years.

Although the numbers in these tables describe the long-term growth of congressional staff, they do not reveal the many roles staff members play in the legislative process. The infinite variety of staffing arrangements that exists in members' offices and on committees and the influence exercised by various staff members become apparent only through close examination of individual offices and committees. The role played by staff within individual offices may also change over time with the ebb and flow of political tides. President Reagan's ability to make Congress focus on budget issues, for example, greatly reduced the number of bills Congress passed, as did the focus President Clinton placed on health care reform in 1993 (see Chapter 6). That meant less chance for members to use their staffs as policy entrepreneurs. Still, although the number of bills passed in the early 1990s declined, most committees claimed some jurisdiction over the health care reform issue and had their staffers working on it fervently. In short, it is difficult, if not impossible, to generalize about staffing roles and patterns solely on the basis of gross figures.

The costs of running Congress have grown along with the staff. Today's Congress is now more than a $2 billion enterprise. Although that may appear small when compared with the executive branch, it has grown at a dramatic pace from what it once was. In the years between 1946 and 1996, legislative branch appropriations increased 3830.4 percent. Over the same period, the consumer price index went up "only" 703.2 percent (see Table 5-9). As recently as the mid-1960s, the cost of operating Congress was less than one-ninth of what it is today. Recent years have shown signs of more legislative self-control: in the years between FY1976, when Congress first approached the billion dollar threshold, and FY1994, legislative branch appropriations went up only 140 percent, while the consumer price index increased by 160 percent. In fact, the FY1996 overall budget reflects a $178.8 million decrease since 1992.

The figures summarizing legislative branch appropriations include much more than the cost of House and Senate operations. It also includes the expenses of such agencies as the Library of Congress, the Government Printing Office, the General Accounting Office, the Botanic Garden, and the Copyright Royalty Commission, which make up a large portion of the spending. In fact, actual House and Senate appropriations comprise under 50 percent of total legislative branch appropriations. And, while overall spending has fluctuated significantly through the years, figures within these other components have remained relatively stable over the last decade. (See Table 5-10.)

Table 5-11 traces one of the perquisites of office available to members of Congress—use of the frank to send materials pertaining to the official business of Congress through the U.S. mails. In 1993 the cost of the congressional franking privilege was $67.7 million. Until 1981, the main reasons for the growing use of the frank were a more liberal law, permitting members of Congress to send mail (including newsletters and questionnaires) addressed to "occupant," and the increased value that legislators attach to communications with their constituents. The explosive growth since 1981 is a reflection of grass-roots lobbying. In other words, the first wave of growth was stimulated by members, the second by constituents. The rules have now changed to limit use of the frank and to prevent members from using the frank as a campaign tool. And, the House Oversight Committee of the 104th Congress voted to cut franking authorization by one-third of the 1994 figures.

Tables 5-12 and 5-13 summarize the allowances available to representatives and senators for operating their offices and outline the changes in those allowances since 1977. In the past, expenses for such things as postage, stationery, office furnishings, equipment, and travel were governed by strict individual spending limits. The House in 1978 and the Senate in 1973 consolidated their office expense allowances into one account to give members greater flexibility in using their expense allowances.The House Republicans went further in 1995 by consolidating all expenses into one account (see Table 5-12.) Because Congress is a labor intensive enterprise, however, the largest share of the congressional allowance is for staff.

NOTE: In the source notes to the tables in this chapter, two kinds of frequently cited legislative appropriations documents are abbreviated as follows: (1) *House LBA Hearings for 19xx* = U.S. Congress, House of Representatives, Committee on Appropriations, Subcommittee on Legislative Branch Appropriations, *Hearings on Legislative Branch Appropriations for 19xx.* (2) *Senate LBA Hearings for 19xx* = U.S. Congress, Senate, Committee on Appropriations, *Hearings on Legislative Branch Appropriations for 19xx.* The year in the citation is the fiscal year covered by the appropriation hearing, not the calendar year that may appear in the table.

**Table 5-1** Congressional Staff, 1979-1997

| | *1979* | *1981* | *1983* | *1985* | *1987* | *1989* | *1991* | *1993* | *1995* | *1997* |
|---|---|---|---|---|---|---|---|---|---|---|
| House | | | | | | | | | | |
| Committee staff[a] | 2,027 | 1,917 | 2,068 | 2,146 | 2,136 | 2,267 | 2,321 | 2,147[b] | 1,266 | 1,276 |
| Personal staff | 7,067 | 7,487 | 7,606 | 7,528 | 7,584 | 7,569 | 7,278 | 7,400 | 7,186 | 7,282 |
| Leadership staff[c] | 162 | 127 | 135 | 144 | 138 | 133 | 149 | 132 | 134 | 126 |
| Officers of the House, staff[d] | 1,487 | 1,686 | 1,728 | 1,818 | 1,845 | 1,215 | 1,293 | 1,194 | 1,327 | 1,146 |
| Subtotal, House | 10,743 | 11,217 | 11,537 | 11,636 | 11,703 | 11,184 | 11,041 | 10,878 | 9,913 | 9,830 |
| Senate | | | | | | | | | | |
| Committee staff[a] | 1,410 | 1,150 | 1,176 | 1,178 | 1,207 | 1,116 | 1,154 | 994 | 796 | 1,216 |
| Personal staff | 3,593 | 3,945 | 4,059 | 4,097 | 4,075 | 3,837 | 4,294 | 4,138 | 4,247 | 4,410 |
| Leadership staff[c] | 91 | 106 | 120 | 118 | 103 | 105 | 125 | 132 | 126 | 148 |
| Officers of the Senate, staff[d] | 828 | 878 | 948 | 976 | 904 | 926 | 1,092 | 1,165 | 994 | 958 |
| Subtotal, Senate | 5,922 | 6,079 | 6,303 | 6,369 | 6,289 | 5,984 | 6,665 | 6,429 | 6,163 | 6,732 |
| Joint committee staffs | 138 | 126 | 123 | 131 | 132 | 138 | 145 | 145 | 108 | 120 |
| Support agencies[e] | | | | | | | | | | |
| General Accounting Office | 5,303 | 5,182 | 4,960 | 5,042 | 5,016 | 5,063 | 5,054 | 4,958 | 4,342 | 3,500 |
| Congressional Research Service | 847 | 849 | 853 | 860 | 860 | 860 | 831 | 814 | 746 | 747 |
| Congressional Budget Office | 207 | 218 | 211 | 222 | 226 | 226 | 226 | 230 | 214 | 232 |
| Office of Technology Assessment | 145 | 130 | 130 | 143 | 143 | 143 | 143 | 143 | n.a.[f] | n.a. |
| Subtotal, support agencies | 6,502 | 6,379 | 6,154 | 6,267 | 6,245 | 6,292 | 6,254 | 6,145 | 5,302 | 4,479 |
| Miscellaneous | | | | | | | | | | |
| Architect | 2,296 | 1,986 | 2,061 | 2,073 | 2,412 | 2,088 | 2,099 | 2,060 | 2,151 | 1,854 |
| Capitol Police[g] | 1,167 | 1,163 | 1,148 | 1,227 | 1,250 | 1,259 | 1,265 | 1,159 | 1,076 | 1,076 |
| Subtotal | 3,463 | 3,149 | 3,209 | 3,300 | 3,662 | 3,347 | 3,364 | 3,219 | 3,227 | 2,930 |
| Total | 26,768 | 26,950 | 27,326 | 27,703 | 28,031 | 26,945 | 27,469 | 26,816 | 24,713 | 24,091 |

*(Table continues)*

**Table 5-1** *(Continued)*

*Note:* Totals for Tables 5-1 through 5-8 reflect number of full-time paid employees.

[a] Includes select and special committee staffs. Figures therefore do not agree with those in Table 5-5.

[b] In addition to the staffs (twenty-nine members) of the Permanent Select Committee on Intelligence and the Joint Committee on the Organization of Congress, which retained twenty-nine staff members, there were three other select committees in operation in 1993. These committees, the Select Committee on Aging, the Select Committee on Children, Youth, and Families, and the Special and Select Committee on Funerals, were not reauthorized by the 104th Congress. However, the committees stayed on for a few months to complete previous business. Although the committees did little business in 1993, it should be noted that they retained small staffs during this time.

[c] Includes legislative counsels' offices.

[d] Doorkeepers, parliamentarians, sergeants-at-arms, clerk of the House, Senate majority and minority secretaries, and postmasters.

[e] Adjustments were made in this edition to reflect the current division of labor among the various support agencies. Today approximately 80 percent of GAO's work is done directly for Congress; the Congressional Research Service is the branch of the Library of Congress that serves Congress most directly.

[f] The Office of Technology Assessment was eliminated in 1995.

[g] Sworn officers only.

*Sources:* For 1979, *Report of the Clerk of the House,* July 1, 1979-September 30, 1979; *Report of the Secretary of the Senate,* April 1, 1979-September 30, 1979; U.S. Office of Personnel Management, Work Force Analysis and Statistics Branch, *Federal Civilian Workforce Statistics,* monthly release, October 31, 1979, 6. For 1981, U.S. Congress, House, Committee on Appropriations, Subcommittee on Legislative Branch Appropriations, *Hearings on Legislative Branch Appropriations for 1983,* pt. 1, 24-28; U.S. Congress, Senate, Committee on Appropriations, *Hearings on Legislative Branch Appropriations for 1982,* 117, 253, 266; Senate Committee on Rules and Administration, *Senate Committee Funding,* 97th Cong., 1st sess., 1981, Committee Print 2; *Report of the Secretary of the Senate,* October 1, 1981-March 31, 1982, 1-23. For 1983, *House LBA Hearings for 1985,* pt. 1, 23-27; Office of the Clerk of the House; Senate Committee on Rules and Administration, *Senate Committee Funding,* 98th Cong., 2d sess., 1984, Committee Print 3; *Senate LBA Hearings for 1984,* 47, 276; Office of the U.S. Capitol Police. For 1985, *House LBA Hearings for 1987,* pt. 1, 22-27; *Report of the Clerk of the House,* October 1, 1985-December 31, 1985; Senate Committee on Rules and Administration, *Senate Committee Funding,* 99th Cong., 2d sess., 1986, Committee Print 2; *Senate LBA Hearings for 1986; Report of the Secretary of the Senate,* October 1, 1985-March 31, 1986; Office of the U.S. Capitol Police. For 1987, *House LBA Hearings for 1989,* pt. 2; Office of the Clerk of the House; *Senate LBA Hearings for 1988; Report of the Secretary of the Senate,* October 1, 1987-March 31, 1988; Bureau of the Census, *Statistical Abstract of the United States 1989* (Washington, D.C.: U.S. Government Printing Office, 1989), 252; Office of the Architect of the Capitol; Office of the U.S. Capitol Police. For 1989, *House LBA Hearings for 1991,* pt. 1; Office of the Clerk of the House; *Senate LBA Hearings for 1990; Report of the Secretary of the Senate,* October 1, 1989-March 31, 1990. For 1991, *House LBA Hearings for 1993,* pt. 1; *Report of the Clerk of the House,* October 1, 1991-December 31, 1991; *Senate LBA Hearings for 1992; Report of the Secretary of the Senate,* October 1, 1991-March 31, 1992. For 1993, *House LBA Hearings for 1995,* pt. 1; *Report of the Clerk of the House,* October 1, 1993-December 31, 1993; House Office of Finance; *Senate LBA Hearings for 1994; Report of the Secretary of the Senate,* October 1, 1993-March 31, 1994. For 1995, LBA for 1997, report of the Secretary of the Senate October 1, 1995-March 31-1996, House Office of Finance. For 1997, *Report of the Secretary of the Senate,* October 1, 1996-March 31, 1997; *Statement of Disbursements of the House,* January 1, 1997-March 31, 1997; Legislative Branch Appropriations for 1998.

**Table 5-2** Staffs of Members of the House and the Senate, 1891–1997

| *Year* | *Employees in House* | *Employees in Senate* | *Year* | *Employees in House* | *Employees in Senate* |
|---|---|---|---|---|---|
| 1891 | n.a. | 39 | 1983 | 7,606 | 4,059 |
| 1914 | n.a. | 72 | 1984 | 7,385 | 3,949 |
| 1930 | 870 | 280 | 1985 | 7,528 | 4,097 |
| 1935 | 870 | 424 | 1986 | 7,920[a] | 3,774[a] |
| 1947 | 1,440 | 590 | 1987 | 7,584 | 4,075 |
| 1957 | 2,441 | 1,115 | 1988 | 7,564 | 3,977 |
| 1967 | 4,055 | 1,749 | 1989 | 7,569 | 3,837 |
| 1972 | 5,280 | 2,426 | 1990 | 7,496 | 4,162 |
| 1976 | 6,939 | 3,251 | 1991 | 7,278 | 4,294 |
| 1977 | 6,942 | 3,554 | 1992 | 7,597 | 4,249 |
| 1978 | 6,944 | 3,268 | 1993 | 7,400 | 4,138 |
| 1979 | 7,067 | 3,593 | 1994 | 7,390 | 4,200 |
| 1980 | 7,371 | 3,746 | 1995 | 7,186 | 4,247 |
| 1981 | 7,487 | 3,945 | 1996 | 7,288 | 4,151 |
| 1982 | 7,511 | 4,041 | 1997 | 7,282 | 4,410 |

n.a. = not available.

[a] Senate figures reflect the period immediately after Gramm-Rudman mandated staffing cuts. House figures are for the entire fiscal year, thus averaging post-Gramm-Rudman staffing levels with previous, higher levels.

*Sources:* For 1891 through 1976, Harrison W. Fox, Jr., and Susan W. Hammond, *Congressional Staffs: The Invisible Force in American Lawmaking* (New York: Free Press, 1977), 171. For 1977 and 1978, Judy Schneider, "Congressional Staffing, 1947–78," Congressional Research Service, Library of Congress, August 24, 1979, reprinted in U.S. Congress, House, Select Committee on Committees, *Final Report,* 96th Cong., 2d sess., 1980, 540. For 1977, 1978, and 1979 House, *Report of the Clerk of the House.* For 1979 Senate, *Report of the Secretary of the Senate.* For 1980, *House LBA Hearings for 1982,* pt. 1, 25; *Senate LBA Hearings for 1981,* pt. 1, 26. For 1981, *House LBA Hearings for 1983,* pt. 1, 24–28; *Report of the Secretary of the Senate,* October 1, 1981–March 31, 1982. For 1982, *House LBA Hearings for 1984,* pt. 1, 25; *Report of the Secretary of the Senate,* October 1, 1982–March 31, 1983. For 1983, *House LBA Hearings for 1985,* pt. 1, 24; *Report of the Secretary of the Senate,* October 1, 1983–March 31, 1984. For 1984, *House LBA Hearings for 1986,* pt. 1, 22; *Report of the Secretary of the Senate,* October 1, 1984–March 31, 1985. For 1985–1986, *House LBA Hearings for 1987,* pt. 1, 23; *Report of the Secretary of the Senate,* October 1, 1985–March 31, 1986. For 1987, *House LBA Hearings for 1989,* pt. 2; *Senate LBA Hearings for 1988; Report of the Secretary of the Senate,* October 1, 1987–March 31, 1988. For 1988, *House LBA Hearings for 1990,* pt. 2; *Report of the Secretary of the Senate,* April–September 1989, pt. 1. For 1989, *House LBA Hearings for 1991,* pt. 2; *Report of the Secretary of the Senate,* October 1, 1989–March 31, 1990. For 1990, *House LBA Hearings for 1992,* pt. 2; *Report of the Secretary of the Senate,* October 1, 1990–March 31, 1991. For 1991, *House LBA Hearings for 1993,* pt. 2; *Report of the Secretary of the Senate,* October 1, 1991–March 31, 1992. For 1992, House Appropriations Committee; *Report of the Secretary of the Senate,* October 1, 1992–March 31, 1993. For 1993, House Office of Finance; *Report of the Secretary of the Senate,* October 1, 1993–March 31, 1994; for 1994, House Office of Finance; *Report of the Secretary of the Senate,* October 1, 1995–March 31, 1996.

Figure 5-1 Staff of Members and of Committees in Congress, 1891–1997

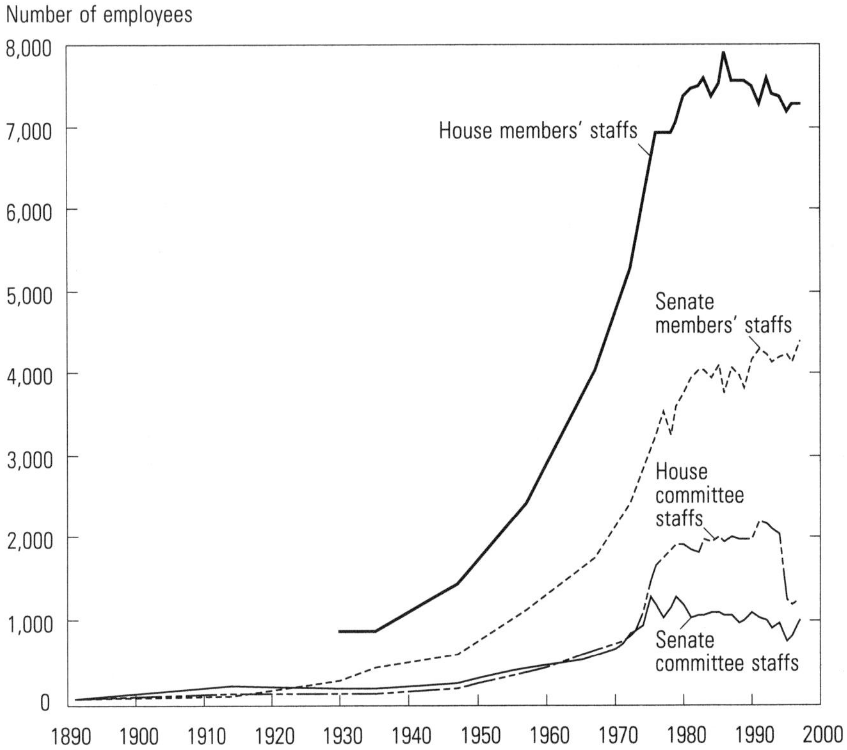


*Sources:* Tables 5-2 and 5-5.

**Table 5-3** House Staff Based in District Offices, 1970–1997

| *Year* | *Employees* | *Percentage of total personal staffs in district offices* |
|---|---|---|
| 1970 | 1,035 | n.a. |
| 1971 | 1,121 | n.a. |
| 1972 | 1,189 | 22.5 |
| 1973 | 1,347 | n.a. |
| 1974 | 1,519 | n.a. |
| 1975 | 1,732 | n.a. |
| 1976 | 1,943 | 28.0 |
| 1977 | 2,058 | 29.6 |
| 1978 | 2,317 | 33.4 |
| 1979 | 2,445 | 34.6 |
| 1980 | 2,534 | 34.4 |
| 1981 | 2,702 | 36.1 |
| 1982 | 2,694 | 35.8 |
| 1983 | 2,785 | 36.6 |
| 1984 | 2,872 | 38.9 |
| 1985 | 2,871 | 38.1 |
| 1986 | 2,940 | 43.6 |
| 1987 | 2,503 | 33.0 |
| 1988 | 2,954 | 39.6 |
| 1989 | 2,916 | 38.5 |
| 1990 | 3,027 | 40.4 |
| 1991 | 3,022 | 41.5 |
| 1992 | 3,128 | 41.2 |
| 1993 | 3,130 | 42.3 |
| 1994 | 3,335 | 45.1 |
| 1995 | 3,459 | 48.1 |
| 1996 | 3,144 | 43.1 |
| 1997 | 3,209 | 44.1 |

n.a. = not available.

*Sources:* For 1970–1978, Schneider, "Congressional Staffing, 1947–78." For 1979–1988, Charles B. Brownson, *Congressional Staff Directory* (Washington, D.C.: Congressional Staff Directory, annual editions). For 1989–1997, Ann Brownson, *Congressional Staff Directory.*

**Table 5-4** Senate Staff Based in State Offices, 1972–1997

| *Year* | *Employees* | *Percentage of total personal staffs in state offices* |
|---|---|---|
| 1972 | 303 | 12.5 |
| 1978 | 816 | 25.0 |
| 1979 | 879 | 24.4 |
| 1980 | 953 | 25.4 |
| 1981 | 937 | 25.8 |
| 1982 | 1,053 | 26.1 |
| 1983 | 1,132 | 27.9 |
| 1984 | 1,140 | 28.9 |
| 1985 | 1,180 | 28.8 |
| 1986 | 1,249 | 33.1 |
| 1987 | 1,152 | 28.3 |
| 1988 | 1,217 | 30.6 |
| 1989 | 1,200 | 31.3 |
| 1990 | 1,293 | 31.1 |
| 1991 | 1,316 | 30.6 |
| 1992 | 1,368 | 32.2 |
| 1993 | 1,335 | 32.3 |
| 1994 | 1,345 | 32.0 |
| 1995 | 1,278 | 30.1 |
| 1996 | 1,290 | 31.1 |
| 1997 | 1,366 | 31.0 |

*Source:* Brownson, *Congressional Staff Directory* and *Report of the Secretary of the Senate.*

**Table 5-5** Staffs of House and Senate Standing Committees, 1891–1997

| *Year* | *Employees in House* | *Employees in Senate* | *Year* | *Employees in House* | *Employees in Senate* |
|---|---|---|---|---|---|
| 1891 | 62 | 41 | 1980 | 1,917 | 1,191 |
| 1914 | 105 | 198 | 1981 | 1,843 | 1,022 |
| 1930 | 112 | 163 | 1982 | 1,839 | 1,047 |
| 1935 | 122 | 172 | 1983 | 1,970 | 1,075 |
| 1947 | 167 | 232 | 1984 | 1,944 | 1,095 |
| 1950 | 246 | 300 | 1985 | 2,009 | 1,080 |
| 1955 | 329 | 386 | 1986 | 1,954 | 1,075 |
| 1960 | 440 | 470 | 1987 | 2,024 | 1,074 |
| 1965 | 571 | 509 | 1988 | 1,976 | 970 |
| 1970 | 702 | 635 | 1989 | 1,986 | 1,013 |
| 1971 | 729 | 711 | 1990 | 1,993 | 1,090 |
| 1972 | 817 | 844 | 1991 | 2,201 | 1,030 |
| 1973 | 878 | 873 | 1992 | 2,178 | 1,008 |
| 1974 | 1,107 | 948 | 1993 | 2,118 | 897 |
| 1975 | 1,460 | 1,277 | 1994 | 2,046 | 958 |
| 1976 | 1,680 | 1,201 | 1995 | 1,246 | 732 |
| 1977 | 1,776 | 1,028 | 1996 | 1,177 | 793 |
| 1978 | 1,844 | 1,151 | 1997 | 1,250 | 1,002 |
| 1979 | 1,909 | 1,269 | | | |

*Note:* Figures for 1947–1986 are for the statutory and investigative staffs of standing committees. They do not include select committee staffs, which varied between 31 and 238 in the House and between 62 and 172 in the Senate during the 1970s. For this reason, the numbers do not agree with those in Table 5-1. In an attempt to provide further accuracy, we have counted certain individuals as .5 of a staff member based on the length of employment and salary received. Rounding of these numbers then means that figures in this table do not necessarily equal those of the individual committees in Tables 5-6 and 5-7.

*Sources:* For 1891–1935, Fox and Hammond, *Congressional Staffs,* 171. For 1947–1978, Schneider, "Congressional Staffing, 1947–78." For 1979–1980 Senate, U.S. Congress, Senate, Committee on Rules and Administration, *Senate Inquiries and Investigations,* 96th Cong., 2d sess., 1980, Committee Print 2, March 5, 1980. For 1981–1986 Senate, U.S. Congress, Senate, Committee on Rules and Administration, *Senate Committee Funding,* annual committee prints. For 1981 House, *House LBA Hearings for 1983,* pt. 2, 107. For 1982 House, *House LBA Hearings for 1984,* pt. 2, 77. For 1983–1984 House, Office of the Clerk of the House. For 1985 House, *Report of the Clerk of the House,* October 1, 1985–December 31, 1985. For 1986 House, *Report of the Clerk of the House,* October 1, 1986–December 31, 1986. For 1987 House, *Report of the Clerk of the House,* October 1, 1987–December 31, 1987; Senate, Committee on Rules and Administration. For 1988 House, *Report of the Clerk of the House,* October 1, 1988–December 31, 1988; Senate, *Report of the Secretary of the Senate,* April–September 1989, pt. 1. For 1989 House, *Report of the Clerk of the House,* October 1, 1989–December 31, 1989; Senate, *Report of the Secretary of the Senate,* October 1, 1989–March 31, 1990, pt. 1. For 1990 House, *Report of the Clerk of the House,* October 1, 1990–December 31, 1990; Senate, *Report of the Secretary of the Senate,* October 1, 1990–March 31, 1991. For 1991 House, *Report of the Clerk of the House,* October 1, 1991–December 31, 1991; Senate, *Report of the Secretary of the Senate,* October 1, 1991–March 31, 1992. For 1992 House, *Report of the Clerk of the House,* October 1, 1992–December 31, 1992; Senate, *Report of the Secretary of the Senate,* October 1, 1992–March 31, 1993. For 1993 House, *Report of the Clerk of the House,* October 1, 1993–December 31, 1993; Senate, *Report of the Secretary of the Senate,* October 1, 1993–March 31, 1994. For 1994 House, *Report of the Clerk of the House,* October 1, 1994–December 31, 1994; Senate, *Report of the Secretary of the Senate,* October 1, 1994–March 31, 1995. For 1995 House, *Report of the Clerk of the House,* October 1, 1995–December 31, 1995; Senate, *Report of the Secretary of the Senate,* April 1, 1995–September 30, 1995. *Report of the Secretary of the Senate,* October 1, 1996–March 31, 1997; *Statement of Disbursements of the House,* October 1, 1996–December 31, 1996; January 1, 1997–March 31, 1997.

**Table 5-6** Staffs of House Standing Committees, 1947–1997

| *Committee* | *1947* | *1960* | *1970* | *1975* | *1981* | *1985* | *1987* | *1989* | *1991* | *1993* | *1994* | *1995* | *1996* | *1997* |
|---|---|---|---|---|---|---|---|---|---|---|---|---|---|---|
| Appropriations | 29 | 59 | 71 | 98 | 127 | 182 | 188 | 196 | 218 | 227 | 202 | 126 | 143 | 156 |
| Government Reform and Oversight (Government Operations) | 9 | 54 | 60 | 68 | 84 | 86 | 80 | 82 | 90 | 86 | 82 | 75 | 100 | 120 |
| Commerce (Energy and Commerce) | 10 | 45 | 42 | 112 | 151 | 162 | 153 | 138 | 155 | 140 | 139 | 67 | 93 | 94 |
| Judiciary | 7 | 27 | 35 | 69 | 75 | 81 | 81 | 80 | 71 | 75 | 74 | 47 | 61 | 85 |
| Transportation and Infrastructure (Public Works) | 6 | 32 | 40 | 88 | 86 | 84 | 83 | 83 | 97 | 89 | 87 | 70 | 74 | 84 |
| Economic and Educational Opportunities (Education and Labor) | 10 | 25 | 77 | 114 | 121 | 119 | 127 | 114 | 117 | 112 | 114 | 66 | 75 | 77 |
| International Relations (Foreign Affairs ) | 10 | 14 | 21 | 54 | 84 | 97 | 101 | 98 | 104 | 96 | 98 | 62 | 69 | 73 |
| Resources (Natural Resources) | 4 | 10 | 14 | 57 | 70 | 73 | 71 | 67 | 85[c] | 71 | 66 | 56 | 62 | 71 |
| Ways and Means | 12 | 22 | 24 | 63 | 91 | 99 | 108 | 94 | 94 | 142 | 122 | 60 | 67 | 65 |
| Banking and Financial Services (Banking) | 4 | 14 | 50 | 85 | 87 | 90 | 99 | 108 | 112 | 100 | 98 | 46 | 56 | 64 |
| Science (Science, Space and Technology) | b | 17 | 26 | 47 | 74 | 78 | 78 | 79 | 84 | 87 | 86 | 48 | 56 | 63 |
| Agriculture | 9 | 10 | 17 | 48 | 62 | 67 | 69 | 69 | 69 | 70 | 66 | 48 | 50 | 62 |
| Budget | b | b | b | 67 | 93 | 109 | 124 | 96 | 101 | 98 | 98 | 61 | 67 | 61 |
| National Security (Armed Services) | 10 | 15 | 37 | 38 | 49 | 64 | 70 | 66 | 82 | 76 | 78 | 44 | 70 | 60 |
| Rules | 4 | 2 | 7 | 18 | 43 | 45 | 43 | 41 | 49 | 48 | 47 | 37 | 36 | 41 |
| Small Business | b | b | b | 27 | 54 | 53 | 62 | 54 | 53 | 45 | 40 | 24 | 28 | 40 |
| House Oversight (House Administration)[a] | 7 | 4 | 25 | 217 | 252 | 275 | 228 | 275 | 317 | 317 | 316 | 270 | 33 | 36 |
| Veterans' Affairs | 7 | 18 | 18 | 26 | 34 | 32 | 44 | 41 | 44 | 46 | 45 | 28 | 28 | 27 |

| | | | | | | | | | | | | | | |
|---|---|---|---|---|---|---|---|---|---|---|---|---|---|---|
| Standards of Official Conduct | b | b | 5 | 5 | 9 | 9 | 11 | 8 | 11 | 9 | 9 | 10 | 9 | 11 |
| Post Office and Civil Service | 6 | 9 | 46 | 61 | 74 | 83 | 85 | 83 | 87 | 76 | 70 | 6 | d | d |
| Merchant Marine and Fisheries | 6 | 9 | 21 | 28 | 82 | 79 | 77 | 74 | 76 | 75 | 75 | 6 | d | d |
| District of Columbia | 7 | 8 | 15 | 43 | 41 | 42 | 42 | 39 | 40 | 34 | 36 | 6 | d | d |

*Note:* Many of the committee names and jurisdictions changed in the 104th Congress. For continuity we have included the old committee names in parentheses. The committees are ranked in order of their staff size in 1997. Through 1991, numbers ending in .5 are rounded up.

[a] After 1972, figures include employees of House Informations Systems, the House of Representatives' central computer facility.

[b] Not a standing committee.

[c] In 1993 the Natural Resources Committee was created out of the old Interior Committee. The staff figures for 1947–1991 are actually those of the Interior Committee.

[d] These three committees were eliminated in the first few weeks of the 104th Congress. The jurisdictions of the Post Office and Civil Service Committee and District of Columbia Committee became part of the Government Reform and Oversight Committee. The jurisdiction of the Merchant Marine and Fisheries Committee was divided among several other committees.

*Sources:* For 1947–1975, Schneider, "Congressional Staffing, 1947–78." For 1979, *House LBA Hearings for 1981,* pt. 2, 136. For 1981, *House LBA Hearings for 1983,* pt. 2, 107. For 1983, Office of the Clerk of the House. For 1985, *Report of the Clerk of the House,* October 1, 1985–December 31, 1985. For 1987, *Report of the Clerk of the House,* October 1, 1987–December 31, 1987. For 1989, *Report of the Clerk of the House,* October 1, 1989–December 31, 1989. For 1991, *Report of the Clerk of the House,* October 1, 1991–December 31, 1991. For 1993, *Report of the Clerk of the House,* October 1, 1993–December 31, 1993. For 1994 House, *Report of the Clerk of the House,* October 1, 1994–December 31, 1994; Senate, *Report of the Secretary of the Senate,* October 1, 1994–March 31, 1995. For 1995 House, *Report of the Clerk of the House,* October 1, 1995–December 31, 1995; Senate, *Report of the Secretary of the Senate,* April 1, 1995–September 30, 1995. For 1996–1997, *Statement of Disbursements of the House,* October 1, 1996–December 31, 1996; January 1, 1997–March 31, 1997.

**Table 5-7** Staffs of Senate Standing Committees, 1947–1997

| *Committee* | *1947* | *1960* | *1970* | *1975* | *1979* | *1981* | *1985* | *1989* | *1993* | *1994* | *1995* | *1996* | *1997* |
|---|---|---|---|---|---|---|---|---|---|---|---|---|---|
| Governmental Affairs | 29 | 47 | 55 | 144 | 179 | 153 | 131 | 111 | 96 | 95 | 66 | 63 | 147 |
| Judiciary | 19 | 137 | 190 | 251 | 223 | 134 | 141 | 127 | 108 | 110 | 74 | 100 | 141 |
| Labor and Human Resources | 9 | 28 | 69 | 150 | 155 | 119 | 127 | 122 | 108 | 117 | 80 | 83 | 94 |
| Appropriations | 23 | 31 | 42 | 72 | 80 | 79 | 82 | 80 | 72 | 70 | 60 | 59 | 76 |
| Commerce, Science, and Transportation | 8 | 52 | 53 | 111 | 96 | 78 | 93 | 76 | 68 | 70 | 56 | 65 | 63 |
| Foreign Relations | 8 | 25 | 31 | 62 | 75 | 59 | 61 | 58 | 54 | 58 | 42 | 50 | 54 |
| Finance | 6 | 6 | 16 | 26 | 67 | 50 | 54 | 55 | 46 | 54 | 46 | 49 | 51 |
| Banking, Housing, and Urban Affairs | 9 | 22 | 23 | 55 | 48 | 39 | 38 | 51 | 51 | 58 | 44 | 47 | 51 |
| Armed Services | 10 | 23 | 19 | 30 | 31 | 36 | 48 | 51 | 50 | 45 | 43 | 49 | 49 |
| Budget | a | a | a | 90 | 91 | 82 | 81 | 66 | 58 | 66 | 46 | 46 | 48 |
| Agriculture | 3 | 10 | 7 | 22 | 34 | 34 | 34 | 42 | 29 | 35 | 28 | 33 | 47 |
| Energy and Natural Resources (Interior) | 7 | 26 | 22 | 53 | 55 | 50 | 57 | 50 | 46 | 47 | 39 | 37 | 39 |
| Environment and Public Works | 10 | 11 | 34 | 70 | 74 | 56 | 56 | 50 | 40 | 44 | 37 | 34 | 39 |
| Rules and Administration | 41 | 15 | 13 | 29 | 37 | 31 | 28 | 27 | 24 | 24 | 20 | 25 | 27 |
| Small Business | a | a | a | a | a | a | 24 | 22 | 24 | 26 | 20 | 20 | 27 |
| Indian Affairs | a | a | a | a | a | a | a | a | a | 22 | 15 | 16 | 23 |
| Veterans' Affairs | a | a | a | 32 | 24 | 22 | 25 | 25 | 24 | 14 | 14 | 17 | 21 |

*Note:* Committees are ranked in the order of their staff size in 1997. Through 1991, numbers ending in .5 are rounded up.

[a] Committee not in existence.

*Sources:* For 1947–1975, Schneider, "Congressional Staffing, 1947–78." For 1979–1987, U.S. Congress, Senate, Committee on Rules and Administration, *Senate Committee Funding* (this annual committee print lists the number of positions authorized for each committee; the number actually employed at any one time may be less). For 1989, *Report of the Secretary of the Senate,* October 1, 1989–March 31, 1990, pt. 1. For 1991, *Report of the Secretary of the Senate,* October 1, 1991–March 31, 1992, pt. 1. For 1993, *Report of the Secretary of the Senate,* October 1, 1993–March 31, 1994, pt. 1. For 1996–1997, *Report of the Secretary of the Senate,* October 1, 1996–March 31, 1997.

**Table 5-8** Staffs of Congressional Support Agencies, FY1946–1997

| *Year* | *Library of Congress* | *Congressional Research Service only*[a] | *General Accounting Office*[b] | *Congressional Budget Office* | *Office of Technology Assessment*[c] |
|---|---|---|---|---|---|
| 1946 | — | — | 14,219 | — | — |
| 1947 | 1,898 | 160 | 10,695 | — | — |
| 1950 | 1,973 | 161 | 7,876 | — | — |
| 1955 | 2,459 | 166 | 5,776 | — | — |
| 1960 | 2,779 | 183 | 5,074 | — | — |
| 1965 | 3,390 | 231 | 4,278 | — | — |
| 1970 | 3,848 | 332 | 4,704 | — | — |
| 1971 | 3,963 | 386 | 4,718 | — | — |
| 1972 | 4,135 | 479 | 4,742 | — | — |
| 1973 | 4,375 | 596 | 4,908 | — | — |
| 1974 | 4,504 | 687 | 5,270 | — | 10 |
| 1975 | 4,649 | 741 | 4,905 | 193 | 54 |
| 1976 | 4,880 | 806 | 5,391 | 203 | 103 |
| 1977 | 5,075 | 789 | 5,315 | 201 | 139 |
| 1978 | 5,231 | 818 | 5,476 | 203 | 164 |
| 1979 | 5,390 | 847 | 5,303 | 207 | 145 |
| 1980 | 5,047 | 868 | 5,196 | 218 | 122 |
| 1981 | 4,799 | 849 | 5,182 | 218 | 130 |
| 1982 | 4,803 | 849 | 5,027 | 218 | 130 |
| 1983 | 4,815 | 853 | 4,960 | 211 | 130 |
| 1984 | 4,802 | 858 | 4,985 | 210 | 139 |
| 1985 | 4,809 | 860 | 5,042 | 222 | 143 |
| 1986 | 4,806 | 860 | 5,019 | 222 | 143 |
| 1987 | 4,983 | 860 | 5,016 | 226 | 143 |
| 1988 | 4,874 | 825 | 5,042 | 211 | 143 |
| 1989 | 4,793 | 860 | 5,063 | 226 | 143 |
| 1990 | 4,659 | 797 | 5,066 | 226 | 143 |
| 1991 | 5,043 | 831 | 5,054 | 226 | 143 |
| 1992 | 5,050 | 838 | 5,062 | 218 | 143 |
| 1993 | 5,033 | 814 | 4,958 | 230 | 143 |
| 1994 | 4,701 | 740 | 4,572 | 218 | 143 |
| 1995 | 4,572 | 746 | 4,572 | 214 | 143[c] |
| 1996 | 4,399 | 747 | 3,677 | 232 | [c] |
| 1997 | 4,299 | 747 | 3,500 | 232 | [c] |

[a] Legislative Reference Service through 1970.

[b] Before 1950 the GAO was responsible for auditing all individual federal transactions and keeping a record of them. Legislation in 1950 transferred these responsibilities to the executive branch. The staff reductions through 1965 result from this 1950 change. *See* Frederich C. Mosher, *The GAO: The Quest for Accountability in American Government* (Boulder, Colo.: Westview Press, 1979), 124.

[c] OTA's research activities were terminated at the end of FY95. For FY96, OTA was given an appropriation sufficient to conduct agency closeout activities and the authority to employ seventeen staff members for that purpose.

*(Notes continue)*

**Table 5-8** *(Continued)*

*Sources:* For Library of Congress and CRS 1946–1993, Library of Congress, *Annual Reports of the Librarian of Congress.* For GAO 1946–1965, *Annual Reports of the Comptroller General of the United States.* For CBO 1975, Joel Havemann, *Congress and the Budget* (Bloomington: Indiana University Press, 1978), 109. (Data are as of October 1975. The CBO's director took office on February 24, 1975.) For OTA 1974–1976, *Appendixes of the Budget of the United States,* fiscal 1976, 18; 1977, 18; 1978, 40. For GAO 1970–1978, CBO 1976–1978, and OTA 1977–1978, Schneider, "Congressional Staffing, 1947–78"; for 1979–1997 see sources in Table 5-1.

**Table 5-9** Legislative Branch Appropriations and the Consumer Price Index, 1946–1996

| *Year* | *Appropriation (dollars)* | *Increase (percent)* | *Consumer Price Index*[a] | *Increase (percent)* |
|---|---|---|---|---|
| 1946 | 54,065,614 | — | 58.5 | — |
| 1947 | 61,825,020 | 14.4 | 66.9 | 14.4 |
| 1948 | 62,119,714 | 0.5 | 72.1 | 7.8 |
| 1949 | 62,057,678 | –0.1 | 71.4 | –1.0 |
| 1950 | 64,313,460 | 3.6 | 72.1 | 1.0 |
| 1951 | 71,888,244 | 11.8 | 77.8 | 7.9 |
| 1952 | 75,673,896 | 5.3 | 79.5 | 2.2 |
| 1953 | 77,670,076 | 2.6 | 80.1 | 0.8 |
| 1954 | 70,925,361 | –8.7 | 80.5 | 0.5 |
| 1955 | 86,304,923 | 21.7 | 80.2 | –0.4 |
| 1956 | 94,827,986 | 9.9 | 81.4 | 1.5 |
| 1957 | 120,775,798 | 27.4 | 84.3 | 3.6 |
| 1958 | 107,785,560 | –10.8 | 86.6 | 2.7 |
| 1959 | 136,153,580 | 26.3 | 87.3 | 0.8 |
| 1960 | 131,055,385 | –3.7 | 88.7 | 1.6 |
| 1961 | 140,930,781 | 7.5 | 89.6 | 1.0 |
| 1962 | 136,686,715 | –3.0 | 90.6 | 1.1 |
| 1963 | 150,426,185 | 10.1 | 91.7 | 1.2 |
| 1964 | 168,467,869 | 12.0 | 92.9 | 1.3 |
| 1965 | 221,904,318 | 31.7 | 94.5 | 1.7 |
| 1966 | 197,965,307 | –10.8 | 97.2 | 2.9 |
| 1967 | 221,715,643 | 12.0 | 100.0 | 2.9 |
| 1968 | 282,003,322 | 27.2 | 104.2 | 4.2 |
| 1969 | 311,542,399 | 10.5 | 109.8 | 5.4 |
| 1970 | 361,024,327 | 15.9 | 116.3 | 5.9 |
| 1971 | 443,104,319 | 22.7 | 121.3 | 4.3 |
| 1972 | 564,107,992 | 27.3 | 125.3 | 3.3 |
| 1973 | 645,127,365 | 14.4 | 133.1 | 6.2 |
| 1974 | 662,180,668 | 2.6 | 147.7 | 11.0 |
| 1975 | 785,618,833 | 18.6 | 161.2 | 9.1 |
| 1976[b] | 947,185,778 | 20.6 | 170.5 | 5.8 |
| 1977 | 963,921,185 | 1.8 | 181.5 | 6.5 |
| 1978 | 1,009,225,350 | 4.7 | 195.4 | 7.7 |
| 1979 | 1,124,766,400 | 11.4 | 217.4 | 11.3 |
| 1980 | 1,199,061,463 | 6.6 | 246.8 | 13.5 |
| 1981 | 1,285,943,826 | 7.2 | 272.4 | 10.4 |
| 1982 | 1,365,272,433 | 6.2 | 289.1 | 6.1 |
| 1983 | 1,467,318,263 | 7.5 | 298.4 | 3.2 |
| 1984 | 1,644,160,600 | 12.0 | 311.1 | 4.3 |
| 1985 | 1,599,977,138 | –2.7 | 322.2 | 3.6 |
| 1986 | 1,783,255,000 | 11.4 | 328.4 | 1.9 |
| 1987 | 1,635,190,214 | –8.3 | 340.4 | 3.6 |
| 1988 | 1,745,201,500 | 6.7 | 354.3 | 4.1 |
| 1989 | 1,804,624,000 | 3.4 | 371.3 | 4.8 |

*(Table continues)*

**Table 5-9** *(Continued)*

| *Year* | *Appropriation (dollars)* | *Increase (percent)* | *Consumer Price Index*[a] | *Increase (percent)* |
|---|---|---|---|---|
| 1990 | 1,968,441,000 | 9.1 | 391.4 | 5.4 |
| 1991 | 2,161,367,000 | 9.8 | 408.0 | 4.2 |
| 1992 | 2,303,844,000 | 6.6 | 420.3 | 3.0 |
| 1993 | 2,302,924,000 | –0.1 | 432.7 | 3.0 |
| 1994 | 2,269,558,000 | –1.4 | 444.0 | 2.6 |
| 1995 | 2,390,600,000 | 5.3 | 456.5 | 2.8 |
| 1996 | 2,125,000,000 | –11.1 | 469.9 | 2.9 |
| 1946-1996 | — | 3,830.4 | — | 703.2 |

*Note:* Appropriations include supplementals, except for 1986; appropriations are for fiscal years, but the consumer price index is the year average for calendar years.

[a] CPI base is 1967=100.

[b] From fiscal year 1946 through fiscal year 1976, the fiscal year began on July 1. Beginning with fiscal year 1977, the start of the fiscal year was shifted to October 1. During the transition quarter of July 1–September 30, 1976, the amount appropriated for legislative branch operations was $207,391,365. This amount is not included.

*Sources:* For 1946–1976, U.S. Congress, House, Committee on House Administration, *Studies Dealing with Budgetary, Staffing, and Administrative Activities of the U.S. House of Representatives, 1947–78,* 95th Cong., 2d sess., 1978. For 1977–1979, *Congressional Quarterly Almanac* (Washington, D.C.: Congressional Quarterly, 1977–1980). For 1980, *House LBA Hearings for 1981,* pt. 1, 10–11; *Senate LBA Hearings for 1981,* pt. 1, 15–23; Public Law 96–304 (July 8, 1980); Public Law 97-51 (October 1, 1981). For 1981, *House LBA Hearings for 1982,* pt. 1, 15–23; *Senate LBA Hearings for 1982,* 268; U.S. Congress, Senate, Committee on Appropriations, *Comparative Statement of New Budget Authority and Outlays—Fiscal Year 1983,* 97th Cong., 2d sess., 1982 (unpublished committee document), 3; Public Law 97-12 (June 5, 1981). For 1982-1986, House Committee on Appropriations, *Comparative Statement of New Budget Authority* (unpublished committee documents). For 1987–1996, *Congressional Quarterly Almanac.* For consumer price index, 1946–1986, *Economic Report of the President,* January 1989. For 1987–1996, U.S. Department of Labor, Bureau of Labor Statistics.

**Table 5-10** Legislative Branch Appropriations, by Category, FY1984–1997 (in thousands of dollars)

| | *1984* | *1985* | *1986*[a] | *1987* | *1988* | *1989* |
|---|---|---|---|---|---|---|
| Senate | 255,856 | 285,930 | 308,834 | 307,658 | 337,314 | 340,677 |
| House of Representatives | 419,784 | 439,398 | 455,431 | 463,907 | 513,786 | 506,068 |
| Joint items[b] | 128,933 | 96,415 | 155,804 | 103,136 | 94,981 | 120,983 |
| Architect of the Capitol[c] | 82,021 | 85,181 | 112,191 | 101,633 | 107,306 | 103,640 |
| Botanic Garden | 2,158 | 2,080 | 2,197 | 2,062 | 2,221 | 2,521 |
| Congressional Budget Office | 16,723 | 17,541 | 18,455 | 17,251 | 17,886 | 18,361 |
| Congressional Research Service | 36,700 | 39,833 | 38,963 | 39,602 | 43,022 | 44,684 |
| Copyright Royalty Commission[d] | 210 | 217 | 227 | 123 | 129 | 123 |
| General Accounting Office | 271,710 | 299,704 | 339,639 | 304,910 | 329,847 | 347,339 |
| Government Printing Office[c] | 125,700 | 122,704 | 122,268 | 94,956 | 89,521 | 85,731 |
| Library of Congress | 228,715 | 228,242 | 242,829 | 183,670 | 191,998 | 199,650 |
| Office of Technology Assessment | 14,831 | 15,692 | 17,000 | 15,532 | 16,901 | 17,937 |
| Office of Compliance | — | — | — | — | — | — |

*(Table continues)*

**Table 5-10** *(Continued)*

| *1990* | *1991* | *1992* | *1993* | *1994* | *1995* | *1996* | *1997* |
|---|---|---|---|---|---|---|---|
| 373,761 | 437,223 | 449,568 | 451,451 | 443,315 | 460,600 | 426,900 | 441,200 |
| 537,207 | 647,675 | 693,970 | 699,109 | 684,696 | 728,700 | 671,600 | 684,000 |
| 170,454 | 114,187 | 80,716 | 80,476 | 78,750 | 86,200 | 86,800 | 85,300 |
| 116,221 | 139,806 | 151,633 | 149,613 | 150,223 | 159,700 | 143,000 | 139,800 |
| 2,638 | 3,519 | 2,862 | 4,906 | 3,008 | 3,200 | 3,100 | 2,900 |
| 19,580 | 21,183 | 22,542 | 22,542 | 22,317 | 23,200 | 24,300 | 24,500 |
| 46,895 | 52,743 | 56,583 | 57,291 | 56,718 | 60,100 | 60,100 | 62,600 |
| 101 | 127 | 130 | 130 | 128 | — | — | — |
| 364,720 | 419,130 | 442,647 | 435,167 | 430,815 | 449,400 | 374,000 | 332,500 |
| 98,018 | 79,615 | 91,591 | 89,591 | 29,082 | 32,200 | 83,800 | 81,700 |
| 211,100 | 239,924 | 248,308 | 252,808 | 250,813 | 263,100 | 264,600 | 269,100 |
| 18,900 | 19,557 | 21,025 | 21,025 | 21,315 | 22,000 | — | — |
| — | — | — | — | — | — | — | 2,600 |

*Note:* Includes supplemental appropriations, except for 1986.

[a] Figures for 1986 are prior to Gramm-Rudman-Hollings sequestration.
[b] Includes such items as joint committees and the Capitol Police. Prior to 1991, official mail costs were also included in this category.
[c] Figures for the Architect of the Capitol and Government Printing Office include appropriations for legislative activities only.
[d] The commission was abolished after FY1994. Its duties have been taken over by a Copyright Office Panel; therefore, there is no further appropriation.

*Sources:* For 1982-1986, House Committee on Appropriations, *Comparative Statement of New Budget Authority*. For 1987, *Congressional Quarterly Almanac,* vol. 43 (1988). For 1988, *Congressional Quarterly Almanac,* vol. 44 (1989). For 1989, *Congressional Quarterly Almanac,* vol. 45 (1990). For 1990, *Congressional Quarterly Almanac,* vol. 46 (1991). For 1991, *Congressional Quarterly Almanac,* vol. 47 (1992). For 1992, *Congressional Quarterly Almanac,* vol. 48 (1993). For 1993, *Congressional Quarterly Almanac,* vol. 49 (1994). For 1994, *Congressional Quarterly Almanac,* vol. 50 (1995). For 1995, *Congressional Quarterly Almanac,* vol. 51 (1996). For 1996, *Congressional Quarterly Almanac,* vol. 52 (1997). The projected numbers for 1997, *Congressional Quarterly Almanac,* vol. 52 (1997).

**Table 5-11** Costs of Official Mail, 1971–1993

| *Year* | *Appropriations (dollars)* | *Average unit cost of franked mail (cents)* |
|---|---|---|
| 1971 | 11,244,000 | 8.0 |
| 1972 | 14,594,000 | 8.0 |
| 1972 supplement | 18,400,000 | |
| 1973 | 21,226,480 | 9.0 |
| 1974 | 30,500,000 | 9.9 |
| 1975 | 38,756,015 | 11.4 |
| 1976 | 46,101,000 | 13.2 |
| Transition period[a] | 11,525,000 | |
| 1976 supplement | 16,080,000 | |
| 1977 | 46,904,000 | 13.4 |
| 1978 | 48,926,000 | 11.4 |
| 1979 | 64,944,000 | 12.8 |
| 1980[b] | 50,707,000 | 13.4 |
| 1981 | 52,033,000 | 12.4 |
| 1982 | 75,095,000 | 13.9 |
| 1983 | 93,161,000 | 13.1 |
| 1984 | 117,277,000 | 12.8 |
| 1985 | 85,797,000 | 12.6 |
| 1986 | 95,700,000 | 12.6 |
| 1987 | 91,423,000 | 18.4 |
| 1988 | 82,163,000 | 14.1 |
| 1989 | 85,262,000[c] | 14.9 |
| 1990 | 99,016,000 | 15.3[d] |
| 1991 | 88,834,000 | 15.7 |
| 1992 | 112,000,000 | 14.9 |
| 1993 | 67,700,000 | 15.5 |

*Note:* See Table 6-8 for number of pieces of franked mail.

[a] Reflects change in the fiscal year from July 1 to October 1.
[b] Lower figure reflects decrease in bulk mail rates.
[c] Adjusted to reflect FY89 shortfall in the mail account.
[d] In 1990 the U.S. Postal Service altered its method for calculating the average unit cost. Average figures prior to 1990 are combined House and Senate figures. Figures for 1990 and later are for the House only.

*Sources:* For 1971-1987, Office of the Clerk of the House. For 1988 and 1989, Congressional Research Service Report for Congress, "U.S. Congress Official Mail Costs: FY1972 to FY1991," July 20, 1990. For 1990 and 1991, Congressional Research Service. For 1992–1993, U.S. Postal Service.

**Table 5-12** Allowances for Representatives, 1977–1997

| *Category* | *1977* | *1981* | *1983* | *1985* |
|---|---|---|---|---|
| Clerk-hire | $238,580 | $336,384 | $366,648 | $394,680 |
| Postage | $211 | b | b | b |
| Stationery | $6,500 | b | b | b |
| Travel (round trips) | 33 | b | b | b |
| Telephone/telegraph | $5,200 for equipment 15,000 long-distance minutes | b | b | b |
| District and state offices rental | 2,500 sq. ft. | b | b | b |
| Furnishings (one-time) | $27,000 | b | b | b |
| Official expenses | $7,000 | $66,200–248,601 | $588,850–279,470 | $105,513–306,509 |
| Constituent communications (begun in 1975) | $5,000 | b | b | b |
| Equipment lease | $9,000 | b | b | b |
| Members' representational allowance | d | d | d | d |

[a] Each member is entitled to an annual clerk-hire allowance of the designated amount for a staff not to exceed twenty-two employees, four of whom must fit into five categories: (1) shared payroll—employees, such as computer experts, who are shared by members; (2) interns; (3) employees on leave without pay; (4) part-time employees; (5) temporary employees—employees hired for a specific purpose for not more than ninety days.

[b] As of January 3, 1978, previous individual allowances for travel, office equipment lease, district office lease, stationery, telecommunications, mass mailings, postage, computer services, and other official expenses were consolidated in a single allowance category—the official expenses allowance. Members may budget funds for each category as they see fit. The average allowance for 1995 was $193,000.

[c] Each member is entitled to a base official expenses allowance of $122,500. In addition, there are three variables that determine the total amount allotted for official expenses: (1) transportation costs, (2) telecommunications costs, and (3) cost of office space. The amount allotted for travel is computed as follows: 64 multiplied by the rate per mile multiplied by the mileage between the District of Columbia and the farthest point in the member's district. The minimum amount allotted for travel in 1995 was $6,200 per member.

The amount allotted for telecommunications is computed as follows: 15,000 times the highest long-distance rate per minute from the District of Columbia to the member's district. The minimum amount allotted for telecommunications in 1995 was $6,000 per member. If the member has elected to use WATS or a similar service in his office, the 15,000-minute multiplier will be reduced by one-half.

The amount allotted for office space costs is computed as follows: 2,500 square feet multiplied by the highest applicable rate per square foot charged by the administrator of the General Services Administration to federal agencies in the district for rental of office space.

The official expenses allowance may not be used for:

1. expenses relating to the hiring and employment of individuals, including, but not limited to,employment service fees, transportation of interviewees to and from employment interviews, and cost of relocation upon acceptance or termination of employment

2. items purchased from other than the House stationery store that have a useful life greater than the current term of the member and that would have a residual value of more than $25 upon the expiration of the current term of the member

| *1987* | *1989* | *1991* | *1993* | *1995* | *1997* |
|---|---|---|---|---|---|
| $406,560 | $431,760[a] | $475,000[a] | $557,400[a] | 568,560[a] | |
| b | b | b | b | b | |
| b | b | b | b | b | |
| b | b | b | b | b | |
| b | b | b | b | b | |
| b | b | b | b | b | |
| b | b | b | b | b | |
| $105,513–306,509[c] | $108,400–306,500 | $135,000–317,000 | $152,128–302,008 | 152,128–334,629 | |
| b | b | b | b | b | |
| b | b | b | b | b | |
| d | d | d | d | d | $814,090–1,233,780 (901,771) |

3. holiday greeting cards, flowers, and trophies
4. personal advertisements (other than meeting or appearance notices)
5. donations of any type, except flags of the United States flown over the Capitol and items purchased for use as gifts when on official travel
6. dues other than to legislative support organizations as approved by the Committee on House Administration
7. educational expenses for courses of study or information or training programs unless the benefit accrues primarily to the House and the skill or knowledge is not commonly available
8. purchases of radio and television time
9. parking for member and employees at district offices, except when included as an integral part of the lease or occupancy agreement for the district office space.

Each member may allocate up to $40,000 from the clerk-hire allowance to supplement the official expenses allowance. A member also may allocate up to $40,000 from the official expenses allowance to supplement the clerk-hire allowance, provided that monthly clerk-hire disbursements not exceed 10 percent of the total clerk-hire allowance.

[d] On September 1, 1995, members' three former expense allowances (clerk-hire, official expenses, and official mail allowances) were consolidated into one members' representational allowance (MRA). Although the MRA is calculated based on these three components, members may spend the MRA as they see fit. Within the MRA, each member's expenditures for franked mail may not exceed the total amount allocated by the Committee on House Oversight for official mail expenses, plus an additional $25,000, transferable within the MRA at the member's discretion according to the procedures under the previous allowance structure. The 1997 mean MRA was $901,771.

*Sources:* For 1977 and 1979, Committee on House Administration, *Studies Dealing with Budgetary, Staffing and Administrative Activities of the U.S. House of Representatives, 1946–1978.* For 1981, 1983, and 1985, U.S. House of Representatives, *Congressional Handbook.* For 1987, "Salaries and Allowances: The Congress," Congressional Research Service, Library of Congress, Washington, D.C., July 15, 1987, update. For 1989, Office of the Clerk of the House. For 1991 and 1993, Committee on House Administration. For 1995, House Oversight Committee. For 1997, *Congressional Handbook,* 104th Congress, Committee on House Oversight.

## Table 5-13 Allowances for Senators, 1977-1997

| Category | 1977 | 1979 | 1981 | 1983 | 1985 |
|---|---|---|---|---|---|
| Clerk-hire | $311,577–588,145[a] | $508,221–1,021,167[a] | $592,608–1,190,724[a] | $645,897–1,297,795[a] | $695,244–1,396,947[a] |
| Legislative assistance | n.a. | $157,626[b] | $183,801[b] | $200,328[b] | $215,634[b] |
| Postage | $1,215–1,520 | c | c | c | c |
| Stationery | $3,600–5,000 | c | c | c | c |
| Travel (round trips) | 20–22 | c | c | c | c |
| District and state offices rental | n.a. | 4,800–8,000 sq. ft.[d] | 4,800–8,000 sq. ft.[d] | 4,800–8,000 sq. ft.[d] | 4,800–8,000 sq. ft.[d] |
| Furnishings, state offices | n.a. | $22,550–31,350 | $22,550–31,350 | $22,550–31,350 | $22,550–31,350 |
| Official office expense account | n.a. | $33,000–143,000[f] | $33,000–143,000[f] | $36,000–156,000[f] | $36,000–156,000[f] |

n.a. = not applicable.

[a] There is no limit on the number of employees a senator may hire. He or she must, however, use only the clerk-hire or legislative assistance allowance to pay staff salaries. The clerk-hire allowance varies according to state population.

[b] In addition to clerk-hire, each senator has a legislative assistance allowance worth $385,050 in 1997. This allowance is reduced for any committee chairman or ranking minority member of a committee. It is also reduced for any other senator authorized by a committee chairman to recommend or approve any individuals for appointment to the committee staff who will assist that senator "solely and directly" in his duties as a member of the committee. The reduction requirements were waived for the 99th and 100th Congresses.

[c] This allowance is one of the allocations of the consolidated office expense allowance. Before January 1, 1973, senators were authorized individually controlled allowances for six expense categories as follows: transportation expenses for the senator and his staff; stationery; air mail and special delivery postage; long-distance telephone calls; telegram charges; and home state expenses, which include home state office expenses; telephone service charges incurred outside Washington, D.C.; subscriptions to newspapers, magazines, periodicals, and clipping or similar services; and home state office rent (repealed effective July 1, 1974).

Effective January 1, 1973, the Supplemental Appropriations Act, 1973, provided for the consolidation of these same allowances to provide flexibility to senators in the management of the same dollars provided for their expense allowances. No limit was imposed on any expense category by this authorization. The allowance was designated as the consolidated office expense allowance. Effective January 1, 1977, the Legislative Branch Appropriation Act redesignated the consolidated office expense allowance as the official office expense account.

[d] Effective July 1, 1974, the Legislative Branch Appropriations Act, 1975, provided a formula for the allowable aggregate square feet of office space in the home state of a senator. There is no limit on the number of offices that may be established by a senator in his home state, but the designated square footage may not be exceeded. The cost of office space in the home state is not chargeable to the official office expense account.

[e] An aggregate furniture and furnishings allowance is provided through the General Services Administration for one or more state offices in either federal or privately owned buildings. The

| 1987 | 1989 | 1991 | 1993 | 1995 | 1997 |
|---|---|---|---|---|---|
| $716,102–1,438,856[a] | $754,000–1,636,000[a] | $814,000–1,760,000[a] | $1,540,000–1,914,000[a] | $1,660,000–1,935,000[a] | $1,087,597–1,974,051[a] |
| $243,543[b] | $248,000[b] | $269,000[b] | $374,000[b] | $377,400[b] | $385,050[b] |
| c | c | c | c | c | c |
| c | c | c | c | c | c |
| c | c | c | c | c | c |
| 4,800–8,000 sq. ft. | 4,800–8,000 sq. ft.[d] | 4,800–8,000 sq. ft.[d] | 4,800–8,000 sq. ft.[d] | 4,800–8,000 sq. ft.[d] | 4,800–8,000 sq. ft.[d] |
| $30,000–41,744 | $30,000–41,744[e] | $30,000–41,744[e] | $30,000–41,744[e] | $30,000–41,744[e] | $30,000–41,744[e] |
| $36,000–156,000 | $33,000–156,000[f] | $47,000–122,000[f] | $44,000–200,000[f] | $90,000–250,000[f] | $95,825–245,000[f] |

$30,000 minimum allowance for office space not greater than 4,800 square feet is increased by $734 for each authorized increase of 200 square feet of space.

[f] The expense account may be used for the following expenses (2 U.S.C. 58[a], as amended):

1. official telegrams and long-distance phone calls and related services
2. stationery and other office supplies purchased through the stationery room for official business
3. costs incurred in the mailing or delivery of matters relating to official business
4. official office expenses in home state, other than equipment or furniture (purchase of office equipment beyond stated allocations may be made through 10 percent funds listed under item 9 below)
5. official telephone charges incurred outside Washington, D.C.
6. subscriptions to newspapers, magazines, periodicals, or clipping or similar services
7. travel expenses incurred by a senator or staff member, subject to certain limitations
8. expenses incurred by individuals selected by a senator to serve on panels or other bodies making recommendations for nominees to service academies or federal judgeships
9. other official expenses as the senator determines are necessary, including (a) additional office equipment for Washington, D.C., or state offices; (b) actual transportation expenses incurred by the senator and employees for official business in the Washington metropolitan area (this is also allowed to employees assigned to a state office for actual transportation expenses in the general vicinity of the office to which assigned but is not available for a change of assignment within the state or for commuting between home and office).

The total reimbursement expense for the calendar year may not exceed 10 percent of the total official office expense account.

Beginning with fiscal year 1981, each senator was also allowed to transfer funds from the administrative, clerical, and legislative assistance allowances to the official office expense account.

*Sources:* For 1972, *Senate LBA Hearings for 1980.* For 1979-1985, U.S. Senate, *Congressional Handbook.* For 1987, "Salaries and Allowances: The Congress." For 1989, Office of the Secretary of the Senate; Office of the Sergeant-at-Arms. For 1991 and 1993, Senate Disbursing Office. For 1995, Senate Disbursing Office and Sergeant-at-Arms. For 1997, *Senate LBA.*

# 6

# Workload

The tables in this chapter provide a picture of an institution in which the workload increased dramatically in the 1970s, peaking in about 1976 or 1977, and then began to decline, although not back to its level in the 1950s. The overall number of bills, votes, hours in session, meetings, and hearings multiplied during the 1960s and 1970s (see Tables 6-1 and 6-2). Paradoxically, however, through much of the 1970s the number of bills passed by the House and the Senate and the number of bills enacted into law decreased. More and more activity was combined with fewer and fewer products. Since 1980 the workload—hearings, meetings, and so on—has slowed, while output has increased, yet there is still a decided gap between activity and output. In the 104th Congress, the first Republican House in forty years, showed a distinctive workload pattern. Bills introduced and passed went down sharply, while debate, votes, and time in session went sharply up.

## Bills Introduced

The number of bills introduced in the House has had several pronounced increases or decreases. From an average of about 10,000 per Congress in the 1940s and early 1950s, the number jumped to 13,169 in the Eighty-fourth Congress (1955–1956). It remained at approximately 14,000 until the Eighty-ninth Congress (1965–1966), when it jumped to nearly 20,000. In the 1970s bills introduced declined steadily, to 15,587 in the Ninety-fifth Congress, in part because of changes in the rules regarding cosponsorship, which reduced the need to introduce multiple numbers of an identical bill. The numbers dropped dramatically in the Ninety-sixth Congress—by 42 percent—and have continued to decline. But the steep decrease to around six or seven thousand bills dropped to 4,542 bills in the 104th Congress—just one-fifth the total of the modern high in 1967–1968. The One-hundredth Congress had the lowest total in forty years; the average increased slightly for the 101st Congress, and by a larger margin for the 102d, but then declined again slightly in the 103d and 104th, all the while remaining well below 10,000 bills. The Senate has shown no such distinct ebbs and flows. While there was a real decline between the Ninety-fifth and the One-hundredth Congresses, the total number of bills introduced then rose steadily until the 103rd and 104th Congresses. As with the House, the 104th Senate had a modern low of bills introduced, 2,226, about half the average of the 1970s. It remains to be seen if this is a new pattern or an aberration.

## Bills Passed

An examination of bills passed in both houses shows a definite decline in the 1960s and again in the 1970s, though not in a uniform fashion, stabilizing in the 1980s at roughly half the total of the 1950s. Overall, bills passed in each house went from a rough average of 2,000 per Congress in the 1950s to 1,500 in the 1960s, to 1,000 in the 1970s, and to 950 or so in the 1980s and early 1990s, then dropping sharply in the 103d and 104th Congresses to roughly 600 in the Republican 104th. (The Ninety-seventh Congress, the first under Ronald Reagan and with a Republican Senate, had a distinctly lower total.) Tables 6-1 and 6-2 also examine the ratio of bills passed to bills introduced. Although the significance of these figures is limited because some bills are introduced by more than one member and some that are passed may originally have been introduced in the other body, the ratios can be used for comparisons over time. In both institutions, there has been a steady and marked decline since 1947 in the proportion of bills passed. A bill introduced now has about half the chance of success that it would have had in the Eightieth Congress. While the batting averages were on the rise in the mid- to late-1980s, recent years have witnessed a decline.

At the heart of the decline in bills introduced and the more substantial decline in number of bills passed in the House and the Senate in the 103d and 104th Congresses, is the overwhelming domination of one major piece of legislation each year—the Clinton economic package in 1993, failed health care reform in 1994, and intensely partisan budget battles in 1995 and 1996.

## Recorded Votes

The number of recorded votes remained quite low in the House through the 1940s and 1950s, increased somewhat in the mid-1960s, and jumped dramatically in the 1970s with each Congress from the Ninety-second (1971–1972) through the Ninety-fifth (1977–1978). A rules change in 1971, which permitted recorded teller votes and thereby expanded the opportunities for recorded votes on amendments, was clearly a major factor in increasing the number of recorded votes in the House. The Senate also showed a marked though not as great increase in recorded votes beginning in 1971, even though no comparable procedural reform was introduced there. In the Ninety-fifth Congress the House for the first time had more recorded votes than the Senate. It appears that both procedural reforms and a decentralization of power and initiative in the House and Senate contributed to the trend toward increased numbers of recorded votes. The increase in both houses in the 104th Congress reflected in part the increased partisanship in the newly Republican Congress.

Table 6-3, which breaks down recorded votes by year, shows a small but relatively steady decline in the votes in the Senate since 1977, with steep decreases in the late 1970s and again in the 1980s. The House rates declined significantly in 1979 and 1980, dropped sharply in 1981 to levels of a decade earlier, then increased somewhat to a rough average of 450 per year. Although long-term future trends are difficult to discern, it seems likely that the number of recorded votes in both chambers will stabilize at levels below the peak years of the mid-1970s but above those of the 1960s. In the 104th Congress, the fast, early pace, crowded agenda, and use of more open rules in the House promised a jump in the number of recorded votes, which might prove a temporary phenomenon.

## Time in Session

As Tables 6-1 and 6-2 indicate, there has been substantial fluctuation in the numbers of days in session per Congress, with no particular longitudinal pattern until recently; Congress has been in session fewer days, but distinctly longer hours. This pattern is true of both houses. The House went from an average of 4.2 hours per day in the 1950s to 4.4 in the 1960s and 5.3 in the 1970s, with an average of 5.8 hours per day in 1979–1980. The numbers increased in the 101st–103d Congresses, then jumped sharply to 8.5 hours per day in the 104th to an average of just over 6.5 hours per day.

In the Senate, where floor procedures have always been looser and more informal and filibusters have periodically extended the time in session, sessions in the 1970s and 1980s have consistently been long, only once falling below 2,000 hours. In the earlier period they demonstrated considerably more fluctuation, with only five of the twelve sessions between 1947 and 1970 running over 2,000 hours. The average hours per day in session jumped in the Ninety-ninth Senate to 8.1 and reached its highest level in at least forty-six years (8.6 hours) in the 103d Senate. The 104th dropped slightly, to 8.4 hours.

## Committee and Subcommittee Meetings

The number of committee and subcommittee meetings and hearings rose consistently in the House of Representatives beginning in 1965–1966, the most substantial increases occurring in the mid-to-late 1970s. The 1977–1978 figures for the House were more than double the average number per Congress in the 1950s and 1960s. The expansion of power and initiative of subcommittees and the wider distribution of chairmanships probably account for much of this change. But the figures for the 1980s and early 1990s indicate a marked cutback in committee and subcommittee activity to levels of a decade or more earlier, with another significant decline in the 104th.

The Senate numbers also increased, but then peaked and declined earlier than in the House. The number of meetings and hearings jumped substantially in the late 1960s and early 1970s, beginning especially with the famous "Great Society" Eighty-ninth Congress (1965–1966) and reaching a peak a decade later in the Ninety-fourth Congress (1975–1976) of 4,265, some 70 percent higher than in the 1950s. Beginning in 1977, however—after the committee system reorganization that sharply cut back the number of subcommittees and assignments (see Chapter 4)—the number of meetings and hearings began to decline steadily, to 2,373 in the Ninety-ninth Congress, a number comparable to levels in the 1950s and 1960s. With the exception of the One-hundredth Congress, the number has continued to decline since then, with the 104th Congress contributing another decline to 1,601 meetings.

## Laws and Other Output

Table 6-4, focusing more directly on congressional output, shows the number of public and private bills enacted into law (that is, passed by both the House and the Senate and signed by the president) and the number of pages of enacted bills. The number of bills enacted has fluctuated from Congress to Congress, but broader patterns are evident. An average of 900 or so bills per Congress in the 1950s went to 700 or so bills in the 1960s and 600 or so in the 1970s and 1980s. The numbers dropped significantly in each of the 102d through 104th Congresses, down to a modern low of 333 in the 104th. Indeed, the first year output of that Congress—85 laws—was a particularly low point. But as the numbers of bills declined, their average length increased. From the 1950s through the mid-1960s, the average number of pages per statute was approximately 2.5. The average jumped to approximately 5 pages in the mid-1970s, reached 7 pages in the Ninety-fourth Congress, and jumped to between 8 and 9 pages in the Ninety-fifth through Ninety-eighth Congresses. That more than doubled to 19.1 pages per statute in the 104th Congress. Divided government, when fewer bills have a chance of being enacted, often results in the inclusion of various issues and interests in a single piece of legislation that has a reasonable likelihood of becoming law. It is important to understand that a handful of these omnibus measures (megabills) account for a large proportion of total statute pages.

Actions of Congress, in votes and laws, affect the workload, job difficulty, and output of the federal executive as well. Table 6-5 shows the number of pages in the *Federal Register* per year since 1971, along with those of some earlier years for comparison. As the average length of statutes increased in Congress in the 1970s, the number of pages in the *Federal Register*—which among other things displays regulations mandated by these statutes—jumped correspondingly. In 1981, as deregulation proceeded in the Reagan administration and the number of substantive bills declined, the total pages in the *Federal Register* dropped by 27 percent—to the level of 1977–1978, at the beginning of the Carter administration. The number of pages dropped further during the Reagan administration, reaching a level of 47,418 pages in 1986, the lowest in twelve years. The page count then rose during the Bush administration and has continued to rise. Although the number of bills enacted fell during the 104th Congress, the number of pages reached more than 69,000.

Table 6-6 describes the postwar record of presidential vetoes and veto overrides. President Truman exercised his veto power far more than any of his successors; the record shows a total of seventy-five vetoes in the so-called "Do-Nothing" Eightieth Congress. The number of presidential vetoes is generally higher when presidents face Congresses with opposition party majorities, as Truman did in the Eightieth Congress. With a split Congress during his first six years in office, President Reagan showed a much lower propensity to veto than his Republican predecessors. But even after Democrats took back the Senate in the One-hundredth Congress, Reagan vetoed fewer bills than he had in either of the two previous Congresses.

Presidents Nixon and Ford faced the greatest resistance from Congress. The Ninety-third and Ninety-fourth Congresses attempted a much higher number of veto overrides than any of the other Congresses in the previous thirty years, and a large number of their attempts were successful. The first three Congresses under Reagan did not show any particular inclination to override his vetoes, but the last picked up a bit, overriding 37.5 percent of Reagan's vetoes. President Bush's use of the veto was comparable to his most recent predecessors in terms of numbers. However, Bush tended to reserve the veto for crucial pieces of legislation, such as the Civil Rights Act of 1990, and had impressive success sustaining them in his first two years.

President Clinton, however, became the first president since 1853 not to veto a single bill during an entire Congress. Having a Democratic House and Senate certainly diminished his need or willingness to use the veto, yet zero vetoes is highly unusual. Clinton seemed to be a president much more prone to compromise than to confrontation. But this did not last for long. The Republican takeover of Congress in 1994 transformed executive-congressional relations, ensuring a substantial number of vetoes during the 104th Congress, though still less than Presidents Reagan or Bush applied.

Table 6-7 examines the use of filibusters (measured by the number of cloture votes) in the Senate since the Sixty-sixth Congress (1919–1920). The table shows that the filibuster was a rarely exercised privilege until the 1960s, when the civil rights debates increased the average number of cloture votes from one or two to six or seven per Congress. The number of filibusters and cloture votes increased strikingly in the 1970s, after Majority Leader Mike Mansfield introduced a "two-track" system to enable the Senate to conduct other business as a filibuster proceeded. The increased use of filibusters on a wider variety of issues led the Senate to amend the rules in 1975, changing the number of votes required to invoke cloture from two-thirds of those present and voting to three-fifths of the total Senate. This did not reduce the number of filibusters or cloture votes, but the success rate for cloture votes appears to have increased. Note that, except for the Nixon-Ford years, filibusters are generally more prevalent in the second session of a Congress, when delaying tactics have a greater likelihood of succeeding. Republican filibusters were used routinely in the 103d Congress to frustrate President Clinton's agenda; Democrats immediately returned the favor on the Contract With America and intensified their efforts at the beginning of the 105th Congress.

Table 6-8 examines outgoing congressional mail. It shows that the amount of franked mail generated by Congress increased tremendously from the 1960s through the 1980s, averaging approximately 700 million pieces per year from 1984–1989. The record was 924.6 million pieces in the election year of 1984. In light of these escalating numbers, in 1990 Congress came under considerable pressure to adopt reforms in an attempt to curb the use of franked mail. The House imposed new restrictions on franked mailings including a requirement that each member adhere to an individual mail budget and that all expenditures be publicly disclosed. These restrictions have succeeded in not only lowering the overall cost of official mail, but also reducing the amount of mail being sent by members. These changes are reflected in the drastically reduced number of mailings for 1991—down 54 percent—from 1990's total. Despite these overall reductions, note that we still see increases in the amount of franked mail in election years and the decline in off years—despite House rules that limit newsletter production and distribution as the election nears. For example, after 1991's figure of 259.8 million pieces, it jumped by more than 76 percent to 458 million pieces in the 1992 election year and declined once again in 1993, to just over 200 million.

Over the years the system for counting incoming mail has been changed so much that reliable data cannot be compiled.

**Table 6-1** House Workload, 80th–104th Congresses, 1947–1996

| *Congress* | | *Bills introduced*[a] | *Average no. of bills introduced per member* | *Bills passed* | *Ratio of bills passed to bills introduced* | *Recorded votes*[b] | *Time in session* | | *Hours per day in session* | *Committee, subcommittee meetings*[c] |
|---|---|---|---|---|---|---|---|---|---|---|
| | | | | | | | Days | Hours | | |
| 80th | (1947-48) | 7,611 | 17.5 | 1,739 | 0.228 | 159 | 254 | 1,224 | 4.8 | n.a. |
| 81st | (1949–50) | 10,502 | 24.1 | 2,482 | 0.236 | 275 | 345 | 1,501 | 4.4 | n.a. |
| 82d | (1951–52) | 9,065 | 20.8 | 2,008 | 0.222 | 181 | 274 | 1,163 | 4.2 | n.a. |
| 83d | (1953–54) | 10,875 | 25.0 | 2,129 | 0.196 | 147 | 240 | 1,033 | 4.3 | n.a. |
| 84th | (1955–56) | 13,169 | 30.3 | 2,360 | 0.179 | 147 | 230 | 937 | 4.1 | 3,210 |
| 85th | (1957–58) | 14,580 | 33.5 | 2,064 | 0.142 | 193 | 276 | 1,147 | 4.2 | 3,750 |
| 86th | (1959–60) | 14,112 | 32.4 | 1,636 | 0.116 | 180 | 265 | 1,039 | 3.9 | 3,059 |
| 87th | (1961–62) | 14,328 | 32.9 | 1,927 | 0.134 | 240 | 304 | 1,227 | 4.0 | 3,402 |
| 88th | (1963–64) | 14,022 | 32.2 | 1,267 | 0.090 | 232 | 334 | 1,251 | 3.7 | 3,596 |
| 89th | (1965–66) | 19,874 | 45.7 | 1,565 | 0.079 | 394 | 336 | 1,547 | 4.6 | 4,367 |
| 90th | (1967–68) | 22,060 | 50.7 | 1,213 | 0.055 | 478 | 328 | 1,595 | 4.9 | 4,386 |
| 91st | (1969–70) | 21,436 | 49.3 | 1,130 | 0.053 | 443 | 350 | 1,613 | 4.6 | 5,066 |
| 92d | (1971–72) | 18,561 | 42.7 | 970 | 0.052 | 649 | 298 | 1,429 | 4.8 | 5,114 |
| 93d | (1973–74) | 18,872 | 43.4 | 923 | 0.049 | 1,078 | 318 | 1,487 | 4.7 | 5,888 |
| 94th | (1975–76) | 16,982 | 39.0 | 968 | 0.057 | 1,273 | 311 | 1,788 | 5.7 | 6,975 |
| 95th | (1977–78) | 15,587 | 35.8 | 1,027 | 0.066 | 1,540 | 323 | 1,898 | 5.9 | 7,896 |
| 96th | (1979–80) | 9,103 | 20.9 | 929 | 0.102 | 1,276 | 326 | 1,876 | 5.8 | 7,033 |
| 97th | (1981–82) | 8,094 | 18.6 | 704 | 0.087 | 812 | 303 | 1,420 | 4.7 | 6,078 |
| 98th | (1983–84) | 7,105 | 16.3 | 978 | 0.137 | 906 | 266 | 1,705 | 6.4 | 5,661 |
| 99th | (1985–86) | 6,499 | 14.9 | 973 | 0.150 | 890 | 281 | 1,794 | 6.4 | 5,272 |
| 100th | (1987–88) | 6,263 | 14.4 | 1,061 | 0.169 | 939 | 298 | 1,659 | 5.6 | 5,388 |
| 101st | (1989–90) | 6,683 | 15.4 | 968 | 0.145 | 915 | 281 | 1,688 | 6.0 | 5,305 |

| | | | | | | | | | | |
|---|---|---|---|---|---|---|---|---|---|---|
| 102d | (1991–92) | 7,771 | 17.9 | 932 | 0.120 | 932 | 277 | 1,795 | 6.5 | 5,152 |
| 103d | (1993–94) | 6,647 | 15.3 | 749 | 0.113 | 1,122 | 265 | 1,887 | 7.1 | 4,304 |
| 104th | (1995–96) | 4,542 | 10.4 | 611 | 0.134 | 1,340 | 289 | 2,444 | 8.5 | 3,796 |

*Note:* n.a. = not available.

[a] All bills and joint resolutions introduced.
[b] Includes all quorum calls, yea and nay votes, and recorded votes.
[c] Figures do not include the House Appropriations Committee for the Eighty-fourth to Eighty-eighth Congresses. House Appropriations included in subsequent Congresses numbered 584 in the Eighty-ninth Congress, 705 in the Ninetieth, 709 in the Ninety-first, 854 in the Ninety-second, and 892 in the Ninety-third.

*Sources:* Arthur G. Stevens, "Indicators of Congressional Workload and Activity," staff report, Congressional Research Service, Library of Congress, Washington, D.C., May 30, 1979; U.S. Congress, *Congressional Record—Daily Digest,* "Resume of Congressional Activity," vol. 126, no. 180, December 30, 1980; vol. 127, no. 188, pt. 3, December 16, 1981; vol. 130, no. 136, November 14, 1984; vol. 133, no. 1, January 6, 1987; vol. 134, no. 152, November 10, 1988; vol. 135, no. 165, pt. 4, November 21, 1989; vol. 136, no. 151, November 2, 1990; vol. 139, no. 1, January 5, 1993; vol. 140, no. 150, December 20, 1994. *Congressional Quarterly Almanac* (Washington, D.C.: Congressional Quarterly, various years); Roger H. Davidson and Carol Hardy, "Indicators of Congressional Workload and Activity," staff report, Congressional Research Service, Library of Congress, Washington, D.C., June 8, 1987; Office of the Official Reporters to House Committees, U.S. House of Representatives.

**Table 6-2** SenateWorkload, 80th–104th Congresses, 1947–1996

| *Congress* | | *Bills introduced*[a] | *Average no. of bills introduced per member* | *Bills passed* | *Ratio of bills passed to bills introduced* | *Recorded votes*[b] | *Time in session* | | *Hours per day in session* | *Committee, subcommittee meetings*[c] |
|---|---|---|---|---|---|---|---|---|---|---|
| | | | | | | | Days | Hours | | |
| 80th | (1947–48) | 3,186 | 33.2 | 1,670 | 0.524 | 248 | 257 | 1,462 | 5.7 | n.a. |
| 81st | (1949–50) | 4,486 | 46.7 | 2,362 | 0.527 | 455 | 389 | 2,410 | 6.2 | n.a. |
| 82d | (1951–52) | 3,665 | 38.2 | 1,849 | 0.505 | 331 | 287 | 1,648 | 5.7 | n.a. |
| 83d | (1953–54) | 4,077 | 42.5 | 2,231 | 0.547 | 270 | 294 | 1,962 | 6.7 | n.a. |
| 84th | (1955–56) | 4,518 | 47.1 | 2,550 | 0.564 | 224 | 224 | 1,362 | 6.1 | 2,607 |
| 85th | (1957–58) | 4,532 | 47.2 | 2,202 | 0.486 | 313 | 271 | 1,876 | 6.9 | 2,748 |
| 86th | (1959–60) | 4,149 | 42.3 | 1,680 | 0.405 | 422 | 280 | 2,199 | 7.9 | 2,271 |
| 87th | (1961–62) | 4,048 | 40.5 | 1,953 | 0.482 | 434 | 323 | 2,164 | 6.7 | 2,532 |
| 88th | (1963–64) | 3,457 | 34.6 | 1,341 | 0.388 | 541 | 375 | 2,395 | 6.4 | 2,493 |
| 89th | (1965–66) | 4,129 | 41.3 | 1,636 | 0.396 | 497 | 345 | 1,814 | 5.3 | 2,889 |
| 90th | (1967–68) | 4,400 | 44.0 | 1,376 | 0.313 | 595 | 358 | 1,961 | 5.5 | 2,892 |
| 91st | (1969–70) | 4,867 | 48.7 | 1,271 | 0.261 | 667 | 384 | 2,352 | 6.1 | 3,264 |
| 92d | (1971–72) | 4,408 | 44.1 | 1,035 | 0.235 | 955 | 348 | 2,294 | 6.6 | 3,559 |
| 93d | (1973–74) | 4,524 | 45.2 | 1,115 | 0.246 | 1,138 | 334 | 2,028 | 6.1 | 4,067 |
| 94th | (1975–76) | 4,114 | 41.1 | 1,038 | 0.252 | 1,290 | 320 | 2,210 | 6.9 | 4,265 |
| 95th | (1977–78) | 3,800 | 38.0 | 1,070 | 0.282 | 1,151 | 337 | 2,510 | 7.4 | 3,960 |
| 96th | (1979–80) | 3,480 | 34.8 | 977 | 0.281 | 1,043 | 333 | 2,324 | 7.0 | 3,790 |
| 97th | (1981–82) | 3,396 | 34.0 | 803 | 0.236 | 966 | 312 | 2,158 | 6.9 | 3,236 |
| 98th | (1983–84) | 3,454 | 34.5 | 936 | 0.271 | 673 | 281 | 1,951 | 6.9 | 2,471 |
| 99th | (1985–86) | 3,386 | 33.9 | 940 | 0.278 | 740 | 313 | 2,531 | 8.1 | 2,373 |
| 100th | (1987–88) | 3,325 | 33.3 | 1,002 | 0.301 | 799 | 307 | 2,342 | 7.6 | 2,493 |
| 101st | (1989–90) | 3,669 | 36.7 | 980 | 0.267 | 638 | 274 | 2,254 | 8.2 | 2,340[c] |

| | | | | | | | | | |
|---|---|---|---|---|---|---|---|---|---|
| 102d (1991–92) | 4,245 | 42.5 | 947 | 0.223 | 550 | 287 | 2,291 | 8.0 | 2,039 |
| 103d (1993–94) | 3,177 | 31.8 | 682 | 0.215 | 724 | 291 | 2,513 | 8.6 | 2,043 |
| 104th (1995–96) | 2,266 | 22.7 | 518 | 0.229 | 919 | 343 | 2,876 | 8.4 | 1,601 |

*Note:* n.a. = not available.

[a] All bills and joint resolutions introduced.
[b] All yea and nay votes.
[c] Where final legislative calendars were not available, figures were compiled from *Congressional Information Service Abstracts* and the *Congressional Record.*

*Sources:* Davidson and Hardy, "Indicators of Congressional Workload and Activity" (1987); "Resume of Congressional Activity," vol. 126, no. 180, December 30, 1980; vol. 127, no. 188, pt. 3, December 16, 1981; vol. 130, no. 136, November 14, 1984; vol. 133, no. 1, January 6, 1987; vol. 134, no. 152, November 10, 1988; vol. 135, no. 165, pt. 4, November 21, 1989; vol. 136, no. 151, November 2, 1990; vol. 139, no. 1, January 5, 1993; vol. 140, no. 150, December 20, 1994. *Congressional Quarterly Almanac,* various years; final legislative calendars for each committee, 100th and 101st Congresses.

Figure 6-1 Ratio of Bills Passed to Bills Introduced, 80th–104th Congresses, 1947–1996

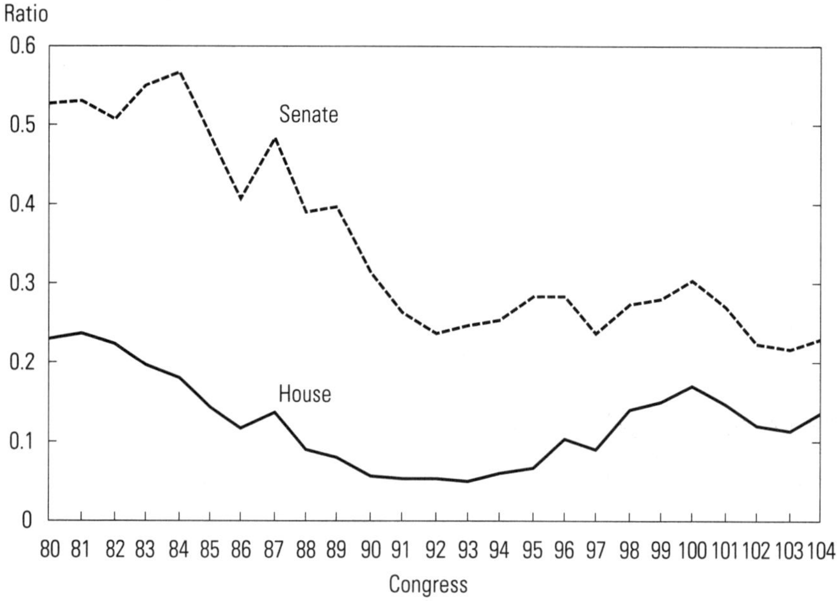


*Sources:* Tables 6-1 and 6-2.

Figure 6-2 Recorded Votes in the House and the Senate, 80th–104th Congresses, 1947–1996

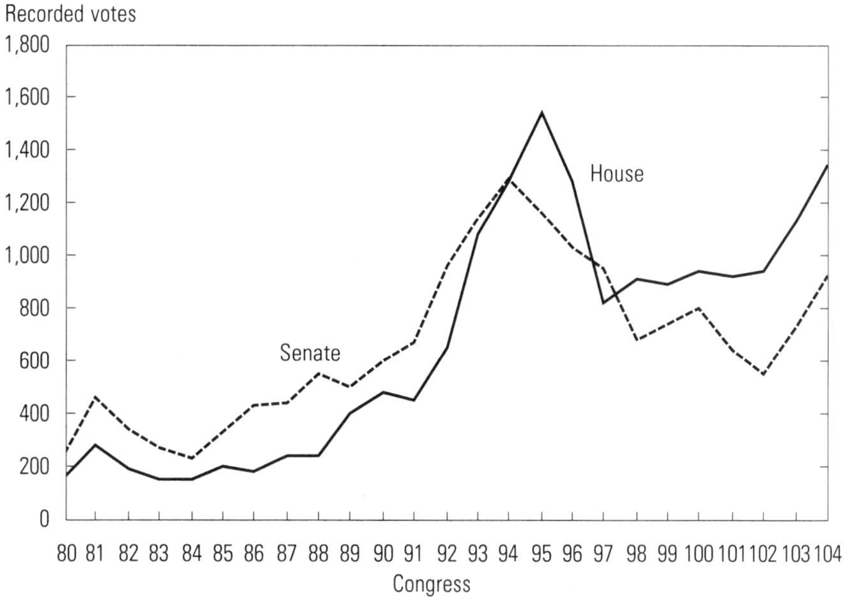


*Sources:* Tables 6-1 and 6-2.

**Table 6-3** Recorded Votes in the House and the Senate, 1947–1996

| *Year* | *House* | *Senate* | *Year* | *House* | *Senate* |
|---|---|---|---|---|---|
| 1947 | 84 | 138 | 1972 | 329 | 532 |
| 1948 | 75 | 110 | 1973 | 541 | 594 |
| 1949 | 121 | 226 | 1974 | 537 | 544 |
| 1950 | 154 | 229 | 1975 | 612 | 602 |
| 1951 | 109 | 202 | 1976 | 661 | 688 |
| 1952 | 72 | 129 | 1977 | 706 | 635 |
| 1953 | 71 | 89 | 1978 | 834 | 516 |
| 1954 | 76 | 181 | 1979 | 672 | 497 |
| 1955 | 73 | 88 | 1980 | 604 | 546 |
| 1956 | 74 | 136 | 1981 | 353 | 497 |
| 1957 | 100 | 111 | 1982 | 459 | 469 |
| 1958 | 93 | 202 | 1983 | 498 | 381 |
| 1959 | 87 | 215 | 1984 | 408 | 292 |
| 1960 | 93 | 207 | 1985 | 439 | 381 |
| 1961 | 116 | 207 | 1986 | 451 | 359 |
| 1962 | 124 | 227 | 1987 | 488 | 420 |
| 1963 | 119 | 229 | 1988 | 451 | 379 |
| 1964 | 113 | 312 | 1989 | 379 | 312 |
| 1965 | 201 | 259 | 1990 | 536 | 326 |
| 1966 | 193 | 238 | 1991 | 444 | 280 |
| 1967 | 245 | 315 | 1992 | 488 | 270 |
| 1968 | 233 | 280[a] | 1993 | 615 | 395 |
| 1969 | 177 | 245 | 1994 | 507 | 329 |
| 1970 | 266 | 422 | 1995 | 885 | 613 |
| 1971 | 320 | 423 | 1996 | 455 | 306 |

*Note:* House figures reflect the total number of quorum calls, yea and nay votes, and recorded votes, while Senate figures include only yea and nay votes.

[a] This figure does not include one yea and nay vote that was ruled invalid for lack of a quorum.

*Sources:* "Resume of Congressional Activity," vol. 130, no. 136, November 14, 1984; vol. 133, no. 1, January 6, 1987; vol. 134, no. 152, November 10, 1988; vol. 137, no. 1, January 3, 1991; vol. 139, no. 1, January 5, 1993; vol. 140, no. 150, December 20, 1994. *Congressional Quarterly Almanac,* various years. *Congressional Monitor,* October 7, 1996, 5.

**Table 6-4** Congressional Workload, 80th–104th Congresses, 1947–1996

| | Public bills | | | Private bills | | |
|---|---|---|---|---|---|---|
| *Congress* | No. of bills enacted | Total pages of statutes | Average pages per statute | No. of bills enacted | Total pages of statutes | Average pages per statute |
| 80th (1947–48) | 906 | 2,236 | 2.5 | 458 | 182 | 0.40 |
| 81st (1949–50) | 921 | 2,314 | 2.5 | 1,103 | 417 | 0.38 |
| 82d (1951–52) | 594 | 1,585 | 2.7 | 1,023 | 360 | 0.35 |
| 83d (1953–54) | 781 | 1,899 | 2.4 | 1,002 | 365 | 0.36 |
| 84th (1955–56) | 1,028 | 1,848 | 1.8 | 893 | 364 | 0.41 |
| 85th (1957–58) | 936 | 2,435 | 2.6 | 784 | 349 | 0.45 |
| 86th (1959–60) | 800 | 1,774 | 2.2 | 492 | 201 | 0.41 |
| 87th (1961–62) | 885 | 2,078 | 2.3 | 684 | 255 | 0.37 |
| 88th (1963–64) | 666 | 1,975 | 3.0 | 360 | 144 | 0.40 |
| 89th (1965–66) | 810 | 2,912 | 3.6 | 473 | 188 | 0.40 |
| 90th (1967–68) | 640 | 2,304 | 3.6 | 362 | 128 | 0.35 |
| 91st (1969–70) | 695 | 2,927 | 4.2 | 246 | 104 | 0.42 |
| 92d (1971–72) | 607 | 2,330 | 3.8 | 161 | 67 | 0.42 |
| 93d (1973–74) | 649 | 3,443 | 5.3 | 123 | 48 | 0.39 |
| 94th (1975–76) | 588 | 4,121 | 7.0 | 141 | 75 | 0.53 |
| 95th (1977–78) | 633 | 5,403 | 8.5 | 170 | 60 | 0.35 |
| 96th (1979–80) | 613 | 4,947 | 8.1 | 123 | 63 | 0.51 |
| 97th (1981–82) | 473 | 4,343 | 9.2 | 56 | 25 | 0.45 |
| 98th (1983–84) | 623 | 4,893 | 7.8 | 54 | 26 | 0.48 |
| 99th (1985–86) | 664 | 7,198 | 10.8 | 24 | 13 | 0.54 |
| 100th (1987–88) | 713 | 4,839 | 6.8 | 48 | 29 | 0.60 |
| 101st (1989–90) | 650 | 5,767 | 8.9 | 16 | 9 | 0.56 |
| 102d (1991–92) | 590 | 7,544 | 12.8 | 20 | 11 | 0.55 |
| 103d (1993–94) | 465 | 7,542 | 16.2 | 8 | 9 | 1.10 |
| 104th (1995–96) | 333 | 6,369 | 19.1 | 4 | 4 | 1.00 |

*Sources:* Stevens, "Indicators of Congressional Workload and Activity"; *U.S. Code Congressional and Administrative News,* volumes for 97th, 98th, 99th, and 100th Congresses; Office of the Law Revision Counsel, U.S. House of Representatives. For the 101st, 102d, and 103d Congresses, Office of the Law Revision Counsel; *Federal Register.*

**Table 6-5** Pages in the *Federal Register,* 1936–1996

| *Year* | *Pages* | *Year* | *Pages* | *Year* | *Pages* |
|---|---|---|---|---|---|
| 1936 | 2,355 | 1977 | 63,629 | 1988 | 53,376 |
| 1946 | 14,736 | 1978 | 61,261 | 1989 | 53,821 |
| 1956 | 10,528 | 1979 | 77,497 | 1990 | 53,618 |
| 1966 | 16,850 | 1980 | 87,012 | 1991 | 67,715 |
| 1969 | 20,464 | 1981 | 63,554 | 1992 | 62,919 |
| 1971 | 25,442 | 1982 | 58,493 | 1993 | 69,684 |
| 1972 | 28,920 | 1983 | 57,703 | 1994 | 68,107 |
| 1973 | 35,586 | 1984 | 50,997 | 1995 | 68,108 |
| 1974 | 45,422 | 1985 | 53,479 | 1996 | 69,368 |
| 1975 | 60,221 | 1986 | 47,418 | | |
| 1976 | 57,072 | 1987 | 49,654 | | |

Figure 6-3 Public Bills in the Congressional Workload, 80th–104th Congresses, 1947–1996

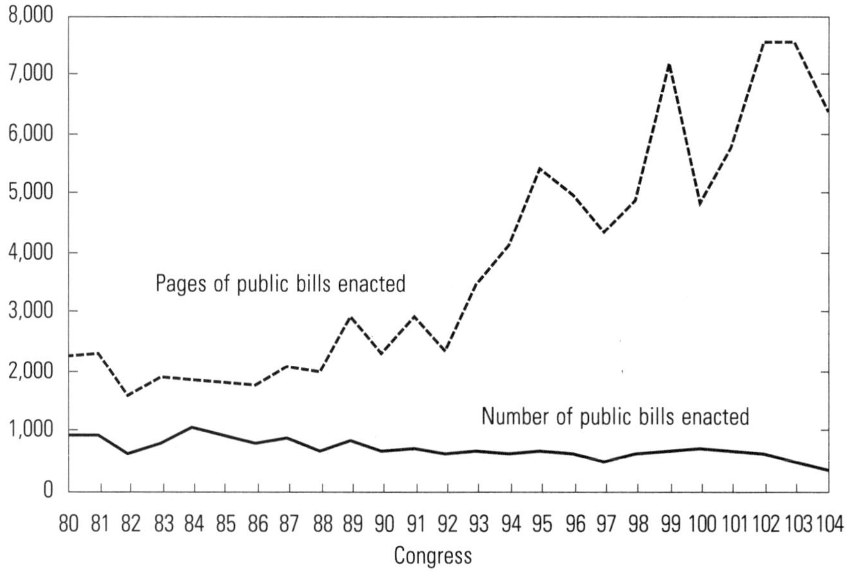


*Source:* Table 6-4.

**Table 6-6** Vetoes and Overrides, 80th–104th Congresses, 1947–1996

| *Congress* | | *Total no. of presidential vetoes* | *No. of regular vetoes* | *No. of pocket vetoes* | *Vetoes overridden* Total | *Vetoes overridden* Percentage of regular vetoes | *House attempts to override vetoes* | *Senate attempts to override vetoes* |
|---|---|---|---|---|---|---|---|---|
| 80th | (1947–48) | 75 | 42 | 33 | 6 | 14.3 | 8 | 8 |
| 81st | (1949–50) | 79 | 70 | 9 | 3 | 4.3 | 5 | 5 |
| 82d | (1951–52) | 22 | 14 | 8 | 3 | 21.4 | 4 | 4 |
| 83d | (1953–54) | 52 | 21 | 31 | 0 | — | 0 | 0 |
| 84th | (1955–56) | 34 | 12 | 22 | 0 | — | 1 | 1 |
| 85th | (1957–58) | 51 | 18 | 33 | 0 | — | 1 | 1 |
| 86th | (1959–60) | 44 | 22 | 22 | 2 | 9.1 | 5 | 6 |
| 87th | (1961–62) | 20 | 11 | 9 | 0 | — | 0 | 0 |
| 88th | (1963–64) | 9 | 5 | 4 | 0 | — | 0 | 0 |
| 89th | (1965–66) | 14 | 10 | 4 | 0 | — | 0 | 0 |
| 90th | (1967–68) | 8 | 2 | 6 | 0 | — | 0 | 0 |
| 91st | (1969–70) | 11 | 7 | 4 | 2 | 28.6 | 4 | 4 |
| 92d | (1971–72) | 20 | 6 | 14 | 2 | 33.3 | 3 | 4 |
| 93d | (1973–74) | 39 | 27 | 12 | 5 | 18.5 | 12 | 10 |
| 94th | (1975–76) | 37 | 32 | 5 | 8 | 25.0 | 17 | 15 |
| 95th | (1977–78) | 19 | 6 | 13 | 0 | — | 2 | 0 |
| 96th | (1979–80) | 12 | 7 | 5 | 2 | 28.6 | 2 | 2 |
| 97th | (1981–82) | 15 | 9 | 6 | 2 | 22.2 | 4 | 3 |
| 98th | (1983–84) | 24 | 9 | 15 | 2 | 22.2 | 2 | 2 |
| 99th | (1985–86) | 20 | 13 | 7 | 2 | 15.4 | 3 | 3 |

*(Table continues)*

**Table 6-6** *(Continued)*

| *Congress* | | *Total no. of presidential vetoes* | *No. of regular vetoes* | *No. of pocket vetoes* | *Vetoes overridden* | | *House attempts to override vetoes* | *Senate attempts to override vetoes* |
|---|---|---|---|---|---|---|---|---|
| | | | | | Total | Percentage of regular vetoes | | |
| 100th | (1987–88) | 19 | 8 | 11 | 3 | 37.5 | 5 | 4 |
| 101st | (1989–90) | 21 | 16 | 5 | 0 | — | 9 | 5 |
| 102d | (1991–92) | 25 | 15 | 10[a] | 1 | 6.7 | 3 | 3 |
| 103d | (1993–94) | 0 | 0 | 0 | 0 | 0 | 0 | 0 |
| 104th | (1995–96) | 17 | 17 | 0 | 1 | 5.9 | 6 | 1 |

[a] President Bush asserted that he had pocket-vetoed S1176, although some members in Congress dispute that on the grounds that bills can be pocket-vetoed only after Congress has adjourned, not during a recess.

*Sources:* Roger H. Davidson and Carol Hardy, "Indicators of Congressional Workload and Activity," staff report, Congressional Research Service, Library of Congress, Washington, D.C., 1989. For 1989–1990, Congressional Quarterly Research Query Service. For 1991–1992, *Congressional Quarterly Weekly Report,* December 19, 1992, 3925–3926. For 1993–1994, *Congressional Quarterly Weekly Report,* December 31, 1994, 3623. For 1995–1996, *Congressional Quarterly Weekly Report,* December 14, 1996, 3386.

**Table 6-7** Attempted and Successful Cloture Votes in the Senate, 1919–1996

| | *1st session* | | *2d session* | | *Total* | |
|---|---|---|---|---|---|---|
| *Congress* | attempted | successful | attempted | successful | attempted | successful |
| 66th (1919-20) | 1 | 1 | 0 | 0 | 1 | 1 |
| 67th (1921-22) | 1 | 0 | 1 | 0 | 2 | 0 |
| 68th (1923-24) | 0 | 0 | 0 | 0 | 0 | 0 |
| 69th (1925-26) | 0 | 0 | 2 | 1 | 2 | 1 |
| 70th (1927-28) | 5 | 2 | 0 | 0 | 5 | 2 |
| 71st (1929-30) | 0 | 0 | 0 | 0 | 0 | 0 |
| 72d (1931-32) | 0 | 0 | 0 | 0 | 0 | 0 |
| 73d (1933-34) | 1 | 0 | 0 | 0 | 1 | 0 |
| 74th (1935-36) | 0 | 0 | 0 | 0 | 0 | 0 |
| 75th (1937-38) | 0 | 0 | 2 | 0 | 2 | 0 |
| 76th (1939-40) | 0 | 0 | 0 | 0 | 0 | 0 |
| 77th (1941-42) | 0 | 0 | 1 | 1 | 1 | 1 |
| 78th (1943-44) | 0 | 0 | 1 | 1 | 1 | 0 |
| 79th (1945-46) | 0 | 0 | 4 | 0 | 4 | 0 |
| 80th (1947-48) | 0 | 0 | 0 | 0 | 0 | 0 |
| 81st (1949-50) | 0 | 0 | 2 | 0 | 2 | 0 |
| 82d (1951-52) | 0 | 0 | 0 | 0 | 0 | 0 |
| 83d (1953-54) | 0 | 0 | 1 | 0 | 1 | 0 |
| 84th (1955-56) | 0 | 0 | 0 | 0 | 0 | 0 |
| 85th (1957-58) | 0 | 0 | 0 | 0 | 0 | 0 |
| 86th (1959-60) | 0 | 0 | 1 | 0 | 1 | 0 |
| 87th (1961-62) | 1 | 0 | 3 | 1 | 4 | 1 |
| 88th (1963-64) | 1 | 0 | 2 | 1 | 3 | 1 |
| 89th (1965-66) | 2 | 1 | 5 | 0 | 7 | 1 |
| 90th (1967-68) | 1 | 0 | 5 | 1 | 6 | 1 |
| 91st (1969-70) | 2 | 0 | 4 | 0 | 6 | 0 |
| 92d (1971-72) | 10 | 2 | 10 | 2 | 20 | 4 |
| 93d (1973-74) | 10 | 2 | 21 | 7 | 31 | 9 |
| 94th (1975-76) | 23 | 13 | 4 | 4 | 27 | 17 |
| 95th (1977-78) | 5 | 1 | 8 | 2 | 13 | 3 |
| 96th (1979-80) | 4 | 1 | 17 | 9 | 21 | 10 |
| 97th (1981-82) | 7 | 2 | 20 | 7 | 27 | 9 |
| 98th (1983-84) | 7 | 2 | 12 | 9 | 19 | 11 |
| 99th (1985-86) | 9 | 1 | 14 | 9 | 23 | 10 |
| 100th (1987-88) | 24 | 6 | 20 | 6 | 44 | 12 |
| 101st (1989-90) | 9 | 6 | 15 | 5 | 24 | 11 |
| 102d (1991-92) | 21 | 9 | 28 | 14 | 49 | 23 |
| 103d (1993-94) | 20 | 4 | 22 | 10 | 42 | 14 |
| 104th (1995-96) | 21 | 4 | 29 | 5 | 50 | 9 |

*Note:* The number of votes required to invoke cloture was changed March 7, 1975, from two-thirds of those present and voting to three-fifths of the total Senate membership, as Rule XXII of the standing rules of the Senate was amended.

*Sources:* Davidson and Hardy, "Indicators of Congressional Workload and Activity" (1989). For 1989-1992, Congressional Research Service, Library of Congress-Government Division. For 1993, *Congressional Quarterly Almanac* 1994, 14. For 1994, *Congressional Monitor*, October 11, 1994, 17; October 7, 1996, 24.

**Table 6-8** Congressional Mailings, 1954–1993

| *Fiscal year* | *Millions of pieces* | *Increase or decrease (%)* |
|---|---|---|
| 1954 | 43.5 | — |
| 1955 | 45.6 | 4.8 |
| 1956 | 58.2 | 27.6 |
| 1957 | 59.6 | 2.4 |
| 1958 | 65.4 | 9.7 |
| 1959 | 86.5 | 32.3 |
| 1960 | 108.0 | 24.9 |
| 1961 | 85.1 | –21.2 |
| 1962 | 110.1 | 29.4 |
| 1963 | 94.7 | –14.0 |
| 1964 | 110.5 | 16.7 |
| 1965 | 120.9 | 9.4 |
| 1966 | 197.5 | 63.4 |
| 1967 | 192.9 | –2.3 |
| 1968 | 178.2 | –7.6 |
| 1969 | 190.0 | 6.6 |
| 1970 | 201.0 | 5.8 |
| 1971 | 238.4 | 18.6 |
| 1972 | 308.9 | 29.6 |
| 1973 | 310.6 | 0.6 |
| 1974 | 321.0 | 3.3 |
| 1975 | 312.4 | –2.7 |
| 1976 | 401.4 | 28.5 |
| Transition quarter | 159.9 | — |
| 1977 | 293.3 | –26.9 |
| 1978 | 430.2 | 46.7 |
| 1979 | 409.9 | –4.7 |
| 1980 | 511.3 | 24.7 |
| 1981 | 395.6 | –22.6 |
| 1982 | 771.8 | 95.1 |
| 1983 | 556.8 | –27.9 |
| 1984 | 924.6 | 60.3 |
| 1985 | 675.0 | –27.9 |
| 1986 | 758.7 | 12.4 |
| 1987 | 494.7 | –34.8 |
| 1988 | 804.9 | 62.7 |
| 1989 | 598.6 | –25.6 |
| 1990 | 564.2 | –5.7 |
| 1991 | 259.8 | –54.0 |
| 1992 | 458.0 | 76.3 |
| 1993 | 200.7 | –56.3 |

*Sources:* For 1954-1978, U.S. Congress, House, Committee on Appropriations, Subcommittee on Legislative Branch Appropriations, *Hearings on Legislative Branch Appropriations for 1980,* pt. 2; for 1979, *House LBA Hearings for 1981,* pt. 2; for 1980–1983, Office of the Clerk of the House; for 1984, *House LBA Hearings for 1986,* pt. 2; for 1985, *House LBA Hearings for 1987,* pt. 2; for 1986, *House LBA Hearings for 1988,* pt. 2; for 1987, *House LBA Hearings for 1989,* pt. 2; for 1988, *House LBA Hearings for 1990,* pt. 2; for 1989, Congressional Research Service Report for Congress, "U.S. Congress Official Mail Costs: FY1972 to FY1991"; for 1990–1991, Congressional Research Service, "U.S. Congress Official Mail Costs: FY1972 to FY1993 (Est.)"; for 1992–1993, U.S. Postal Service.

# 7

# Budgeting

The Constitution gives Congress the power to levy taxes and to appropriate money. Accordingly, the executive branch can raise and spend money only to the extent and in the manner authorized by Congress. In addition to its taxing and appropriating power, Congress makes financial decisions through its authorizations and budget processes. The authorizations process is anchored in the rules of the House (and, to a lesser extent, those of the Senate), which require that agencies and programs be authorized in law before funds are appropriated for them. The budget process was established by the Congressional Budget Act of 1974, which provided that Congress adopt two budget resolutions each year to coordinate the numerous fiscal decisions made in separate revenue, spending, and debt legislation. A succession of reforms, including two versions of Gramm/Rudman/Hollings among other changes, have not altered the basics.

In recent years, however, Congress has adopted only a single budget resolution. The process itself came under reexamination in the last few years with proposed legislation for biennial budgeting and a constitutional amendment requiring a balanced budget. The 104th Congress passed a statutory line-item veto, and all of this came during heated, partisan budget battles. It is not clear that any of the other reforms will happen in the near future, and the line-item veto, while actively employed in the 105th Congress, could well be ruled unconstitutional. However, there is no doubt that the budget has been one of the most important issues of recent Congresses.

---

Allen Schick, then-professor of public policy at the University of Maryland, wrote and assembled the original version of Chapter 7 for *Vital Statistics in Congress 1980*. This is an updated version of Schick's essay.

## Budget Resolutions

Since the inception of the congressional budget process, voting on the resolutions has reflected a sharp split in the House between the Democratic and Republican parties. Table 7-1 shows remarkable Republican cohesion until 1989, when more members began to break party ranks. During the 1976-1981 fiscal years, approximately 95 percent of House Republicans voted against adoption of the budget resolutions. For the fiscal 1982 and 1983 budgets, however, the Republicans (despite their minority status in the House) gained control of the budget process, and most of them voted in favor of budget resolutions supported by Republican president Ronald Reagan. When they lost control of the fiscal 1984 resolution, the Republicans reverted to opposition and persisted in opposing all budget resolutions until the 1989 agreement resulted in a GOP split and a wide margin of victory for the resolution. A similar pattern held in 1990; however, 1991 saw renewed opposition, which continued for several years. The Republicans were unanimously opposed to the 1993, 1994, and 1995 budgets. The pattern continued in reverse after the Republican takeover of Congress, with Republicans nearly unanimously supporting the 1996 and 1997 budgets over near unanimous opposition from the Democrats.

Because House Democrats have generally not been as united as the Republicans, the latter sometimes prevailed on budget resolutions when they were in the minority. At various times majority Democrats from both the liberal and the conservative wings of the party opposed the position taken by most of their colleagues. Nevertheless, during the 1976-1981 fiscal years, House Democrats supplied sufficient votes to pass the budget resolutions, although on two occasions (the first resolution for fiscal 1978 and the second resolution for fiscal 1980) only after the initial version was rejected. In voting on the 1982 and 1983 budget resolutions, most House Democrats opposed the president's position and, when their view was rejected, voted against adoption of the budget resolutions. But in subsequent years Democrats managed remarkable unity and passed resolutions without GOP help for each fiscal year from 1984 through 1988. In 1989 the split in the Republican vote resulted in a large, bipartisan margin of victory, breaking the previous vote mold. Democrats supported the resolutions of 1990 and 1991, but by smaller margins. Democratic defections combined with Republican solidarity nearly caused the majority to lose the vote on 1993's budget resolution. The Democrats squeezed out a narrow victory (209-207), in which the Speaker cast an extremely rare floor vote.

The 1994 and 1995 budgets were based on a budget request from a Democratic president for the first time in twelve years. Democrats demonstrated early support for Clinton by passing the 1994 resolution swiftly and by a wide margin (243-183). The much more difficult vote, a cliff-hanger in both the House and the Senate, was on the reconciliation package to implement the deficit reduction agreement. It finally passed by a single vote in each house without any Republican support. The FY1995 budget was routine, following the five-year plan approved the year before. Debate over the next budget quickly degenerated into a party standoff that was not completely resolved until the latter half of 1997. The budget resolution for FY1998 seemed to resolve some of the dispute, although there is deep disagreement about whether or not the long-term spending cuts for projects will be implemented.

Until the 1982 fiscal year, the Senate displayed a different voting pattern, one in which a bipartisan coalition of Republicans and Democrats passed resolutions by a wide margin (see Table 7-2). The two parties were polarized on the 1982 and 1983 budgets, and in both years a majority of Senate Democrats voted against approval of the budget resolution. Growing Democratic opposition was matched by increasing Republican support for the resolutions, a pattern that reversed when the Democrats regained control of the Senate before the 1988 fiscal year. As in the House, the 1989 resolution won a comfortable bipartisan majority, built on a unified Democratic vote and a split GOP. Democrats were much less unified in 1990 and 1991; Republicans remained split. The resolutions from 1992 through 1995 passed largely on the basis of unified Democratic support, with the majority of Republican senators opposing both. As in the House, the pattern simply reversed itself in the 104th Congress.

In voting on the budget resolutions, Congress goes on record with respect to key budget aggregates (total revenues, budget authority, outlays, and deficit) and functional allocations. Table 7-3 compares congressional decisions on the aggregates with presidential budget recommendations and with the actual results for each fiscal year from 1976 through 1995. During the early years of the budget process, actual spending and the deficit tended to be below those set by Congress in its budget resolutions. In 1980, however, the final results began to consistently show higher spending. The level of disparity varied with the largest occurring with the 1991 deficit—projected at $64 billion in the budget resolution and actually totaling $268.7 billion. Working within the confines of the 1990 Budget Enforcement Act, budget writers were forced to make more realistic deficit projections in 1992 and 1993. In 1993 the actual deficit as well as all key budget aggregates were below that of Congress's resolution for the first time since the 1980 trend began. The actual deficit dropped again in 1994, once more falling below that set by Congress. Strong economic growth and smaller than expected increases in health outlays made the 1997 budget deals possible and produced a fiscal 1997 deficit of $22 billion, the lowest in more than two decades. A strong economy may be the driving force behind producing a revenue surplus in the coming years.

## Congressional Control of the Budget

Although Congress holds the power of the purse, its ability to effectively exercise this power has been hampered by the rise of uncontrollable spending.

During fiscal years 1967-1992 "relatively uncontrollable" outlays soared from less than $100 billion to more than $1 trillion and from less than 60 percent of total outlays to nearly 80 percent (see Table 7-4). In the early 1990s, this proportion remained stable with the major increases in outlays once again occurring in Social Security, Medicare, and Medicaid, although with low inflation, the increases slowed by the mid-1990s.

Most uncontrollables are in the form of entitlements: provisions of law that mandate payments to eligible recipients. Most entitlements are open-ended and cannot be controlled through budgetary or appropriations actions. Moreover, many entitlements are indexed to the rate of inflation, so that payments are adjusted to increases in the cost of living without congressional action. Entitlements can only be controlled by changing the laws that mandate the payments. Congress developed the reconciliation process in 1980 as a means of reducing certain entitlements that would then, lawmakers hoped, bring expenditures for them in line with congressional budget decisions. But this method proved ineffective, and as deficit reduction became a greater national priority, the massive growth of entitlement spending, especially that of Social Security, Medicare, and Medicaid gained much attention.

In 1993 and 1994, Medicare and Medicaid spending came under intense scrutiny during the debate over health care reform. But when discussion of cuts began, legislators were quickly reminded of the wide public support of these programs. The future of Social Security expenditures brought much contention to the 1995 debate over an amendment requiring a balanced federal budget. Senate Democrats demanded that legislation proposed by Republicans include a measure protecting Social Security from budget cuts. Both of these measures were a prelude for the all-out warfare of the latter half of 1995. The controversy seems cooler today in the wake of the 1997 budget deal, which included plans for a bipartisan commission on Medicaid. But any significant changes in it or in Social Security remain problematic.

## The Appropriations Process

A budget resolution is advisory. No funds can be spent by government agencies pursuant to the amounts set in a resolution. The actual provision of funds occurs in appropriation bills, of which there are supposed to be thirteen regular bills and a number of supplemental measures each year.

The Appropriations committees see themselves as guardians of the Treasury, a role that is reflected in their determination to appropriate less money than has been requested by the president. Table 7-5, drawn from the official records of the House Appropriations Committee, shows that in almost every year the total amount appropriated is below the president's budget request. These figures do not include permanent appropriations (which are not reviewed by the Appropriations committees) or "backdoor" authority provided in other legislation.

Although the Appropriations committees provide less money than the president requests, they also enact sizable supplemental appropriations each year (see Table 7-6). Supplemental appropriations are made for a number of reasons: to provide for agencies not funded in the regular appropriation bills, to pay for the salary increases of federal employees, to supplement the funds for agencies facing a deficiency, to finance new or expanded programs, to pay for natural disasters like floods or hurricanes, and, as in 1991, to finance major military operations such as Desert Shield/Desert Storm for which an additional $42.6 billion was appropriated. The number of supplemental bills and their amounts rose after the congressional budget process was introduced, but both have declined in the past five fiscal years to where they cannot be considered ways to evade budget limits. Indeed, with the focus on deficit reduction, it has become increasingly difficult to pass supplemental spending. In recent years, Republicans and conservative Democrats demanded that the bulk of the supplementals be offset by spending cuts elsewhere. In 1995 all of the supplementals were offset for the first time since at least 1964.

Historically, budget cutting has been concentrated in the House, which, under long-standing precedent, considers appropriation bills before they are taken up by the Senate. This role depends largely on the ability of the House Appropriations Committee to protect its bills against floor amendments to provide additional funds. But as Table 7-7 shows, from 1965 through 1980 there was a steady rise in the number of amendments proposed and the number agreed to by the House.

One important factor in this upward trend was the Legislative Reorganization Act of 1970, which provided for recorded votes in the Committee of the Whole, where most House action on appropriation bills (and other measures) takes place. Another reason for the increase in floor amendments has been the practice of attaching "limitations" to appropriation bills. Although the rules bar the insertion of legislation in such bills, limitations that restrict the use of appropriated funds are permissible. The House adopted three times as many limitation amendments in the 1970s as it did in the 1960s. Some of the most contentious issues, such as U.S. policy in Vietnam, school busing, aid to the Nicaraguan contras, and abortions, have been considered as limitations in appropriation bills.

Although the data in Table 7-7 do not show it, there appears to have been a downturn in the number of limiting amendments because of a change in rules adopted by the House at the start of the Ninety-eighth Congress in 1983. The new rule makes it easier for the House to avoid consideration of these amendments, but if a House majority wants to do so, it can still use appropriation bills as an effective means of controlling government policy by limiting the use of appropriated funds.

The Congressional Budget Act of 1974 established a timetable designed to ensure enactment of all regular appropriation bills by October 1, when the new fiscal year begins. Despite the legislative schedule, Congress has had difficulty in completing its work on regular appropriation bills by the start of the fiscal year. As a consequence, it has been compelled to provide stopgap funding through continuing appropriations (see Table 7-8). There have only been three fiscal years—1977, 1989, and 1995—when it has not been necessary to rely on continuing appropriations. Only three of the thirteen regular appropriation bills for fiscal 1980 were enacted by the start of the fiscal year; only one regular appropriation bill for fiscal 1981 was enacted on time; and none of these bills had been enacted into law when fiscal 1982 began. The record improved slightly in subsequent years, with one bill enacted by the start of fiscal 1983 and four bills by the start of fiscal 1984 and 1985, but then Congress failed to enact any regular appropriation bills at the start of fiscal 1986, 1987, 1988, 1990, and 1991. That record makes passage of all thirteen bills for 1989 all the more remarkable, reflecting a broad bipartisan agreement to get things done in the presidential election year, while putting off the hottest and most controversial budget issues to the next administration. Nevertheless, congressional activity quickly reverted back to normal, and no appropriation bills were passed by the start of FY1990 or FY1991. Yet, another surge came with the passage of all bills before FY1995 commenced. It seems that the swiftness can only last one year at a time though. The budget battles of the 104th Congress intensified the old passions, and although the immediate future looks calm, it is unlikely to stay that way. The major controversies on appropriations bills in 1997 were driven by the line-item veto. Its vigorous exercise by President Clinton in a few targeted areas spurred howls of protest by many lawmakers, including a large number who had been the veto's most vociferous proponents. The line-item vetoes had far more impact on small but key priorities of individual legislators than they did on overall budget numbers.

## The Budgetary Work of Congress

To an extraordinary degree, the business of Congress is related to the budget. Tables 7-9 and 7-10 show a steep increase between 1955 and 1982 in the number of House and Senate roll calls dealing with budgetary issues. Budget-related votes include all roll calls on appropriation bills, tax legislation (other than tax treaties and tariffs), budget resolutions, and reconciliation bills, as well as votes pertaining to the level of authorizations. The number of budget-related votes has escalated in both chambers during the past quarter of a century, but the increase has been especially striking in the Senate. With the exception of 1988, consistently nearly 50 percent of House roll calls each year have been budget related, reaching 59 percent in 1993 and declining in 1995 and 1996 to around 54 percent. In the Senate, budget-related roll call votes hit

71 percent in 1981 and leveled off at 60 percent. They declined a bit from 1986 to 1992, but then climbed back to 62 percent in 1993 and 69 percent in 1996.

One interesting pattern that emerges from the data in Tables 7-9 and 7-10 is that despite the establishment of the congressional budget process, Congress still gives a great deal of attention to authorizations, appropriations, and tax legislation. Congressional budget activity—especially in the Senate—was extraordinary during the 1981 session, which coincided with Ronald Reagan's first year in office. The new president organized his domestic agenda around the federal budget and called for major changes in economic policies and spending priorities. Inevitably, Congress increased its budget activity. In subsequent years, budget activity was more normal, though the increase that began in 1993 continued into the next few years because the budget remained such a high priority.

## Rescissions and Deferrals

One of the key purposes of the congressional budget process is to ensure that congressional spending priorities prevail when they are in conflict with those of the president. To achieve this end, the Impoundment Control Act established procedures for congressional review of presidential proposals to defer or rescind funds provided by Congress. When a president proposes rescission, Congress has a forty-five-day period during which it can pass a bill rescinding the funds; if Congress fails to act during this period, the president is required to make the funds available for expenditure. The deficit control mentality of the 1990s led many members, mostly Republicans but also some Democrats, to call for passage of a presidential line-item veto. The 104th Congress passed a line-item veto provision, which was actually more an enhanced rescission, that allows the president to veto specific sections of appropriations bills and requires a two-thirds vote by Congress to overturn them. President Clinton, as we noted, exercised the veto several times in the fall of 1997. The veto is sure to eventually face a Court test, but until then it remains to be seen if the bill will actually limit pork-barrel spending or if it will drastically change the balance of power between the two branches.

Table 7-11 shows that the use of the rescission process varies sharply from year to year. In 1975 and 1976 President Gerald Ford proposed billions of dollars in rescissions, but Congress actually rescinded less than 10 percent of the amount. During Jimmy Carter's administration, rescissions dropped sharply. Reagan resorted to rescissions to implement his budget policy, however, and 90 percent of the amount he proposed to rescind in fiscal 1981 was approved by Congress. The approval rate and dollar amounts of Reagan's proposed rescissions dropped substantially in later years until fiscal 1986, when Reagan sharply increased his use of rescissions and deferrals. Congress also rescinded several billion dollars in 1986. In the last two years of the Reagan administration, however, the president found that Congress voted down all but 1 percent of his proposed rescissions, and in the last year, he did not propose any. President Bush proposed only seventeen rescissions in his first two years in office, with Congress rescinding less than 1 percent of the funds requested. Bush relied on rescissions to a much greater extent in 1991 and 1992. While he had little success in 1991, in 1992, 26 percent of the nearly $8 billion he proposed to rescind was approved by Congress. In 1993 and 1994 deficit cutting was such a top priority for most members that Congress went far beyond approving President Clinton's proposed rescissions. They initiated seventy-four of their own in 1993 and eighty-one in 1994. Then in 1995 the new Republican Congress forced the president to accept more than $16 billion in FY1995 rescissions.

When a president proposes deferrals, either the House or the Senate can approve an "impoundment resolution" compelling the release of the affected funds. The constitutional status of this procedure was questioned by the June 1983 decision of the Supreme Court that invalidated all legislative vetoes. Because the president now proposes only nonpolicy deferrals, Congress usually disapproves only a small portion of them. In fact, from 1988 through 1994, Congress accepted all of the president's proposed deferrals.

**Table 7-1** House Votes on Adoption of Budget Resolutions, by Party, Fiscal Years 1976–1997

| | | *Total* | | *Democrats* | | *Republicans* | |
|---|---|---|---|---|---|---|---|
| *Fiscal year* | *Resolution* | Yes | No | Yes | No | Yes | No |
| 1976 | First | 200 | 196 | 197 | 68 | 3 | 128 |
| | Second | 225 | 191 | 214 | 67 | 11 | 124 |
| 1977 | First | 221 | 155 | 208 | 44 | 13 | 111 |
| | Second | 227 | 151 | 215 | 38 | 12 | 113 |
| | Third | 239 | 169 | 225 | 50 | 14 | 119 |
| 1978 | First (first round) | 84 | 320 | 82 | 185 | 2 | 135 |
| | First (second round) | 213 | 179 | 206 | 58 | 7 | 121 |
| | Second | 199 | 188 | 195 | 59 | 4 | 129 |
| 1979 | First | 201 | 197 | 198 | 61 | 3 | 136 |
| | Second | 217 | 178 | 215 | 42 | 2 | 136 |
| 1980 | First | 220 | 184 | 211 | 50 | 9 | 134 |
| | Second (first round) | 192 | 213 | 188 | 67 | 4 | 146 |
| | Second (second round) | 212 | 206 | 212 | 52 | 0 | 154 |
| | Third[a] | 241 | 174 | 218 | 45 | 23 | 129 |
| 1981 | First | 225 | 193 | 203 | 62 | 22 | 131 |
| | Second | 203 | 191 | 201 | 45 | 2 | 146 |
| 1982 | First | 270 | 154 | 84 | 153 | 186 | 1 |
| | Second | 206 | 200 | 70 | 150 | 136 | 50 |
| 1983 | First | 219 | 206 | 63 | 174 | 156 | 32 |
| 1984 | First | 229 | 196 | 225 | 36 | 4 | 160 |
| 1985 | First | 250 | 168 | 229 | 29 | 21 | 139 |
| 1986 | First | 258 | 170 | 234 | 15 | 24 | 155 |
| 1987 | First | 245 | 179 | 228 | 19 | 17 | 160 |
| 1988 | First | 215 | 201 | 212 | 34 | 3 | 167 |
| 1989 | First | 319 | 102 | 227 | 24 | 92 | 78 |
| 1990 | First | 263 | 157 | 157 | 96 | 106 | 61 |
| 1991 | First | 218 | 208 | 218 | 34 | 0 | 174 |
| 1992 | First | 239 | 181[b] | 231 | 25 | 8 | 155 |
| 1993 | First | 209 | 207[b] | 209 | 47 | 0 | 159 |
| 1994 | First | 243[b] | 183 | 242 | 11 | 0 | 172 |
| 1995 | First | 223[b] | 175 | 222 | 11 | 0 | 164 |
| 1996 | First | 238 | 194[b] | 8 | 191 | 230 | 1 |
| 1997 | First | 216 | 211[b] | 4 | 191 | 212 | 19 |

*Note:* These votes are on passage of the resolutions in the House, not on adoption of the conference report. Beginning with the 1983 fiscal year, Congress has adopted only one budget resolution each year, rather than the two originally prescribed by the Congressional Budget Act.

[a] The third resolution for fiscal 1980 was part of the first resolution for the 1981 fiscal year, but it was voted on separately in the House.

[b] Total includes Bernard Sanders (I-Vt.).

*Sources: Congressional Record; Congressional Quarterly Almanac* (Washington, D.C.: Congressional Quarterly, various years); *Congressional Quarterly Weekly Report,* May 6, 1989, May 5, 1990, May 25, 1991, May 23, 1992, March 20, 1993, March 19, 1994, May 20, 1995, June 15, 1996.

**Table 7-2** Senate Votes on Adoption of Budget Resolutions, by Party, Fiscal Years 1976–1997

| | | *Total* | | *Democrats* | | *Republicans* | |
|---|---|---|---|---|---|---|---|
| *Fiscal year* | *Resolution* | Yes | No | Yes | No | Yes | No |
| 1976 | First | 69 | 22 | 50 | 4 | 19 | 18 |
| | Second | 69 | 23 | 50 | 8 | 19 | 15 |
| 1977 | First | 62 | 22 | 45 | 6 | 17 | 16 |
| | Second | 55 | 23 | 41 | 5 | 14 | 18 |
| | Third | 72 | 20 | 55 | 3 | 17 | 17 |
| 1978 | First | 56 | 31 | 41 | 14 | 15 | 17 |
| | Second | 63 | 21 | 46 | 8 | 17 | 13 |
| 1979 | First | 64 | 27 | 48 | 8 | 16 | 19 |
| | Second | 56 | 18 | 42 | 6 | 14 | 12 |
| 1980 | First | 64 | 20 | 44 | 5 | 20 | 15 |
| | Second | 62 | 36 | 45 | 14 | 17 | 22 |
| 1981 | First | 68 | 28 | 49 | 6 | 19 | 22 |
| | Second | 48 | 46 | 33 | 21 | 15 | 25 |
| 1982 | First | 78 | 20 | 28 | 18 | 50 | 2 |
| | Second | 49 | 48 | 2 | 44 | 47 | 4 |
| 1983 | First | 49 | 43 | 3 | 41 | 46 | 2 |
| 1984 | First | 50 | 49 | 29 | 17 | 21 | 32 |
| 1985 | First | 41 | 34 | 1 | 31 | 40 | 3 |
| 1986 | First | 50 | 49 | 1 | 45 | 49[a] | 4 |
| 1987 | First | 70 | 25 | 38 | 6 | 32 | 19 |
| 1988 | First | 53 | 46 | 50 | 3 | 3 | 43 |
| 1989 | First | 69 | 26 | 44 | 6 | 25 | 20 |
| 1990 | First | 68 | 31 | 38 | 17 | 30 | 14 |
| 1991 | First[b] | — | — | — | — | — | — |
| 1992 | First | 57 | 41 | 49 | 7 | 8 | 34 |
| 1993 | First | 52 | 41 | 36 | 16 | 16 | 25 |
| 1994 | First | 54 | 45 | 54 | 2 | 0 | 43 |
| 1995 | First | 57 | 40 | 55 | 0 | 2 | 40 |
| 1996 | First | 57 | 42 | 3 | 42 | 54 | 0 |
| 1997 | First | 53 | 46 | 0 | 46 | 53 | 0 |

*Note:* These votes are on passage of the resolutions in the Senate, not on adoption of the conference report. Beginning with the 1983 fiscal year, Congress has adopted only one budget resolution each year, rather than the two originally prescribed by the Congressional Budget Act.

[a] Vice President George Bush cast the deciding vote for the Republicans.
[b] The Senate Budget Resolution (S. Con. Res. 110) was approved by voice vote on June 14, 1990.

*Sources: Congressional Record; Congressional Quarterly Almanac,* various years; *Congressional Quarterly Weekly Report,* May 6, 1989, June 16, 1990, May 25, 1991, May 23, 1992, March 27, 1993, April 2, 1994, May 27, 1995, June 15, 1996.

**Table 7-3** Budgeted and Actual Revenues, Budget Authority, Outlays, and Deficits, Fiscal Years 1976–1997 (billions of dollars)

| | *Revenues* | *Budget authority* | *Budget outlays* | *Budget deficit* |
|---|---|---|---|---|
| 1976 | | | | |
| President's budget | 297.7 | 385.8 | 349.4 | 51.7 |
| First budget resolution | 298.2 | 395.8 | 367.0 | 68.8 |
| Second budget resolution | 300.8 | 408.0 | 374.9 | 74.1 |
| Actual | 300.0 | 415.3 | 366.4 | 66.4 |
| 1977 | | | | |
| President's budget | 351.3 | 433.4 | 394.2 | 42.9 |
| First budget resolution | 362.5 | 454.2 | 413.3 | 50.8 |
| Second budget resolution | 362.5 | 451.6 | 413.1 | 50.6 |
| Third budget resolution | 347.7 | 472.9 | 417.5 | 69.8 |
| Fourth budget resolution | 356.6 | 470.2 | 409.2 | 52.6 |
| Actual | 357.8 | 464.4 | 402.7 | 44.9 |
| 1978 | | | | |
| Ford budget | 393.0 | 480.4 | 440.0 | 47.0 |
| Carter budget | 401.6 | 507.3 | 459.4 | 57.8 |
| First budget resolution | 396.3 | 503.5 | 461.0 | 64.7 |
| Second budget resolution | 397.0 | 500.1 | 458.3 | 61.3 |
| Actual | 402.0 | 500.4 | 450.8 | 48.8 |
| 1979 | | | | |
| President's budget | 439.6 | 568.2 | 500.2 | 60.6 |
| First budget resolution | 447.9 | 568.9 | 498.8 | 50.9 |
| Second budget resolution | 448.7 | 555.7 | 487.5 | 38.8 |
| Third budget resolution | 461.0 | 559.2 | 494.5 | 33.5 |
| Actual | 465.9 | 556.7 | 493.6 | 27.7 |
| 1980 | | | | |
| President's budget | 502.6 | 615.5 | 531.6 | 29.0 |
| First budget resolution | 509.0 | 604.4 | 532.0 | 23.0 |
| Second budget resolution | 517.8 | 638.0 | 547.6 | 29.8 |
| Third budget resolution | 525.7 | 658.9 | 572.7 | 47.0 |
| Actual | 520.0 | 658.8 | 579.6 | 59.6 |
| 1981 | | | | |
| President's budget | 600.0 | 696.1 | 615.8 | 15.8 |
| Revised budget | 628.0 | 691.3 | 611.5 | –16.5 |
| First budget resolution | 613.8 | 697.2 | 613.6 | –0.2 |
| Second budget resolution | 605.0 | 694.6 | 632.4 | 27.4 |
| Third budget resolution | 603.3 | 717.5 | 661.4 | 58.1 |
| Actual | 599.3 | 718.4 | 657.2 | 57.9 |
| 1982 | | | | |
| Carter budget | 711.8 | 809.8 | 739.3 | 27.5 |
| Reagan budget | 650.3 | 772.4 | 695.3 | 45.0 |
| Budget resolution | 657.8 | 770.9 | 695.5 | 37.7 |
| Revised resolution | 628.4 | 777.7 | 734.1 | 105.7 |
| Actual | 617.8 | 779.9 | 728.4 | 110.6 |

*(Table continues)*

**Table 7-3** *(Continued)*

| | *Revenues* | *Budget authority* | *Budget outlays* | *Budget deficit* |
|---|---|---|---|---|
| 1983 | | | | |
| President's budget | 666.1 | 801.9 | 757.6 | 91.5 |
| Budget resolution | 665.9 | 822.4 | 769.8 | 103.9 |
| Actual | 600.6 | 866.7 | 796.0 | 195.4 |
| 1984 | | | | |
| President's budget | 659.7 | 900.1 | 848.5 | 188.8 |
| Budget resolution[a] | 679.6 | 919.5 | 849.5 | 169.9 |
| | | 928.7 | 858.9 | 179.3 |
| Revised resolution | 672.9 | 918.9 | 845.6 | 172.7 |
| Actual | 666.5 | 949.8 | 851.8 | 185.3 |
| 1985 | | | | |
| President's budget | 745.1 | 1,006.5 | 925.5 | 180.4 |
| Budget resolution | 750.9 | 1,021.4 | 932.1 | 181.2 |
| Actual | 734.1 | 1,074.1 | 946.3 | 212.2 |
| 1986 | | | | |
| President's budget | 793.7 | 1,060.0 | 973.7 | 180.0 |
| Budget resolution | 795.7 | 1,069.7 | 967.6 | 171.9 |
| Actual | 769.1 | 1,072.8 | 989.8 | 220.7 |
| 1987 | | | | |
| President's budget | 850.4 | 1,102.0 | 994.0 | 143.6 |
| Budget resolution | 852.4 | 1,093.4 | 995.0 | 142.6 |
| Actual | 854.1 | 1,099.9 | 1,003.8 | 149.7 |
| 1988 | | | | |
| President's budget | 916.6 | 1,142.2 | 1,024.4 | 107.8 |
| Budget resolution | 921.6 | 1,153.2 | 1,055.5 | 133.9 |
| Actual | 909.0 | 1,185.5 | 1,064.0 | 155.0 |
| 1989 | | | | |
| President's budget | 964.7 | 1,222.1 | 1,094.2 | 129.5 |
| Budget resolution | 964.3 | 1,232.0 | 1,098.2 | 133.9 |
| Actual | 990.7 | 1,309.9 | 1,144.1 | 153.4 |
| 1990 | | | | |
| President's budget | 1,059.3 | 1,331.2 | 1,151.8 | 92.5 |
| Budget resolution | 1,065.5 | 1,350.9 | 1,165.3 | 99.8 |
| Actual | 1,031.3 | 1,368.5 | 1,251.7 | 220.4 |
| 1991 | | | | |
| President's budget | 1,170.2 | 1,396.5 | 1,233.3 | 63.1 |
| Budget resolution | 1,172.9 | 1,485.6 | 1,236.9 | 64.0 |
| Actual | 1,054.3 | 1,398.2 | 1,323.0 | 268.7 |
| 1992 | | | | |
| President's budget | 1,172.2 | 1,579.3 | 1,442.2 | 270.0 |
| Budget resolution | 1,169.2 | 1,590.1 | 1,448.0 | 278.8 |
| Actual | 1,091.7 | 1,469.2 | 1,381.9 | 290.2 |

| | *Revenues* | *Budget authority* | *Budget outlays* | *Budget deficit* |
|---|---|---|---|---|
| 1993 | | | | |
| President's budget | 1,171.2 | 1,516.8 | 1,503.0 | 331.8 |
| Budget resolution | 1,173.4 | 1,516.4 | 1,500.0 | 326.6 |
| Actual | 1,153.5 | 1,473.6 | 1,408.7 | 255.1 |
| 1994 | | | | |
| President's budget | 1,242.1 | 1,512.6 | 1,500.6 | 258.5 |
| Budget resolution | 1,241.8 | 1,507.1 | 1,495.6 | 253.8 |
| Actual | 1,257.7 | 1,528.4 | 1,460.9 | 203.2 |
| 1995 | | | | |
| President's budget | 1,353.8 | 1,537.0 | 1,518.9 | 165.1[b] |
| Budget resolution | 1,338.2 | 1,540.7 | 1,513.6 | 175.4 |
| Actual | 1,351.8 | 1,543.3 | 1,515.7 | 163.9 |
| 1996 | | | | |
| President's budget | 1,415.5 | 1,613.8 | 1,612.1 | 196.7 |
| Budget resolution | 1,417.2 | 1,591.7 | 1,587.5 | 170.3 |
| Actual | 1,453.1 | 1,581.1 | 1,560.3 | 107.3 |
| 1997 | | | | |
| President's budget | 1,495.2 | 1,638.4 | 1,635.3 | 140.1 |
| Budget resolution | 1,469.0 | 1,633.0 | 1,622.0 | 153.4 |

[a] Larger figures for authority, outlays, and deficit assumed enactment of programs in a reserve fund.

[b] Assumed enactment of president's health care reforms.

*Sources:* Congressional Budget Office; *The Budget of the United States Government* for fiscal years 1984-1996; *Congressional Quarterly Almanac,* vols. 39-40; *Congressional Quarterly Weekly Report,* 1985-1987, and March 26, 1988; *Congressional Record,* vol. 136, no. 131, October 7, 1990. For 1992, *Congressional Quarterly Weekly Report,* May 25, 1991; for 1993, Congressional Budget Office; for 1994, *Congressional Quarterly Weekly Report,* April 3, 1993; for 1995, *Congressional Quarterly Weekly Report,* May 7, 1994; for 1996, *Congressional Quarterly Weekly Report,* February 11, 1995, May 20, 1995; for 1997, *Congressional Quarterly Weekly Report,* March 23, 1996, *U.S. Budget History* Tables 1.1 and 5.1 FY1998.

**Table 7-4** Relatively Uncontrollable Federal Outlays under Present Law, Fiscal Years 1967–1997 (billions of dollars)

| *Fiscal year* | *Social Security and other retirement* | *Medical care* | *Other payments to individuals* | *Net interest* | *Outlays from prior obligations* | *Other uncon-trollables* | *Total uncon-trollables* | *Percent budget uncontrollable* |
|---|---|---|---|---|---|---|---|---|
| 1967 | 26.3 | 4.6 | 10.7 | 10.3 | 37.0 | 4.7 | 93.5 | 59.1 |
| 1968 | 29.1 | 7.2 | 11.4 | 11.1 | 42.3 | 6.2 | 107.3 | 60.0 |
| 1969 | 33.1 | 8.9 | 12.9 | 12.4 | 41.9 | 6.9 | 116.1 | 63.1 |
| 1970 | 36.9 | 9.9 | 15.4 | 14.4 | 41.5 | 7.6 | 125.7 | 64.0 |
| 1971 | 43.8 | 11.2 | 22.3 | 14.8 | 40.2 | 8.0 | 140.4 | 66.4 |
| 1972 | 49.2 | 13.4 | 25.8 | 15.5 | 39.2 | 10.4 | 153.5 | 66.2 |
| 1973 | 63.6 | 14.1 | 18.3 | 17.3 | 41.4 | 13.9 | 168.6 | 68.7 |
| 1974 | 72.5 | 17.2 | 21.4 | 21.4 | 46.0 | 11.9 | 190.4 | 70.8 |
| 1975 | 86.7 | 21.6 | 34.3 | 23.2 | 53.3 | 9.3 | 228.4 | 70.4 |
| 1976 | 97.2 | 26.3 | 43.5 | 26.7 | 53.7 | 10.1 | 257.5 | 70.7 |
| 1977 | 111.5 | 31.4 | 39.6 | 29.9 | 58.8 | 12.4 | 283.5 | 70.8 |
| 1978 | 122.8 | 35.9 | 36.9 | 35.4 | 76.9 | 15.8 | 323.7 | 72.2 |
| 1979 | 136.7 | 41.6 | 46.5 | 42.6 | 85.3 | 12.0 | 364.7 | 72.3 |
| 1980 | 156.5 | 49.0 | 47.0 | 52.5 | 103.2 | 16.2 | 424.4 | 73.6 |
| 1981 | 183.7 | 59.3 | 51.5 | 68.7 | 108.6 | 13.2 | 485.0 | 73.8 |
| 1982 | 201.8 | 65.6 | 53.2 | 85.0 | 121.5 | 15.1 | 542.1 | 74.4 |
| 1983 | 219.1 | 73.5 | 61.2 | 89.8 | 128.7 | 21.3 | 593.6 | 74.6 |
| 1984 | 228.3 | 79.9 | 49.2 | 111.1 | 145.3 | 10.3 | 624.1 | 73.3 |
| 1985 | 238.2 | 91.0 | 49.7 | 129.4 | 162.2 | 17.3 | 689.5 | 72.9 |
| 1986 | 252.8 | 97.8 | 52.0 | 136.0 | 181.3 | 25.5 | 745.4 | 76.2 |
| 1987 | 263.8 | 105.6 | 52.1 | 138.6 | 185.2 | 23.8 | 769.1 | 76.6 |
| 1988 | 279.6 | 114.7 | 53.7 | 151.7 | 186.8 | 20.9 | 807.4 | 76.5 |
| 1989 | 285.9 | 133.4 | 52.3 | 169.1 | 210.4 | 16.9 | 868.0 | 75.9 |
| 1990 | 304.8 | 155.8 | 57.4 | 184.2 | 231.6 | 12.0 | 945.8 | 75.6 |

| | | | | | | | | |
|---|---|---|---|---|---|---|---|---|
| 1991 | 329.2 | 175.7 | 69.9 | 194.5 | 233.8 | 15.2 | 1,018.3 | 77.0 |
| 1992 | 349.7 | 208.5 | 84.7 | 199.4 | 233.8 | 15.2 | 1,091.3 | 79.0 |
| 1993 | 368.8 | 230.0 | 87.8 | 198.8 | 236.7 | 20.4 | 1,142.5 | 81.1 |
| 1994 | 386.6 | 251.9 | 75.0 | 203.0 | 228.2 | 15.1 | 1,159.8 | 79.4 |
| 1995 | 405.7 | 275.3 | 77.9 | 232.2 | 233.2 | 9.8 | 1,234.1 | 81.2 |
| 1996 | 418.1 | 293.6 | 76.9 | 241.1 | 227.9 | 9.2 | 1,266.8 | 81.2 |
| 1997 (est.) | 439.2 | 321.9 | 76.4 | 247.4 | 225.7 | 10.2 | 1,320.8 | 81.0 |

*Note:* From time to time the Office of Management and Budget reclassifies or redefines uncontrollables; hence the figures in this table may not be consistent with those published in some budget documents.

*Sources:* For the 1967–1972 fiscal years, *The Budget of the United States Government Fiscal Year 1977,* table 16; for the 1973–1981 fiscal years, *The Budget of the United States Government Fiscal Year 1983;* for the 1982–1983 fiscal years, *The Budget of the United States Government Fiscal Year 1985,* table 20; for the 1984–1985 fiscal years, *The Budget of the United States Government Fiscal Year 1986,* table 18; for the 1986 fiscal year, *The Budget of the United States Government Fiscal Year 1987,* table 16; for the 1987 fiscal year, *The Budget of the United States Government Fiscal Year 1989,* table 16; for the 1988 and 1989 fiscal years, *The Budget of the United States Government Fiscal Year 1990,* table 14; for fiscal years 1990–1991, *The Budget of the United States Government Fiscal Year 1992,* tables 1-1 and 1-2; for fiscal years 1992–1993, *The Budget of the United States Government Fiscal Year 1994,* Appendix; for fiscal years 1994–1995, *The Budget of the United States Government,* Analytical Perspectives, table 6-2. For FY 1996–1997, *Budget of the United States Government* budget table 31-2 and historical table 3-2.

**Table 7-5** President's Budget Requests and Congressional Appropriations, 1968–1996 (thousands of dollars)

| *Year* | *Budget requests* | *Appropriations* | *Appropriations compared with requests* |
|---|---|---|---|
| 1968 | 147,908,613 | 133,339,869 | –14,568,744 |
| 1969 | 142,701,346 | 134,431,463 | –8,269,883 |
| 1970 | 147,765,358 | 144,273,529 | –3,491,830 |
| 1971 | 167,874,625 | 165,225,662 | –2,648,963 |
| 1972 | 185,431,805 | 178,960,107 | –6,471,698 |
| 1973 | 177,959,504 | 174,901,434 | –3,058,070 |
| 1974 | 213,667,190 | 204,012,312 | –9,654,878 |
| 1975 | 267,224,774 | 259,852,322 | –7,372,452 |
| 1976 | 282,142,432 | 282,536,695 | 394,263 |
| 1977 | 364,867,240 | 354,025,781 | –10,841,459 |
| 1978 | 348,506,125 | 337,859,467 | –10,646,658 |
| 1979 | 397,653,766 | 386,822,093 | –10,831,673 |
| 1980 | 340,339,447 | 333,695,164 | –6,644,283 |
| 1981 | 440,398,235 | 442,215,128 | 1,816,893 |
| 1982 | 507,740,133 | 514,832,375 | 7,092,242 |
| 1983 | 542,956,652 | 551,620,505 | 8,663,853 |
| 1984 | 576,343,258 | 559,151,835 | –17,191,422 |
| 1985 | 588,698,503 | 583,446,885 | –5,251,618 |
| 1986 | 590,345,199 | 577,279,102 | –13,066,097 |
| 1987 | 595,071,473 | 584,399,770 | –10,671,703 |
| 1988 | 607,213,694 | 606,443,182[a] | –770,511 |
| 1989 | 652,138,432 | 666,211,681 | 14,073,249 |
| 1990 | 704,510,962 | 697,257,740 | –7,253,222 |
| 1991[b] | 720,178,246 | 712,696,380 | –7,481,866 |
| 1992[b/c] | 736,231,270 | 715,697,705 | –20,533,566 |
| 1993 | 798,046,000 | 782,150,000 | –15,896,000 |
| 1994 | 782,753,000 | 779,375,000 | –3,378,000 |
| 1995 | 804,207,430 | 761,097,096 | –43,110,334 |
| 1996 | 801,214,439 | 793,403,352 | –7,811,087 |

*Note:* The years are calendar, not fiscal, years. The amounts shown are for budget authority provided in appropriations acts and do not include permanent appropriations or budget authority provided in legislative acts.

[a] Includes defense rescission of –3,531,030.
[b] Excludes Desert Shield/Desert Storm contributed funds.
[c] Includes rescission of Desert Shield/Desert Storm funds.

*Source:* House Committee on Appropriations.

**Table 7-6** Supplemental Appropriations, Fiscal Years 1964–1996

| *Fiscal year* | *Number of supplemental bills*[a] | *Amount of budget authority*[b] *(millions of dollars)* |
|---|---|---|
| 1964 | 1 | 290 |
| 1965 | 4 | 5,645 |
| 1966 | 4 | 21,889 |
| 1967 | 3 | 19,420 |
| 1968 | 5 | 8,218 |
| 1969 | 4 | 5,835 |
| 1970 | 2 | 5,993 |
| 1971 | 4 | 9,870 |
| 1972 | 7 | 11,599 |
| 1973 | 5 | 11,371 |
| 1974 | 5 | 14,796 |
| 1975 | 7 | 27,587 |
| 1976 | 5 | 24,636 |
| 1977 | 5 | 49,835 |
| 1978 | 9 | 16,053 |
| 1979 | 1 | 13,845 |
| 1980 | 6 | 19,683 |
| 1981 | 2 | 20,960 |
| 1982 | 4 | 27,442 |
| 1983 | 2 | 22,655 |
| 1984 | 4 | 16,307 |
| 1985 | 3 | 14,804 |
| 1986 | 3 | 8,191 |
| 1987 | 1 | 9,400 |
| 1988 | 1 | 672 |
| 1989 | 1 | 3,294 |
| 1990 | 1 | 4,344 |
| 1991 | 3 | 48,639 |
| 1992 | 2 | 9,786 |
| 1993 | 5 | 11,957 |
| 1994 | 2 | 9,291 |
| 1995 | 0 | –[c] |
| 1996 | 1[d] | 2,125 |

[a] The number of supplemental bills does not include regular and continuing appropriations in which supplemental budget authority was provided.
[b] The amount of budget authority does include, for fiscal year 1976 and subsequent years, supplementals provided in regular or continuing appropriation bills. The figure represents supplemental spending after accounting for offsetting cuts.
[c] All 1995 supplemental spending was offset.
[d] The supplementals fell under ten regular appropriations bills but were lumped into the omnibus FY96 appropriation bill (HR 3019).

*Sources:* For the 1964–1969 fiscal years, Louis Fisher, "Supplemental Appropriations History, Controls, Recent Record," Congressional Research Service, Library of Congress, Washington, D.C., April 12, 1979; for the 1970–1980 fiscal years, Congressional Budget Office, *Supplemental Appropriations in the 1970s,* Staff Working Paper, July 1981; for the 1981–1983 and 1987-1988 fiscal years, *Congressional Quarterly Almanac;* for the 1984–1988 fiscal years, House Committee on Appropriations; for 1989–1994, *Congressional Quarterly Weekly Report,* June 30, 1989, November 3, 1990, December 7, 1991, November 5, 1994; for 1992–1994, House Committee on Appropriations; for 1995, *Congressional Quarterly Almanac;* for 1996, *Congressional Quarterly Weekly Report,* May 25, 1996, 1488.

**Table 7-7** House Amendments to Appropriation Bills, 1963–1982

| *Year* | *Total amendments* | *Amendments adopted* | *Limitation amendments*[a] | *Limitation amendments adopted* |
|---|---|---|---|---|
| 1963 | 47 | 15 | 17 | 7 |
| 1964 | 27 | 9 | 11 | 2 |
| 1965 | 26 | 9 | 11 | 1 |
| 1966 | 56 | 10 | 8 | 1 |
| 1967 | 70 | 15 | 16 | 4 |
| 1968 | 75 | 24 | 20 | 7 |
| 1969 | 89 | 27 | 20 | 10 |
| 1970 | 51 | 11 | 13 | 1 |
| 1971 | 83 | 34 | 23 | 7 |
| 1972 | 89 | 15 | 26 | 5 |
| 1973 | 99 | 31 | 31 | 12 |
| 1974 | 109 | 53 | 34 | 15 |
| 1975 | 106 | 52 | 34 | 12 |
| 1976 | 122 | 68 | 33 | 13 |
| 1977 | 107 | 54 | 44 | 24 |
| 1978 | 135 | 61 | 44 | 25 |
| 1979 | 165 | 74 | 52 | 31 |
| 1980 | 168 | 100 | 74 | 57 |
| 1981 | 143 | 87 | 47 | 33 |
| 1982 | 59 | 33 | 21 | 14 |

*Note:* The years are calendar, not fiscal, years. No new data available after 1982.

[a] Limitation amendments are amendments that bar the use of appropriated funds for specified purposes.

*Sources:* For 1963–1977, Democratic Study Group, Special Report No. 95-12 (Washington, D.C., February 14, 1978); for 1978–1982, Richard S. Beth, Daniel P. Strickland, and Stanley Bach, "Limitation and Other House Amendments to General Appropriation Bills: Fiscal Years 1979–1983," Congressional Research Service, Library of Congress, Washington, D.C., December 28, 1982. The two sources may not be completely consistent in their scope and definition of amendments.

**Table 7-8** Continuing Appropriations, Fiscal Years 1972–1997

| *Fiscal year* | *Regular appropriation bills not enacted by start of fiscal year*[a] | *Continuing resolutions enacted for fiscal year* |
|---|---|---|
| 1972 | 5 | 5 |
| 1973 | 4 | 5 |
| 1974 | 10 | 2 |
| 1975 | 6 | 4 |
| 1976 | 11 | 3 |
| 1977[b] | 0[c] | 2 |
| 1978 | 4 | 3 |
| 1979 | 8 | 1 |
| 1980 | 10 | 2 |
| 1981 | 12 | 2 |
| 1982 | 13 | 5 |
| 1983 | 12 | 2 |
| 1984 | 9 | 4 |
| 1985 | 9 | 4 |
| 1986 | 13 | 5 |
| 1987 | 13 | 1 |
| 1988 | 13 | 5 |
| 1989 | 0[d] | 0 |
| 1990 | 13 | 3 |
| 1991 | 13 | 5 |
| 1992 | 10 | 3 |
| 1993 | 12 | 1 |
| 1994 | 11 | 3 |
| 1995 | 0 | 0 |
| 1996 | 11 | 14 |
| 1997 | 0 | 0 |

[a] In calendar year 1976, the start of the fiscal year was changed from July 1 to October 1.
[b] Although all regular appropriation bills were enacted by the start of the fiscal year, continuing appropriations were needed for certain items not provided for in these bills.
[c] The appropriation was signed into law on the first day of the fiscal year.
[d] Congress cleared and sent all bills to the president by the beginning of the fiscal year, but not all bills were signed until the following day.

*Sources:* Robert A. Keith, "An Overview of the Use of Continuing Appropriations," Congressional Research Service, Library of Congress, Washington, D.C., September 26, 1980; Congressional Budget Office, "Consideration of Appropriation Bills," unpublished memorandum, August 21, 1979; data for the 1980–1989 fiscal years are taken from the House calendars; for 1990–1997, *Congressional Quarterly Weekly Report,* November 20, 1989, November 3, 1990, November 16, 1991, October 31, 1992, December 11, 1993, November 5, 1994, April 27, 1996; October 5, 1996.

**Table 7-9** Budget-related Roll Call Votes in the House, Selected Years, 1955–1996

| *Measure* | *1955* | *1960* | *1965* | *1970* | *1975* | *1980* | *1981* | *1983* |
|---|---|---|---|---|---|---|---|---|
| Authorizations | 27 | 28 | 78 | 77 | 147 | 105 | 70 | 129 |
| Appropriations | 6 | 16 | 21 | 39 | 94 | 111 | 85 | 112 |
| Tax legislation | 3 | 3 | 3 | 1 | 48 | 14 | 7 | 9 |
| Budget resolutions | — | — | — | — | 12 | 30 | 13 | 4 |
| Reconciliation bills | — | — | — | — | — | 6 | 12 | 2 |
| Debt ceilings | 1 | 2 | 2 | 2 | 11 | 7 | 2 | 3 |
| Miscellaneous | 0 | 1 | 0 | 2 | 8 | 4 | 7 | 3 |
| Total budget-related roll calls | 37 | 50 | 104 | 121 | 320 | 277 | 196 | 262 |
| Total roll calls | 76 | 93 | 201 | 266 | 612 | 604 | 353 | 498 |
| Percentage budget-related | 49 | 54 | 52 | 45 | 52 | 46 | 56 | 53 |

*Sources:* For 1955–1982, Allen Schick, "Legislation, Appropriations, and Budgets: The Development of Spending Decision-Making in Congress," Congressional Research Service, Library of Congress, Washington, D.C., 1984; for 1983-1986, House Appropriations Committee; for 1987-1996, based on Congressional Quarterly roll call vote index.

| *1985* | *1987* | *1989* | *1990* | *1991* | *1992* | *1993* | *1994* | *1995* | *1996* |
|---|---|---|---|---|---|---|---|---|---|
| 95 | 118 | 68 | 116 | 83 | 38 | 94 | 94 | 57 | 40 |
| 82 | 86 | 95 | 110 | 101 | 129 | 176 | 121 | 294 | 146 |
| 11 | 0 | 0 | 0 | 11 | 21 | 6 | 6 | 20 | 18 |
| 10 | 8 | 7 | 8 | 9 | 10 | 8 | 9 | 23 | 8 |
| 10 | 6 | 14 | 5 | 0 | 0 | 9 | 0 | 9 | 8 |
| 11 | 7 | 3 | 6 | 0 | 0 | 0 | 1 | 13 | 10 |
| 1 | 2 | 0 | 8 | 4 | 16 | 12 | 34 | 65 | 11 |
| | | | | | | | | | |
| 220 | 227 | 187 | 253 | 208 | 214 | 305 | 265 | 481 | 241 |
| 439 | 488 | 359 | 497 | 414 | 459 | 513 | 500 | 885 | 455 |
| | | | | | | | | | |
| 50 | 46 | 52 | 51 | 50 | 47 | 59 | 53 | 54 | 53 |

**Table 7-10** Budget-related Roll Call Votes in the Senate, Selected Years, 1955–1996

| *Measure* | *1955* | *1960* | *1965* | *1970* | *1975* | *1980* | *1981* | *1983* |
|---|---|---|---|---|---|---|---|---|
| Authorizations | 22 | 48 | 87 | 83 | 96 | 82 | 55 | 58 |
| Appropriations | 12 | 28 | 27 | 77 | 87 | 128 | 130 | 107 |
| Tax legislation | 2 | 10 | 10 | 6 | 48 | 10 | 56 | 13 |
| Budget resolutions | — | — | — | — | 8 | 50 | 26 | 34 |
| Reconciliation bills | — | — | — | — | — | 4 | 63 | 2 |
| Debt ceilings | 0 | 2 | 1 | 3 | 3 | 6 | 12 | 15 |
| Miscellaneous | 1 | 0 | 0 | 1 | 4 | 3 | 2 | 9 |
| Total budget-related roll calls | 37 | 88 | 125 | 170 | 246 | 283 | 344 | 238 |
| Total roll calls | 87 | 207 | 258 | 418 | 602 | 531 | 483 | 381 |
| Percentage budget-related | 42 | 42 | 48 | 41 | 41 | 53 | 71 | 62 |

[a] 597 is the total number of roll call votes listed in the *Congressional Quarterly Weekly Report* index. It does not accord with "yeas" and "nays" according to *Congressional Record* and Congressional Quarterly's final vote number. That number was 613.

*Sources:* For 1955–1982, Schick, "Legislation, Appropriations, and Budgets"; for 1983-1986, Senate Appropriations Committee; for 1987–1996, based on Congressional Quarterly roll call vote index.

| *1985* | *1987* | *1989* | *1990* | *1991* | *1992* | *1993* | *1994* | *1995* | *1996* |
|---|---|---|---|---|---|---|---|---|---|
| 67 | 84 | 42 | 81 | 73 | 20 | 27 | 68 | 38 | 33 |
| 59 | 66 | 75 | 58 | 66 | 64 | 114 | 108 | 113 | 80 |
| 7 | 0 | 5 | 0 | 5 | 41 | 27 | 3 | 27 | 10 |
| 39 | 17 | 8 | 1 | 12 | 14 | 46 | 15 | 56 | 42 |
| 23 | 8 | 2 | 6 | 0 | 0 | 6 | 0 | 48 | 31 |
| 29 | 17 | 0 | 1 | 0 | 0 | 0 | 0 | 4 | 2 |
| 6 | 3 | 6 | 10 | 3 | 9 | 16 | 9 | 58 | 15 |
| 230 | 195 | 138 | 157 | 159 | 148 | 236 | 203 | 344 | 213 |
| 381 | 420 | 302 | 337 | 287 | 267 | 383 | 330 | 597[a] | 308 |
| 60 | 46 | 46 | 46 | 55 | 55 | 62 | 62 | 58 | 69 |

**Table 7-11** Rescissions, Fiscal Years 1975–1996

| *Fiscal year* | *Number of rescissions* | *Amount proposed ($ thousands)* | *Amount approved ($ thousands)* | *Amount rescinded (percent)* | *Proposals approved, wholly or in part (percent)* |
|---|---|---|---|---|---|
| 1975 | 91 | 3,328,500 | 391,295 | 12 | 43 |
| 1976[a] | 50 | 3,608,363 | 138,331 | 4 | 14 |
| 1977 | 21 | 1,835,602 | 1,271,040 | 69 | 48 |
| 1978 | 8 | 644,055 | 55,255 | 9 | 38 |
| 1979 | 11 | 908,692 | 723,609 | 80 | 80 |
| 1980 | 59 | 1,618,061 | 778,127 | 48 | 58 |
| 1981 | 208 | 16,204,936 | 14,509,878 | 90 | 67 |
| 1982 | 34 | 9,484,941 | 5,974,966 | 63 | 21 |
| 1983 | 21 | 1,569,015 | 0 | 0 | 0 |
| 1985 | 244 | 1,855,000 | 212,000 | 11 | 39 |
| 1986 | 83 | 10,121,548 | 18,876,367[b] | 188[b] | — |
| 1987 | 73 | 5,835,800 | 36,090 | 1 | 3 |
| 1988 | 0 | 0 | 0 | — | — |
| 1989 | 6 | 143,096 | 2,053 | 1 | 17 |
| 1990 | 11 | 554,258 | 0 | 0 | 0 |
| 1991 | 30 | 4,859,300 | 0 | 0 | 0 |
| 1992 | 128 | 7,879,500 | 2,066,900 | 26 | 20 |
| 1993 | 7 | 356,000 | 2,411,587[b] | 677 | — |
| 1994 | 65 | 3,172,180 | 3,667,895[b] | 116 | — |
| 1995 | 25 | 1,199,824 | 19,713,689 | 1,643 | — |
| 1996 | 16 | 963,500 | 4,170,246 | 433 | — |

[a] Fiscal 1976 data include the transition quarter. A proposal to rescind or defer funds in both fiscal 1976 and the transition quarter counted as a single proposal.
[b] Some approved amounts are higher than proposals because Congress added its own rescissions.

*Source:* House Appropriations Committee; Senate Budget Committee.

**Table 7-12** Deferrals, Fiscal Years 1975–1996

| *Fiscal year* | *Number of deferrals* | *Amount proposed ($ thousands)* | *Amount disapproved ($ thousands)* | *Number of deferrals disapproved* | *Amount disapproved (percent)* | *Deferrals disapproved (percent)* |
|---|---|---|---|---|---|---|
| 1975 | 159 | 24,574,236 | 9,318,217 | 16 | 38 | 10 |
| 1976[a] | 119 | 9,209,780 | 393,081 | 24[b] | 4 | 20 |
| 1977 | 68 | 6,831,194 | 25,600 | 3 | 0.4 | 4 |
| 1978 | 66 | 4,910,114 | 69,531 | 6 | 1 | 9 |
| 1979 | 70 | 4,696,056 | 13,852 | 2 | 0.3 | 3 |
| 1980 | 73 | 9,846,235 | 3,663,448 | 2 | 37 | 3 |
| 1981 | 131 | 7,535,493 | 367,359 | 15 | 5 | 12 |
| 1982 | 267 | 7,562,078 | 386,347 | 15 | 5 | 6 |
| 1983 | 87 | 9,957,186 | 4,119,590 | 16 | 41 | 19 |
| 1985 | 78 | 8,476,000 | 0 | 0 | 0 | 0 |
| 1986 | 70 | 24,767,151 | 2,828,276 | [c] | 11.4 | [c] |
| 1987 | 57 | 11,494,600 | 174,300 | [c] | 1.5 | [c] |
| 1988 | 22 | 9,320,100 | 0 | 0 | 0 | 0 |
| 1989 | 14 | 9,156,174 | 0 | 0 | 0 | 0 |
| 1990 | 28 | 11,071,540 | 0 | 0 | 0 | 0 |
| 1991 | 11 | 10,347,800 | 0 | 0 | 0 | 0 |
| 1992 | 12 | 5,791,800 | 0 | 0 | 0 | 0 |
| 1993 | 12 | 2,921,080 | 0 | 0 | 0 | 0 |
| 1994 | 12 | 7,334,903 | 0 | 0 | 0 | 0 |
| 1995 | 7 | 3,525,000 | 0 | 0 | 0 | 0 |
| 1996 | 6 | 3,700,000 | 0 | 0 | 0 | 0 |

[a] Fiscal 1976 data include the transition quarter. A proposal to rescind or defer funds in both fiscal 1976 and the transition quarter counted as a single proposal.
[b] Two fiscal 1976 deferrals that were disapproved by both the House and the Senate are counted here once each.
[c] Figures cannot be listed because in many cases Congress deferred only partial amounts.

*Sources:* House Appropriations Committee; Senate Budget Committee.

# 8

# Voting Alignments

Three important patterns to track regarding voting on the floor of the House and the Senate are support for the president, the cohesion of the parties, and the strength of the ideological coalitions that cut across party lines. This chapter provides a description of the dynamics of these forces in congressional decision making since the 1950s, using the measures compiled annually by Congressional Quarterly.

## Presidential Success and Support

Table 8-1 shows the annual percentages of presidential victories on votes on which the president took clear-cut positions. Congressional Quarterly determines what the president wants in the way of legislative action by analyzing his messages to Congress, press conference remarks, and other public statements and documents. The measure combines the significant and the trivial, the controversial and the consensual; moreover, it reflects the position of the president at the time of a vote, even though that position may reflect a major concession from an earlier stand.

Despite these limitations, the measure does give a rough indication of the state of relations between the president and Congress. Table 8-1 provides an overall success score, as well as the president's success averages in the House and Senate. Presidential success is mainly a function of the number of seats in Congress held by the president's party. When one party controls both branches, success never drops below 75 percent; with divided government, presidents average well below that level of success.

With the Democrats in control of the House, Senate, and presidency during Bill Clinton's first two years in office, presidential success scores reached 86.4 percent, the highest level since Lyndon Johnson's Great Society. In 1993 the president and the Democratic Congress achieved many genuine legislative victories. But in 1994 the high rate of success can largely be attributed to the fact that most of the president's controversial legislation became so stymied that it never reached a vote. The second Congress of Clinton's presidency was not nearly as supportive. In 1995, amid budget and policy battles, the House and Senate supported the president only 36 percent of the time, the lowest score ever. This fits with the pattern of previous presidencies. President Eisenhower's score dropped twenty-four percentage points after the Democratic victory in the 1958 elections. President Johnson achieved a modern high of 93 percent in the session following the 1964 elections. And, after his smashing victory in 1980, President Reagan enjoyed a level of support seven percentage points higher than that of his predecessor's first year in office. But Reagan's support plummeted in the Senate after the Democrats regained control in the 1986 elections. For President Clinton, the pattern shifted again in the second half of the 104th Congress. Although still low compared with previous years, there was nearly double the support of 1995. Some of that can be attributed to avoiding votes on the difficult issues and waiting for an election to resolve them; and a resolve by Congress to go into the election looking cooperative, not confrontational.

Over the course of his four years in office, George Bush won an average of 51.6 of the roll call votes on which he took a stand. This marked the lowest score of any first term president since Congressional Quarterly began keeping track in 1953. Bush's score reached a low point in 1992 when he lost the support of many Senate Republicans and could claim victory on only 43 percent of the votes where he held a clear position. Although higher, the scores of many of Bush's predecessors similarly reflect the struggle that often accompanies divided government (Ronald Reagan, 61.9 percent; Gerald Ford, 57.6 percent; Richard Nixon, 67.2 percent; Dwight D. Eisenhower after 1954, 67.7 percent). The anomaly is 1981, when the Republicans controlled the presidency and the Senate but not the House. Ronald Reagan's overall success score of 82.3 percent in 1981 ranks with presidents whose party has controlled both houses; his score in the Senate places him alongside Eisenhower in 1953 and Lyndon Johnson in 1964. After that initial year, however, Reagan's overall success dropped sharply, due almost entirely to the collapse of his support in the Democrat-controlled House.

Success rates usually deteriorate over the course of a presidency (Johnson, Nixon, Reagan, and Bush), but at times they remain relatively stable (Carter) or even increase (Kennedy). It should be noted that presidential success cannot be measured by the outcome of roll call votes alone. These do not account for the many other ways in which a president can influence the legislative process. For example, on numerous occasions President Bush effectively used the veto and the threat of vetoes to affect legislative outcomes. Clinton, who did not use the veto once during his first two years, subsequently wielded it skillfully in his battles with the Republicans.

The base for computing presidential scores varies widely, from a low of 34 House votes in 1953 and 1956 to a high of 185 Senate votes in 1973. The average number of votes on which presidents have taken clear-cut positions has increased over time, but the percentage has declined. In 1979 President Carter made his position known on only 22 percent of all House recorded votes and 19 percent of Senate votes. The comparable figures for President Eisenhower's third year are 56 percent in the House and 59 percent in the Senate. The congressional liaison workload of the White House has increased, but so too has the relative independence of Congress.

Table 8-2 presents presidential support scores (adjusted to remove the effects of absences) for all Democrats, southern Democrats, and Republicans in the House and Senate. Senate Republicans have usually been more supportive of presidents, Republican and Democratic, than their House counterparts. No such consistent pattern is evident among Democrats. Whereas Democrats in the Senate were more supportive of Carter than their party colleagues in the House, the pattern was just the opposite under Presidents Kennedy and Johnson. The voting of southern Democrats is at least partly responsible for this change. Among southern Democratic members, President Kennedy fared better in the House than in the Senate, but President Carter received more support among these members in the Senate.

The sharpest trend in Table 8-2 is the decline in support for Republican presidents among southern Democrats, particularly in the House. The steady decline in success by President Reagan after 1981 mirrors the collapse in support for his proposals by House Democrats south of the Mason-Dixon line. While Bush regained some support among southern Democrats in both houses during his first year in office, that support eroded over time, and, in fact, reached a low point in the Senate in 1992. In 1993 Clinton received the highest support score recorded among southern Democrats in the House and Senate, in part because of his own southern roots and in part because of the changing character of the southern Democrats. But the House score dropped almost fifteen percentage points in 1994, foreshadowing the Republican takeover of that region. Clinton's scores among Republicans were lower than for most Democratic presidents. The high scores in 1994 were artificial because many items did not come to a vote. Clinton's scores with Republicans are better reflected in the last two years of his first term when the Republicans supported him only 22 percent of the time in the House and only 29 percent in the Senate in 1995. Facing an election they agreed to compromises that slightly raised his scores in 1996.

## Party Unity

One important component of the structure of congressional voting is party-line voting. Table 8-3 presents for both the House and the Senate the percentage of all recorded votes on which a majority of voting Democrats opposed a majority of voting Republicans. In the House the trend in that measure had been downward beginning with Johnson's troubles with the war in Vietnam. Under Presidents Nixon and Ford, about 35 percent of all roll call votes produced a party split, down from an average of nearly 50 percent under President Eisenhower. The number rose to 40 percent during Carter's four years in office and then dropped back to 37 percent in Reagan's first year. By 1983, however, voting in the House had taken on a distinctively partisan cast. Four years later the percentage of party votes in the House reached its highest point in the postwar period, at 64 percent. After declining slightly over the next few years, party unity votes again reached that postwar high in 1992, and continued to rise in 1993 to 65 percent in the House (67 percent in the Senate) as the first Democratic White House and Congress in twelve years worked to advance several measures along partisan lines. Party unity scores then dropped in 1994, falsely giving the picture of a less partisan Congress. Actually, Congress was so split along party lines that many bills never made it to a House vote. The partisanship carried over into the Republican-controlled 104th Congress and may be part of a longer trend.

There also appears to be an election year cycle in these figures, especially in recent years. The percentage of party votes increases in off years and declines in subsequent election years. This may reflect the efforts of congressional leaders during election years to avoid sharply partisan votes that may hurt members back home, or an effort by members to put party interests aside and vote with their constituents' interests in mind.

The Senate figures on party voting in Table 8-3 are less patterned than the House figures. The percentage of party votes grew under Carter and Reagan, reached new highs in 1990 under Bush, and skyrocketed to 67 and then 69 percent—the highest percentages of any recent president—under Clinton.

Table 8-4 presents other information needed to gauge the level of party voting: the cohesion of the parties on those votes that elicit a party split. Party unity among Democrats declined after the Kennedy and the early Johnson years, more so in the House (about ten percentage points) than in the Senate (about five percentage points). A decline in party unity also was registered among Republicans during this period, although in the House they appear to have turned the corner by the late 1970s and in the Senate they rebounded in 1981 to a high of 85 percent. Party unity among House Democrats also increased after the election of Ronald Reagan, and Democratic cohesion in both the House and the Senate reached postwar highs during the last two years of his presidency. Cohesion among Democrats remained fairly consistent during the Bush presidency, while Republican unity increased steadily. Since 1992, GOP unity scores in both houses have been over 80 percent reaching peaks of 89 percent in the Senate and 91 percent in the House in 1996 and 1995 respectively.

However important the decline in party voting during the 1960s and 1970s or the post-1980 resurgence, it pales in significance when compared with the long-term decline in party voting. During the years 1890–1910, two-thirds of all votes evoked a party split, and in several sessions more than half the roll calls found 90 percent of one party opposing 90 percent of the other. Since 1946 the percentage of votes showing such extreme partisan division has not gone above 10 percent.

## Conservative Coalition

One reason for the decline in cohesion among the Democrats was the emergence in the late 1930s of a set of issues that brought together southern Democrats and Republicans and pitted them against northern Democrats. Since that time this "conservative coalition" has proved itself a formidable opponent to Democratic presidents.

Table 8-5 shows the percentage of all recorded votes in which the coalition has appeared (a majority of voting southern Democrats and a majority of voting Republicans oppose the stand taken by a majority of voting northern Democrats). It also shows the percentage of those votes won by the coalition.

Over the past several decades the conservative coalition appeared more often in the Senate than in the House, although its record of success was no greater in the Senate (with the important exception of the Reagan era of split-party control of Congress). Its percentage of success reached an all-time low in the House during the Eighty-ninth Congress, after the 1964 Democratic landslide, and a modern-day high in 1981, rivaling its record in the 1940s and 1950s.[1] But much more significant is the virtual disappearance of the conservative coalition during the last two years of the Reagan presidency. This trend has continued into the 1990s, with a coalition appearing on no more than 14 percent of roll call votes in either house since 1987. As one political scientist put it, "The conservative coalition as a working political force is really a statistical artifact."[2] While the percentage of conservative coalition votes dropped to its lowest level in 1993 and 1994, its success rate reached 98 percent and then 100 percent in the House in the 104th Congress.

The coalition's success after the 1980 elections was due both to the increase in the number of Republicans in both chambers and to the increasingly conservative cast of Senate Republicans. Conservative coalition support scores (adjusted for absences) for northern Democrats, southern Democrats, and Republicans are presented in Table 8-6. In the House there was a steady increase in the degree of support for the coalition among northern Democrats beginning in the early 1970s and running through 1981. That support waned somewhat during the 1980s, but was back above 30 percent by the end of 1992, and reached its highest level of 39 percent in 1994. Among northern Democrats in the Senate, support has remained fairly constant since the late 1970s. (By definition, the conservative coalition support among northern Democrats overall cannot exceed 50 percent.) Among southern Democrats in both houses, support declined after the late 1960s and early 1970s, although 1981 and 1982 saw a temporary increase in support.

Conservative coalition support scores are perhaps most useful for gauging how ideologically representative smaller groups of members are of their party and of the entire chamber. Tables 8-7 and 8-8 present the mean conservative coalition support scores for House and Senate committees between 1959 and 1995. Scores are presented for all committee members as well as for Democratic and Republican members separately. Overall scores reflecting the average conservative coalition support among all members in the chamber and in each party caucus provide a view of the relative conservatism of each committee. The absolute scores are less reliable than the relative standing of the committees and their parent chamber over time.

The ideological makeup of some committees changed dramatically even before there was a shift in party control. In the House, the District of Columbia Committee, one of the most conservative committees in 1959, became one of the most liberal (with only a 6 percent support score among Democrats on the committee in 1991). Not surprisingly, it was among the first committees to be eliminated by the Republicans when they took control after the 1994 elections. (Its duties have been folded into the new Government Reform and Oversight Committee.) A similar though less dramatic change occurred in the Ways and Means and Energy and Commerce committees, while Education and Labor grew more conservative. Other committees did not transform their philosophical base but moved further toward the ideological poles. Armed Services, always conservative, became the most conservative committee in the House. There have been dramatic changes in the ideological makeup of House committees in 1995, due to the Republican takeover and their reforms in committee sizes and jurisdiction. Virtually all committees shifted in a conservative direction, especially the Rules and Appropriations committees.

Similar patterns can be discerned for Senate committees in Table 8-8, at least before the 1980 elections. Between 1959 and 1979 the Finance and the Appropriations committees moved from right to center, Energy and Public Works from left to center. Armed Services and Agriculture remained more conservative than the Senate; Foreign Relations and Labor continued to be more liberal. In 1981, after the infusion of conservative Republicans from the 1980 election, the Senate shifted distinctively to the right, upsetting many patterns of behavior, including those of its committees. Every committee shifted in a conservative direction.

In 1981 nine Senate committees were still more liberal than the average, but two-thirds of these were more conservative than the average in the preceding Congress. Even the liberal Labor and Human Resources Committee had shifted by fifteen percentage points in a more conservative direction and its average score was more than 50 percent for the first time in at least three decades. The change came from the Republicans, with their great increase in numbers and the greater conservatism of the new members. The Democrats barely changed in ideology from the Ninety-sixth to the Ninety-seventh Congress, averaging in both Congresses 43 percent or 44 percent in conservative coalition support. Republican support, however, went up substantially, from an average of 74 percent to an average of 84 percent.

The partisan ideological gap within committees also grew. As Table 8-8 shows, the change was greater on some committees than others but was particularly significant among the most prestigious committees, such as Appropriations, Finance, Budget, and Foreign Relations. Some already polarized committees, like Labor and Banking, became even more polarized. Partisan conflict also increased in the important Energy and Environment committees.

The Senate chamber shifted back to the left after the Democrats regained majority control in the 1986 elections, and remained fairly consistent through 1993. Three-fourths of the committees either became more liberal or remained at their 1993 level in 1994. All of the committee Conservative Coalition scores went up in 1995 with the Republican takeover; the Appropriations and Environment committees showed especially notable change. Across the board they have reached some of their highest levels ever, making this Congress one of the most conservative in the past few generations.

## NOTES

1. John F. Manley, "The Conservative Coalition in Congress," *American Behavioral Scientist,* vol. 17, no. 2 (1973).
2. Quote by Burdett Loomis, *Congressional Quarterly Weekly Report,* December 28, 1991, 3759.

**Table 8-1** Presidential Victories on Votes in Congress, 1953–1996

| *President and year* | *House and Senate (%)* | *House (%)* | *No. of Votes* | *Senate (%)* | *No. of Votes* |
|---|---|---|---|---|---|
| Eisenhower | | | | | |
| 1953 | 89.2 | 91.2 | 34 | 87.8 | 49 |
| 1954 | 82.8 | n.a. | n.a. | n.a. | n.a. |
| 1955 | 75.3 | 63.4 | 41 | 84.6 | 52 |
| 1956 | 69.7 | 73.5 | 34 | 67.7 | 65 |
| 1957 | 68.4 | 58.3 | 60 | 78.9 | 57 |
| 1958 | 75.7 | 74.0 | 50 | 76.5 | 98 |
| 1959 | 52.0 | 55.5 | 54 | 50.4 | 121 |
| 1960 | 65.1 | 65.0 | 43 | 65.1 | 86 |
| Average | 72.2 | | | | |
| Kennedy | | | | | |
| 1961 | 81.5 | 83.1 | 65 | 80.6 | 124 |
| 1962 | 85.4 | 85.0 | 60 | 85.6 | 125 |
| 1963 | 87.1 | 83.1 | 71 | 89.6 | 115 |
| Average | 84.6 | | | | |
| Johnson | | | | | |
| 1964 | 87.9 | 88.5 | 52 | 87.6 | 97 |
| 1965 | 93.1 | 93.8 | 112 | 92.6 | 162 |
| 1966 | 78.9 | 91.3 | 103 | 68.8 | 125 |
| 1967 | 78.8 | 75.6 | 127 | 81.2 | 165 |
| 1968 | 74.5 | 83.5 | 103 | 68.9 | 164 |
| Average | 82.6 | | | | |
| Nixon | | | | | |
| 1969 | 74.8 | 72.3 | 47 | 76.4 | 72 |
| 1970 | 76.9 | 84.6 | 65 | 71.4 | 91 |
| 1971 | 74.8 | 82.5 | 57 | 69.5 | 82 |
| 1972 | 66.3 | 81.1 | 37 | 54.3 | 46 |
| 1973 | 50.6 | 48.0 | 125 | 52.4 | 185 |
| 1974 | 59.6 | 67.9 | 53 | 54.2 | 83 |
| Average | 67.2 | | | | |
| Ford | | | | | |
| 1974 | 58.2 | 59.3 | 54 | 57.4 | 68 |
| 1975 | 61.0 | 50.6 | 89 | 71.0 | 93 |
| 1976 | 53.8 | 43.1 | 51 | 64.2 | 53 |
| Average | 57.6 | | | | |
| Carter | | | | | |
| 1977 | 75.4 | 74.7 | 79 | 76.1 | 88 |
| 1978 | 78.3 | 69.6 | 112 | 84.8 | 151 |
| 1979 | 76.8 | 71.7 | 145 | 81.4 | 161 |
| 1980 | 75.1 | 76.9 | 117 | 73.3 | 116 |
| Average | 76.4 | | | | |

*(Table continues)*

**Table 8-1** *(Continued)*

| *President and year* | *House and Senate (%)* | *House (%)* | *No. of Votes* | *Senate (%)* | *No. of Votes* |
|---|---|---|---|---|---|
| Reagan | | | | | |
| 1981 | 82.3 | 72.4 | 76 | 88.3 | 128 |
| 1982 | 72.4 | 55.8 | 77 | 83.2 | 119 |
| 1983 | 67.1 | 47.6 | 82 | 85.9 | 85 |
| 1984 | 65.8 | 52.2 | 113 | 85.7 | 77 |
| 1985 | 59.9 | 45.0 | 80 | 71.6 | 102 |
| 1986 | 56.5 | 34.1 | 88 | 81.2 | 80 |
| 1987 | 43.5 | 33.3 | 99 | 56.4 | 78 |
| 1988 | 47.4 | 32.7 | 104 | 64.8 | 88 |
| Average | 61.9 | | | | |
| Bush | | | | | |
| 1989 | 62.6 | 50.0 | 86 | 73.3 | 101 |
| 1990 | 46.8 | 32.4 | 108 | 63.4 | 93 |
| 1991 | 54.2 | 43.0 | 111 | 69.0 | 81 |
| 1992 | 43.0 | 37.0 | 105 | 53.0 | 60 |
| Average | 51.6 | | | | |
| Clinton | | | | | |
| 1993 | 86.4 | 87.2 | 102 | 85.4 | 89 |
| 1994 | 86.4 | 87.2 | 78 | 85.5 | 62 |
| 1995 | 36.2 | 26.3 | 133 | 49.0 | 102 |
| 1996 | 55.1 | 53.2 | 79 | 57.6 | 59 |
| Average | 66.0 | | | | |

n.a. = not available.

*Note:* Percentages indicate number of congressional votes supporting the president divided by the total number of votes on which the president had taken a position.

The findings for 1956, 1981, 1982, and 1983 differ slightly from previous editions due to recalculation and corrections in the *Congressional Quarterly Almanac*. The *Congressional Quarterly Almanac* frequently rounds off House and Senate percentages of these votes, but figures in *Vital Statistics* are not rounded here.

*Sources: Congressional Quarterly Almanac* (Washington, D.C.: Congressional Quarterly, various years); *Congressional Quarterly Weekly Report,* January 2, 1982; December 31, 1983; October 27, 1984; January 11, 1986; October 25, 1986, 2690; January 16, 1988; November 19, 1988; December 30, 1989; January 6, 1990; December 22, 1990; December 28, 1991; December 19, 1992; December 18, 1993; December 31, 1994; January 27, 1996; December 21, 1996. Some percentages recalculated.

Figure 8-1 Presidential Victories on Votes in Congress, 1953–1996

*Note:* Percentages indicate number of congressional votes supporting the president divided by the total number of votes on which the president has taken a position.
*Source:* Table 8-1.

**Table 8-2** Congressional Voting in Support of the President's Position, 1954–1996 (percent)

| | *House* | | | *Senate* | | |
|---|---|---|---|---|---|---|
| *President and year* | All Democrats | Southern Democrats | Republicans | All Democrats | Southern Democrats | Republicans |
| Eisenhower | | | | | | |
| 1954 | 54 | n.a. | n.a. | 45 | n.a. | 82 |
| 1955 | 58 | n.a. | 67 | 65 | n.a. | 85 |
| 1956 | 58 | n.a. | 79 | 44 | n.a. | 80 |
| 1957 | 54 | n.a. | 60 | 60 | n.a. | 80 |
| 1958 | 63 | n.a. | 65 | 51 | n.a. | 77 |
| 1959 | 44 | n.a. | 76 | 44 | n.a. | 80 |
| 1960 | 49 | n.a. | 63 | 52 | n.a. | 76 |
| Kennedy | | | | | | |
| 1961 | 81 | n.a. | 41 | 73 | n.a. | 42 |
| 1962 | 83 | 71 | 47 | 76 | 63 | 48 |
| 1963 | 84 | 71 | 36 | 77 | 65 | 52 |
| Johnson | | | | | | |
| 1964 | 84 | 70 | 42 | 73 | 63 | 52 |
| 1965 | 83 | 65 | 46 | 75 | 60 | 55 |
| 1966 | 81 | 64 | 45 | 71 | 59 | 53 |
| 1967 | 80 | 65 | 51 | 73 | 69 | 63 |
| 1968 | 77 | 63 | 59 | 64 | 50 | 57 |
| Nixon | | | | | | |
| 1969 | 56 | 55 | 65 | 55 | 56 | 74 |
| 1970 | 64 | 64 | 79 | 56 | 62 | 74 |
| 1971 | 53 | 69 | 79 | 48 | 59 | 76 |
| 1972 | 56 | 59 | 74 | 52 | 71 | 77 |
| 1973 | 39 | 49 | 67 | 42 | 55 | 70 |
| 1974 | 52 | 64 | 71 | 44 | 60 | 65 |
| Ford | | | | | | |
| 1974 | 48 | 52 | 59 | 45 | 55 | 67 |
| 1975 | 40 | 48 | 67 | 53 | 67 | 76 |
| 1976 | 36 | 52 | 70 | 47 | 61 | 73 |
| Carter | | | | | | |
| 1977 | 69 | 58 | 46 | 77 | 71 | 58 |
| 1978 | 67 | 54 | 40 | 74 | 61 | 47 |
| 1979 | 70 | 58 | 37 | 75 | 66 | 51 |
| 1980 | 71 | 63 | 44 | 71 | 69 | 50 |
| Reagan | | | | | | |
| 1981 | 46 | 60 | 72 | 52 | 63 | 84 |
| 1982 | 43 | 55 | 70 | 46 | 57 | 77 |
| 1983 | 30 | 45 | 74 | 45 | 46 | 77 |
| 1984 | 37 | 47 | 64 | 45 | 58 | 81 |

| *President and year* | *House* All Demo-crats | Southern Demo-crats | Repub-licans | *Senate* All Demo-crats | Southern Demo-crats | Repub-licans |
|---|---|---|---|---|---|---|
| 1985 | 31 | 43 | 69 | 36 | 46 | 80 |
| 1986 | 26 | 37 | 69 | 39 | 56 | 90 |
| 1987 | 26 | 36 | 64 | 38 | 42 | 67 |
| 1988 | 27 | 34 | 61 | 51 | 58 | 73 |
| Bush | | | | | | |
| 1989 | 38 | 49 | 72 | 56 | 66 | 84 |
| 1990 | 26 | 35 | 65 | 39 | 49 | 72 |
| 1991 | 35 | 43 | 74 | 42 | 53 | 83 |
| 1992 | 27 | 38 | 75 | 33 | 41 | 75 |
| Clinton | | | | | | |
| 1993 | 80 | 81 | 39 | 87 | 84 | 30 |
| 1994 | 78 | 68 | 49 | 88 | 88 | 44 |
| 1995 | 75 | 69 | 22 | 81 | 78 | 29 |
| 1996 | 74 | 70 | 38 | 83 | 75 | 37 |

n.a. = not available.

*Note:* Percentages indicate number of congressional votes supporting the president divided by the total number of votes on which the president had taken a position. The percentages are normalized to eliminate the effects of absences, as follows: support = (support)/(support + opposition).

*Sources: Congressional Quarterly Almanac,* various years; *Congressional Quarterly Weekly Report,* January 2, 1982; October 27, 1984; January 11, 1986; October 25, 1986, 2690-2693; January 16, 1988; November 19, 1988; December 30, 1989; January 6, 1990; December 22, 1990; December 28, 1991; December 19, 1992; December 18, 1993; December 31, 1994; January 27, 1996; December 21, 1996.

**Table 8-3** Party Unity Votes in Congress, 1953–1996 (percentage of all votes)

| *Year* | *House* | *Senate* | *Year* | *House* | *Senate* |
|---|---|---|---|---|---|
| 1953 | 52 | n.a. | 1975 | 48 | 48 |
| 1954 | 38 | 47 | 1976 | 36 | 37 |
| 1955 | 41 | 30 | 1977 | 42 | 42 |
| 1956 | 44 | 53 | 1978 | 33 | 45 |
| 1957 | 59 | 36 | 1979 | 47 | 47 |
| 1958 | 40 | 44 | 1980 | 38 | 46 |
| 1959 | 55 | 48 | 1981 | 37 | 48 |
| 1960 | 53 | 37 | 1982 | 36 | 43 |
| 1961 | 50 | 62 | 1983 | 56 | 44 |
| 1962 | 46 | 41 | 1984 | 47 | 40 |
| 1963 | 49 | 47 | 1985 | 61 | 50 |
| 1964 | 55 | 36 | 1986 | 57 | 52 |
| 1965 | 52 | 42 | 1987 | 64 | 41 |
| 1966 | 41 | 50 | 1988 | 47 | 42 |
| 1967 | 36 | 35 | 1989 | 55 | 35 |
| 1968 | 35 | 32 | 1990 | 49 | 54 |
| 1969 | 31 | 36 | 1991 | 55 | 49 |
| 1970 | 27 | 35 | 1992 | 64 | 53 |
| 1971 | 38 | 42 | 1993 | 65 | 67 |
| 1972 | 27 | 36 | 1994 | 62 | 52 |
| 1973 | 42 | 40 | 1995 | 73 | 69 |
| 1974 | 29 | 44 | 1996 | 56 | 62 |

n.a. = not available.

*Note:* Data indicate the percentage of all recorded votes on which a majority of voting Democrats opposed a majority of voting Republicans.

*Sources: Congressional Quarterly Almanac,* various years; *Congressional Quarterly Weekly Report,* January 9, 1982; January 15, 1983, 107; December 31, 1983, 2790; October 27, 1984, 2810; January 11, 1986, 87; November 15, 1986, 2902; January 16, 1988; November 19, 1988; December 30, 1989; December 22, 1990; December 28, 1991; December 19, 1992; December 18, 1993; December 31, 1994; January 27, 1996; December 21, 1996.

**Table 8-4** Party Unity Scores in Congressional Voting, 1954–1996 (percent)

| | *House* | | | *Senate* | | |
|---|---|---|---|---|---|---|
| *Year* | All Democrats | Southern Democrats | Republicans | All Democrats | Southern Democrats | Republicans |
| 1954 | 80 | n.a. | 84 | 77 | n.a. | 89 |
| 1955 | 84 | 68 | 78 | 82 | 78 | 82 |
| 1956 | 80 | 79 | 78 | 80 | 75 | 80 |
| 1957 | 79 | 71 | 75 | 79 | 81 | 81 |
| 1958 | 77 | 67 | 73 | 82 | 76 | 74 |
| 1959 | 85 | 77 | 85 | 76 | 63 | 80 |
| 1960 | 75 | 62 | 77 | 73 | 60 | 74 |
| 1961 | n.a. | n.a. | n.a. | n.a. | n.a. | n.a. |
| 1962 | 81 | n.a. | 80 | 80 | n.a. | 81 |
| 1963 | 85 | n.a. | 84 | 79 | n.a. | 79 |
| 1964 | 82 | n.a. | 81 | 73 | n.a. | 75 |
| 1965 | 80 | 55 | 81 | 75 | 55 | 78 |
| 1966 | 78 | 55 | 82 | 73 | 52 | 78 |
| 1967 | 77 | 53 | 82 | 75 | 59 | 73 |
| 1968 | 73 | 48 | 76 | 71 | 57 | 74 |
| 1969 | 71 | 47 | 71 | 74 | 53 | 72 |
| 1970 | 71 | 52 | 72 | 71 | 49 | 71 |
| 1971 | 72 | 48 | 76 | 74 | 56 | 75 |
| 1972 | 70 | 44 | 76 | 72 | 43 | 73 |
| 1973 | 75 | 55 | 74 | 79 | 52 | 74 |
| 1974 | 72 | 51 | 71 | 72 | 41 | 68 |

*(Table continues)*

**Table 8-4** *(Continued)*

| | *House* | | | *Senate* | | |
|---|---|---|---|---|---|---|
| *Year* | All Democrats | Southern Democrats | Republicans | All Democrats | Southern Democrats | Republicans |
| 1975 | 75 | 53 | 78 | 76 | 48 | 71 |
| 1976 | 75 | 52 | 75 | 74 | 46 | 72 |
| 1977 | 74 | 55 | 77 | 72 | 48 | 75 |
| 1978 | 71 | 53 | 77 | 75 | 54 | 66 |
| 1979 | 75 | 60 | 79 | 76 | 62 | 73 |
| 1980 | 78 | 64 | 79 | 76 | 64 | 74 |
| 1981 | 75 | 57 | 80 | 77 | 64 | 85 |
| 1982 | 77 | 62 | 76 | 76 | 62 | 80 |
| 1983 | 82 | 67 | 80 | 76 | 70 | 79 |
| 1984 | 81 | 68 | 77 | 75 | 61 | 83 |
| 1985 | 86 | 76 | 80 | 79 | 68 | 81 |
| 1986 | 86 | 76 | 76 | 74 | 59 | 80 |
| 1987 | 88 | 78 | 79 | 85 | 80 | 78 |
| 1988 | 88 | 81 | 80 | 85 | 78 | 74 |
| 1989 | 86 | 77 | 76 | 79 | 69 | 79 |
| 1990 | 86 | 78 | 78 | 82 | 75 | 77 |
| 1991 | 86 | 78 | 81 | 83 | 73 | 83 |
| 1992 | 86 | 79 | 84 | 82 | 70 | 83 |
| 1993 | 88 | 84 | 87 | 87 | 78 | 86 |

| | | | | | | |
|---|---|---|---|---|---|---|
| 1994 | 88 | 83 | 87 | 86 | 77 | 81 |
| 1995 | 80 | 72 | 91 | 81 | 74 | 89 |
| 1996 | 80 | 71 | 87 | 84 | 73 | 89 |

n.a. = not available.

*Note:* Data show percentage of members voting with a majority of their party on party unity votes. Party unity votes are those roll calls on which a majority of a party votes on one side of the issue and a majority of the other party votes on the other side. The percentages are normalized to eliminate the effects of absences, as follows: party unity = (unity)/(unity + opposition).

*Sources: Congressional Quarterly Almanac,* various years; *Congressional Quarterly Weekly Report,* January 9, 1982; January 15, 1983, 108; October 27, 1984, 2804–2805; January 11, 1986, 88; November 15, 1986, 2902–2906; January 16, 1988; November 19, 1988; December 30, 1989; January 6, 1990; December 22, 1990; December 28, 1991, 3790–3792; December 19, 1992, 3907–3909, December 18, 1993, 3481–3483; December 31, 1994, 3660–3662; January 27, 1996; December 21, 1996.

**Table 8-5** Conservative Coalition Votes and Victories in Congress, 1957–1996 (percent)

| | *House* | | *Senate* | |
|---|---|---|---|---|
| *Year* | Votes | Victories | Votes | Victories |
| 1957 | 16 | 81 | 11 | 100 |
| 1958 | 15 | 64 | 19 | 86 |
| 1959 | 13 | 91 | 19 | 65 |
| 1960 | 20 | 35 | 22 | 67 |
| 1961 | 30 | 74 | 32 | 48 |
| 1962 | 13 | 44 | 15 | 71 |
| 1963 | 13 | 67 | 19 | 44 |
| 1964 | 11 | 67 | 17 | 47 |
| 1965 | 25 | 25 | 24 | 39 |
| 1966 | 19 | 32 | 30 | 51 |
| 1967 | 22 | 73 | 18 | 54 |
| 1968 | 22 | 63 | 25 | 80 |
| 1969 | 25 | 71 | 28 | 67 |
| 1970 | 17 | 70 | 26 | 64 |
| 1971 | 31 | 79 | 28 | 86 |
| 1972 | 25 | 79 | 29 | 63 |
| 1973 | 25 | 67 | 21 | 54 |
| 1974 | 22 | 67 | 30 | 54 |
| 1975 | 28 | 52 | 28 | 48 |
| 1976 | 17 | 59 | 26 | 58 |
| 1977 | 22 | 60 | 29 | 74 |
| 1978 | 20 | 57 | 23 | 46 |
| 1979 | 21 | 73 | 18 | 65 |
| 1980 | 16 | 67 | 20 | 75 |

*Note:* "Votes" is the percentage of all roll call votes on which a majority of voting southern Democrats and a majority of voting Republicans—the conservative coalition—opposed the stand taken by a majority of voting northern Democrats. "Victories" is the percentage of conservative coalition votes won by the coalition.

*Sources: Congressional Quarterly Almanac,* various years; *Congressional Quarterly Weekly Report,* January 9, 1982; January 15, 1983; December 31, 1983; October 27, 1984, 2821; January 11, 1986, 76-77, 81; November 15, 1986, 2908–2909; January 16, 1988; November 19, 1988; December 30, 1989; January 6, 1990; December 22, 1990; December 28, 1991; December 19, 1992; December 18, 1993, 3485; December 31, 1994, 3663; January 27, 1996; December 21, 1996.

| *Year* | *House* | | *Senate* | |
|---|---|---|---|---|
| | Votes | Victories | Votes | Victories |
| 1981 | 21 | 88 | 21 | 95 |
| 1982 | 16 | 78 | 20 | 90 |
| 1983 | 18 | 71 | 12 | 89 |
| 1984 | 14 | 75 | 17 | 94 |
| 1985 | 13 | 84 | 16 | 93 |
| 1986 | 11 | 78 | 20 | 93 |
| 1987 | 9 | 88 | 8 | 100 |
| 1988 | 8 | 82 | 10 | 97 |
| 1989 | 11 | 80 | 12 | 95 |
| 1990 | 10 | 74 | 11 | 95 |
| 1991 | 9 | 86 | 14 | 95 |
| 1992 | 10 | 88 | 14 | 87 |
| 1993 | 7 | 98 | 10 | 90 |
| 1994 | 7 | 92 | 10 | 72 |
| 1995 | 13 | 100 | 9 | 95 |
| 1996 | 51 | 100 | 38 | 97 |

**Table 8-6** Voting in Support of the Conservative Coalition, 1959–1996 (percent)

| | *House* | | | *Senate* | | |
|---|---|---|---|---|---|---|
| | Northern Democrats | Southern Democrats | Republicans | Northern Democrats | Southern Democrats | Republicans |
| 1959 | 17 | 85 | 87 | 23 | 69 | 80 |
| 1960 | 8 | 66 | 77 | 21 | 77 | 74 |
| 1961 | 15 | 69 | 83 | 15 | 74 | 75 |
| 1962 | 14 | 65 | 75 | 29 | 77 | 79 |
| 1963 | 13 | 70 | 78 | 20 | 73 | 76 |
| 1964 | 13 | 72 | 76 | 20 | 78 | 72 |
| 1965 | 10 | 69 | 81 | 19 | 71 | 81 |
| 1966 | 13 | 69 | 82 | 17 | 75 | 80 |
| 1967 | 15 | 75 | 81 | 24 | 76 | 72 |
| 1968 | 16 | 77 | 75 | 31 | 77 | 74 |
| 1969 | 21 | 79 | 75 | 24 | 77 | 73 |
| 1970 | 19 | 79 | 78 | 21 | 74 | 72 |
| 1971 | 25 | 76 | 80 | 38 | 80 | 79 |
| 1972 | 24 | 75 | 79 | 20 | 78 | 74 |
| 1973 | 22 | 69 | 77 | 17 | 74 | 76 |
| 1974 | 24 | 72 | 69 | 19 | 79 | 69 |
| 1975 | 22 | 69 | 81 | 19 | 79 | 69 |
| 1976 | 25 | 72 | 80 | 21 | 73 | 76 |
| 1977 | 25 | 68 | 82 | 26 | 75 | 80 |
| 1978 | 26 | 68 | 79 | 24 | 70 | 69 |
| 1979 | 29 | 70 | 85 | 29 | 75 | 74 |
| 1980 | 27 | 69 | 81 | 26 | 72 | 74 |
| 1981 | 30 | 75 | 82 | 29 | 76 | 84 |

| | | | | | | |
|---|---|---|---|---|---|---|
| 1982 | 27 | 73 | 81 | 30 | 76 | 81 |
| 1983 | 22 | 68 | 81 | 30 | 69 | 81 |
| 1984 | 23 | 68 | 84 | 27 | 74 | 85 |
| 1985 | 23 | 67 | 84 | 30 | 72 | 82 |
| 1986 | 27 | 70 | 83 | 26 | 70 | 83 |
| 1987 | 27 | 71 | 87 | 30 | 70 | 79 |
| 1988 | 27 | 67 | 88 | 29 | 72 | 80 |
| 1989 | 27 | 68 | 87 | 31 | 69 | 84 |
| 1990 | 27 | 69 | 85 | 29 | 70 | 83 |
| 1991 | 30 | 69 | 90 | 33 | 71 | 84 |
| 1992 | 31 | 67 | 87 | 27 | 67 | 79 |
| 1993 | 31 | 63 | 87 | 31 | 70 | 84 |
| 1994 | 39 | 58 | 89 | 30 | 69 | 81 |
| 1995 | 28 | 57 | 90 | 24 | 68 | 87 |
| 1996 | 31 | 63 | 85 | 30 | 66 | 88 |

*Note:* Data indicate the percentage of conservative coalition votes on which members voted in agreement with the position of the conservative coalition. Conservative coalition votes are those on which a majority of northern Democrats voted against a majority of southern Democrats and Republicans—the conservative coalition. The percentages are normalized to eliminate the effects of not voting as follows: conservative coalition support = (support)/(support + opposition).

*Sources: Congressional Quarterly Almanac,* various years; *Congressional Quarterly Weekly Report,* January 9, 1982; January 15, 1983, 102; October 27, 1984, 2821; January 11, 1986, 76; November 15, 1986, 2908–2912; January 16, 1988; November 19, 1988; December 30, 1989; January 6, 1990; December 22, 1990; December 28, 1991, 3795–3797; December 19, 1992, 3902–3904; December 18, 1993, 3486–3488; December 31, 1994, 3665–3667; January 27, 1996; December 21, 1996.

**Table 8-7** House Committee Support of the Conservative Coalition, 1959–1995 (percent)

| *Committee* | *1959* | *1969* | *1977* | *1981* | *1983* | *1985* | *1987* | *1989* | *1991* | *1993* | *1995* |
|---|---|---|---|---|---|---|---|---|---|---|---|
| Agriculture | | | | | | | | | | | |
| All members | 79 | 80 | 56 | 70 | 60 | 65 | 69 | 70 | 73 | 66 | 76 |
| Democrats | 69 | 72 | 44 | 58 | 48 | 52 | 56 | 58 | 62 | 51 | 53 |
| Republicans | 97 | 90 | 81 | 86 | 81 | 84 | 89 | 89 | 93 | 88 | 96 |
| Appropriations | | | | | | | | | | | |
| All members | 69 | 63 | 56 | 56 | 52 | 53 | 58 | 57 | 57 | 64 | 72 |
| Democrats | 55 | 54 | 42 | 42 | 37 | 36 | 41 | 39 | 39 | 47 | 42 |
| Republicans | 90 | 76 | 83 | 78 | 79 | 81 | 86 | 85 | 88 | 90 | 95 |
| Armed Services | | | | | | | | | | | |
| All members | 68 | 69 | 69 | 80 | 74 | 75 | 74 | 73 | 72 | 74 | 81 |
| Democrats | 55 | 63 | 59 | 71 | 65 | 67 | 63 | 62 | 59 | 61 | 62 |
| Republicans | 90 | 79 | 90 | 91 | 90 | 86 | 90 | 89 | 92 | 92 | 95 |
| Banking, Finance, and Urban Affairs | | | | | | | | | | | |
| All members | 44 | 50 | 45 | 52 | 50 | 52 | 58 | 56 | 57 | 50 | 59 |
| Democrats | 26 | 37 | 33 | 34 | 34 | 34 | 39 | 35 | 39 | 26 | 23 |
| Republicans | 75 | 68 | 68 | 77 | 76 | 79 | 86 | 87 | 88 | 85 | 89 |
| Budget | | | | | | | | | | | |
| All members | n.a. | n.a. | 43 | 63 | 50 | 55 | 56 | 56 | 60 | 59 | 67 |
| Democrats | n.a. | n.a. | 26 | 47 | 32 | 34 | 33 | 34 | 43 | 45 | 38 |
| Republicans | n.a. | n.a. | 79 | 87 | 85 | 87 | 89 | 88 | 88 | 81 | 89 |
| District of Columbia | | | | | | | | | | | |
| All members | 72 | 62 | 41 | 39 | 40 | 31 | 44 | 39 | 42 | 43 | n.a. |
| Democrats | 65 | 54 | 37 | 17 | 15 | 15 | 17 | 7 | 6 | 14 | n.a. |
| Republicans | 85 | 72 | 49 | 78 | 79 | 66 | 91 | 96 | 96 | 86 | n.a. |
| Education and Labor | | | | | | | | | | | |
| All members | 39 | 40 | 42 | 44 | 39 | 42 | 49 | 44 | 46 | 48[a] | 66 |
| Democrats | 16 | 17 | 26 | 25 | 25 | 21 | 28 | 19 | 23 | 26 | 24 |
| Republicans | 86 | 72 | 73 | 70 | 71 | 73 | 82 | 84 | 88 | 85[a] | 90 |
| Energy and Commerce | | | | | | | | | | | |
| All members | 65 | 60 | 48 | 58 | 50 | 56 | 57 | 60 | 60 | 59 | 66 |
| Democrats | 49 | 41 | 31 | 38 | 31 | 35 | 36 | 39 | 41 | 39 | 37 |
| Republicans | 92 | 84 | 81 | 85 | 84 | 87 | 87 | 93 | 94 | 86 | 94 |
| Foreign Affairs | | | | | | | | | | | |
| All members | 48 | 42 | 41 | 51 | 42 | 45 | 50 | 45 | 47 | 50 | 63 |
| Democrats | 32 | 20 | 25 | 38 | 25 | 21 | 28 | 22 | 24 | 29 | 31 |
| Republicans | 78 | 68 | 73 | 70 | 74 | 79 | 81 | 80 | 81 | 80 | 89 |

| *Committee* | *1959* | *1969* | *1977* | *1981* | *1983* | *1985* | *1987* | *1989* | *1991* | *1993* | *1995* |
|---|---|---|---|---|---|---|---|---|---|---|---|
| Government Operations | | | | | | | | | | | |
| All members | 55 | 37 | 47 | 54 | 53 | 54 | 57 | 50 | 53 | 50 | 67 |
| Democrats | 37 | 25 | 32 | 37 | 40 | 31 | 40 | 30 | 36 | 28 | 40 |
| Republicans | 81 | 55 | 78 | 77 | 78 | 86 | 85 | 83 | 85 | 83 | 88 |
| House Administration | | | | | | | | | | | |
| All members | 61 | 55 | 49 | 58 | 49 | 53 | 52 | 57 | 55 | 61 | 71 |
| Democrats | 52 | 37 | 32 | 41 | 30 | 32 | 38 | 35 | 31 | 42 | 42 |
| Republicans | 78 | 79 | 87 | 83 | 82 | 88 | 92 | 94 | 95 | 94 | 92 |
| Judiciary[b] | | | | | | | | | | | |
| All members | 58 | 43 | 45 | 51 | 47 | 50 | 52 | 49 | 52 | 52 | 62 |
| Democrats | 45 | 28 | 36 | 30 | 26 | 26 | 26 | 24 | 30 | 30 | 21 |
| Republicans | 83 | 63 | 62 | 79 | 85 | 87 | 90 | 87 | 88 | 86 | 93 |
| Merchant Marine and Fisheries | | | | | | | | | | | |
| All members | 54 | 52 | 49 | 63 | 53 | 61 | 61 | 65 | 66 | 61 | n.a. |
| Democrats | 39 | 41 | 29 | 51 | 39 | 47 | 46 | 52 | 50 | 45 | n.a. |
| Republicans | 82 | 67 | 71 | 79 | 76 | 83 | 84 | 85 | 91 | 88 | n.a. |
| Natural Resources[c] | | | | | | | | | | | |
| All members | 56 | 57 | 51 | 57 | 54 | 55 | 57 | 54 | 58 | 54 | 71 |
| Democrats | 36 | 36 | 33 | 34 | 33 | 30 | 36 | 31 | 37 | 32 | 35 |
| Republicans | 86 | 85 | 88 | 91 | 91 | 92 | 92 | 93 | 95 | 90 | 93 |
| Post Office and Civil Service | | | | | | | | | | | |
| All members | 57 | 49 | 43 | 49 | 47 | 42 | 40 | 38 | 42 | 51 | n.a. |
| Democrats | 40 | 28 | 24 | 23 | 21 | 14 | 17 | 17 | 21 | 31 | n.a. |
| Republicans | 88 | 77 | 84 | 83 | 87 | 83 | 78 | 71 | 79 | 81 | n.a. |
| Public Works and Transportation | | | | | | | | | | | |
| All members | 58 | 63 | 62 | 66 | 56 | 54 | 60 | 67 | 67 | 64 | 70 |
| Democrats | 45 | 45 | 53 | 51 | 39 | 34 | 42 | 49 | 53 | 50 | 46 |
| Republicans | 82 | 86 | 80 | 87 | 83 | 83 | 86 | 90 | 91 | 85 | 89 |
| Rules | | | | | | | | | | | |
| All members | 63 | 54 | 47 | 54 | 48 | 45 | 53 | 48 | 52 | 55 | 77 |
| Democrats | 44 | 39 | 26 | 36 | 28 | 25 | 35 | 32 | 32 | 38 | 35 |
| Republicans | 100 | 85 | 56 | 94 | 92 | 92 | 95 | 87 | 98 | 94 | 96 |
| Science, Space and Technology | | | | | | | | | | | |
| All members | 52 | 58 | 56 | 58 | 55 | 60 | 64 | 62 | 69 | 67[a] | 72 |
| Democrats | 34 | 46 | 47 | 49 | 43 | 47 | 52 | 52 | 58 | 56 | 52 |
| Republicans | 85 | 73 | 73 | 70 | 74 | 80 | 82 | 77 | 86 | 84[a] | 89 |
| Small Business | | | | | | | | | | | |
| All members | n.a. | n.a. | n.a. | 59 | 55 | 60 | 63 | 61 | 61 | 59 | 66 |
| Democrats | n.a. | n.a. | n.a. | 44 | 47 | 43 | 48 | 46 | 43 | 39 | 38 |
| Republicans | n.a. | n.a. | n.a. | 79 | 71 | 84 | 88 | 85 | 91 | 89 | 91 |

*(Table continues)*

**Table 8-7** *(Continued)*

| *Committee* | *1959* | *1969* | *1977* | *1981* | *1983* | *1985* | *1987* | *1989* | *1991* | *1993* | *1995* |
|---|---|---|---|---|---|---|---|---|---|---|---|
| Standards of Official Conduct | | | | | | | | | | | |
| All members | n.a. | n.a. | 70 | 63 | 55 | 63 | 63 | 62 | 55 | 56 | 59 |
| Democrats | n.a. | n.a. | 67 | 57 | 29 | 37 | 38 | 38 | 22 | 31 | 25 |
| Republicans | n.a. | n.a. | 74 | 82 | 82 | 90 | 88 | 87 | 88 | 81 | 92 |
| Veterans' Affairs | | | | | | | | | | | |
| All members | 53 | 63 | 62 | 73 | 65 | 65 | 65 | 69 | 74 | 64 | 74 |
| Democrats | 46 | 54 | 53 | 65 | 53 | 51 | 52 | 56 | 62 | 47 | 50 |
| Republicans | 65 | 74 | 80 | 83 | 85 | 84 | 86 | 89 | 92 | 93 | 95 |
| Ways and Means | | | | | | | | | | | |
| All members | 62 | 56 | 54 | 60 | 54 | 53 | 55 | 55 | 55 | 54 | 65 |
| Democrats | 42 | 38 | 39 | 45 | 38 | 34 | 36 | 37 | 34 | 35 | 27 |
| Republicans | 95 | 83 | 86 | 87 | 85 | 87 | 87 | 86 | 91 | 86 | 91 |
| Chamber average | | | | | | | | | | | |
| All members | 59 | 56 | 51 | 61 | 55 | 56 | 60 | 56 | 60 | 60[a] | 67 |
| Democrats | 44 | 42 | 38 | 45 | 39 | 36 | 41 | 37 | 42 | 42 | 38 |
| Republicans | 86 | 75 | 78 | 82 | 81 | 84 | 87 | 87 | 90 | 87[a] | 91 |

n.a. = not available.

*Note:* Data indicate the percentage of conservative coalition votes on which members voted in agreement with the position of the conservative coalition. Conservative coalition votes are those on which a majority of northern Democrats voted against a majority of southern Democrats and Republicans—the conservative coalition. The percentages are normalized to eliminate the effects of not voting as follows: conservative coalition support = (support)/(support + opposition).

[a] Vacancy left by the death of Rep. Paul B. Henry (R-Mich.) on July 31, 1993. Henry was eligible for eighteen conservative coalition votes in 1993. Support score adjusted for absences was zero percent.

[b] Frederick Boucher (D-Va.) replaced Harold Washington (D-Ill.), who resigned from Congress to become mayor of Chicago, April 1983.

[c] In 1993 the Interior and Insular Affairs Committee was renamed Natural Resources. The figures for 1959-1991 are actually for the members of the Interior and Insular Affairs Committee.

*Sources: Congressional Directory* (Washington, D.C.: Government Printing Office, various years); *Congressional Quarterly Almanac,* various years; *Congressional Quarterly Weekly Report,* January 6, 1990; December 28, 1991; December 19, 1992; December 18, 1993, 3486–3487; January 27, 1996.

Figure 8-2 House Committee Support of the Conservative Coalition, 1959, 1977, 1981, 1989, 1991, and 1995

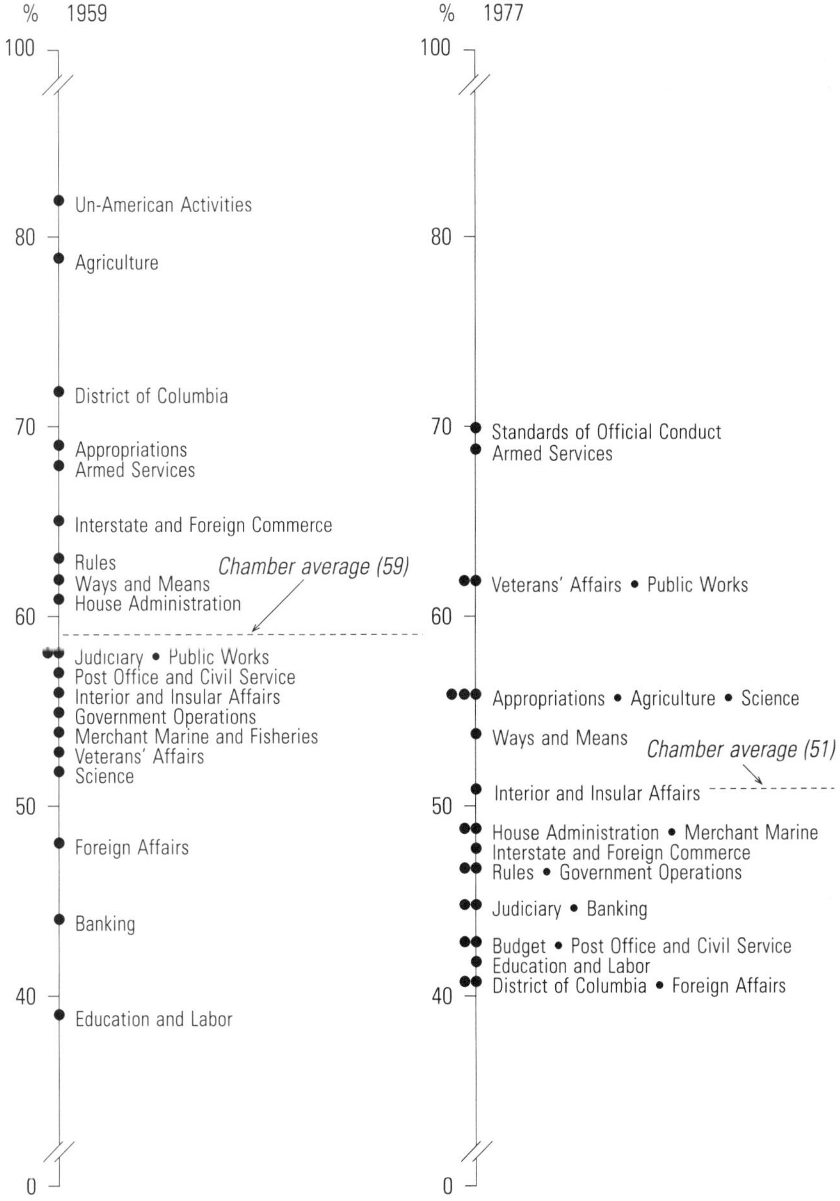


*Note:* Percentage of conservative coalition votes on which members voted in agreement with the position of the conservative coalition. Conservative coalition votes are those on which a majority of northern Democrats voted against a majority of southern Democrats and Republicans—the conservative coalition.

*Source:* Table 8-7.

Figure 8-2 (continued)

% 1981
100
80
Armed Services
Veterans' Affairs
70
Agriculture
Public Works
Chamber average (61)
Standards of Official Conduct • Budget
• Merchant Marine and Fisheries
60
Ways and Means
Small Business
Energy & Commerce • Science • House Admin.
Interior and Insular Affairs
Appropriations
Rules • Government Operations
Banking
Foreign Affairs • Judiciary
50
Post Office and Civil Service
Education and Labor
40
District of Columbia
0
% 1989
100
80
Armed Services
70
Agriculture
Veterans' Affairs
Public Works
Merchant Marine
Science • Standards of Official Conduct
Small Business
60
Energy and Commerce
Chamber average (56)
Appropriations • House Administration
Banking • Budget
Ways and Means
Interior
50
Government Operations
Judiciary
Rules
Foreign Affairs
Education and Labor
40
District of Columbia
Post Office
0

Figure 8-2 (continued)

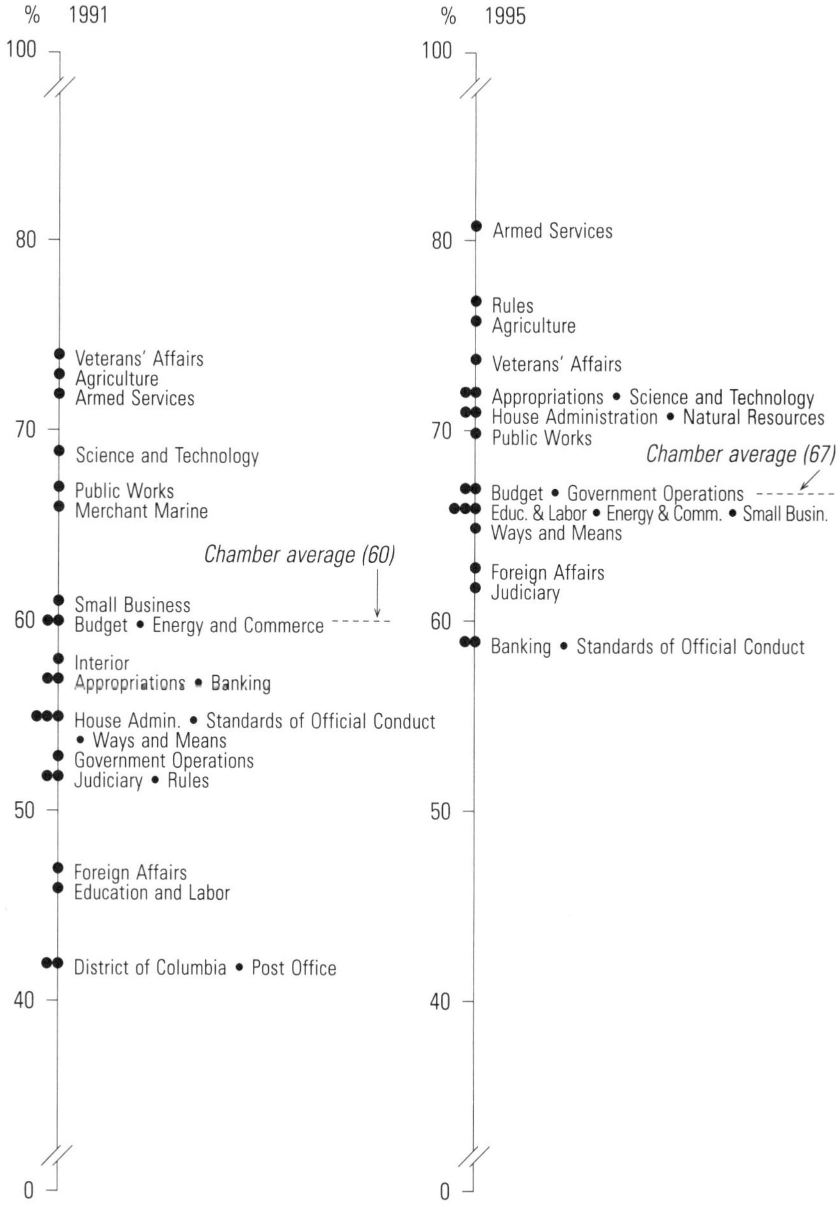

**Table 8-8** Senate Committee Support of the Conservative Coalition, 1959–1995 (percent)

| *Committee* | *1959* | *1969* | *1977* | *1981* | *1983* | *1985* | *1987* | *1989* | *1991* | *1993* | *1995* |
|---|---|---|---|---|---|---|---|---|---|---|---|
| Agriculture, Nutrition, and Forestry | | | | | | | | | | | |
| All members | 63 | 81 | 67 | 77 | 75 | 72 | 72 | 67 | 70 | 68 | 68 |
| Democrats | 51 | 78 | 51 | 62 | 61 | 53 | 54 | 46 | 52 | 48 | 40 |
| Republicans | 85 | 83 | 91 | 90 | 86 | 90 | 92 | 90 | 93 | 93 | 93 |
| Appropriations | | | | | | | | | | | |
| All members | 65 | 67 | 50 | 68 | 66 | 66 | 59 | 57 | 62 | 62 | 66 |
| Democrats | 55 | 58 | 47 | 53 | 49 | 49 | 44 | 38 | 45 | 42 | 41 |
| Republicans | 85 | 79 | 55 | 83 | 83 | 81 | 76 | 81 | 83 | 86 | 90 |
| Armed Services[a] | | | | | | | | | | | |
| All members | 70 | 65 | 66 | 76 | 70 | 69 | 68 | 70 | 69 | 69 | 66 |
| Democrats | 68 | 55 | 47 | 58 | 46 | 47 | 56 | 55 | 54 | 53 | 41 |
| Republicans | 84 | 77 | 96 | 92 | 89 | 88 | 83 | 89 | 88 | 87 | 91 |
| Banking, Housing, and Urban Affairs | | | | | | | | | | | |
| All members | 49 | 49 | 46 | 55 | 59 | 60 | 58 | 58 | 60 | 59 | 60 |
| Democrats | 35 | 29 | 27 | 23 | 27 | 31 | 41 | 41 | 43 | 38 | 20 |
| Republicans | 76 | 57 | 74 | 83 | 84 | 85 | 80 | 82 | 85 | 89 | 95 |
| Budget | | | | | | | | | | | |
| All members | n.a. | n.a. | 53 | 69 | 63 | 65 | 67 | 64 | 64 | 60 | 62 |
| Democrats | n.a. | n.a. | 36 | 44 | 40 | 43 | 50 | 47 | 44 | 40 | 32 |
| Republicans | n.a. | n.a. | 82 | 89 | 81 | 83 | 87 | 86 | 89 | 87 | 89 |
| Commerce, Science, and Transportation | | | | | | | | | | | |
| All members | 55 | 52 | 58 | 72 | 58 | 70 | 61 | 73 | 72 | 70 | 71 |
| Democrats | 40 | 38 | 45 | 58 | 43 | 56 | 46 | 64 | 61 | 58 | 54 |
| Republicans | 83 | 72 | 80 | 84 | 71 | 83 | 78 | 84 | 85 | 85 | 89 |
| Energy and Natural Resources[b] | | | | | | | | | | | |
| All members | 45 | 52 | 54 | 62 | 58 | 65 | 62 | 64 | 67 | 69 | 66 |
| Democrats | 23 | 29 | 34 | 37 | 38 | 44 | 48 | 43 | 52 | 56 | 39 |
| Republicans | 75 | 78 | 76 | 83 | 71 | 82 | 77 | 87 | 86 | 85 | 84 |
| Environment and Public Works | | | | | | | | | | | |
| All members | 40 | 53 | 51 | 63 | 60 | 58 | 51 | 61 | 51 | 52 | 64 |
| Democrats | 22 | 36 | 35 | 38 | 38 | 35 | 37 | 46 | 34 | 33 | 32 |
| Republicans | 75 | 78 | 76 | 85 | 77 | 78 | 68 | 80 | 73 | 79 | 92 |
| Finance | | | | | | | | | | | |
| All members | 67 | 63 | 51 | 67 | 63 | 67 | 55 | 59 | 59 | 58 | 65 |
| Democrats | 53 | 47 | 35 | 51 | 49 | 53 | 43 | 40 | 47 | 43 | 39 |
| Republicans | 94 | 90 | 74 | 80 | 74 | 78 | 70 | 81 | 76 | 76 | 89 |

| *Committee* | *1959* | *1969* | *1977* | *1981* | *1983* | *1985* | *1987* | *1989* | *1991* | *1993* | *1995* |
|---|---|---|---|---|---|---|---|---|---|---|---|
| Foreign Relations | | | | | | | | | | | |
| All members | 44 | 45 | 36 | 55 | 52 | 54 | 50 | 56 | 55 | 51 | 58 |
| Democrats | 29 | 39 | 26 | 26 | 25 | 23 | 18 | 30 | 27 | 27 | 25 |
| Republicans | 71 | 55 | 51 | 78 | 76 | 82 | 86 | 85 | 89 | 84 | 87 |
| Governmental Affairs[c] | | | | | | | | | | | |
| All members | 55 | 55 | 48 | 61 | 60 | 63 | 64 | 58 | 59 | 61 | 63 |
| Democrats | 39 | 43 | 41 | 47 | 44 | 51 | 52 | 42 | 47 | 48 | 38 |
| Republicans | 88 | 71 | 55 | 73 | 73 | 73 | 79 | 78 | 78 | 83 | 87 |
| Judiciary | | | | | | | | | | | |
| All members | 53 | 55 | 42 | 63 | 61 | 63 | 49 | 55 | 55 | 53 | 58 |
| Democrats | 43 | 36 | 35 | 36 | 38 | 38 | 28 | 30 | 32 | 29 | 27 |
| Republicans | 74 | 72 | 69 | 85 | 80 | 83 | 76 | 88 | 87 | 84 | 86 |
| Labor and Human Resources | | | | | | | | | | | |
| All members | 35 | 34 | 36 | 54 | 56 | 53 | 41 | 48 | 46 | 43 | 54 |
| Democrats | 12 | 14 | 18 | 14 | 23 | 18 | 16 | 18 | 23 | 22 | 16 |
| Republicans | 71 | 62 | 62 | 85 | 82 | 81 | 74 | 86 | 78 | 74 | 87 |
| Rules and Administration | | | | | | | | | | | |
| All members | 56 | 71 | 51 | 64 | 60 | 62 | 56 | 60 | 63 | 60 | 60 |
| Democrats | 43 | 65 | 39 | 38 | 36 | 41 | 33 | 41 | 45 | 40 | 40 |
| Republicans | 82 | 79 | 74 | 82 | 77 | 79 | 86 | 84 | 88 | 87 | 89 |
| Veterans' Affairs | | | | | | | | | | | |
| All members | n.a. | n.a. | n.a. | 63 | 59 | 66 | 48 | 61 | 53 | 55 | 65 |
| Democrats | n.a. | n.a. | n.a. | 34 | 38 | 40 | 31 | 42 | 34 | 40 | 34 |
| Republicans | n.a. | n.a. | n.a. | 84 | 74 | 84 | 68 | 85 | 78 | 76 | 82 |
| Chamber average | | | | | | | | | | | |
| All members | 54 | 55 | 51 | 65 | 62 | 63 | 60 | 61 | 61 | 60 | 64 |
| Democrats | 41 | 42 | 37 | 44 | 42 | 41 | 43 | 42 | 44 | 41 | 35 |
| Republicans | 80 | 73 | 73 | 84 | 79 | 82 | 79 | 84 | 84 | 84 | 87 |

n.a. = not available.

*Note:* Data indicate the percentage of conservative coalition votes on which members voted in agreement with the position of the conservative coalition. Conservative coalition votes are those on which a majority of northern Democrats voted against a majority of southern Democrats and Republicans—the conservative coalition. The percentages are normalized to eliminate the effects of not voting as follows: conservative coalition support = (support)/(support + opposition).

[a] Alan Dixon (D-Ill.) filled the seat vacated by the death of Henry Jackson (D-Wash.), September 1, 1983.

[b] Daniel Evans (R-Wash.) replaced Henry Jackson (D-Wash.) in 1983.

[c] David Pryor (D-Ark.) replaced Henry Jackson (D-Wash.) in 1983.

*Sources: Congressional Directory,* various years; *Congressional Quarterly Almanac,* various years; *Congressional Quarterly Weekly Report,* January 6, 1990; December 28, 1991; December 19, 1992; December 18, 1993, 3488; January 27, 1996.

Figure 8-3 Senate Committee Support of the Conservative Coalition, 1959, 1977, 1981, 1989, 1991, and 1995

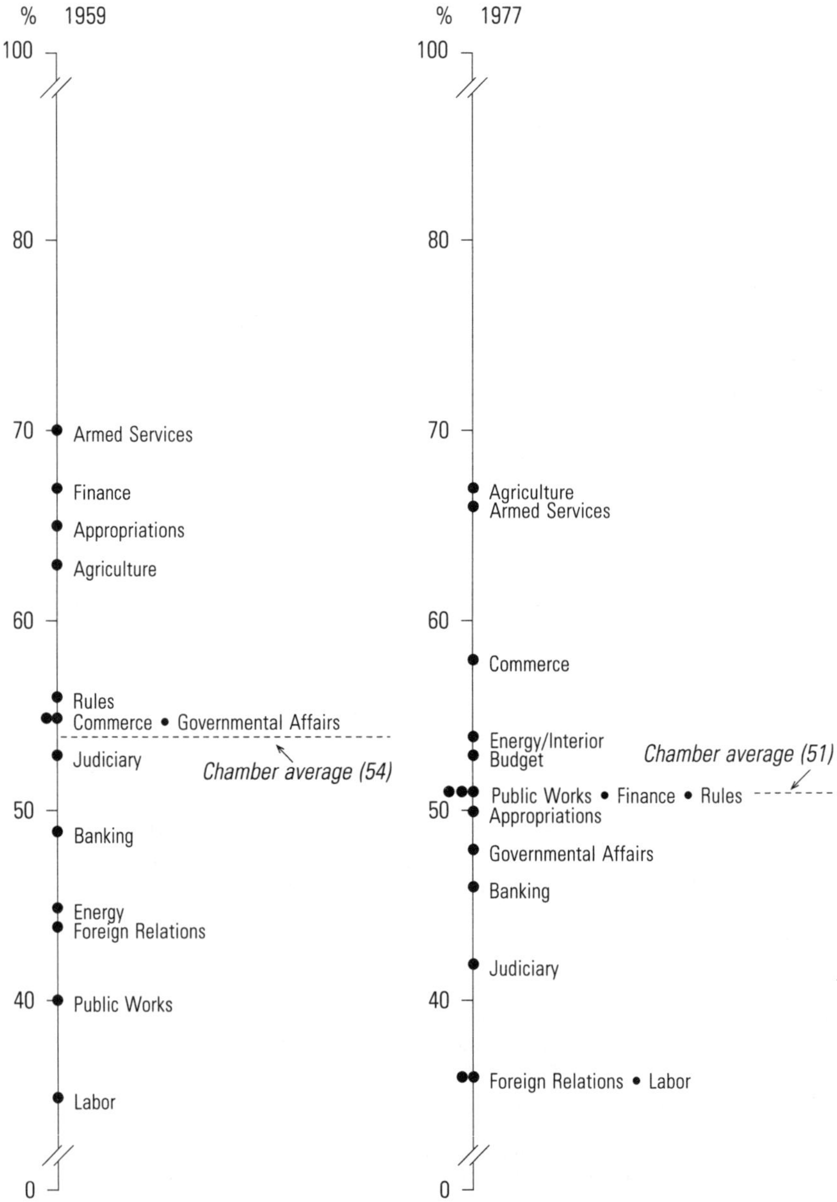


*Note:* Percentage of conservative coalition votes on which members voted in agreement with the position of the conservative coalition. Conservative coalition votes are those on which a majority of northern Democrats voted against a majority of southern Democrats and Republicans—the conservative coalition.

*Source:* Table 8-8.

Figure 8-3 (continued)

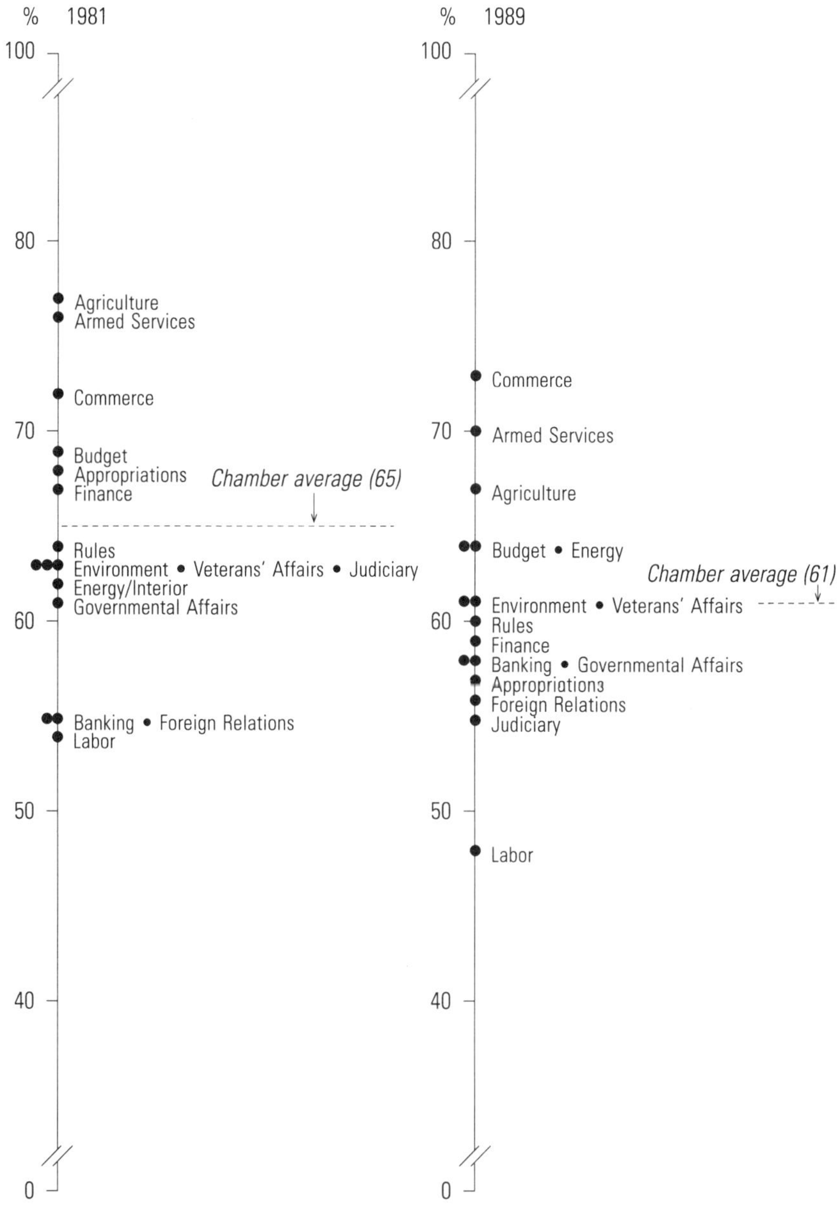

Figure 8-3 (continued)

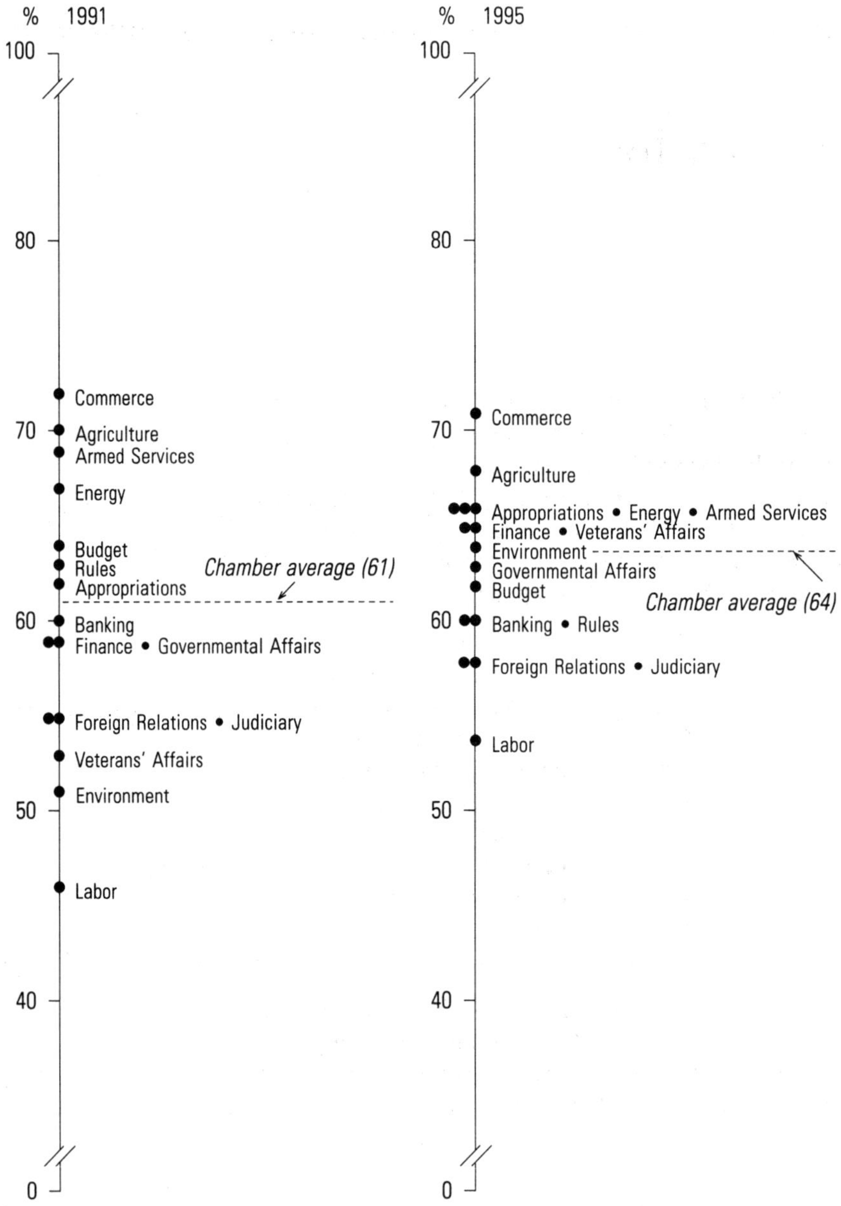

# Appendix

The appendix contains data on individual members of the 105th and 104th Congresses. Tables A-1 and A-3 show years of service, age, returns of the most recent election participated in (for House Members, 1996), and various voting ratings for each member of the 105th House (A-1) and Senate (A-3) all based on the year 1996. Tables A-2 and A-4 give comparable data on members of the 104th Congress, based on the year 1994. The following abbreviations are used throughout the tables in the appendix:

| | |
|---|---|
| ACU | American Conservative Union |
| ADA | Americans for Democratic Action |
| AL | at large |
| CC | conservative coalition |
| conv. | nominated by convention |
| D | Democrat |
| I | Independent |
| PU | party unity |
| PS | presidential support |
| R | Republican |
| unopp. | unopposed |

Note that the conservative coalition, party unity, and presidential support scores, all derived from Congressional Quarterly measures, have been recalculated to eliminate the effect of absences. Americans for Democratic Action and American Conservative Union scores have not been so altered.

**Table A-1** House of Representatives, 105th Congress, 1997

| State, district | Representative | Party | Years of service[a] | Age | % vote in 1996 | | 1996 voting ratings | | | | | |
|---|---|---|---|---|---|---|---|---|---|---|---|---|
| | | | | | Primary | General | CC | PU | PS | ADA | ACU | ACU (career) |
| Alabama | | | | | | | | | | | | |
| 1 | S. Callahan | R | 12 | 64 | unopp. | 64 | 100 | 94 | 38 | 0 | 100 | 94 |
| 2 | T. Everett | R | 4 | 59 | unopp. | 63 | 100 | 95 | 34 | 5 | 100 | 97 |
| 3 | B. Riley | R | 0 | 52 | 64 | 51 | — | — | — | — | — | — |
| 4 | R. B. Aderholt | R | 0 | 31 | 49 | 50 | — | — | — | — | — | — |
| 5 | R.E. Cramer | D | 6 | 49 | unopp. | 56 | 98 | 59 | 65 | 40 | 55 | 44 |
| 6 | S. Bachus | R | 4 | 49 | unopp. | 71 | 98 | 93 | 38 | 5 | 95 | 96 |
| 7 | E.F. Hilliard | D | 4 | 54 | unopp. | 71 | 39 | 93 | 80 | 85 | 15 | 15 |
| Alaska | | | | | | | | | | | | |
| AL | D. Young | R | 24 | 63 | 58 | 59 | 100 | 91 | 40 | 0 | 89 | 74 |
| Arizona | | | | | | | | | | | | |
| 1 | M. Salmon | R | 2 | 38 | unopp. | 60 | 92 | 92 | 33 | 10 | 100 | 96 |
| 2 | E. Pastor | D | 6 | 53 | unopp. | 65 | 44 | 90 | 79 | 85 | 5 | 6 |
| 3 | B. Stump | R | 20 | 69 | unopp. | 67 | 98 | 97 | 34 | 0 | 100 | 96 |
| 4 | J. Shadegg | R | 2 | 47 | 74 | 67 | 90 | 96 | 30 | 5 | 100 | 96 |
| 5 | J. Kolbe | R | 12 | 54 | 70 | 69 | 86 | 88 | 49 | 5 | 90 | 80 |
| 6 | J. D. Hayworth | R | 2 | 38 | unopp. | 48 | 94 | 96 | 37 | 0 | 100 | 100 |
| Arkansas | | | | | | | | | | | | |
| 1 | M. Berry | D | 0 | 54 | 52 | 53 | — | — | — | — | — | — |
| 2 | V. Snyder | D | 0 | 49 | 51 | 52 | — | — | — | — | — | — |
| 3 | A. Hutchinson | R | 0 | 46 | — | 56 | — | — | — | — | — | — |
| 4 | J. Dickey | R | 4 | 57 | unopp. | 64 | 92 | 96 | 25 | 0 | 100 | 96 |

| | | | | | | | | | | | | |
|---|---|---|---|---|---|---|---|---|---|---|---|---|
| California | | | | | | | | | | | | |
| 1 | F. Riggs | R | 2 | 46 | unopp. | 50 | 80 | 86 | 40 | 10 | 85 | 73 |
| 2 | W. Herger | R | 10 | 51 | 84 | 61 | 94 | 96 | 33 | 0 | 100 | 98 |
| 3 | V. Fazio | D | 18 | 54 | 82 | 54 | 57 | 89 | 84 | 80 | 0 | 6 |
| 4 | J. T. Doolittle | R | 6 | 46 | unopp. | 60 | 100 | 95 | 28 | 5 | 100 | 100 |
| 5 | R.T. Matsui | D | 18 | 55 | unopp. | 70 | 42 | 93 | 87 | 85 | 0 | 6 |
| 6 | L. C. Woolsey | D | 4 | 59 | unopp. | 62 | 4 | 98 | 84 | 95 | 0 | 2 |
| 7 | G. Miller | D | 22 | 51 | unopp. | 72 | 4 | 96 | 81 | 90 | 0 | 22 |
| 8 | N. Pelosi | D | 9 | 56 | unopp. | 84 | 2 | 98 | 83 | 95 | 0 | 1 |
| 9 | R. V. Dellums | D | 26 | 61 | 85 | 77 | 2 | 97 | 76 | 100 | 0 | 6 |
| 10 | E. O. Tauscher | D | 0 | 45 | 75 | 49 | — | — | — | — | — | — |
| 11 | R. W. Pombo | R | 4 | 35 | unopp. | 59 | 98 | 95 | 29 | 5 | 100 | 100 |
| 12 | T. Lantos | D | 16 | 68 | unopp. | 72 | 15 | 97 | 87 | 95 | 0 | 8 |
| 13 | P. Stark | D | 24 | 65 | unopp. | 65 | 0 | 95 | 74 | 80 | 0 | 5 |
| 14 | A. G. Eshoo | D | 4 | 54 | unopp. | 65 | 12 | 92 | 83 | 85 | 0 | 5 |
| 15 | T. Campbell | R | 2 | 44 | unopp. | 59 | 43 | 73 | 54 | 40 | 60 | 58 |
| 16 | Z. Lofgren | D | 2 | 49 | unopp. | 66 | 16 | 91 | 77 | 85 | 5 | 7 |
| 17 | S. Farr | D | 4 | 55 | 88 | 59 | 27 | 94 | 84 | 90 | 0 | 3 |
| 18 | G. A. Condit | D | 8 | 48 | unopp. | 66 | 82 | 52 | 53 | 35 | 70 | 48 |
| 19 | G. P. Radanovich | R | 2 | 41 | unopp. | 67 | 98 | 96 | 34 | 0 | 100 | 98 |
| 20 | C. Dooley | D | 6 | 42 | unopp. | 57 | 67 | 74 | 81 | 55 | 15 | 11 |
| 21 | W. M. Thomas | R | 18 | 55 | 79 | 66 | 100 | 90 | 42 | 5 | 90 | 79 |
| 22 | W. Capps | D | 0 | 62 | unopp. | 48 | — | — | — | — | — | — |
| 23 | E. Gallegly | R | 10 | 52 | unopp. | 60 | 94 | 95 | 38 | 0 | 100 | 91 |
| 24 | B. Sherman | D | 0 | 42 | 54 | 50 | — | — | — | — | — | — |
| 25 | H. P. "Buck" McKeon | R | 4 | 57 | 85 | 62 | 96 | 95 | 33 | 0 | 100 | 96 |
| 26 | H. L. Berman | D | 14 | 45 | 84 | 66 | 21 | 94 | 88 | 90 | 0 | 6 |
| 27 | J. E. Rogan | R | 0 | 39 | 88 | 50 | — | — | — | — | — | — |
| 28 | D. Dreier | R | 16 | 44 | unopp. | 61 | 98 | 98 | 33 | 0 | 100 | 94 |

*(Table continues)*

**Table A-1** *(Continued)*

| *State, district* | *Representative* | *Party* | *Years of service*[a] | *Age* | *% vote in 1996* | | *1996 voting ratings* | | | | | |
|---|---|---|---|---|---|---|---|---|---|---|---|---|
| | | | | | Primary | General | CC | PU | PS | ADA | ACU | ACU (career) |
| 29 | H. A. Waxman | D | 22 | 57 | unopp. | 68 | 6 | 97 | 83 | 90 | 0 | 5 |
| 30 | X. Becerra | D | 4 | 38 | unopp. | 72 | 9 | 98 | 84 | 85 | 0 | 3 |
| 31 | M. G. Martinez | D | 14 | 67 | unopp. | 67 | 57 | 78 | 79 | 80 | 10 | 8 |
| 32 | J. C. Dixon | D | 18 | 62 | unopp. | 82 | 40 | 91 | 84 | 90 | 0 | 5 |
| 33 | L. Roybal-Allard | D | 4 | 55 | unopp. | 82 | 12 | 97 | 83 | 90 | 0 | 2 |
| 34 | E. E. Torres | D | 14 | 66 | unopp. | 68 | 27 | 95 | 84 | 100 | 0 | 3 |
| 35 | M. Waters | D | 6 | 58 | unopp. | 86 | 13 | 95 | 74 | 85 | 0 | 4 |
| 36 | J. Harman | D | 4 | 51 | unopp. | 52 | 66 | 75 | 67 | 60 | 26 | 22 |
| 37 | J. Millender-McDonald[b] | D | 1 | 58 | 27 | 85 | 28 | 93 | 84 | 83 | 0 | 0 |
| 38 | S. Horn | R | 4 | 65 | unopp. | 53 | 73 | 72 | 50 | 40 | 63 | 60 |
| 39 | E. Royce | R | 4 | 45 | unopp. | 63 | 74 | 90 | 34 | 15 | 100 | 98 |
| 40 | J. Lewis | R | 18 | 62 | 77 | 65 | 100 | 88 | 46 | 5 | 83 | 84 |
| 41 | J. C. Kim | R | 4 | 57 | 58 | 59 | 98 | 98 | 34 | 0 | 100 | 95 |
| 42 | G. E. Brown Jr. | D | 32 | 76 | 78 | 50 | 26 | 96 | 90 | 90 | 0 | 6 |
| 43 | K. Calvert | R | 4 | 43 | 74 | 55 | 98 | 93 | 33 | 0 | 95 | 91 |
| 44 | S. Bono | R | 2 | 61 | unopp. | 58 | 98 | 94 | 37 | 0 | 95 | 96 |
| 45 | D. Rohrabacher | R | 8 | 49 | unopp. | 61 | 78 | 92 | 28 | 15 | 100 | 95 |
| 46 | L. Sanchez | D | 0 | 36 | 35 | 47 | — | — | — | — | — | — |
| 47 | C. Cox | R | 8 | 44 | unopp. | 66 | 91 | 97 | 31 | 5 | 100 | 98 |
| 48 | R. Packard | R | 14 | 65 | unopp. | 66 | 96 | 93 | 40 | 0 | 94 | 93 |
| 49 | B. Bilbray | R | 2 | 45 | unopp. | 53 | 73 | 82 | 45 | 20 | 74 | 73 |
| 50 | B. Filner | D | 4 | 54 | 55 | 62 | 12 | 97 | 86 | 90 | 0 | 6 |
| 51 | R. "Duke" Cunningham | R | 6 | 55 | 86 | 65 | 91 | 95 | 31 | 10 | 100 | 96 |
| 52 | D.L. Hunter | R | 16 | 48 | unopp. | 65 | 98 | 96 | 30 | 10 | 100 | 95 |

| | | | | | | | | | | | | |
|---|---|---|---|---|---|---|---|---|---|---|---|---|
| Colorado | | | | | | | | | | | | |
| 1 | D. DeGette | D | 0 | 39 | 56 | 57 | — | — | — | — | — | — |
| 2 | D. E. Skaggs | D | 10 | 53 | unopp. | 57 | 33 | 93 | 85 | 90 | 0 | 7 |
| 3 | S. McInnis | R | 4 | 43 | unopp. | 69 | 88 | 92 | 38 | 5 | 100 | 89 |
| 4 | B. Schaffer | R | 0 | 34 | 40 | 56 | — | — | — | — | — | — |
| 5 | J. Hefley | R | 10 | 61 | 77 | 72 | 94 | 95 | 30 | 10 | 100 | 96 |
| 6 | D. Schaefer | R | 14 | 60 | unopp. | 62 | 98 | 97 | 33 | 0 | 100 | 90 |
| Connecticut | | | | | | | | | | | | |
| 1 | B. B. Kennelly | D | 15 | 60 | unopp. | 74 | 50 | 87 | 84 | 80 | 10 | 6 |
| 2 | S. Gejdenson | D | 16 | 48 | unopp. | 52 | 33 | 92 | 83 | 90 | 0 | 4 |
| 3 | R. DeLauro | D | 6 | 53 | unopp. | 71 | 29 | 93 | 84 | 85 | 0 | 3 |
| 4 | C. Shays | R | 9 | 51 | unopp. | 60 | 33 | 69 | 53 | 30 | 60 | 42 |
| 5 | J. H. Maloney | D | 0 | 48 | unopp. | 52 | — | — | — | — | — | — |
| 6 | N. L. Johnson | R | 14 | 61 | unopp. | 50 | 78 | 74 | 58 | 20 | 55 | 51 |
| Delaware | | | | | | | | | | | | |
| AL | M. N. Castle | R | 4 | 57 | unopp. | 70 | 71 | 74 | 57 | 25 | 60 | 65 |
| Florida | | | | | | | | | | | | |
| 1 | J. Scarborough | R | 2 | 33 | unopp. | 73 | 79 | 89 | 31 | 10 | 95 | 96 |
| 2 | A. Boyd | D | 0 | 51 | 64 | 59 | — | — | — | — | — | — |
| 3 | C. Brown | D | 4 | 50 | unopp. | 61 | 59 | 90 | 84 | 90 | 0 | 10 |
| 4 | T. Fowler | R | 4 | 54 | 89 | unopp. | 96 | 92 | 36 | 10 | 95 | 87 |
| 5 | K. L. Thurman | D | 4 | 45 | unopp. | 62 | 75 | 84 | 77 | 75 | 15 | 19 |
| 6 | C. Stearns | R | 8 | 55 | unopp. | 67 | 90 | 94 | 33 | 5 | 100 | 94 |
| 7 | J. L. Mica | R | 4 | 53 | unopp. | 62 | 94 | 96 | 33 | 0 | 100 | 96 |
| 8 | B. McCollum | R | 16 | 52 | unopp. | 67 | 96 | 94 | 33 | 0 | 95 | 91 |
| 9 | M. Bilirakis | R | 14 | 66 | 80 | 69 | 90 | 91 | 33 | 5 | 90 | 85 |
| 10 | C. W. B. Young | R | 26 | 66 | unopp. | 67 | 90 | 92 | 40 | 5 | 88 | 84 |

*(Table continues)*

**Table A-1** *(Continued)*

| State, district | Representative | Party | Years of service[a] | Age | % vote in 1996 Primary | % vote in 1996 General | 1996 voting ratings CC | PU | PS | ADA | ACU | ACU (career) |
|---|---|---|---|---|---|---|---|---|---|---|---|---|
| 11 | J. Davis | D | 0 | 39 | 56 | 58 | — | — | — | — | — | — |
| 12 | C. T. Canady | R | 4 | 42 | unopp. | 62 | 94 | 93 | 37 | 5 | 85 | 88 |
| 13 | D. Miller | R | 4 | 54 | unopp. | 64 | 82 | 92 | 39 | 10 | 95 | 88 |
| 14 | P. J. Goss | R | 8 | 58 | unopp. | 73 | 84 | 92 | 39 | 10 | 95 | 87 |
| 15 | D. Weldon | R | 2 | 43 | unopp. | 51 | 94 | 93 | 38 | 5 | 100 | 98 |
| 16 | M. Foley | R | 2 | 42 | unopp. | 64 | 78 | 84 | 43 | 10 | 90 | 87 |
| 17 | C. Meek | D | 4 | 70 | unopp. | 89 | 46 | 91 | 81 | 85 | 5 | 6 |
| 18 | I. Ros-Lehtinen | R | 8 | 44 | unopp. | unopp. | 76 | 77 | 48 | 30 | 60 | 73 |
| 19 | R. Wexler | D | 0 | 35 | 65 | 66 | — | — | — | — | — | — |
| 20 | P. Deutsch | D | 4 | 39 | unopp. | 65 | 46 | 87 | 84 | 70 | 18 | 20 |
| 21 | L. Diaz-Balart | R | 4 | 42 | unopp. | unopp. | 90 | 77 | 51 | 30 | 60 | 70 |
| 22 | E. C. Shaw Jr. | R | 16 | 57 | unopp. | 62 | 92 | 90 | 40 | 10 | 95 | 85 |
| 23 | A. L. Hastings | D | 4 | 60 | unopp. | 73 | 47 | 93 | 86 | 95 | 0 | 4 |
| Georgia | | | | | | | | | | | | |
| 1 | J. Kingston | R | 4 | 41 | unopp. | 68 | 90 | 92 | 31 | 5 | 100 | 99 |
| 2 | S.D. Bishop Jr. | D | 4 | 47 | 59 | 54 | 90 | 75 | 73 | 60 | 30 | 22 |
| 3 | M. Collins | R | 4 | 52 | unopp. | 61 | 98 | 98 | 32 | 5 | 100 | 97 |
| 4 | C. McKinney | D | 4 | 41 | 67 | 58 | 4 | 98 | 80 | 100 | 0 | 3 |
| 5 | J. Lewis | D | 10 | 56 | unopp. | unopp. | 10 | 98 | 84 | 100 | 0 | 3 |
| 6 | N. Gingrich | R | 18 | 53 | unopp. | 58 | 100 | 97 | 25 | 0 | 100 | 90 |
| 7 | B. Barr | R | 2 | 48 | unopp. | 58 | 98 | 97 | 30 | 5 | 100 | 96 |
| 8 | S. Chambliss | R | 2 | 53 | unopp. | 53 | 100 | 96 | 35 | 0 | 100 | 98 |
| 9 | N. Deal | R | 4 | 54 | unopp. | 66 | 94 | 92 | 37 | 5 | 90 | 74 |

| | | | | | | | | | | | | |
|---|---|---|---|---|---|---|---|---|---|---|---|---|
| 10 | C. Norwood | R | 2 | 55 | unopp. | 52 | 100 | 98 | 31 | 0 | 100 | 100 |
| 11 | J. Linder | R | 4 | 54 | unopp. | 64 | 98 | 96 | 35 | 0 | 100 | 96 |
| Hawaii | | | | | | | | | | | | |
| 1 | N. Abercrombie | D | 6 | 58 | 72 | 50 | 47 | 90 | 78 | 90 | 0 | 2 |
| 2 | P. T. Mink | D | 19 | 69 | 60 | 60 | 25 | 95 | 78 | 95 | 5 | 3 |
| Idaho | | | | | | | | | | | | |
| 1 | H. Chenoweth | R | 2 | 58 | 68 | 50 | 92 | 92 | 28 | 10 | 95 | 93 |
| 2 | M. D. Crapo | R | 4 | 45 | 86 | 69 | 96 | 95 | 36 | 0 | 95 | 91 |
| Illinois | | | | | | | | | | | | |
| 1 | B. L. Rush | D | 4 | 50 | 89 | 86 | 10 | 96 | 84 | 95 | 0 | 2 |
| 2 | J. Jackson Jr. | D | 2 | 31 | unopp. | 94 | 12 | 96 | 85 | 100 | 0 | 0 |
| 3 | W. O. Lipinski | D | 14 | 59 | unopp. | 65 | 59 | 63 | 65 | 70 | 40 | 38 |
| 4 | L. V. Gutierrez | D | 4 | 43 | 71 | 94 | 6 | 95 | 83 | 100 | 0 | 5 |
| 5 | R. R. Blagojevich | D | 0 | 39 | 50 | 64 | — | — | — | — | — | — |
| 6 | H. J. Hyde | R | 22 | 72 | 84 | 64 | 94 | 93 | 39 | 10 | 90 | 87 |
| 7 | D. K. Davis | D | 0 | 55 | 33 | 82 | — | — | — | — | — | — |
| 8 | P. M. Crane | R | 27 | 66 | 75 | 62 | 96 | 98 | 35 | 0 | 100 | 99 |
| 9 | S. R. Yates | D | 46 | 87 | 84 | 63 | 7 | 96 | 79 | 85 | 0 | 4 |
| 10 | J. E. Porter | R | 17 | 61 | 68 | 69 | 58 | 81 | 42 | 25 | 80 | 64 |
| 11 | J. Weller | R | 2 | 39 | unopp. | 52 | 84 | 84 | 41 | 5 | 84 | 87 |
| 12 | J. F. Costello | D | 9 | 47 | unopp. | 72 | 60 | 75 | 67 | 70 | 30 | 31 |
| 13 | H. W. Fawell | R | 12 | 67 | unopp. | 60 | 78 | 85 | 43 | 10 | 85 | 80 |
| 14 | D. Hastert | R | 10 | 54 | unopp. | 64 | 100 | 96 | 37 | 0 | 100 | 91 |
| 15 | T. W. Ewing | R | 6 | 61 | unopp. | 57 | 94 | 94 | 35 | 0 | 100 | 96 |
| 16 | D. Manzullo | R | 4 | 52 | unopp. | 60 | 82 | 94 | 33 | 5 | 100 | 99 |
| 17 | L. Evans | D | 14 | 45 | unopp. | 52 | 14 | 95 | 75 | 95 | 0 | 4 |
| 18 | R. LaHood | R | 2 | 51 | unopp. | 59 | 76 | 84 | 39 | 10 | 80 | 76 |

*(Table continues)*

**Table A-1** *(Continued)*

| *State, district* | *Representative* | *Party* | *Years of service*[a] | *Age* | *% vote in 1996* Primary | General | *1996 voting ratings* CC | PU | PS | ADA | ACU | ACU (career) |
|---|---|---|---|---|---|---|---|---|---|---|---|---|
| 19 | G. Poshard | D | 8 | 51 | unopp. | 67 | 63 | 68 | 61 | 70 | 45 | 35 |
| 20 | J. M. Shimkus | R | 0 | 38 | 51 | 50 | — | — | — | — | — | — |
| Indiana | | | | | | | | | | | | |
| 1 | P. J. Visclosky | D | 12 | 47 | 84 | 69 | 41 | 82 | 75 | 85 | 15 | 9 |
| 2 | D. McIntosh | R | 2 | 38 | 86 | 58 | 96 | 95 | 36 | 0 | 100 | 100 |
| 3 | T. Roemer | D | 6 | 40 | unopp. | 58 | 63 | 64 | 68 | 60 | 40 | 14 |
| 4 | M. Souder | R | 2 | 46 | 82 | 58 | 92 | 92 | 37 | 10 | 95 | 98 |
| 5 | S. Buyer | R | 4 | 38 | unopp. | 65 | 98 | 94 | 37 | 5 | 95 | 96 |
| 6 | D. Burton | R | 14 | 58 | unopp. | 75 | 94 | 96 | 35 | 10 | 100 | 97 |
| 7 | E. A. Pease | R | 0 | 45 | 30 | 62 | — | — | — | — | — | — |
| 8 | J. N. Hostettler | R | 2 | 35 | 82 | 50 | 90 | 91 | 38 | 20 | 95 | 90 |
| 9 | L. H. Hamilton | D | 32 | 65 | 86 | 56 | 88 | 56 | 63 | 45 | 45 | 23 |
| 10 | J. M. Carson | D | 0 | 58 | 49 | 53 | — | — | — | — | — | — |
| Iowa | | | | | | | | | | | | |
| 1 | J. Leach | R | 20 | 54 | unopp. | 53 | 59 | 69 | 58 | 40 | 37 | 41 |
| 2 | J. Nussle | R | 6 | 36 | unopp. | 53 | 90 | 96 | 33 | 5 | 95 | 83 |
| 3 | L. L. Boswell | D | 0 | 62 | 58 | 49 | — | — | — | — | — | — |
| 4 | G. Ganske | R | 2 | 47 | unopp. | 52 | 61 | 84 | 45 | 20 | 83 | 78 |
| 5 | T. Latham | R | 2 | 48 | unopp. | 65 | 94 | 96 | 32 | 0 | 95 | 90 |
| Kansas | | | | | | | | | | | | |
| 1 | J. Moran | R | 0 | 42 | 76 | 73 | — | — | — | — | — | — |
| 2 | J. Ryun[c] | R | 0 | 49 | 62 | 52 | — | — | — | — | — | — |

| | | | | | | | | | | | | |
|---|---|---|---|---|---|---|---|---|---|---|---|---|
| 3 | V. Snowbarger | R | 0 | 47 | 44 | 50 | — | — | — | — | — | — |
| 4 | T. Tiahrt | R | 2 | 45 | unopp. | 50 | 88 | 93 | 34 | 5 | 100 | 100 |
| Kentucky | | | | | | | | | | | | |
| 1 | E. Whitfield | R | 2 | 53 | unopp. | 54 | 98 | 89 | 38 | 5 | 85 | 89 |
| 2 | R. Lewis | R | 3 | 50 | unopp. | 58 | 96 | 95 | 37 | 5 | 100 | 97 |
| 3 | A. M. Northup | R | 0 | 48 | unopp. | 50 | — | — | — | — | — | — |
| 4 | J. Bunning | R | 10 | 65 | unopp. | 68 | 98 | 96 | 33 | 5 | 100 | 96 |
| 5 | H. Rogers | R | 16 | 59 | unopp. | unopp. | 100 | 91 | 39 | 10 | 95 | 84 |
| 6 | S. Baesler | D | 4 | 55 | unopp. | 56 | 76 | 70 | 73 | 60 | 25 | 31 |
| Louisiana | | | | | | | | | | | | |
| 1 | B. Livingston | R | 20 | 53 | unopp. | d | 98 | 92 | 39 | 0 | 95 | 88 |
| 2 | W. J. Jefferson | D | 6 | 49 | unopp. | d | 54 | 90 | 79 | 85 | 5 | 6 |
| 3 | W. J. "Billy" Tauzin | R | 17 | 53 | unopp. | d | 98 | 93 | 35 | 0 | 90 | 71 |
| 4 | J. McCrery | R | 9 | 47 | 71 | d | 98 | 92 | 37 | 0 | 95 | 6 |
| 5 | J. Cooksey | R | 0 | 55 | 34 | 58 | — | — | — | — | — | — |
| 6 | R. Baker | R | 10 | 48 | 69 | d | 100 | 94 | 34 | 0 | 95 | 92 |
| 7 | C. John | D | 0 | 36 | 26 | 53 | — | — | — | — | — | — |
| Maine | | | | | | | | | | | | |
| 1 | T. H. Allen | D | 0 | 51 | 52 | 55 | — | — | — | — | — | — |
| 2 | J. E. Baldacci | D | 2 | 41 | unopp. | 72 | 47 | 89 | 86 | 80 | 10 | 15 |
| Maryland | | | | | | | | | | | | |
| 1 | W. T. Gilchrest | R | 6 | 49 | 65 | 62 | 76 | 84 | 46 | 20 | 80 | 66 |
| 2 | R. L. Ehrlich Jr. | R | 2 | 39 | 83 | 62 | 96 | 94 | 33 | 10 | 100 | 82 |
| 3 | B. L. Cardin | D | 10 | 53 | 90 | 67 | 38 | 87 | 83 | 75 | 11 | 6 |
| 4 | A. R. Wynn | D | 4 | 45 | 85 | 85 | 37 | 91 | 86 | 90 | 0 | 4 |
| 5 | S. H. Hoyer | D | 16 | 57 | 84 | 57 | 69 | 87 | 86 | 85 | 5 | 6 |
| 6 | R. G. Bartlett | R | 4 | 70 | 85 | 57 | 96 | 95 | 30 | 0 | 100 | 100 |

*(Table continues)*

**Table A-1** *(Continued)*

| *State, district* | *Representative* | *Party* | *Years of service*[a] | *Age* | *% vote in 1996* Primary | General | *1996 voting ratings* CC | PU | PS | ADA | ACU | ACU (career) |
|---|---|---|---|---|---|---|---|---|---|---|---|---|
| 7 | E. E. Cummings[e] | D | 1 | 45 | 37 | 83 | 18 | 94 | 76 | 92 | 0 | 4 |
| 8 | C. A. Morella | R | 10 | 65 | 65 | 61 | 38 | 56 | 73 | 50 | 30 | 25 |
| Massachusetts | | | | | | | | | | | | |
| 1 | J. W. Olver | D | 6 | 60 | unopp. | 53 | 6 | 98 | 85 | 95 | 0 | 2 |
| 2 | R. E. Neal | D | 8 | 47 | unopp. | 72 | 18 | 93 | 81 | 75 | 11 | 9 |
| 3 | J. P. McGovern | D | 0 | 46 | unopp. | 53 | — | — | — | — | — | — |
| 4 | B. Frank | D | 16 | 56 | unopp. | 72 | 4 | 94 | 79 | 100 | 0 | 4 |
| 5 | M. T. Meehan | D | 4 | 40 | 85 | unopp. | 8 | 93 | 87 | 85 | 0 | 16 |
| 6 | J. F. Tierney | D | 0 | 45 | 86 | 48 | — | — | — | — | — | — |
| 7 | E. J. Markey | D | 20 | 50 | unopp. | 70 | 0 | 97 | 81 | 95 | 0 | 4 |
| 8 | J. P. Kennedy II | D | 10 | 44 | unopp. | 84 | 4 | 95 | 84 | 95 | 0 | 5 |
| 9 | J. J. Moakley | D | 24 | 69 | unopp. | 72 | 12 | 93 | 78 | 65 | 6 | 7 |
| 10 | W. D. Delahunt | D | 0 | 55 | 37 | 54 | — | — | — | — | — | — |
| Michigan | | | | | | | | | | | | |
| 1 | B. Stupak | D | 4 | 44 | unopp. | 71 | 37 | 84 | 73 | 75 | 20 | 22 |
| 2 | P. Hoekstra | R | 4 | 43 | unopp. | 65 | 66 | 91 | 34 | 10 | 95 | 88 |
| 3 | V. J. Ehlers | R | 3 | 62 | unopp. | 69 | 63 | 79 | 43 | 25 | 79 | 78 |
| 4 | D. Camp | R | 5 | 43 | unopp. | 65 | 72 | 89 | 37 | 0 | 95 | 88 |
| 5 | J. A. Barcia | D | 4 | 44 | unopp. | 97 | 75 | 69 | 71 | 45 | 47 | 46 |
| 6 | F. Upton | R | 10 | 43 | unopp. | 52 | 55 | 82 | 39 | 10 | 85 | 72 |
| 7 | N. Smith | R | 4 | 62 | 75 | 55 | 77 | 89 | 35 | 10 | 95 | 95 |
| 8 | D. Stabenow | D | 0 | 46 | unopp. | 54 | — | — | — | — | — | — |
| 9 | D. E. Kildee | D | 20 | 67 | unopp. | 59 | 51 | 85 | 76 | 75 | 15 | 9 |

| | | | | | | | | | | | | |
|---|---|---|---|---|---|---|---|---|---|---|---|---|
| 10 | D. E. Bonior | D | 20 | 51 | unopp. | 54 | 19 | 95 | 79 | 95 | 5 | 4 |
| 11 | J. Knollenberg | R | 4 | 63 | unopp. | 61 | 98 | 93 | 38 | 0 | 95 | 95 |
| 12 | S. M. Levin | D | 14 | 65 | unopp. | 57 | 31 | 94 | 89 | 85 | 0 | 3 |
| 13 | L. Rivers | D | 2 | 40 | unopp. | 57 | 18 | 91 | 77 | 95 | 5 | 11 |
| 14 | J. Conyers Jr. | D | 32 | 67 | unopp. | 86 | 2 | 97 | 76 | 90 | 0 | 5 |
| 15 | C. C. Kilpatrick | D | 0 | 51 | 51 | 88 | — | — | — | — | — | — |
| 16 | J. D. Dingell | D | 41 | 70 | unopp. | 62 | 52 | 85 | 78 | 70 | 25 | 9 |
| Minnesota | | | | | | | | | | | | |
| 1 | G. Gutknecht | R | 2 | 45 | unopp. | 53 | 81 | 89 | 37 | 5 | 100 | 98 |
| 2 | D. Minge | D | 4 | 54 | unopp. | 55 | 30 | 78 | 73 | 70 | 15 | 20 |
| 3 | J. Ramstad | R | 6 | 50 | unopp. | 70 | 48 | 79 | 46 | 35 | 70 | 70 |
| 4 | B. F. Vento | D | 20 | 56 | unopp. | 57 | 6 | 97 | 89 | 95 | 0 | 3 |
| 5 | M. O. Sabo | D | 18 | 58 | unopp. | 64 | 18 | 96 | 87 | 90 | 0 | 3 |
| 6 | B. Luther | D | 2 | 51 | unopp. | 56 | 22 | 84 | 81 | 80 | 0 | 12 |
| 7 | C. C. Peterson | D | 6 | 52 | unopp. | 68 | 63 | 61 | 61 | 55 | 53 | 41 |
| 8 | J. L. Oberstar | D | 22 | 62 | unopp. | 67 | 22 | 88 | 76 | 80 | 20 | 8 |
| Mississippi | | | | | | | | | | | | |
| 1 | R. F. Wicker | R | 2 | 45 | unopp. | 68 | 100 | 96 | 35 | 0 | 100 | 90 |
| 2 | B. G. Thompson | D | 4 | 48 | unopp. | 60 | 64 | 91 | 81 | 90 | 5 | 10 |
| 3 | C. W. "Chip" Pickering Jr. | R | 0 | 33 | 56 | 61 | — | — | — | — | — | — |
| 4 | M. Parker | R | 8 | 47 | unopp. | 61 | 100 | 95 | 37 | 0 | 100 | 71 |
| 5 | G. Taylor | D | 8 | 43 | 94 | 58 | 86 | 45 | 53 | 80 | 30 | 77 |
| Missouri | | | | | | | | | | | | |
| 1 | W. L. "Bill" Clay | D | 28 | 65 | 78 | 70 | 12 | 96 | 76 | 80 | 6 | 4 |
| 2 | J. M. Talent | R | 4 | 40 | unopp. | 61 | 90 | 93 | 32 | 10 | 100 | 97 |
| 3 | R. A. Gephardt | D | 20 | 55 | 75 | 59 | 35 | 93 | 82 | 85 | 6 | 11 |
| 4 | I. Skelton | D | 20 | 65 | unopp. | 64 | 100 | 58 | 66 | 40 | 50 | 52 |
| 5 | K. McCarthy | D | 2 | 49 | unopp. | 67 | 22 | 87 | 84 | 80 | 5 | 15 |

*(Table continues)*

**Table A-1** *(Continued)*

| State, district | Representative | Party | Years of service[a] | Age | % vote in 1996 Primary | % vote in 1996 General | 1996 voting ratings CC | PU | PS | ADA | ACU | ACU (career) |
|---|---|---|---|---|---|---|---|---|---|---|---|---|
| 6 | P. Danner | D | 4 | 62 | 77 | 69 | 63 | 67 | 63 | 55 | 45 | 27 |
| 7 | R. Blunt | R | 0 | 46 | 56 | 65 | — | — | — | — | — | — |
| 8 | J. A. Emerson[f] | R | 0 | 46 | — | 50 | — | — | — | — | — | — |
| 9 | K. Hulshof | R | 0 | 38 | 50 | 49 | — | — | — | — | — | — |
| Montana | | | | | | | | | | | | |
| AL | R. Hill | R | 0 | 49 | 44 | 52 | — | — | — | — | — | — |
| Nebraska | | | | | | | | | | | | |
| 1 | D. Bereuter | R | 18 | 57 | unopp. | 70 | 82 | 82 | 51 | 50 | 60 | 69 |
| 2 | J. Christensen | R | 2 | 33 | 97 | 57 | 90 | 94 | 35 | 5 | 100 | 96 |
| 3 | B. Barrett | R | 6 | 67 | unopp. | 77 | 96 | 92 | 41 | 0 | 95 | 90 |
| Nevada | | | | | | | | | | | | |
| 1 | J. Ensign | R | 2 | 38 | unopp. | 50 | 68 | 80 | 40 | 5 | 85 | 91 |
| 2 | J. Gibbons | R | 0 | 51 | 42 | 59 | — | — | — | — | — | — |
| New Hampshire | | | | | | | | | | | | |
| 1 | J. E. Sununu | R | 0 | 32 | 28 | 50 | — | — | — | — | — | — |
| 2 | C. F. Bass | R | 2 | 44 | 66 | 50 | 80 | 91 | 34 | 0 | 100 | 86 |
| New Jersey | | | | | | | | | | | | |
| 1 | R. E. Andrews | D | 6 | 39 | unopp. | 76 | 43 | 83 | 77 | 65 | 25 | 27 |
| 2 | F. A. LoBiondo | R | 2 | 50 | unopp. | 60 | 53 | 76 | 44 | 25 | 70 | 75 |
| 3 | J. Saxton | R | 12 | 53 | unopp. | 64 | 83 | 85 | 40 | 15 | 84 | 79 |
| 4 | C. H. Smith | R | 16 | 43 | unopp. | 64 | 76 | 82 | 46 | 30 | 80 | 54 |

| | | | | | | | | | | | | |
|---|---|---|---|---|---|---|---|---|---|---|---|---|
| 5 | M. Roukema | R | 16 | 67 | 75 | 71 | 44 | 68 | 53 | 50 | 53 | 50 |
| 6 | F. Pallone Jr. | D | 8 | 45 | unopp. | 61 | 25 | 91 | 81 | 90 | 10 | 21 |
| 7 | B. Franks | R | 4 | 45 | unopp. | 55 | 40 | 72 | 52 | 35 | 63 | 62 |
| 8 | W. J. Pascrell Jr. | D | 0 | 59 | unopp. | 51 | — | — | — | — | — | — |
| 9 | S. R. Rothman | D | 0 | 44 | 79 | 56 | — | — | — | — | — | — |
| 10 | D. M. Payne | D | 8 | 62 | 82 | 84 | 6 | 98 | 78 | 95 | 0 | 4 |
| 11 | R. Frelinghuysen | R | 2 | 50 | unopp. | 66 | 81 | 80 | 54 | 30 | 75 | 68 |
| 12 | M. Pappas | R | 0 | 35 | 38 | 50 | — | — | — | — | — | — |
| 13 | R. Menendez | D | 4 | 43 | 93 | 79 | 27 | 94 | 80 | 85 | 5 | 9 |
| New Mexico | | | | | | | | | | | | |
| 1 | S. H. Schiff | R | 8 | 49 | unopp. | 57 | 87 | 76 | 56 | 25 | 63 | 72 |
| 2 | J. Skeen | R | 16 | 69 | 70 | 56 | 98 | 89 | 42 | 5 | 90 | 83 |
| 3 | B. Richardson[g] | D | 14 | 49 | unopp. | — | — | — | — | — | — | 18 |
| New York | | | | | | | | | | | | |
| 1 | M. P. Forbes | R | 2 | 44 | unopp. | 55 | 91 | 76 | 43 | 15 | 84 | 82 |
| 2 | R. A. Lazio | R | 4 | 38 | unopp. | 64 | 76 | 76 | 46 | 15 | 75 | 68 |
| 3 | P. T. King | R | 4 | 52 | 88 | 55 | 85 | 83 | 49 | 20 | 79 | 79 |
| 4 | C. McCarthy | D | 0 | 52 | unopp. | 57 | — | — | — | — | — | — |
| 5 | G. L. Ackerman | D | 14 | 54 | unopp. | 64 | 33 | 96 | 89 | 85 | 0 | 4 |
| 6 | F. H. Flake | D | 8 | 51 | unopp. | 85 | 26 | 94 | 86 | 80 | 6 | 2 |
| 7 | T. J. Manton | D | 12 | 64 | unopp. | 71 | 66 | 80 | 75 | 65 | 26 | 14 |
| 8 | J. Nadler | D | 4 | 49 | 82 | 82 | 4 | 96 | 77 | 100 | 0 | 4 |
| 9 | C. E. Schumer | D | 16 | 46 | unopp. | 75 | 24 | 91 | 83 | 90 | 5 | 4 |
| 10 | E. Towns | D | 14 | 62 | unopp. | 91 | 9 | 97 | 79 | 85 | 0 | 3 |
| 11 | M. R. Owens | D | 14 | 60 | unopp. | 92 | 2 | 98 | 80 | 95 | 0 | 3 |
| 12 | N. M. Velazquez | D | 4 | 43 | unopp. | 85 | 2 | 96 | 79 | 100 | 0 | 3 |
| 13 | S. Molinari | R | 7 | 38 | unopp. | 62 | 81 | 84 | 41 | 20 | 88 | 72 |
| 14 | C. B. Maloney | D | 4 | 48 | unopp. | 72 | 13 | 96 | 86 | 85 | 5 | 2 |

*(Table continues)*

**Table A-1** *(Continued)*

| State, district | Representative | Party | Years of service[a] | Age | % vote in 1996: Primary | % vote in 1996: General | 1996 voting ratings: CC | PU | PS | ADA | ACU | ACU (career) |
|---|---|---|---|---|---|---|---|---|---|---|---|---|
| 15 | C. B. Rangel | D | 26 | 66 | unopp. | 91 | 8 | 97 | 82 | 95 | 0 | 5 |
| 16 | J. E. Serano | D | 7 | 53 | unopp. | 96 | 12 | 96 | 82 | 95 | 0 | 2 |
| 17 | E. L. Engel | D | 8 | 49 | 77 | 85 | 22 | 95 | 84 | 95 | 0 | 6 |
| 18 | N. M. Lowey | D | 8 | 59 | unopp. | 64 | 10 | 95 | 86 | 90 | 0 | 5 |
| 19 | S. Kelly | R | 2 | 60 | 53 | 46 | 84 | 83 | 47 | 10 | 70 | 67 |
| 20 | B. A. Gilman | R | 24 | 74 | unopp. | 57 | 78 | 63 | 61 | 35 | 45 | 45 |
| 21 | M. R. McNulty | D | 8 | 49 | 57 | 66 | 39 | 83 | 72 | 60 | 22 | 26 |
| 22 | G. B. H. Solomon | R | 18 | 66 | unopp. | 60 | 98 | 96 | 37 | 5 | 95 | 89 |
| 23 | S. L. Boehlert | R | 14 | 60 | 65 | 64 | 78 | 68 | 56 | 50 | 50 | 35 |
| 24 | J. M. McHugh | R | 4 | 48 | unopp. | 71 | 88 | 85 | 42 | 10 | 79 | 82 |
| 25 | J. T. Walsh | R | 8 | 49 | unopp. | 55 | 96 | 79 | 47 | 20 | 68 | 67 |
| 26 | M. D. Hinchey | D | 4 | 58 | unopp. | 55 | 20 | 93 | 78 | 95 | 5 | 6 |
| 27 | B. Paxon | R | 8 | 42 | unopp. | 60 | 100 | 98 | 35 | 0 | 100 | 92 |
| 28 | L. M. Slaughter | D | 10 | 67 | unopp. | 57 | 18 | 94 | 84 | 90 | 5 | 7 |
| 29 | J. J. LaFalce | D | 22 | 57 | unopp. | 62 | 24 | 91 | 82 | 80 | 5 | 14 |
| 30 | J. Quinn | R | 4 | 45 | unopp. | 55 | 80 | 70 | 58 | 35 | 58 | 63 |
| 31 | A. Houghton | R | 10 | 70 | unopp. | 72 | 83 | 77 | 61 | 20 | 60 | 59 |
| North Carolina | | | | | | | | | | | | |
| 1 | E. Clayton | D | 4 | 62 | unopp. | 66 | 38 | 94 | 86 | 100 | 5 | 4 |
| 2 | B. Etheridge | D | 0 | 55 | unopp. | 53 | — | — | — | — | — | — |
| 3 | W. B. Jones Jr. | R | 2 | 53 | unopp. | 63 | 94 | 93 | 30 | 5 | 100 | 98 |
| 4 | D. E. Price[h] | D | 0 | 56 | unopp. | 54 | — | — | — | — | — | — |
| 5 | R. Burr | R | 2 | 40 | unopp. | 62 | 96 | 96 | 32 | 5 | 100 | 94 |
| 6 | H. Coble | R | 12 | 65 | unopp. | 73 | 88 | 95 | 30 | 15 | 90 | 88 |

| | | | | | | | | | | | | |
|---|---|---|---|---|---|---|---|---|---|---|---|---|
| 7 | M. McIntyre | D | 0 | 40 | 52 | 53 | — | — | — | — | — | — |
| 8 | W. G. "Bill" Hefner | D | 22 | 66 | unopp. | 55 | 94 | 76 | 71 | 55 | 30 | 30 |
| 9 | S. Myrick | R | 2 | 55 | unopp. | 63 | 92 | 96 | 33 | 10 | 100 | 98 |
| 10 | C. Ballenger | R | 10 | 70 | unopp. | 70 | 100 | 95 | 33 | 0 | 100 | 90 |
| 11 | C. H. Taylor | R | 6 | 55 | unopp. | 58 | 100 | 95 | 33 | 5 | 100 | 94 |
| 12 | M. L. Watt | D | 4 | 51 | unopp. | 71 | 16 | 98 | 84 | 90 | 0 | 4 |
| North Dakota | | | | | | | | | | | | |
| AL | E. Pomeroy | D | 4 | 44 | unopp. | 55 | 67 | 80 | 81 | 80 | 11 | 18 |
| Ohio | | | | | | | | | | | | |
| 1 | S. Chabot | R | 2 | 43 | unopp. | 54 | 67 | 87 | 35 | 15 | 100 | 100 |
| 2 | R. Portman | R | 4 | 41 | unopp. | 72 | 90 | 92 | 37 | 10 | 100 | 90 |
| 3 | T. P. Hall | D | 18 | 54 | unopp. | 64 | 52 | 79 | 71 | 65 | 15 | 15 |
| 4 | M. G. Oxley | R | 16 | 52 | unopp. | 65 | 98 | 93 | 37 | 5 | 100 | 89 |
| 5 | P. E. Gillmor | R | 8 | 57 | unopp. | 61 | 73 | 91 | 40 | 15 | 84 | 81 |
| 6 | T. Strickland [i] | D | 0 | 55 | unopp. | 51 | — | — | — | — | — | — |
| 7 | D. L. Hobson | R | 6 | 60 | 86 | 68 | 94 | 90 | 38 | 0 | 90 | 78 |
| 8 | J. A. Boehner | R | 6 | 47 | unopp. | 70 | 98 | 97 | 34 | 0 | 100 | 97 |
| 9 | M. Kaptur | D | 14 | 50 | unopp. | 77 | 31 | 84 | 75 | 75 | 15 | 11 |
| 10 | D. J. Kucinich | D | 0 | 50 | 77 | 49 | — | — | — | — | — | — |
| 11 | L. Stokes | D | 28 | 71 | unopp. | 81 | 14 | 95 | 80 | 65 | 0 | 6 |
| 12 | J. R. Kasich | R | 14 | 44 | 88 | 64 | 86 | 91 | 41 | 15 | 95 | 86 |
| 13 | S. Brown | D | 4 | 44 | unopp. | 60 | 6 | 96 | 84 | 95 | 0 | 14 |
| 14 | T. C. Sawyer | D | 10 | 51 | 80 | 54 | 37 | 93 | 88 | 90 | 0 | 3 |
| 15 | D. Pryce | R | 4 | 45 | 86 | 71 | 88 | 89 | 40 | 5 | 85 | 78 |
| 16 | R. Regula | R | 24 | 72 | 84 | 69 | 94 | 86 | 48 | 15 | 75 | 56 |
| 17 | J. A. Traficant Jr. | D | 12 | 55 | unopp. | 91 | 92 | 51 | 57 | 55 | 50 | 20 |
| 18 | B. Ney | R | 2 | 42 | unopp. | 50 | 88 | 90 | 39 | 10 | 85 | 85 |

*(Table continues)*

**Table A-1** *(Continued)*

| *State, district* | *Representative* | *Party* | *Years of service*[a] | *Age* | *% vote in 1996* Primary | General | *1996 voting ratings* CC | PU | PS | ADA | ACU | ACU (career) |
|---|---|---|---|---|---|---|---|---|---|---|---|---|
| 19 | S. LaTourette | R | 2 | 42 | unopp. | 55 | 90 | 85 | 45 | 15 | 80 | 80 |
| Oklahoma | | | | | | | | | | | | |
| 1 | S. Largent | R | 2 | 41 | unopp. | 68 | 92 | 96 | 30 | 10 | 100 | 100 |
| 2 | T. Coburn | R | 2 | 47 | unopp. | 55 | 86 | 91 | 29 | 10 | 89 | 95 |
| 3 | W. Watkins[j] | R | 0 | 57 | 79 | 51 | — | — | — | — | — | — |
| 4 | J.C. Watts Jr. | R | 2 | 39 | unopp. | 58 | 98 | 93 | 32 | 0 | 100 | 98 |
| 5 | E. J. Istook | R | 4 | 46 | unopp. | 70 | 98 | 96 | 32 | 10 | 100 | 98 |
| 6 | F. D. Lucas | R | 3 | 36 | unopp. | 64 | 100 | 96 | 34 | 0 | 100 | 96 |
| Oregon | | | | | | | | | | | | |
| 1 | E. Furse | D | 4 | 60 | unopp. | 52 | 12 | 93 | 81 | 80 | 5 | 9 |
| 2 | R. F. "Bob" Smith[k] | R | 0 | 65 | 82 | 62 | — | — | — | — | — | — |
| 3 | E. Blumenauer | D | 0 | 48 | 78 | 68 | — | — | — | — | — | — |
| 4 | P.A. DeFazio | D | 10 | 49 | unopp. | 66 | 18 | 89 | 71 | 95 | 5 | 9 |
| 5 | D. Hooley | D | 0 | 57 | 51 | 51 | — | — | — | — | — | — |
| Pennsylvania | | | | | | | | | | | | |
| 1 | T. M. Foglietta | D | 16 | 68 | 73 | 88 | 9 | 96 | 86 | 85 | 5 | 3 |
| 2 | C. Fattah | D | 2 | 40 | unopp. | 88 | 6 | 98 | 83 | 95 | 0 | 2 |
| 3 | R. A. Borski | D | 14 | 48 | 91 | 69 | 37 | 86 | 82 | 80 | 10 | 13 |
| 4 | R. Klink | D | 4 | 45 | unopp. | 64 | 62 | 75 | 63 | 65 | 30 | 29 |
| 5 | J. E. Peterson | R | 0 | 57 | 38 | 60 | — | — | — | — | — | 64 |
| 6 | T. Holden | D | 4 | 39 | unopp. | 59 | 78 | 62 | 61 | 45 | 47 | 44 |
| 7 | C. Weldon | R | 10 | 49 | 83 | 67 | 88 | 85 | 45 | 15 | 84 | 68 |
| 8 | J. Greenwood | R | 4 | 45 | 60 | 59 | 80 | 78 | 49 | 25 | 60 | 68 |

| | | | | | | | | | | | | |
|---|---|---|---|---|---|---|---|---|---|---|---|---|
| 9 | B. Shuster | R | 24 | 64 | unopp. | 74 | 92 | 93 | 34 | 0 | 100 | 93 |
| 10 | J. M. McDade | R | 34 | 65 | 53 | 60 | 95 | 87 | 42 | 5 | 75 | 59 |
| 11 | P. E. Kanjorski | D | 12 | 59 | unopp. | 68 | 55 | 78 | 68 | 65 | 30 | 22 |
| 12 | J. P. Murtha | D | 23 | 64 | unopp. | 70 | 90 | 65 | 77 | 55 | 25 | 36 |
| 13 | J. D. Fox | R | 2 | 49 | unopp. | 49 | 66 | 77 | 44 | 35 | 65 | 73 |
| 14 | W. J. Coyne | D | 16 | 60 | 66 | 61 | 10 | 94 | 81 | 100 | 0 | 3 |
| 15 | P. McHale | D | 4 | 46 | unopp. | 55 | 53 | 77 | 72 | 70 | 20 | 21 |
| 16 | J. R. Pitts | R | 0 | 57 | 45 | 59 | — | — | — | — | — | — |
| 17 | G. W. Gekas | R | 14 | 66 | unopp. | 72 | 98 | 96 | 35 | 0 | 100 | 85 |
| 18 | M. Doyle | D | 2 | 43 | 74 | 56 | 63 | 66 | 66 | 55 | 32 | 34 |
| 19 | W. F. Goodling | R | 22 | 69 | 55 | 63 | 88 | 88 | 37 | 10 | 95 | 75 |
| 20 | F. Mascara | D | 2 | 66 | unopp. | 54 | 76 | 70 | 70 | 60 | 35 | 38 |
| 21 | P. English | R | 2 | 40 | unopp. | 51 | 83 | 81 | 46 | 10 | 74 | 79 |
| Rhode Island | | | | | | | | | | | | |
| 1 | P. Kennedy | D | 2 | 29 | unopp. | 69 | 35 | 86 | 75 | 85 | 10 | 13 |
| 2 | R. A. Weygand | D | 0 | 48 | 48 | 64 | — | — | — | — | — | — |
| South Carolina | | | | | | | | | | | | |
| 1 | M. Sanford | R | 2 | 36 | unopp. | 96 | 63 | 84 | 44 | 10 | 95 | 92 |
| 2 | F. Spence | R | 26 | 68 | unopp. | 90 | 100 | 96 | 35 | 5 | 100 | 89 |
| 3 | L. Graham | R | 2 | 41 | unopp. | 60 | 98 | 96 | 35 | 0 | 100 | 98 |
| 4 | B. Inglis | R | 4 | 37 | unopp. | 71 | 94 | 95 | 34 | 10 | 100 | 98 |
| 5 | J. M. Spratt Jr. | D | 14 | 54 | unopp. | 54 | 75 | 80 | 73 | 60 | 25 | 24 |
| 6 | J. E. Clyburn | D | 4 | 56 | 88 | 69 | 65 | 91 | 84 | 95 | 5 | 13 |
| South Dakota | | | | | | | | | | | | |
| AL | J. R. Thune | R | 0 | 35 | 59 | 58 | — | — | — | — | — | — |
| Tennessee | | | | | | | | | | | | |
| 1 | W. L. "Bill" Jenkins | R | 0 | 59 | 18 | 64 | — | — | — | — | — | — |

*(Table continues)*

**Table A-1** *(Continued)*

| *State, district* | *Representative* | *Party* | *Years of service*[a] | *Age* | *% vote in 1996* | | *1996 voting ratings* | | | | | |
|---|---|---|---|---|---|---|---|---|---|---|---|---|
| | | | | | Primary | General | CC | PU | PS | ADA | ACU | ACU (career) |
| 2 | J. J. Duncan Jr. | R | 8 | 49 | unopp. | 71 | 60 | 82 | 32 | 30 | 85 | 87 |
| 3 | Z. Wamp | R | 2 | 39 | unopp. | 56 | 75 | 89 | 31 | 15 | 100 | 100 |
| 4 | V. Hilleary | R | 2 | 37 | unopp. | 58 | 86 | 93 | 32 | 0 | 95 | 98 |
| 5 | B. Clement | D | 9 | 53 | unopp. | 72 | 86 | 69 | 73 | 60 | 30 | 27 |
| 6 | B. Gordon | D | 12 | 47 | 89 | 54 | 80 | 66 | 63 | 45 | 50 | 21 |
| 7 | E. Bryant | R | 2 | 48 | unopp. | 64 | 98 | 96 | 35 | 0 | 100 | 100 |
| 8 | J. Tanner | D | 8 | 52 | unopp. | 67 | 100 | 63 | 67 | 45 | 47 | 44 |
| 9 | H. E. Ford Jr. | D | 0 | 26 | 60 | 61 | — | — | — | — | — | — |
| Texas | | | | | | | | | | | | |
| 1 | M. Sandlin | D | 0 | 44 | 56 | 52 | — | — | — | — | — | — |
| 2 | J. Turner | D | 0 | 50 | 59 | 52 | — | — | — | — | — | — |
| 3 | S. Johnson | R | 6 | 66 | unopp. | 73 | 98 | 96 | 38 | 5 | 100 | 98 |
| 4 | R. M. Hall | D | 16 | 73 | unopp. | 64 | 92 | 29 | 44 | 15 | 90 | 79 |
| 5 | P. Sessions | R | 0 | 41 | | 53 | — | — | — | — | — | 10 |
| 6 | J. Barton | R | 12 | 47 | 89 | 77 | 94 | 94 | 37 | 15 | 89 | 94 |
| 7 | B. Archer | R | 26 | 68 | unopp. | 81 | 96 | 97 | 35 | 5 | 100 | 97 |
| 8 | K. Brady[l] | R | 0 | 41 | | 59 | — | — | — | — | — | 96 |
| 9 | N. Lampson[m] | D | 0 | 51 | | 53 | — | — | — | — | — | 92 |
| 10 | L. Doggett | D | 2 | 50 | unopp. | 56 | 29 | 90 | 90 | 80 | 0 | 4 |
| 11 | C. Edwards | D | 6 | 45 | unopp. | 57 | 92 | 72 | 73 | 60 | 20 | 33 |
| 12 | K. Granger | R | 0 | 53 | 69 | 58 | — | — | — | — | — | 66 |
| 13 | W. M. "Mac" Thornberry | R | 2 | 38 | unopp. | 67 | 100 | 97 | 35 | 0 | 100 | 98 |
| 14 | R. Paul[n] | R | 0 | 61 | 54 | 51 | — | — | — | — | — | 63 |

| | | | | | | | | | | | | |
|---|---|---|---|---|---|---|---|---|---|---|---|---|
| 15 | R. Hinojosa | D | 0 | 56 | 52 | 62 | — | — | — | — | — | 41 |
| 16 | S. Reyes | D | 0 | 51 | 51 | 71 | — | — | — | — | — | 16 |
| 17 | C. W. Stenholm | D | 18 | 58 | unopp. | 52 | 90 | 50 | 53 | 50 | 65 | 77 |
| 18 | S. Jackson-Lee | D | 2 | 46 | unopp. | 77 | 43 | 93 | 88 | 90 | 5 | 3 |
| 19 | L. Combest | R | 12 | 51 | unopp. | 80 | 100 | 96 | 35 | 0 | 95 | 98 |
| 20 | H. B. Gonzalez | D | 35 | 80 | unopp. | 64 | 68 | 84 | 84 | 80 | 15 | 15 |
| 21 | L. Smith | R | 10 | 49 | unopp. | 76 | 98 | 95 | 35 | 10 | 100 | 92 |
| 22 | T. DeLay | R | 12 | 49 | unopp. | 68 | 98 | 96 | 35 | 0 | 100 | 97 |
| 23 | H. Bonilla | R | 4 | 42 | unopp. | 62 | 96 | 90 | 36 | 0 | 85 | 91 |
| 24 | M. Frost | D | 18 | 55 | unopp. | 56 | 90 | 79 | 83 | 65 | 10 | 18 |
| 25 | K. Bentsen | D | 2 | 37 | 64 | 57 | 82 | 78 | 81 | 75 | 10 | 9 |
| 26 | D. Armey | R | 12 | 56 | unopp. | 74 | 96 | 96 | 38 | 0 | 100 | 97 |
| 27 | S. P. Ortiz | D | 14 | 59 | 70 | 65 | 94 | 70 | 67 | 60 | 37 | 32 |
| 28 | F. Tejeda[o] | D | 4 | 51 | unopp. | 72 | — | — | — | — | 37 | 36 |
| 29 | G. Green | D | 4 | 49 | | 68 | 70 | 82 | 78 | 60 | 28 | 20 |
| 30 | E. B. Johnson | D | 4 | 61 | unopp. | 55 | 55 | 91 | 87 | 80 | 0 | 7 |
| Utah | | | | | | | | | | | | |
| 1 | J. V. Hansen | R | 16 | 64 | unopp. | 68 | 98 | 94 | 41 | 0 | 100 | 94 |
| 2 | M. Cook | R | 0 | 50 | 52 | 55 | — | — | — | — | — | — |
| 3 | C. B. Cannon | R | 0 | 46 | 56 | 51 | — | — | — | — | — | — |
| Vermont | | | | | | | | | | | | |
| AL | B. Sanders | I | 6 | 55 | — | 55 | 14 | 93 | 75 | 100 | 0 | 6 |
| Virginia | | | | | | | | | | | | |
| 1 | H. H. Bateman | R | 14 | 68 | 80 | unopp. | 96 | 91 | 41 | 15 | 85 | 80 |
| 2 | O. B. Pickett | D | 10 | 66 | unopp. | 65 | 92 | 57 | 68 | 45 | 50 | 44 |
| 3 | R. C. Scott | D | 4 | 49 | unopp. | 82 | 59 | 90 | 85 | 90 | 0 | 9 |
| 4 | N. Sisisky | D | 14 | 69 | unopp. | 79 | 100 | 52 | 61 | 35 | 55 | 41 |
| 5 | V. H. Goode Jr. | D | 0 | 50 | unopp. | 60 | — | — | — | — | — | 41 |

*(Table continues)*

**Table A-1** *(Continued)*

| *State, district* | *Representative* | *Party* | *Years of service*[a] | *Age* | *% vote in 1996* Primary | General | *1996 voting ratings* CC | PU | PS | ADA | ACU | ACU (career) |
|---|---|---|---|---|---|---|---|---|---|---|---|---|
| 6 | R. W. Goodlatte | R | 4 | 44 | unopp. | 67 | 88 | 93 | 30 | 5 | 95 | 92 |
| 7 | T. Bliley | R | 16 | 64 | unopp. | 75 | 100 | 94 | 34 | 0 | 100 | 91 |
| 8 | J. P. Moran | D | 6 | 51 | unopp. | 66 | 45 | 83 | 77 | 65 | 20 | 15 |
| 9 | R. Boucher | D | 14 | 50 | unopp. | 65 | 72 | 78 | 73 | 65 | 15 | 13 |
| 10 | F. Wolf | R | 16 | 57 | unopp. | 72 | 88 | 90 | 38 | 5 | 95 | 83 |
| 11 | T. Davis | R | 2 | 47 | unopp. | 64 | 84 | 78 | 52 | 15 | 79 | 70 |
| Washington | | | | | | | | | | | | |
| 1 | R. White | R | 2 | 43 | 50 | 54 | 88 | 92 | 44 | 0 | 95 | 84 |
| 2 | J. Metcalf | R | 2 | 69 | 52 | 49 | 80 | 86 | 38 | 0 | 90 | 95 |
| 3 | L. Smith | R | 2 | 46 | 52 | 50 | 90 | 90 | 36 | 5 | 84 | 90 |
| 4 | R. "Doc" Hastings | R | 2 | 55 | 55 | 53 | 98 | 97 | 33 | 0 | 100 | 96 |
| 5 | G. R. Nethercutt | R | 2 | 52 | 51 | 56 | 98 | 94 | 33 | 0 | 95 | 92 |
| 6 | N. D. Dicks | D | 20 | 56 | 67 | 66 | 59 | 84 | 88 | 65 | 0 | 10 |
| 7 | J. McDermott | D | 8 | 60 | 79 | 81 | 8 | 97 | 82 | 95 | 0 | 2 |
| 8 | J. Dunn | R | 4 | 55 | 65 | 65 | 92 | 94 | 38 | 0 | 100 | 90 |
| 9 | A. Smith | D | 0 | 31 | 49 | 50 | — | — | — | — | — | — |
| West Virginia | | | | | | | | | | | | |
| 1 | A. B. Mollohan | D | 14 | 53 | unopp. | unopp. | 77 | 71 | 72 | 65 | 15 | 31 |
| 2 | B. Wise | D | 14 | 48 | 86 | 69 | 64 | 82 | 85 | 70 | 10 | 12 |
| 3 | N. Rahall II | D | 20 | 47 | unopp. | unopp. | 51 | 81 | 70 | 75 | 20 | 16 |
| Wisconsin | | | | | | | | | | | | |
| 1 | M. W. Neumann | R | 2 | 42 | unopp. | 51 | 51 | 85 | 43 | 15 | 95 | 98 |
| 2 | S. Klug | R | 6 | 43 | unopp. | 57 | 51 | 75 | 46 | 40 | 75 | 60 |
| 3 | R. Kind | D | 0 | 33 | 46 | 52 | — | — | — | — | — | — |

| | | | | | | | | | | | | |
|---|---|---|---|---|---|---|---|---|---|---|---|---|
| 4 | G. D. Kleczka | D | 13 | 53 | 85 | 58 | 25 | 84 | 78 | 75 | 10 | 9 |
| 5 | T. M. Barrett | D | 4 | 42 | unopp. | 73 | 2 | 89 | 86 | 85 | 5 | 8 |
| 6 | T. E. Petri | R | 18 | 56 | unopp. | 73 | 65 | 83 | 46 | 20 | 100 | 75 |
| 7 | D. Obey | D | 28 | 58 | unopp. | 57 | 31 | 85 | 77 | 75 | 25 | 7 |
| 8 | J. Johnson | D | 0 | 53 | 59 | 52 | — | — | — | — | — | — |
| 9 | J. Sensenbrenner Jr. | R | 18 | 53 | unopp. | 74 | 61 | 85 | 37 | 20 | 100 | 6 |
| Wyoming | | | | | | | | | | | | |
| AL | B. Cubin | R | 2 | 50 | unopp. | 55 | 98 | 96 | 31 | 0 | 100 | 95 |

[a] Service beginning in or after November in a given year is not counted as a year of service.

[b] Juanita Millender-McDonald (D-Calif., 37th) was elected on March 26, 1996, to replace Walter Tucker III (D) who resigned in December 1995.

[c] Jim Ryun (R-Kan., 2nd) began service on November 27, 1996, as a member of the 104th Congress following the early resignation of Sen. Sam Brownback from the U.S. House of Representatives.

[d] Louisiana has a two-step election process in which candidates of all parties run against one another in a September primary. If no candidate wins 50 percent or more of the vote at that time, the top two candidates run against each other in November. If a clear winner emerges from the September primary, no candidates compete in the November Election.

[e] E. E. Cummings (D-Md., 7th) was elected on April 16, 1996, to replace Kweisi Mfume (D) who resigned in February 1996.

[f] Jo Ann Emerson (R-Mo., 8th) was elected on November 5, 1996, to fill the vacancy created when her husband, Bill Emerson, died of lung cancer. Jo Ann Emerson began service as a member of the 104th Congress on November 8, 1996, and will also serve in the 105th Congress.

[g] Bill Richardson (D-N.M., 3rd) resigned his seat on February 13, 1997, to become U.S. Ambassador to the United Nations.

[h] David E. Price (D-N.C., 4th) was reelected to the U.S. House of Representatives after not serving from 1995-1997. Price had originally been elected to the House in 1986.

[i] Ted Strickland (D-Ohio, 6th) was reelected to the U.S. House of Representatives after not serving from 1995–1997. Strickland had originally been elected to the House in 1992.

[j] Wes Watkins (R-Okla., 3rd) was reelected to the U.S. House of Representatives after not serving from 1991–1997. Watkins had originally been elected to the House in 1976.

[k] Bob Smith (R-Ore., 2nd) was reelected to the U.S. House of Representatives after not serving from 1995–1997. Smith had originally been elected to the House in 1982.

[l] Kevin Brady (R-Texas, 8th) was elected to the U.S. House of Representatives after winning a December 10, 1996, runoff.

[m] Nick Lampson (D-Texas, 9th) was elected to the U.S. House of Representatives after winning a December 10, 1996, runoff.

[n] Ron Paul (R-Texas, 14th) was reelected to the U.S. House of Representatives after not serving from 1977–1979, 1985–1987, 1995–1997. Paul had originally been elected to the House in 1976.

[o] Frank Tejeda (D-Texas, 28th) died of cancer on January 30, 1997. A special election was held on March 15, 1997, to fill the remainder of Tejeda's term.

**Table A-2** House of Representatives, 104th Congress, 1995

| State, district | Representative | Party | Years of service[a] | Age | % vote in 1994 | | 1994 voting ratings | | | | | |
|---|---|---|---|---|---|---|---|---|---|---|---|---|
| | | | | | Primary | General | CC | PU | PS | ADA | ACU | ACU (career) |
| Alabama | | | | | | | | | | | | |
| 1 | S. Callahan | R | 10 | 62 | unopp. | 67.3 | 100 | 88 | 41 | 5 | 100 | 94 |
| 2 | T. Everett | R | 2 | 57 | unopp. | 73.6 | 97 | 80 | 44 | 0 | 100 | 98 |
| 3 | G. Browder | D | 6 | 51 | 84 | 63.6 | 94 | 76 | 77 | 25 | 62 | 8 |
| 4 | T. Bevill | D | 28 | 73 | unopp. | 98.5 | 94 | 85 | 88 | 35 | 50 | 53 |
| 5 | R. E. "Bud" Cramer | D | 4 | 47 | unopp. | 50.5 | 97 | 81 | 86 | 40 | 38 | 39 |
| 6 | S. Bachus | R | 2 | 47 | unopp. | 79.0 | 97 | 94 | 44 | 15 | 95 | 98 |
| 7 | E. F. Hilliard | D | 2 | 52 | unopp. | 76.9 | 39 | 94 | 75 | 80 | 29 | 17 |
| Alaska | | | | | | | | | | | | |
| AL | D. Young | R | 22 | 61 | unopp. | 56.9 | 97 | 83 | 45 | 10 | 100 | 72 |
| Arizona | | | | | | | | | | | | |
| 1 | M. Salmon | R | — | 36 | 39 | 56.0 | — | — | — | — | — | — |
| 2 | E. Pastor | D | 4 | 51 | 74 | 62.3 | 42 | 95 | 84 | 80 | 14 | 7 |
| 3 | B. Stump | R | 18 | 67 | unopp. | 70.1 | 94 | 99 | 27 | 0 | 100 | 96 |
| 4 | J. Shadegg | R | — | 45 | 43 | 60.2 | — | — | — | — | — | — |
| 5 | J. Kolbe | R | 10 | 52 | 80 | 67.7 | 82 | 83 | 51 | 15 | 80 | 81 |
| 6 | J. Hayworth | R | — | 36 | 45 | 54.6 | — | — | — | — | — | — |
| Arkansas | | | | | | | | | | | | |
| 1 | B. Lambert | D | 2 | 34 | unopp. | 53.4 | 67 | 79 | 73 | 60 | 10 | 18 |
| 2 | R. Thornton | D | 10 | 66 | unopp. | 57.4 | 71 | 93 | 90 | 75 | 19 | 19 |
| 3 | T. Hutchinson | R | 2 | 45 | unopp. | 67.7 | 86 | 95 | 38 | 5 | 95 | 98 |
| 4 | J. Dickey | R | 2 | 55 | unopp. | 51.8 | 91 | 93 | 92 | 0 | 95 | 98 |

| | | | | | | | | | | | | |
|---|---|---|---|---|---|---|---|---|---|---|---|---|
| California | | | | | | | | | | | | |
| 1 | F. Riggs | R | — | 44 | 63 | 53.3 | — | — | — | — | — | — |
| 2 | W. Herger | R | 8 | 49 | unopp. | 64.2 | 94 | 97 | 39 | 5 | 100 | 99 |
| 3 | V. Fazio | D | 16 | 52 | 75 | 49.8 | 50 | 95 | 87 | 75 | 14 | 6 |
| 4 | J. T. Doolittle | R | 4 | 44 | unopp. | 61.3 | 97 | 99 | 36 | 5 | 100 | 100 |
| 5 | R. T. Matsui | D | 16 | 53 | unopp. | 68.5 | 37 | 98 | 93 | 75 | 11 | 6 |
| 6 | L. Woolsey | D | 2 | 57 | unopp. | 58.1 | 8 | 99 | 77 | 100 | 0 | 2 |
| 7 | G. Miller | D | 20 | 49 | unopp. | 69.7 | 3 | 98 | 79 | 90 | 0 | 24 |
| 8 | N. Pelosi | D | 7 | 54 | 92 | 81.8 | 0 | 99 | 79 | 90 | 0 | 1 |
| 9 | R. V. Dellums | D | 24 | 59 | unopp. | 72.2 | 0 | 99 | 74 | 100 | 5 | 6 |
| 10 | B. Baker | R | 2 | 54 | 77 | 59.3 | 97 | 98 | 41 | 0 | 100 | 98 |
| 11 | R. W. Pombo | R | 2 | 33 | unopp. | 62.1 | 100 | 87 | 40 | 5 | 100 | 100 |
| 12 | T. Lantos | D | 14 | 66 | unopp. | 67.4 | 46 | 95 | 84 | 70 | 24 | 8 |
| 13 | P. Stark | D | 22 | 63 | 77 | 64.6 | 0 | 98 | 78 | 95 | 0 | 5 |
| 14 | A. G. Eshoo | D | 2 | 52 | 87 | 60.6 | 11 | 98 | 81 | 95 | 0 | 2 |
| 15 | N. Y. Mineta | D | 20 | 63 | unopp. | 59.9 | 15 | 98 | 90 | 90 | 10 | 4 |
| 16 | Z. Lofgren | D | — | 47 | 45 | 65.0 | — | — | — | — | — | — |
| 17 | S. Farr[b] | D | 2 | 53 | 80 | 52.2 | 13 | 99 | 84 | 90 | 0 | 4 |
| 18 | G. A. Condit | D | 6 | 46 | unopp. | 65.5 | 66 | 59 | 66 | 45 | 38 | 42 |
| 19 | G. P. Radanovich | R | — | 39 | 51 | 56.8 | — | — | — | — | — | — |
| 20 | C. Dooley | D | 4 | 40 | unopp. | 56.7 | 71 | 82 | 74 | 55 | 22 | 19 |
| 21 | B. Thomas | R | 16 | 53 | 70 | 68.1 | 94 | 90 | 51 | 10 | 84 | 78 |
| 22 | A. Seastrand | R | — | 53 | 59 | 49.3 | — | — | — | — | — | — |
| 23 | E. Gallegly | R | 8 | 50 | unopp. | 66.2 | 100 | 94 | 54 | 10 | 95 | 91 |
| 24 | A. C. Beilenson | D | 18 | 62 | 87 | 49.4 | 19 | 97 | 85 | 95 | 0 | 7 |
| 25 | H. P. "Buck" McKeon | R | 2 | 55 | 82 | 64.9 | 100 | 96 | 48 | 5 | 95 | 99 |
| 26 | H. L. Berman | D | 12 | 43 | 76 | 62.6 | 15 | 98 | 84 | 90 | 0 | 6 |
| 27 | C. J. Moorhead | R | 22 | 72 | 77 | 53.0 | 97 | 97 | 41 | 0 | 100 | 96 |
| 28 | D. Dreier | R | 14 | 42 | unopp. | 67.1 | 100 | 99 | 38 | 5 | 100 | 95 |

*(Table continues)*

**Table A-2** *(Continued)*

| State, district | Representative | Party | Years of service[a] | Age | % vote in 1994 | | 1994 voting ratings | | | | | |
|---|---|---|---|---|---|---|---|---|---|---|---|---|
| | | | | | Primary | General | CC | PU | PS | ADA | ACU | ACU (career) |
| 29 | H. A. Waxman | D | 20 | 55 | 80 | 68.0 | 3 | 98 | 77 | 90 | 0 | 5 |
| 30 | X. Becerra | D | 2 | 36 | 81 | 66.2 | 13 | 98 | 78 | 100 | 0 | 2 |
| 31 | M. G. Martinez | D | 13 | 65 | 56 | 59.1 | 63 | 94 | 86 | 70 | 15 | 8 |
| 32 | J. C. Dixon | D | 16 | 60 | 90 | 77.6 | 15 | 99 | 91 | 75 | 10 | 5 |
| 33 | L. Roybal-Allard | D | 2 | 53 | 79 | 81.5 | 14 | 99 | 87 | 100 | 0 | 2 |
| 34 | E. E. Torres | D | 12 | 64 | unopp. | 61.7 | 27 | 98 | 93 | 75 | 10 | 3 |
| 35 | M. Waters | D | 4 | 56 | unopp. | 78.1 | 6 | 97 | 75 | 100 | 10 | 4 |
| 36 | J. Harman | D | 2 | 49 | unopp. | 48.0 | 74 | 83 | 88 | 60 | 19 | 18 |
| 37 | W. R. Tucker III | D | 2 | 37 | 84 | 77.4 | 25 | 97 | 77 | 90 | 11 | 8 |
| 38 | S. Horn | R | 2 | 63 | 76 | 58.5 | 85 | 69 | 69 | 30 | 57 | 60 |
| 39 | E. Royce | R | 2 | 43 | unopp. | 66.4 | 82 | 97 | 34 | 10 | 95 | 96 |
| 40 | J. Lewis | R | 16 | 60 | 69 | 70.7 | 91 | 81 | 55 | 0 | 88 | 85 |
| 41 | J. C. Kim | R | 2 | 55 | 41 | 62.1 | 100 | 96 | 44 | 5 | 95 | 94 |
| 42 | G. E. Brown Jr. | D | 30 | 74 | unopp. | 51.1 | 27 | 96 | 89 | 80 | 10 | 6 |
| 43 | K. Calvert | R | 2 | 41 | 51 | 54.7 | 100 | 91 | 58 | 5 | 90 | 93 |
| 44 | S. Bono | R | — | 59 | 49 | 55.6 | — | — | — | — | — | — |
| 45 | D. Rohrabacher | R | 6 | 47 | unopp. | 69.1 | 69 | 97 | 29 | 10 | 86 | 93 |
| 46 | R. K. Dornan | R | 16 | 61 | unopp. | 57.1 | 97 | 97 | 36 | 0 | 100 | 97 |
| 47 | C. Cox | R | 6 | 42 | 85 | 71.7 | 89 | 98 | 37 | 0 | 100 | 98 |
| 48 | R. Packard | R | 12 | 63 | 81 | 73.4 | 97 | 91 | 45 | 0 | 95 | 93 |
| 49 | B. P. Bilbray | R | — | 43 | 51 | 48.5 | — | — | — | — | — | — |
| 50 | B. Filner | D | 2 | 52 | unopp. | 56.7 | 17 | 98 | 79 | 100 | 0 | 4 |
| 51 | R. "Duke" Cunningham | R | 4 | 53 | 86 | 66.9 | 94 | 91 | 55 | 15 | 95 | 96 |
| 52 | D. Hunter | R | 14 | 46 | unopp. | 64.0 | 94 | 93 | 33 | 0 | 100 | 95 |

| | | | | | | | | | | | | |
|---|---|---|---|---|---|---|---|---|---|---|---|---|
| Colorado | | | | | | | | | | | | |
| 1 | P. Schroeder | D | 22 | 54 | 85 | 80.0 | 14 | 83 | 74 | 100 | 5 | 12 |
| 2 | D. E. Skaggs | D | 8 | 51 | unopp. | 56.7 | 20 | 97 | 90 | 80 | 10 | 9 |
| 3 | S. McInnis | R | 2 | 41 | unopp. | 69.6 | 88 | 86 | 43 | 15 | 81 | 84 |
| 4 | W. Allard | R | 4 | 51 | unopp. | 72.3 | 94 | 97 | 40 | 5 | 95 | 95 |
| 5 | J. Hefley | R | 8 | 59 | unopp. | 100.0 | 89 | 96 | 33 | 0 | 100 | 97 |
| 6 | D. Schaefer | R | 12 | 58 | unopp. | 59.8 | 92 | 96 | 35 | 10 | 90 | 89 |
| Connecticut | | | | | | | | | | | | |
| 1 | B. B. Kennelly | D | 13 | 58 | unopp. | 73.4 | 42 | 96 | 90 | 85 | 10 | 5 |
| 2 | S. Gejdenson | D | 14 | 46 | unopp. | 42.6 | 17 | 99 | 87 | 80 | 10 | 4 |
| 3 | R. DeLauro | D | 4 | 51 | unopp. | 63.4 | 31 | 97 | 86 | 90 | 5 | 4 |
| 4 | C. Shays | R | 7 | 49 | unopp. | 74.4 | 42 | 67 | 56 | 55 | 38 | 40 |
| 5 | G. A. Franks | R | 4 | 41 | unopp. | 52.2 | 86 | 74 | 71 | 20 | 70 | 83 |
| 6 | N. L. Johnson | R | 12 | 59 | unopp. | 63.9 | 66 | 62 | 68 | 30 | 52 | 50 |
| Delaware | | | | | | | | | | | | |
| AL | M. N. Castle | R | 2 | 55 | unopp. | 70.7 | 92 | 82 | 71 | 20 | 67 | 71 |
| Florida | | | | | | | | | | | | |
| 1 | J. Scarborough | R | — | 31 | 54 | 61.6 | — | — | — | — | — | — |
| 2 | P. Peterson | D | 4 | 59 | unopp. | 61.3 | 84 | 87 | 84 | 50 | 38 | 23 |
| 3 | C. Brown | D | 2 | 48 | 67 | 57.7 | 47 | 95 | 90 | 85 | 24 | 14 |
| 4 | T. Fowler | R | 2 | 52 | unopp. | unopp. | 94 | 89 | 62 | 15 | 90 | 87 |
| 5 | K. L. Thurman | D | 2 | 43 | unopp. | 57.2 | 69 | 81 | 73 | 65 | 19 | 18 |
| 6 | C. Stearns | R | 6 | 53 | unopp. | 99.1 | 89 | 99 | 35 | 0 | 100 | 92 |
| 7 | J. L. Mica | R | 2 | 51 | unopp. | 73.4 | 97 | 94 | 42 | 10 | 95 | 96 |
| 8 | B. McCollum | R | 14 | 50 | unopp. | 99.7 | 93 | 91 | 44 | 0 | 95 | 91 |
| 9 | M. Bilirakis | R | 12 | 64 | unopp. | 99.9 | 94 | 89 | 50 | 20 | 86 | 85 |
| 10 | C. W. Bill Young | R | 24 | 64 | unopp. | unopp. | 85 | 87 | 55 | 25 | 81 | 84 |

*(Table continues)*

**Table A-2** *(Continued)*

| *State, district* | *Representative* | *Party* | *Years of service*[a] | *Age* | *% vote in 1994* Primary | General | *1994 voting ratings* CC | PU | PS | ADA | ACU | ACU (career) |
|---|---|---|---|---|---|---|---|---|---|---|---|---|
| 11 | S. M. Gibbons | D | 32 | 74 | unopp. | 51.6 | 51 | 94 | 90 | 70 | 16 | 31 |
| 12 | C. T. Canady | R | 2 | 40 | unopp. | 65.0 | 100 | 94 | 54 | 5 | 90 | 95 |
| 13 | D. Miller | R | 2 | 52 | 81 | unopp. | 82 | 96 | 42 | 20 | 90 | 89 |
| 14 | P. J. Goss | R | 6 | 56 | unopp. | unopp. | 89 | 94 | 51 | 10 | 86 | 87 |
| 15 | D. Weldon | R | — | 41 | 54 | 53.7 | — | — | — | — | — | — |
| 16 | M. Foley | R | — | 40 | 60 | 58.1 | — | — | — | — | — | — |
| 17 | C. P. Meek | D | 2 | 68 | unopp. | 100.0 | 32 | 97 | 86 | 95 | 10 | 10 |
| 18 | I. Ros-Lehtinen | R | 6 | 42 | unopp. | unopp. | 72 | 78 | 61 | 25 | 65 | 75 |
| 19 | H. A. Johnston | D | 6 | 63 | unopp. | 66.1 | 14 | 97 | 83 | 90 | 5 | 12 |
| 20 | P. Deutsch | D | 2 | 37 | unopp. | 61.2 | 49 | 92 | 84 | 60 | 19 | 16 |
| 21 | L. Diaz-Balart | R | 2 | 40 | unopp. | 100.0 | 80 | 71 | 61 | 25 | 71 | 73 |
| 22 | E. Clay Shaw Jr. | R | 14 | 55 | 78 | 63.4 | 94 | 89 | 64 | 15 | 74 | 85 |
| 23 | A. L. Hastings | D | 2 | 58 | unopp. | unopp. | 21 | 97 | 78 | 80 | 7 | 6 |
| Georgia | | | | | | | | | | | | |
| 1 | J. Kingston | R | 2 | 39 | unopp. | 76.6 | 97 | 89 | 43 | 5 | 100 | 100 |
| 2 | S. D. Bishop Jr. | D | 2 | 47 | 67 | 66.2 | 70 | 92 | 90 | 75 | 25 | 19 |
| 3 | M. Collins | R | 2 | 50 | unopp. | 65.5 | 86 | 92 | 36 | 0 | 95 | 98 |
| 4 | J. Linder | R | 2 | 52 | unopp. | 57.9 | 100 | 96 | 46 | 0 | 95 | 98 |
| 5 | J. Lewis | D | 8 | 54 | unopp. | 69.1 | 60 | 97 | 73 | 100 | 5 | 2 |
| 6 | N. Gingrich | R | 16 | 51 | 77 | 64.2 | 100 | 95 | 45 | 5 | 100 | 88 |
| 7 | B. Barr | R | — | 46 | 57 | 51.9 | — | — | — | — | — | — |
| 8 | S. Chambliss | R | — | 51 | unopp. | 62.7 | — | — | — | — | — | — |
| 9 | N. Deal[c] | D | 2 | 52 | unopp. | 57.9 | 91 | 63 | 64 | 15 | 67 | 64 |

| | | | | | | | | | | | | |
|---|---|---|---|---|---|---|---|---|---|---|---|---|
| 10 | C. Norwood | R | — | 53 | 51 | 65.2 | — | — | — | — | — | — |
| 11 | C. A. McKinney | D | 2 | 39 | unopp. | 65.6 | 3 | 99 | 77 | 100 | 0 | 0 |
| Hawaii | | | | | | | | | | | | |
| 1 | N. Abercrombie | D | 4 | 56 | 67 | 53.6 | 17 | 98 | 72 | 100 | 0 | 0 |
| 2 | P. T. Mink | D | 17 | 67 | 85 | 70.1 | 3 | 99 | 74 | 100 | 0 | 1 |
| Idaho | | | | | | | | | | | | |
| 1 | H. Chenoweth | R | — | 56 | 48 | 55.4 | — | — | — | — | — | — |
| 2 | M. D. Crapo | R | 2 | 43 | unopp. | 75.0 | 97 | 96 | 40 | 5 | 90 | 93 |
| Illinois | | | | | | | | | | | | |
| 1 | B. L. Rush | D | 2 | 48 | unopp. | 75.7 | 6 | 97 | 74 | 100 | 5 | 3 |
| 2 | M. Reynolds | D | 2 | 42 | 57 | 98.1 | 21 | 99 | 86 | 85 | 0 | 2 |
| 3 | W. O. Lipinski | D | 12 | 57 | unopp. | 54.2 | 71 | 77 | 74 | 45 | 38 | 38 |
| 4 | L. V. Gutierrez | D | 2 | 41 | 64 | 75.2 | 6 | 96 | 69 | 90 | 0 | 2 |
| 5 | M. P. Flanagan | R | — | 32 | 39 | 54.4 | — | — | — | — | — | — |
| 6 | H. J. Hyde | R | 20 | 70 | 82 | 73.5 | 86 | 87 | 54 | 5 | 90 | 88 |
| 7 | C. Collins | D | 22 | 63 | unopp. | 79.6 | 3 | 96 | 70 | 95 | 6 | 3 |
| 8 | P. M. Crane | R | 25 | 64 | 40 | 64.9 | 81 | 98 | 29 | 5 | 100 | 99 |
| 9 | S. R. Yates | D | 44 | 85 | 75 | 66.1 | 0 | 98 | 72 | 100 | 0 | 4 |
| 10 | J. Edward Porter | R | 15 | 59 | 66 | 75.1 | 61 | 73 | 55 | 30 | 52 | 64 |
| 11 | J. Weller | R | — | 37 | 32 | 60.6 | — | — | — | — | — | — |
| 12 | J. F. Costello | D | 7 | 45 | unopp. | 65.9 | 72 | 76 | 73 | 50 | 38 | 31 |
| 13 | H. W. Fawell | R | 10 | 65 | unopp. | 73.1 | 78 | 85 | 51 | 25 | 81 | 81 |
| 14 | D. Hastert | R | 8 | 52 | 80 | 76.5 | 94 | 95 | 47 | 5 | 95 | 90 |
| 15 | T. W. Ewing | R | 4 | 59 | unopp. | 68.2 | 94 | 94 | 43 | 10 | 90 | 95 |
| 16 | D. Manzullo | R | 2 | 50 | unopp. | 70.6 | 94 | 94 | 46 | 5 | 95 | 98 |
| 17 | L. Evans | D | 12 | 43 | unopp. | 54.5 | 6 | 99 | 77 | 100 | 0 | 3 |
| 18 | R. LaHood | R | — | 49 | 50 | 60.2 | — | — | — | — | — | — |

*(Table continues)*

**Table A-2** *(Continued)*

| *State, district* | *Representative* | *Party* | *Years of service*[a] | *Age* | *% vote in 1994* Primary | General | *1994 voting ratings* CC | PU | PS | ADA | ACU | ACU (career) |
|---|---|---|---|---|---|---|---|---|---|---|---|---|
| 19 | G. Poshard | D | 6 | 49 | unopp. | 58.4 | 69 | 65 | 63 | 55 | 38 | 31 |
| 20 | R. J. Durbin | D | 12 | 50 | unopp. | 54.8 | 22 | 98 | 78 | 95 | 0 | 9 |
| Indiana | | | | | | | | | | | | |
| 1 | P. J. Visclosky | D | 10 | 45 | 77 | 56.5 | 36 | 96 | 91 | 75 | 19 | 8 |
| 2 | D. M. McIntosh | R | — | 36 | 43 | 54.5 | — | — | — | — | — | — |
| 3 | T. Roemer | D | 4 | 38 | 86 | 55.2 | 69 | 86 | 83 | 65 | 14 | 3 |
| 4 | M. E. Souder | R | — | 44 | 40 | 55.4 | — | — | — | — | — | — |
| 5 | S. Buyer | R | 2 | 36 | unopp. | 69.5 | 97 | 94 | 50 | 0 | 100 | 100 |
| 6 | D. Burton | R | 12 | 56 | 87 | 77.0 | 97 | 99 | 29 | 0 | 100 | 97 |
| 7 | J. T. Myers | R | 28 | 67 | 54 | 65.1 | 92 | 75 | 42 | 5 | 100 | 83 |
| 8 | J. Hostettler | R | — | 33 | 35 | 52.4 | — | — | — | — | — | — |
| 9 | L. H. Hamilton | D | 30 | 63 | 82 | 52.0 | 69 | 78 | 82 | 60 | 38 | 22 |
| 10 | A. Jacobs Jr. | D | 28 | 62 | 58 | 53.5 | 40 | 62 | 71 | 85 | 30 | 26 |
| Iowa | | | | | | | | | | | | |
| 1 | J. Leach | R | 18 | 52 | unopp. | 60.2 | 69 | 69 | 64 | 40 | 33 | 41 |
| 2 | J. Nussle | R | 4 | 34 | unopp. | 56.0 | 81 | 94 | 43 | 25 | 70 | 79 |
| 3 | J. Ross Lightfoot | R | 10 | 56 | unopp. | 57.8 | 94 | 89 | 51 | 5 | 95 | 85 |
| 4 | G. Ganske | R | — | 45 | 78 | 52.5 | — | — | — | — | — | — |
| 5 | T. Latham | R | — | 46 | 62 | 60.8 | — | — | — | — | — | — |
| Kansas | | | | | | | | | | | | |
| 1 | P. Roberts | R | 14 | 58 | unopp. | 77.4 | 97 | 96 | 40 | 0 | 100 | 86 |
| 2 | S. Brownback | R | — | 38 | 48 | 65.6 | — | — | — | — | — | — |

| | | | | | | | | | | | | |
|---|---|---|---|---|---|---|---|---|---|---|---|---|
| 3 | J. Meyers | R | 10 | 66 | 59 | 56.6 | 78 | 75 | 70 | 30 | 65 | 71 |
| 4 | T. Tiahrt | R | — | 43 | 54 | 52.9 | — | — | — | — | — | — |
| Kentucky | | | | | | | | | | | | |
| 1 | E. Whitfield | R | — | 51 | 52 | 51.0 | — | — | — | — | — | — |
| 2 | R. Lewis[d] | R | 1 | 48 | 55 | 59.8 | 89 | 96 | 40 | n.a. | 86 | 86 |
| 3 | M. Ward | D | — | 43 | 27 | 94.4 | — | — | — | — | — | — |
| 4 | J. Bunning | R | 8 | 63 | unopp. | 74.1 | 83 | 96 | 31 | 5 | 95 | 95 |
| 5 | H. Rogers | R | 14 | 57 | unopp. | 79.4 | 86 | 81 | 49 | 15 | 89 | 83 |
| 6 | S. Baesler | D | 2 | 53 | unopp. | 58.8 | 83 | 83 | 85 | 45 | 33 | 36 |
| Louisiana | | | | | | | | | | | | |
| 1 | R. L. Livingston | R | 18 | 51 | 81 | e | 94 | 84 | 43 | 0 | 95 | 88 |
| 2 | W. J. Jefferson | D | 4 | 47 | 78 | e | 29 | 97 | 89 | 90 | 15 | 5 |
| 3 | W. J. "Billy" Tauzin | D | 15 | 51 | 76 | e | 92 | 51 | 56 | 15 | 76 | 69 |
| 4 | C. Fields | D | 2 | 32 | 70 | e | 25 | 97 | 76 | 90 | 5 | 5 |
| 5 | J. McCrery | R | 7 | 45 | 80 | e | 92 | 86 | 56 | 5 | 90 | 89 |
| 6 | R. H. Baker | R | 8 | 46 | 81 | e | 100 | 94 | 47 | 0 | 100 | 93 |
| 7 | J. Hayes | D | 8 | 48 | 53 | e | 94 | 57 | 60 | 20 | 83 | 60 |
| Maine | | | | | | | | | | | | |
| 1 | J. B. Longley Jr. | R | — | 43 | 42 | 51.9 | — | — | — | — | — | — |
| 2 | J. Baldacci | D | — | 39 | 27 | 45.7 | — | — | — | — | — | — |
| Maryland | | | | | | | | | | | | |
| 1 | W. T. Gilchrest | R | 4 | 47 | 65 | 67.7 | 78 | 72 | 64 | 30 | 62 | 65 |
| 2 | B. Ehrlich Jr. | R | — | 37 | 57 | 62.7 | — | — | — | — | — | — |
| 3 | B. L. Cardin | D | 8 | 51 | 87 | 71.0 | 31 | 96 | 79 | 75 | 10 | 4 |
| 4 | A. R. Wynn | D | 2 | 43 | 84 | 75.0 | 26 | 97 | 98 | 95 | 0 | 2 |
| 5 | S. H. Hoyer | D | 14 | 55 | 82 | 58.8 | 57 | 95 | 86 | 70 | 24 | 8 |
| 6 | R. G. Bartlett | R | 2 | 68 | 84 | 65.9 | 100 | 99 | 40 | 0 | 100 | 100 |

*(Table continues)*

**Table A-2** *(Continued)*

| State, district | Representative | Party | Years of service[a] | Age | % vote in 1994: Primary | % vote in 1994: General | 1994 voting ratings: CC | PU | PS | ADA | ACU | ACU (career) |
|---|---|---|---|---|---|---|---|---|---|---|---|---|
| 7 | K. Mfume | D | 8 | 46 | unopp. | 81.5 | 9 | 96 | 73 | 95 | 0 | 4 |
| 8 | C. A. Morella | R | 8 | 63 | 70 | 70.3 | 51 | 46 | 78 | 70 | 29 | 24 |
| Massachusetts | | | | | | | | | | | | |
| 1 | J. W. Olver | D | 4 | 58 | unopp. | 99.4 | 3 | 99 | 78 | 100 | 0 | 2 |
| 2 | R. E. Neal | D | 6 | 45 | unopp. | 58.6 | 26 | 98 | 79 | 95 | 0 | 8 |
| 3 | P. I. Blute | R | 2 | 38 | unopp. | 54.6 | 78 | 77 | 68 | 20 | 67 | 71 |
| 4 | B. Frank | D | 14 | 54 | 86 | 99.5 | 0 | 98 | 69 | 100 | 0 | 4 |
| 5 | M. T. Meehan | D | 2 | 38 | 77 | 69.9 | 12 | 91 | 70 | 85 | 16 | 17 |
| 6 | P. G. Torkildsen | R | 2 | 36 | unopp. | 50.5 | 78 | 69 | 73 | 15 | 67 | 71 |
| 7 | E. J. Markey | D | 18 | 48 | unopp. | 64.4 | 30 | 99 | 76 | 85 | 0 | 4 |
| 8 | J. P. Kennedy II | D | 8 | 42 | unopp. | 99.0 | 20 | 98 | 78 | 90 | 5 | 5 |
| 9 | J. Moakley | D | 22 | 67 | 86 | 69.8 | 25 | 99 | 78 | 95 | 0 | 7 |
| 10 | G. E. Studds | D | 22 | 57 | 77 | 68.7 | 0 | 99 | 82 | 95 | 0 | 4 |
| Michigan | | | | | | | | | | | | |
| 1 | B. Stupak | D | 2 | 42 | unopp. | 56.9 | 67 | 85 | 72 | 70 | 24 | 21 |
| 2 | P. Hoekstra | R | 2 | 41 | unopp. | 75.3 | 81 | 94 | 40 | 20 | 86 | 87 |
| 3 | V. J. Ehlers[f] | R | 1 | 60 | unopp. | 73.9 | 81 | 77 | 47 | 25 | 81 | 81 |
| 4 | D. Camp | R | 4 | 41 | unopp. | 73.1 | 89 | 92 | 51 | 20 | 95 | 88 |
| 5 | J. A. Barcia | D | 2 | 42 | unopp. | 65.5 | 75 | 70 | 64 | 50 | 43 | 43 |
| 6 | F. Upton | R | 8 | 41 | unopp. | 73.5 | 64 | 83 | 49 | 35 | 67 | 71 |
| 7 | N. Smith | R | 2 | 60 | 67 | 65.1 | 91 | 93 | 47 | 5 | 95 | 92 |
| 8 | D. Chrysler | R | — | 52 | unopp. | 51.6 | — | — | — | — | — | — |
| 9 | D. E. Kildee | D | 18 | 65 | unopp. | 51.2 | 25 | 93 | 77 | 60 | 5 | 7 |

| | | | | | | | | | | | | |
|---|---|---|---|---|---|---|---|---|---|---|---|---|
| 10 | D. E. Bonior | D | 18 | 49 | unopp. | 62.2 | 11 | 99 | 79 | 95 | 5 | 4 |
| 11 | J. Knollenberg | R | 2 | 61 | unopp. | 68.2 | 94 | 96 | 44 | 0 | 100 | 98 |
| 12 | S. M. Levin | D | 12 | 63 | 80 | 52.0 | 28 | 95 | 84 | 85 | 5 | 3 |
| 13 | L. N. Rivers | D | — | 38 | 56 | 51.9 | — | — | — | — | — | — |
| 14 | J. Conyers Jr. | D | 30 | 65 | 50 | 81.5 | 13 | 98 | 74 | 100 | 5 | 5 |
| 15 | B. Collins | D | 4 | 55 | unopp. | 84.1 | 3 | 99 | 69 | 100 | 0 | 0 |
| 16 | J. D. Dingell | D | 39 | 68 | unopp. | 59.1 | 41 | 94 | 82 | 70 | 15 | 8 |
| Minnesota | | | | | | | | | | | | |
| 1 | G. Gutknecht | R | — | 43 | 57 | 55.2 | — | — | — | — | — | — |
| 2 | D. Minge | D | 2 | 52 | unopp. | 52.0 | 61 | 72 | 68 | 60 | 14 | 20 |
| 3 | J. Ramstad | R | 4 | 48 | unopp. | 73.2 | 72 | 82 | 55 | 30 | 62 | 71 |
| 4 | B. F. Vento | D | 18 | 54 | unopp. | 54.9 | 6 | 98 | 78 | 100 | 0 | 3 |
| 5 | M. Olav Sabo | D | 16 | 56 | unopp. | 61.9 | 6 | 99 | 83 | 95 | 10 | 3 |
| 6 | W. P. "Bill" Luther | D | — | 49 | 57 | 49.9 | — | — | — | — | — | — |
| 7 | C. C. Peterson | D | 4 | 50 | unopp. | 51.2 | 74 | 59 | 58 | 45 | 52 | 32 |
| 8 | J. L. Oberstar | D | 20 | 60 | unopp. | 65.7 | 14 | 96 | 74 | 80 | 15 | 7 |
| Mississippi | | | | | | | | | | | | |
| 1 | R. Wicker | R | — | 43 | 53 | 63.1 | — | — | — | — | — | — |
| 2 | B. Thompson[g] | D | 2 | 46 | unopp. | 53.7 | 37 | 96 | 88 | 80 | 20 | 13 |
| 3 | G. V. "Sonny" Montgomery | D | 28 | 74 | unopp. | 67.6 | 97 | 76 | 79 | 35 | 57 | 79 |
| 4 | M. Parker | D | 6 | 45 | 59 | 68.5 | 100 | 62 | 68 | 20 | 67 | 68 |
| 5 | G. Taylor | D | 6 | 41 | unopp. | 60.1 | 97 | 37 | 60 | 15 | 67 | 79 |
| Missouri | | | | | | | | | | | | |
| 1 | W. L. Clay | D | 26 | 63 | 53 | 63.4 | 9 | 86 | 71 | 85 | 14 | 4 |
| 2 | J. M. Talent | R | 2 | 38 | unopp. | 67.3 | 97 | 95 | 51 | 5 | 95 | 96 |
| 3 | R. A. Gephardt | D | 18 | 53 | 77 | 57.7 | 21 | 99 | 91 | 80 | 5 | 11 |
| 4 | I. Skelton | D | 18 | 63 | unopp. | 67.8 | 100 | 70 | 78 | 35 | 62 | 53 |
| 5 | K. McCarthy | D | — | 47 | 41 | 56.6 | — | — | — | — | — | — |

*(Table continues)*

**Table A-2** *(Continued)*

| | | | | | *% vote in 1994* | | *1994 voting ratings* | | | | | |
|---|---|---|---|---|---|---|---|---|---|---|---|---|
| *State, district* | *Representative* | *Party* | *Years of service*[a] | *Age* | Primary | General | CC | PU | PS | ADA | ACU | ACU (career) |
| 6 | P. Danner | D | 2 | 60 | 77 | 66.1 | 77 | 81 | 70 | 70 | 29 | 27 |
| 7 | M. Hancock | R | 6 | 65 | unopp. | 57.3 | 89 | 98 | 29 | 10 | 95 | 99 |
| 8 | B. Emerson | R | 14 | 57 | unopp. | 70.1 | 100 | 88 | 47 | 0 | 10 | 88 |
| 9 | H. L. Volkmer | D | 18 | 63 | 68 | 50.5 | 83 | 78 | 74 | 50 | 48 | 34 |
| Montana | | | | | | | | | | | | |
| AL | P. Williams | D | 16 | 57 | unopp. | 48.7 | 54 | 88 | 74 | 75 | 19 | 10 |
| Nebraska | | | | | | | | | | | | |
| 1 | D. Bereuter | R | 16 | 55 | unopp. | 62.6 | 83 | 78 | 55 | 15 | 71 | 71 |
| 2 | J. Christensen | R | — | 31 | 53 | 49.9 | — | — | — | — | — | — |
| 3 | B. Barrett | R | 4 | 65 | unopp. | 78.7 | 97 | 95 | 47 | 5 | 95 | 90 |
| Nevada | | | | | | | | | | | | |
| 1 | J. Ensign | R | — | 36 | 83 | 48.5 | — | — | — | — | — | — |
| 2 | B. F. Vucanovich | R | 12 | 73 | 78 | 63.5 | 100 | 88 | 53 | 0 | 100 | 93 |
| New Hampshire | | | | | | | | | | | | |
| 1 | B. Zeliff | R | 4 | 58 | unopp. | 65.6 | 94 | 93 | 50 | 5 | 86 | 88 |
| 2 | C. Bass | R | — | 42 | 29 | 51.4 | — | — | — | — | — | — |
| New Jersey | | | | | | | | | | | | |
| 1 | R. E. Andrews | D | 4 | 37 | unopp. | 72.3 | 72 | 69 | 71 | 45 | 26 | 25 |
| 2 | F. A. LoBiondo | R | — | 48 | 55 | 64.6 | — | — | — | — | — | — |
| 3 | H. James Saxton | R | 10 | 51 | unopp. | 66.4 | 89 | 83 | 63 | 15 | 67 | 79 |
| 4 | C. H. Smith | R | 14 | 41 | unopp. | 67.9 | 74 | 66 | 54 | 30 | 70 | 56 |

| | | | | | | | | | | | | |
|---|---|---|---|---|---|---|---|---|---|---|---|---|
| 5 | M. Roukema | R | 14 | 65 | 77 | 74.2 | 67 | 69 | 67 | 35 | 50 | 51 |
| 6 | F. Pallone Jr. | D | 6 | 43 | unopp. | 60.4 | 39 | 89 | 71 | 70 | 14 | 23 |
| 7 | B. Franks | R | 2 | 43 | unopp. | 59.6 | 69 | 77 | 55 | 25 | 62 | 65 |
| 8 | B. Martini | R | — | 47 | unopp. | 49.9 | — | — | — | — | — | — |
| 9 | R. G. Torricelli | D | 12 | 43 | 91 | 62.5 | 50 | 90 | 78 | 65 | 6 | 9 |
| 10 | D. M. Payne | D | 6 | 60 | unopp. | 75.9 | 3 | 98 | 74 | 95 | 10 | 4 |
| 11 | R. Frelinghuysen | R | — | 48 | conv. | 71.2 | — | — | — | — | — | — |
| 12 | D. Zimmer | R | 4 | 50 | unopp. | 58.3 | 67 | 81 | 44 | 25 | 57 | 69 |
| 13 | R. Menendez | D | 2 | 41 | unopp. | 70.9 | 31 | 96 | 79 | 90 | 5 | 7 |
| New Mexico | | | | | | | | | | | | |
| 1 | S. H. Schiff | R | 6 | 47 | unopp. | 73.9 | 89 | 81 | 53 | 15 | 80 | 75 |
| 2 | J. Skeen | R | 14 | 67 | unopp. | 63.3 | 100 | 83 | 53 | 0 | 95 | 82 |
| 3 | B. Richardson | D | 12 | 47 | unopp. | 63.6 | 57 | 94 | 89 | 55 | 26 | 19 |
| New York | | | | | | | | | | | | |
| 1 | M. P. Forbes | R | — | 42 | 56 | 52.5 | — | — | — | — | — | — |
| 2 | R. A. Lazio | R | 2 | 36 | unopp. | 68.2 | 83 | 77 | 72 | 20 | 57 | 64 |
| 3 | P. T. King | R | 2 | 50 | 71 | 59.2 | 83 | 92 | 45 | 5 | 81 | 87 |
| 4 | D. Frisa | R | — | 39 | 51 | 50.2 | — | — | — | — | — | — |
| 5 | G. L. Ackerman | D | 12 | 52 | unopp. | 55.0 | 28 | 96 | 81 | 90 | 0 | 3 |
| 6 | F. H. Flake | D | 8 | 49 | unopp. | 80.4 | 16 | 99 | 84 | 95 | 0 | 2 |
| 7 | T. J. Manton | D | 10 | 62 | unopp. | 87.1 | 49 | 94 | 86 | 70 | 15 | 11 |
| 8 | J. Nadler | D | 2 | 47 | 62 | 82.0 | 6 | 96 | 74 | 100 | 5 | 7 |
| 9 | C. E. Schumer | D | 14 | 44 | unopp. | 72.6 | 31 | 94 | 83 | 90 | 5 | 4 |
| 10 | E. Towns | D | 12 | 60 | unopp. | 89.0 | 16 | 98 | 81 | 85 | 0 | 2 |
| 11 | M. R. Owens | D | 12 | 58 | unopp. | 88.9 | 4 | 97 | 73 | 90 | 0 | 3 |
| 12 | N. M. Velazquez | D | 2 | 41 | 79 | 92.3 | 6 | 98 | 71 | 100 | 0 | 0 |
| 13 | S. Molinari | R | 5 | 36 | unopp. | 71.4 | 83 | 84 | 60 | 20 | 71 | 69 |
| 14 | C. B. Maloney | D | 2 | 46 | 78 | 64.2 | 22 | 94 | 76 | 100 | 0 | 2 |

*(Table continues)*

**Table A-2** *(Continued)*

| *State, district* | *Representative* | *Party* | *Years of service*[a] | *Age* | *% vote in 1994* Primary | General | *1994 voting ratings* CC | PU | PS | ADA | ACU | ACU (career) |
|---|---|---|---|---|---|---|---|---|---|---|---|---|
| 15 | C. B. Rangel | D | 24 | 64 | 58 | 96.5 | 12 | 98 | 80 | 95 | 5 | 5 |
| 16 | J. E. Serrano | D | 5 | 51 | unopp. | 96.3 | 9 | 98 | 73 | 95 | 0 | 1 |
| 17 | E. L. Engel | D | 6 | 47 | 61 | 77.6 | 11 | 97 | 80 | 100 | 0 | 7 |
| 18 | N. M. Lowey | D | 6 | 57 | unopp. | 57.3 | 11 | 98 | 82 | 85 | 10 | 6 |
| 19 | S. W. Kelly | R | — | 58 | 23 | 52.1 | — | — | — | — | — | — |
| 20 | B. A. Gilman | R | 22 | 72 | unopp. | 67.5 | 69 | 45 | 71 | 35 | 52 | 44 |
| 21 | M. R. McNulty | D | 6 | 47 | unopp. | 67.0 | 60 | 84 | 75 | 55 | 42 | 23 |
| 22 | G. B. H. Solomon | R | 16 | 64 | unopp. | 73.4 | 88 | 97 | 35 | 0 | 95 | 89 |
| 23 | S. Boehlert | R | 12 | 58 | unopp. | 70.5 | 63 | 58 | 71 | 50 | 38 | 34 |
| 24 | J. M. McHugh | R | 2 | 46 | unopp. | 78.6 | 89 | 94 | 51 | 10 | 90 | 87 |
| 25 | J. T. Walsh | R | 6 | 47 | unopp. | 57.6 | 86 | 74 | 70 | 20 | 67 | 6 |
| 26 | M. D. Hinchey | D | 2 | 56 | unopp. | 49.1 | 14 | 99 | 79 | 95 | 5 | 5 |
| 27 | B. Paxon | R | 6 | 40 | unopp. | 74.5 | 92 | 98 | 35 | 0 | 100 | 92 |
| 28 | L. M. Slaughter | D | 8 | 65 | unopp. | 56.6 | 14 | 99 | 82 | 95 | 0 | 7 |
| 29 | J. J. LaFalce | D | 20 | 55 | 80 | 55.2 | 53 | 89 | 88 | 80 | 15 | 14 |
| 30 | J. Quinn | R | 2 | 43 | unopp. | 67.0 | 83 | 82 | 64 | 30 | 76 | 80 |
| 31 | A. Houghton | R | 8 | 68 | unopp. | 84.8 | 82 | 61 | 72 | 20 | 68 | 60 |
| North Carolina | | | | | | | | | | | | |
| 1 | E. Clayton | D | 2 | 60 | unopp. | 61.1 | 22 | 98 | 82 | 100 | 0 | 0 |
| 2 | D. Funderburk | R | — | 50 | 54 | 56.0 | — | — | — | — | — | — |
| 3 | W. B. Jones Jr. | R | — | 51 | unopp. | 52.7 | — | — | — | — | — | — |
| 4 | F. K. Heineman | R | — | 65 | 51 | 50.4 | — | — | — | — | — | — |
| 5 | R. M. Burr | R | — | 39 | unopp. | 57.3 | — | — | — | — | — | — |
| 6 | H. Coble | R | 10 | 63 | unopp. | 100.0 | 83 | 97 | 28 | 5 | 95 | 88 |

| | | | | | | | | | | | | |
|---|---|---|---|---|---|---|---|---|---|---|---|---|
| 7 | C. Rose | D | 22 | 55 | unopp. | 51.6 | 57 | 94 | 81 | 75 | 14 | 20 |
| 8 | W. G. "Bill" Hefner | D | 20 | 64 | 66 | 52.4 | 71 | 93 | 79 | 65 | 19 | 31 |
| 9 | S. Myrick | R | — | 53 | 68 | 65.0 | — | — | — | — | — | — |
| 10 | C. Ballenger | R | 8 | 68 | unopp. | 71.5 | 91 | 98 | 36 | 5 | 90 | 89 |
| 11 | C. H. Taylor | R | 4 | 53 | unopp. | 60.1 | 94 | 94 | 36 | 5 | 100 | 94 |
| 12 | M. Watt | D | 2 | 49 | unopp. | 65.8 | 3 | 98 | 73 | 100 | 10 | 5 |
| North Dakota | | | | | | | | | | | | |
| AL | E. Pomeroy | D | 2 | 42 | unopp. | 52.3 | 72 | 86 | 79 | 65 | 14 | 18 |
| Ohio | | | | | | | | | | | | |
| 1 | S. Chabot | R | — | 41 | unopp. | 56.1 | — | — | — | — | — | — |
| 2 | R. Portman[h] | R | 2 | 39 | unopp. | 77.4 | 88 | 94 | 45 | 10 | 86 | 90 |
| 3 | T. P. Hall | D | 16 | 52 | unopp. | 59.3 | 46 | 91 | 81 | 85 | 19 | 15 |
| 4 | M. G. Oxley | R | 14 | 50 | 74 | 100.0 | 91 | 92 | 48 | 0 | 95 | 89 |
| 5 | P. E. Gillmor | R | 6 | 55 | unopp. | 73.4 | 89 | 68 | 64 | 15 | 86 | 80 |
| 6 | F. A. Cremeans | R | 2 | 51 | 50 | 50.9 | — | — | — | — | — | — |
| 7 | D. L. Hobson | R | 4 | 58 | unopp. | 100.0 | 83 | 82 | 58 | 20 | 67 | 77 |
| 8 | J. A. Boehner | R | 4 | 45 | unopp. | 99.9 | 97 | 98 | 38 | 5 | 100 | 98 |
| 9 | M. Kaptur | D | 12 | 48 | unopp. | 75.3 | 58 | 89 | 80 | 60 | 20 | 11 |
| 10 | M. R. Hoke | R | 2 | 42 | unopp. | 51.9 | 88 | 88 | 45 | 15 | 80 | 82 |
| 11 | L. Stokes | D | 26 | 69 | unopp. | 77.2 | 9 | 98 | 72 | 100 | 10 | 6 |
| 12 | J. R. Kasich | R | 12 | 42 | 80 | 66.5 | 86 | 81 | 47 | 10 | 76 | 84 |
| 13 | S. Brown | D | 2 | 42 | unopp. | 49.1 | 36 | 92 | 64 | 75 | 14 | 12 |
| 14 | T. Sawyer | D | 8 | 49 | 69 | 51.9 | 30 | 98 | 92 | 90 | 5 | 3 |
| 15 | D. Pryce | R | 2 | 43 | unopp. | 70.7 | 88 | 90 | 55 | 15 | 67 | 78 |
| 16 | R. Regula | R | 22 | 70 | 86 | 75.0 | 89 | 76 | 59 | 15 | 86 | 54 |
| 17 | J. A. Traficant Jr. | D | 10 | 53 | unopp. | 77.4 | 67 | 80 | 68 | 65 | 33 | 14 |
| 18 | B. Ney | R | unopp. | 40 | 69 | 54.0 | — | — | — | — | — | — |

*(Table continues)*

**Table A-2** *(Continued)*

| State, district | Representative | Party | Years of service[a] | Age | % vote in 1994: Primary | % vote in 1994: General | 1994 voting ratings: CC | PU | PS | ADA | ACU | ACU (career) |
|---|---|---|---|---|---|---|---|---|---|---|---|---|
| 19 | S. LaTourette | R | — | 40 | 54 | 48.5 | — | — | — | — | — | — |
| Oklahoma | | | | | | | | | | | | |
| 1 | S. Largent | R | — | 39 | 51 | 62.7 | — | — | — | — | — | — |
| 2 | T. Coburn | R | — | 46 | 64 | 52.1 | — | — | — | — | — | — |
| 3 | B. Brewster | D | 4 | 53 | 71 | 73.8 | 91 | 73 | 75 | 30 | 60 | 54 |
| 4 | J. C. Watts | R | — | 37 | 52 | 51.6 | — | — | — | — | — | — |
| 5 | E. Jim Istook Jr. | R | 2 | 44 | unopp. | 78.1 | 91 | 96 | 38 | 5 | 95 | 98 |
| 6 | F. D. Lucas[i] | R | 1 | 34 | unopp. | 70.2 | 100 | 93 | 49 | 0 | 100 | 100 |
| Oregon | | | | | | | | | | | | |
| 1 | E. Furse | D | 2 | 58 | unopp. | 47.7 | 22 | 96 | 81 | 95 | 5 | 5 |
| 2 | W. Cooley | R | — | 62 | 23 | 57.3 | — | — | — | — | — | — |
| 3 | R. Wyden | D | 14 | 45 | unopp. | 72.5 | 33 | 96 | 81 | 80 | 0 | 10 |
| 4 | P. A. DeFazio | D | 8 | 47 | unopp. | 66.8 | 34 | 90 | 62 | 70 | 29 | 8 |
| 5 | J. Bunn | R | — | 38 | 43 | 49.8 | — | — | — | — | — | — |
| Pennsylvania | | | | | | | | | | | | |
| 1 | T. M. Foglietta | D | 14 | 66 | 69 | 81.5 | 9 | 99 | 81 | 95 | 0 | 3 |
| 2 | C. Fattah | D | — | 38 | 58 | 85.9 | — | — | — | — | — | — |
| 3 | R. A. Borski | D | 12 | 46 | 86 | 62.7 | 46 | 95 | 86 | 65 | 29 | 13 |
| 4 | R. Klink | D | 2 | 43 | unopp. | 64.2 | 53 | 83 | 72 | 50 | 43 | 34 |
| 5 | W. F. Clinger | R | 16 | 65 | 80 | 99.9 | 97 | 73 | 59 | 15 | 95 | 63 |
| 6 | T. Holden | D | 2 | 37 | unopp. | 56.7 | 72 | 75 | 68 | 45 | 43 | 41 |
| 7 | C. Weldon | R | 8 | 47 | 80 | 69.7 | 81 | 81 | 65 | 10 | 74 | 65 |
| 8 | J. C. Greenwood | R | 2 | 43 | unopp. | 66.1 | 78 | 71 | 69 | 20 | 70 | 77 |

| | | | | | | | | | | | | |
|---|---|---|---|---|---|---|---|---|---|---|---|---|
| 9 | B. Shuster | R | 22 | 62 | unopp. | 99.7 | 94 | 93 | 45 | 0 | 100 | 93 |
| 10 | J. M. McDade | R | 32 | 63 | unopp. | 65.7 | 94 | 73 | 69 | 20 | 83 | 58 |
| 11 | P. E. Kanjorski | D | 10 | 57 | unopp. | 66.5 | 47 | 88 | 82 | 55 | 29 | 21 |
| 12 | J. P. Murtha | D | 21 | 62 | unopp. | 68.9 | 78 | 88 | 85 | 50 | 38 | 38 |
| 13 | J. D. Fox | R | — | 47 | 36 | 49.4 | — | — | — | — | — | — |
| 14 | W. J. Coyne | D | 14 | 58 | unopp. | 64.1 | 3 | 99 | 75 | 100 | 0 | 3 |
| 15 | P. McHale | D | 2 | 44 | unopp. | 47.8 | 69 | 84 | 78 | 45 | 24 | 25 |
| 16 | R. S. Walker | R | 18 | 52 | unopp. | 69.7 | 94 | 98 | 31 | 0 | 100 | 92 |
| 17 | G. W. Gekas | R | 12 | 64 | unopp. | 99.9 | 97 | 93 | 41 | 10 | 95 | 85 |
| 18 | M. Doyle | D | — | 41 | 20 | 54.8 | — | — | — | — | — | — |
| 19 | B. Goodling | R | 20 | 67 | unopp. | 99.5 | 85 | 90 | 46 | 10 | 90 | 73 |
| 20 | F. R. Mascara | D | — | 64 | 50 | 53.1 | — | — | — | — | — | — |
| 21 | P. English | R | — | 38 | 66 | 49.5 | — | — | — | — | — | — |
| Rhode Island | | | | | | | | | | | | |
| 1 | P. J. Kennedy | D | — | 27 | 78 | 54.1 | — | — | — | — | — | — |
| 2 | J. Reed | D | 4 | 45 | unopp. | 68.0 | 28 | 97 | 91 | 85 | 5 | 5 |
| South Carolina | | | | | | | | | | | | |
| 1 | M. Sanford | R | — | 34 | 52 | 66.3 | — | — | — | — | — | — |
| 2 | F. D. Spence | R | 24 | 66 | unopp. | 99.8 | 92 | 89 | 53 | 5 | 95 | 89 |
| 3 | L. Graham | R | — | 39 | 50 | 60.1 | — | — | — | — | — | — |
| 4 | B. Inglis | R | 2 | 35 | unopp. | 73.5 | 92 | 86 | 38 | 5 | 100 | 100 |
| 5 | J. M. Spratt Jr. | D | 12 | 52 | unopp. | 52.1 | 78 | 91 | 82 | 65 | 24 | 25 |
| 6 | J. E. Clyburn | D | 2 | 54 | 86 | 63.8 | 37 | 96 | 89 | 75 | 15 | 4 |
| South Dakota | | | | | | | | | | | | |
| AL | T. Johnson | D | 8 | 48 | unopp. | 59.8 | 62 | 90 | 82 | 55 | 24 | 24 |
| Tennessee | | | | | | | | | | | | |
| 1 | J. H. Quillen | R | 32 | 78 | 78 | 72.9 | 94 | 77 | 49 | 5 | 95 | 86 |

*(Table continues)*

**Table A-2** *(Continued)*

| State, district | Representative | Party | Years of service[a] | Age | % vote in 1994 Primary | % vote in 1994 General | 1994 voting ratings CC | PU | PS | ADA | ACU | ACU (career) |
|---|---|---|---|---|---|---|---|---|---|---|---|---|
| 2 | J. J. "Jimmy" Duncan Jr. | R | 6 | 47 | unopp. | 90.5 | 67 | 95 | 25 | 20 | 76 | 86 |
| 3 | Z. Wamp | R | — | 37 | 68 | 52.3 | — | — | — | — | — | — |
| 4 | V. Hilleary | R | — | 35 | 58 | 56.6 | — | — | — | — | — | — |
| 5 | B. Clement | D | 7 | 51 | unopp. | 60.2 | 82 | 84 | 83 | 35 | 35 | 26 |
| 6 | B. Gordon | D | 10 | 45 | 68 | 50.6 | 79 | 85 | 76 | 55 | 24 | 16 |
| 7 | E. Bryant | R | — | 46 | 35 | 60.2 | — | — | — | — | — | — |
| 8 | J. Tanner | D | 6 | 50 | unopp. | 63.8 | 94 | 69 | 74 | 30 | 67 | 47 |
| 9 | H. E. Ford | D | 20 | 49 | 78 | 57.8 | 24 | 96 | 83 | 75 | 0 | 5 |
| Texas | | | | | | | | | | | | |
| 1 | J. Chapman | D | 10 | 49 | unopp. | 55.3 | 94 | 74 | 73 | 45 | 45 | 34 |
| 2 | C. Wilson | D | 22 | 61 | 68 | 59.0 | 86 | 82 | 75 | 55 | 53 | 44 |
| 3 | S. Johnson | R | 4 | 64 | 89 | 91.0 | 97 | 98 | 37 | 0 | 100 | 99 |
| 4 | R. M. Hall | D | 14 | 71 | 79 | 58.8 | 97 | 37 | 54 | 10 | 95 | 78 |
| 5 | J. Bryant | D | 12 | 47 | unopp. | 50.1 | 50 | 95 | 82 | 80 | 5 | 11 |
| 6 | J. L. Barton | R | 10 | 45 | 90 | 75.6 | 97 | 95 | 38 | 0 | 100 | 95 |
| 7 | B. Archer | R | 24 | 66 | unopp. | 100.0 | 94 | 99 | 33 | 0 | 100 | 98 |
| 8 | J. Fields | R | 14 | 42 | unopp. | 92.0 | 100 | 97 | 39 | 0 | 100 | 96 |
| 9 | S. Stockman | R | — | 38 | 73 | 51.9 | — | — | — | — | — | — |
| 10 | L. Doggett | D | — | 48 | 83 | 56.3 | — | — | — | — | — | — |
| 11 | C. Edwards | D | 4 | 43 | unopp. | 59.2 | 94 | 76 | 82 | 45 | 38 | 37 |
| 12 | P. Geren | D | 6 | 42 | unopp. | 68.7 | 97 | 58 | 69 | 15 | 67 | 65 |
| 13 | W. M. "Mac" Thornberry | R | — | 36 | 75 | 55.4 | — | — | — | — | — | — |
| 14 | G. Laughlin | D | 6 | 52 | unopp. | 55.6 | 87 | 74 | 77 | 50 | 60 | 56 |

| | | | | | | | | | | | | |
|---|---|---|---|---|---|---|---|---|---|---|---|---|
| 15 | E. "Kika" de la Garza | D | 30 | 67 | 60 | 59.0 | 86 | 81 | 78 | 50 | 45 | 41 |
| 16 | R. D. Coleman | D | 12 | 53 | 62 | 57.1 | 62 | 96 | 88 | 80 | 19 | 18 |
| 17 | C. W. Stenholm | D | 16 | 56 | unopp. | 53.7 | 97 | 42 | 53 | 5 | 90 | 80 |
| 18 | S. Jackson-Lee | D | — | 44 | 63 | 73.5 | — | — | — | — | — | — |
| 19 | L. Combest | R | 10 | 49 | unopp. | 100.0 | 97 | 86 | 40 | 0 | 100 | 98 |
| 20 | H. B. Gonzalez | D | 33 | 78 | unopp. | 62.5 | 22 | 96 | 80 | 75 | 15 | 15 |
| 21 | L. Smith | R | 8 | 47 | 82 | 90.0 | 94 | 96 | 43 | 5 | 95 | 92 |
| 22 | T. DeLay | R | 10 | 47 | unopp. | 73.7 | 94 | 98 | 31 | 0 | 100 | 98 |
| 23 | H. Bonilla | R | 2 | 40 | unopp. | 62.6 | 100 | 93 | 44 | 0 | 95 | 96 |
| 24 | M. Frost | D | 16 | 53 | unopp. | 52.8 | 82 | 89 | 86 | 55 | 25 | 18 |
| 25 | K. Bentsen | D | — | 35 | 64 | 52.3 | — | — | — | — | — | — |
| 26 | D. Armey | R | 10 | 54 | unopp. | 76.4 | 94 | 99 | 38 | 0 | 100 | 98 |
| 27 | S. P. Ortiz | D | 12 | 57 | unopp. | 59.4 | 82 | 79 | 79 | 45 | 48 | 32 |
| 28 | F. Tejeda | D | 2 | 49 | unopp. | 70.9 | 86 | 81 | 78 | 50 | 43 | 38 |
| 29 | G. Green | D | 2 | 47 | 55 | 73.4 | 56 | 90 | 78 | 80 | 16 | 15 |
| 30 | E. Bernice Johnson | D | 2 | 59 | unopp. | 72.6 | 29 | 96 | 86 | 85 | 19 | 10 |
| Utah | | | | | | | | | | | | |
| 1 | J. V. Hansen | R | 14 | 62 | unopp. | 64.5 | 100 | 95 | 37 | 0 | 95 | 94 |
| 2 | E. G. Waldholtz | R | — | 36 | unopp. | 45.8 | — | — | — | — | — | — |
| 3 | B. Orton | D | 4 | 46 | unopp. | 59.0 | 86 | 58 | 61 | 25 | 79 | 63 |
| Vermont | | | | | | | | | | | | |
| AL | B. Sanders[j] | I | 4 | 53 | unopp. | 49.9 | 11 | — | 73 | 100 | 0 | 7 |
| Virginia | | | | | | | | | | | | |
| 1 | H. H. Bateman | R | 12 | 66 | conv. | 74.3 | 86 | 69 | 60 | 10 | 90 | 81 |
| 2 | O. B. Pickett | D | 8 | 64 | unopp. | 59.0 | 91 | 70 | 78 | 35 | 48 | 45 |
| 3 | R. C. Scott | D | 2 | 47 | conv. | 79.4 | 28 | 96 | 87 | 80 | 24 | 16 |
| 4 | N. Sisisky | D | 12 | 67 | conv. | 61.6 | 91 | 72 | 81 | 35 | 48 | 41 |
| 5 | L. F. Payne Jr. | D | 7 | 49 | conv. | 53.3 | 89 | 76 | 77 | 25 | 57 | 47 |

*(Table continues)*

**Table A-2** *(Continued)*

| *State, district* | *Representative* | *Party* | *Years of service*[a] | *Age* | *% vote in 1994* Primary | General | *1994 voting ratings* CC | PU | PS | ADA | ACU | ACU (career) |
|---|---|---|---|---|---|---|---|---|---|---|---|---|
| 6 | R. W. Goodlatte | R | 2 | 42 | conv. | 99.9 | 86 | 96 | 39 | 10 | 90 | 93 |
| 7 | T. J. Bliley Jr. | R | 14 | 62 | conv. | 84.0 | 97 | 92 | 44 | 0 | 100 | 91 |
| 8 | J. P. Moran | D | 4 | 49 | conv. | 59.3 | 53 | 91 | 88 | 55 | 29 | 15 |
| 9 | R. Boucher | D | 12 | 48 | conv. | 58.8 | 65 | 91 | 80 | 65 | 30 | 14 |
| 10 | F. R. Wolf | R | 14 | 55 | conv. | 87.3 | 89 | 87 | 53 | 0 | 86 | 83 |
| 11 | T. M. Davis III | R | — | 45 | conv. | 52.9 | — | — | — | — | — | — |
| Washington | | | | | | | | | | | | |
| 1 | R. White | R | — | 41 | 27 | 51.7 | — | — | — | — | — | — |
| 2 | J. Metcalf | R | — | 67 | 25 | 54.7 | — | — | — | — | — | — |
| 3 | L. Smith | R | — | 44 | 27 | 52.0 | — | — | — | — | — | — |
| 4 | R. "Doc" Hastings | R | — | 53 | 49 | 53.3 | — | — | — | — | — | — |
| 5 | G. Nethercutt | R | — | 50 | 30 | 50.9 | — | — | — | — | — | — |
| 6 | N. Dicks | D | 18 | 54 | 59 | 58.3 | 58 | 94 | 91 | 65 | 14 | 12 |
| 7 | J. McDermott | D | 6 | 58 | 72 | 75.1 | 15 | 98 | 79 | 95 | 5 | 2 |
| 8 | J. Dunn | R | 2 | 53 | 70 | 76.1 | 97 | 91 | 55 | 5 | 86 | 89 |
| 9 | R. Tate | R | — | 29 | 52 | 51.8 | — | — | — | — | — | — |
| West Virginia | | | | | | | | | | | | |
| 1 | A. B. Mollohan | D | 12 | 51 | unopp. | 70.3 | 58 | 89 | 75 | 60 | 38 | 32 |
| 2 | B. Wise | D | 12 | 46 | unopp. | 63.7 | 71 | 94 | 82 | 75 | 30 | 13 |
| 3 | N. J. Rahall II | D | 18 | 45 | unopp. | 63.9 | 47 | 87 | 65 | 75 | 24 | 15 |
| Wisconsin | | | | | | | | | | | | |
| 1 | M. W. Neumann | R | — | 40 | unopp. | 49.4 | — | — | — | — | — | — |

| | | | | | | | | | | | | |
|---|---|---|---|---|---|---|---|---|---|---|---|---|
| 2 | S. L. Klug | R | 4 | 41 | unopp. | 69.2 | 61 | 80 | 51 | 45 | 43 | 53 |
| 3 | S. Gunderson | R | 14 | 43 | 63 | 55.7 | 86 | 86 | 53 | 10 | 81 | 66 |
| 4 | G. D. Kleczka | D | 10 | 51 | unopp. | 53.7 | 35 | 94 | 87 | 85 | 5 | 7 |
| 5 | T. M. Barrett | D | 2 | 41 | unopp. | 62.4 | 22 | 90 | 77 | 90 | 0 | 7 |
| 6 | T. Petri | R | 16 | 54 | unopp. | 99.5 | 81 | 93 | 41 | 25 | 76 | 73 |
| 7 | D. R. Obey | D | 26 | 56 | unopp. | 54.3 | 16 | 97 | 72 | 80 | 10 | 6 |
| 8 | T. Roth | R | 16 | 56 | 68 | 63.7 | 77 | 93 | 35 | 15 | 81 | 86 |
| 9 | F. James Sensenbrenner Jr | R | 16 | 51 | unopp. | 99.8 | 69 | 96 | 21 | 20 | 76 | 85 |
| Wyoming | | | | | | | | | | | | |
| AL | B. Cubin | R | — | 48 | 39 | 53.2 | — | — | — | — | — | — |

*Note:* In compiling this table, the conservative coalition, party unity, and presidential support scores were calculated to eliminate the effects of absences, as follows: support = support/(support + opposition).

[a] Service beginning in or after November in a given year is not counted as a year of service.
[b] Sam Farr was elected on June 8, 1993, to replace Leon Panetta (D) who was confirmed as director of the Office of Management and Budget on January 13, 1993.
[c] On April 10, 1994, Nathan Deal switched from the Democratic to the Republican Party.
[d] Ron Lewis was elected on May 24, 1994, to replace William Natcher (D) who died on March 29, 1994.
[e] Louisiana has a two-step election process in which candidates of all parties run against one another in a September primary. If no candidate wins 50 percent or more of the vote at that time, the top two candidates run against each other in November. If a clear winner emerges from the September primary, no candidates compete in the November election.
[f] Vernon Ehlers was elected on December 7, 1993, to replace Paul Henry (R) who died on July 31, 1993.
[g] Bennie Thompson was elected on April 13, 1993, to replace Mike Espy (D) who was confirmed as secretary of Agriculture on January 14, 1993.
[h] Rob Portman was elected on May 4, 1993, to replace Willis Gradison Jr. (R) who resigned in January 1993.
[i] Frank Lucas was elected on May 10, 1994, to replace Glenn English (D) who resigned in January 1994.
[j] Bernard Sanders voted as an Independent. Had he voted as a Democrat, his party unity score, adjusted for absences, would have been 96 percent.

*Sources: Congressional Quarterly Almanac,* various years; *Congressional Directory,* various years; *Congressional Quarterly Weekly Report,* various years; American Conservative Union; Americans for Democratic Action.

**Table A-3** Senate, 105th Congress, 1997

| | | | | Previous Senate election | | | 1996 Voting ratings | | | | | |
|---|---|---|---|---|---|---|---|---|---|---|---|---|
| *State, senator* | *Party* | *Years of Service* | *Age* | Year | Primary (%) | General (%) | CC | PU | PS | ADA | ACU | ACU (Career) |
| Alabama | | | | | | | | | | | | |
| Richard C. Shelby | R | 10 | 62 | 1992 | unopp. | 65 | 92 | 94 | 33 | 5 | 90 | 69 |
| Jeff Sessions | R | 0 | 49 | 1996 | 59 | 52 | — | — | — | — | — | — |
| Alaska | | | | | | | | | | | | |
| Ted Stevens | R | 28 | 73 | 1996 | 59 | 77 | 92 | 90 | 45 | 20 | 80 | 65 |
| Frank H. Murkowski | R | 16 | 63 | 1992 | 81 | 53 | 97 | 96 | 36 | 15 | 95 | 80 |
| Arizona | | | | | | | | | | | | |
| John McCain | R | 10 | 60 | 1992 | unopp. | 56 | 89 | 95 | 32 | 0 | 95 | 88 |
| Jon Kyl | R | 2 | 54 | 1994 | unopp. | 54 | 97 | 98 | 23 | 5 | 100 | 96 |
| Arkansas | | | | | | | | | | | | |
| Dale Bumpers | D | 22 | 71 | 1992 | 65 | 60 | 21 | 91 | 88 | 85 | 0 | 14 |
| Tim Hutchinson | R | 0 | 49 | 1996 | unopp. | 53 | — | — | — | — | — | — |
| California | | | | | | | | | | | | |
| Dianne Feinstein | D | 4 | 63 | 1994 | 74 | 47 | 53 | 81 | 90 | 95 | 20 | 13 |
| Barbara Boxer | D | 4 | 56 | 1992 | 44 | 48 | 18 | 94 | 90 | 100 | 5 | 3 |
| Colorado | | | | | | | | | | | | |
| Ben Nighthorse Campbell | R[a] | 4 | 63 | 1992 | unopp. | 52 | 86 | 82 | 48 | 45 | 78 | 33 |
| Wayne Allard | R | 0 | 52 | 1996 | 57 | 51 | — | — | — | — | — | — |
| Connecticut | | | | | | | | | | | | |
| Christopher J. Dodd | D | 16 | 52 | 1992 | unopp. | 59 | 38 | 89 | 81 | 85 | 10 | 9 |
| Joseph I. Lieberman | D | 8 | 54 | 1994 | unopp. | 67 | 63 | 76 | 90 | 75 | 33 | 21 |

| | | | | | | | | | | | | |
|---|---|---|---|---|---|---|---|---|---|---|---|---|
| Delaware | | | | | | | | | | | | |
| William V. Roth Jr. | R | 26 | 75 | 1994 | unopp. | 56 | 86 | 90 | 43 | 10 | 85 | 69 |
| Joseph R. Biden Jr. | D | 24 | 54 | 1996 | unopp. | 60 | 42 | 79 | 92 | 80 | 20 | 13 |
| Florida | | | | | | | | | | | | |
| Bob Graham | D | 10 | 60 | 1992 | 84 | 65 | 61 | 81 | 86 | 85 | 15 | 21 |
| Connie Mack | R | 8 | 56 | 1994 | unopp. | 70 | 100 | 93 | 34 | 0 | 100 | 95 |
| Georgia | | | | | | | | | | | | |
| Paul Coverdell | R | 4 | 57 | 1992 | 50 | 51 | 97 | 98 | 34 | 5 | 100 | 97 |
| Max Cleland | D | 4 | 47 | 1996 | unopp. | 49 | — | — | — | — | — | — |
| Hawaii | | | | | | | | | | | | |
| Daniel K. Inouye | D | 34 | 72 | 1992 | 76 | 57 | 51 | 87 | 86 | 85 | 11 | 7 |
| Daniel K. Akaka | D | 7 | 72 | 1994 | unopp. | 72 | 26 | 95 | 88 | 95 | 5 | 2 |
| Idaho | | | | | | | | | | | | |
| Larry E. Craig | R | 6 | 51 | 1996 | unopp. | 57 | 97 | 98 | 32 | 0 | 95 | 95 |
| Dirk Kempthorne | R | 4 | 45 | 1992 | 57 | 57 | 97 | 98 | 32 | 0 | 95 | 98 |
| Illinois | | | | | | | | | | | | |
| Carol Moseley-Braun | D | 4 | 49 | 1992 | 38 | 53 | 24 | 89 | 84 | 90 | 5 | 4 |
| Richard J. Durbin | D | 0 | 51 | 1995 | 65 | 56 | — | — | — | — | — | — |
| Indiana | | | | | | | | | | | | |
| Richard G. Lugar | R | 20 | 64 | 1994 | unopp. | 67 | 92 | 90 | 31 | 5 | 95 | 83 |
| Daniel R. Coats | R | 8 | 53 | 1992 | unopp. | 57 | 89 | 96 | 30 | 10 | 100 | 91 |
| Iowa | | | | | | | | | | | | |
| Charles E. Grassley | R | 16 | 63 | 1992 | unopp. | 70 | 82 | 92 | 32 | 15 | 90 | 80 |
| Tom Harkin | D | 12 | 57 | 1996 | unopp. | 52 | 18 | 91 | 85 | 80 | 10 | 9 |

*(Table continues)*

**Table A-3** *(Continued)*

| | | | | *Previous Senate election* | | | *1996 Voting ratings* | | | | | |
|---|---|---|---|---|---|---|---|---|---|---|---|---|
| *State, senator* | *Party* | *Years of Service* | *Age* | Year | Primary (%) | General (%) | CC | PU | PS | ADA | ACU | ACU (Career) |
| Kansas | | | | | | | | | | | | |
| Sam Brownback | R | 0 | 40 | 1996 | 55 | 54 | — | — | — | — | — | — |
| Pat Roberts | R | 0 | 60 | 1996 | 78 | 62 | — | — | — | — | — | — |
| Kentucky | | | | | | | | | | | | |
| Wendell H. Ford | D | 22 | 72 | 1992 | unopp. | 63 | 74 | 79 | 83 | 70 | 40 | 27 |
| Mitch McConnell | R | 12 | 54 | 1996 | 89 | 55 | 95 | 95 | 39 | 10 | 95 | 89 |
| Lousiana | | | | | | | | | | | | |
| John B. Breaux | D | 10 | 52 | 1992 | 73 | unopp. | 84 | 70 | 78 | 60 | 20 | 48 |
| Mary L. Landrieu | D | 0 | 40 | 1996 | 22 | 50 | — | — | — | — | — | — |
| Maine | | | | | | | | | | | | |
| Olympia J. Snowe | R | 2 | 49 | 1994 | unopp. | 60 | 79 | 72 | 53 | 35 | 70 | 51 |
| Susan M. Collins | R | 0 | 43 | 1996 | 55 | 49 | — | — | — | — | — | — |
| Maryland | | | | | | | | | | | | |
| Paul S. Sarbanes | D | 20 | 63 | 1994 | 79 | 59 | 18 | 94 | 90 | 95 | 0 | 6 |
| Barbara A. Mikulski | D | 10 | 60 | 1992 | 77 | 71 | 32 | 92 | 90 | 95 | 0 | 5 |
| Massachusetts | | | | | | | | | | | | |
| Edward M. Kennedy | D | 34 | 64 | 1994 | unopp. | 58 | 8 | 94 | 88 | 90 | 0 | 3 |
| John Kerry | D | 12 | 53 | 1996 | unopp. | 52 | 18 | 92 | 92 | 95 | 25 | 5 |
| Michigan | | | | | | | | | | | | |
| Carl Levin | D | 18 | 62 | 1996 | unopp. | 58 | 29 | 94 | 86 | 85 | 5 | 8 |
| Spencer Abraham | R | 2 | 44 | 1994 | 52 | 52 | 95 | 95 | 37 | 15 | 95 | 9 |

| | | | | | | | | | | | | |
|---|---|---|---|---|---|---|---|---|---|---|---|---|
| Minnesota | | | | | | | | | | | | |
| Paul D. Wellstone | D | 6 | 52 | 1996 | 86 | 50 | 11 | 92 | 85 | 95 | 5 | 4 |
| Rod Grams | R | 2 | 48 | 1994 | 58 | 49 | 92 | 98 | 36 | 5 | 95 | 98 |
| Mississippi | | | | | | | | | | | | |
| Thad Cochran | R | 18 | 58 | 1996 | 95 | 71 | 94 | 93 | 40 | 5 | 94 | 82 |
| Trent Lott | R | 8 | 55 | 1994 | 95 | 69 | 97 | 97 | 34 | 5 | 100 | 94 |
| Missouri | | | | | | | | | | | | |
| Christopher S. Bond | R | 10 | 57 | 1992 | 83 | 52 | 100 | 95 | 37 | 10 | 90 | 82 |
| John Ashcroft | R | 2 | 54 | 1994 | 83 | 60 | 89 | 98 | 29 | 5 | 100 | 96 |
| Montana | | | | | | | | | | | | |
| Max Baucus | D | 18 | 55 | 1996 | unopp. | 50 | 45 | 73 | 90 | 85 | 20 | 12 |
| Conrad Burns | R | 8 | 61 | 1994 | unopp. | 62 | 95 | 97 | 29 | 5 | 100 | 90 |
| Nebraska | | | | | | | | | | | | |
| Bob Kerrey | D | 8 | 53 | 1994 | unopp. | 55 | 32 | 88 | 86 | 85 | 5 | 9 |
| Chuck Hagel | R | 0 | 50 | 1996 | 62 | 56 | — | — | — | — | — | — |
| Nevada | | | | | | | | | | | | |
| Harry Reid | D | 10 | 57 | 1992 | 53 | 51 | 53 | 79 | 78 | 85 | 15 | 23 |
| Richard H. Bryan | D | 8 | 59 | 1994 | unopp. | 51 | 50 | 82 | 78 | 85 | 10 | 22 |
| New Hampshire | | | | | | | | | | | | |
| Robert C. Smith | R | 6 | 55 | 1996 | unopp. | 49 | 92 | 96 | 29 | 5 | 100 | 96 |
| Judd Gregg | R | 4 | 49 | 1992 | 50 | 48 | 89 | 91 | 34 | 5 | 75 | 81 |
| New Jersey | | | | | | | | | | | | |
| Frank R. Lautenberg | D | 14 | 72 | 1994 | 81 | 50 | 11 | 93 | 90 | 95 | 0 | 7 |
| Robert G. Torricelli | D | 0 | 45 | 1996 | unopp. | 53 | — | — | — | — | — | — |

*(Table continues)*

**Table A-3** *(Continued)*

| | | | | *Previous Senate election* | | | *1996 Voting ratings* | | | | | |
|---|---|---|---|---|---|---|---|---|---|---|---|---|
| *State, senator* | *Party* | *Years of Service* | *Age* | Year | Primary (%) | General (%) | CC | PU | PS | ADA | ACU | ACU (Career) |
| New Mexico | | | | | | | | | | | | |
| Pete V. Domenici | R | 24 | 64 | 1996 | unopp. | 65 | 94 | 90 | 42 | 20 | 85 | 69 |
| Jeff Bingaman | D | 14 | 53 | 1994 | unopp. | 54 | 37 | 88 | 84 | 95 | 0 | 13 |
| New York | | | | | | | | | | | | |
| Daniel Patrick Moynihan | D | 20 | 69 | 1994 | 75 | 55 | 19 | 90 | 81 | 90 | 10 | 6 |
| Alfonse M. D'Amato | R | 16 | 59 | 1992 | unopp. | 49 | 89 | 87 | 48 | 25 | 75 | 58 |
| North Carolina | | | | | | | | | | | | |
| Jesse Helms | R | 24 | 75 | 1996 | unopp. | 53 | 97 | 97 | 25 | 5 | 100 | 99 |
| Lauch Faircloth | R | 4 | 68 | 1992 | 48 | 50 | 89 | 96 | 21 | 5 | 95 | 99 |
| North Dakota | | | | | | | | | | | | |
| Kent Conrad | D | 10 | 48 | 1994 | unopp. | 58 | 39 | 87 | 83 | 85 | 15 | 20 |
| Byron L. Dorgan | D | 4 | 54 | 1992 | unopp. | 59 | 37 | 84 | 80 | 85 | 20 | 19 |
| Ohio | | | | | | | | | | | | |
| John Glenn | D | 22 | 75 | 1992 | unopp. | 51 | 18 | 90 | 88 | 95 | 10 | 13 |
| Mike DeWine | R | 2 | 49 | 1994 | 52 | 53 | 92 | 88 | 41 | 15 | 85 | 87 |
| Oklahoma | | | | | | | | | | | | |
| Don Nickles | R | 16 | 48 | 1992 | unopp. | 59 | 97 | 99 | 34 | 0 | 100 | 95 |
| James M. Inhofe | R | 2 | 62 | 1996 | 75 | 57 | 97 | 100 | 28 | 0 | 100 | 97 |
| Oregon | | | | | | | | | | | | |
| Ron Wyden | D | 1 | 47 | 1996 | 80 | 48 | 24 | 92 | 95 | 95 | 15 | 10 |
| Gordon H. Smith | R | 0 | 45 | 1996 | 78 | 50 | — | — | — | — | — | — |

| | | | | | | | | | | | | |
|---|---|---|---|---|---|---|---|---|---|---|---|---|
| Pennsylvania | | | | | | | | | | | | |
| Arlen Specter | R | 16 | 66 | 1992 | 65 | 49 | 66 | 64 | 59 | 50 | 50 | 38 |
| Rick Santorum | R | 2 | 38 | 1994 | 82 | 49 | 92 | 93 | 40 | 15 | 95 | 83 |
| Rhode Island | | | | | | | | | | | | |
| John H. Chafee | R | 20 | 74 | 1994 | 69 | 65 | 68 | 64 | 60 | 40 | 60 | 30 |
| Jack Reed | D | 0 | 46 | 1996 | 86 | 63 | — | — | — | — | — | — |
| South Carolina | | | | | | | | | | | | |
| Strom Thurmond | R | 42 | 93 | 1996 | 60 | 53 | 95 | 97 | 39 | 5 | 95 | 90 |
| Ernest F. Hollings | D | 30 | 74 | 1992 | unopp. | 50 | 59 | 82 | 82 | 70 | 20 | 42 |
| South Dakota | | | | | | | | | | | | |
| Tom Daschle | D | 10 | 48 | 1996 | unopp. | 51 | 24 | 94 | 93 | 90 | 0 | 16 |
| Tim Johnson | D | 0 | 50 | 1996 | unopp. | 51 | — | — | — | — | — | — |
| Tennessee | | | | | | | | | | | | |
| Fred Thompson | R | 2 | 54 | 1996 | 94 | 61 | 92 | 96 | 36 | 0 | 85 | 84 |
| Bill Frist | R | 2 | 44 | 1994 | 44 | 56 | 97 | 96 | 40 | 0 | 95 | 89 |
| Texas | | | | | | | | | | | | |
| Phil Gramm | R | 12 | 54 | 1996 | 85 | 55 | 97 | 99 | 25 | 0 | 100 | 93 |
| Kay Bailey Hutchison | R | 4 | 53 | 1994 | 84 | 61 | 95 | 98 | 34 | 5 | 100 | 94 |
| Utah | | | | | | | | | | | | |
| Orrin G. Hatch | R | 20 | 64 | 1994 | unopp. | 69 | 97 | 94 | 32 | 5 | 100 | 92 |
| Robert F. Bennett | R | 4 | 63 | 1992 | 51 | 55 | 97 | 92 | 36 | 5 | 95 | 91 |
| Vermont | | | | | | | | | | | | |
| Patrick J. Leahy | D | 22 | 56 | 1992 | unopp. | 54 | 33 | 88 | 75 | 90 | 5 | 5 |
| James M. Jeffords | R | 8 | 62 | 1996 | unopp. | 50 | 59 | 58 | 53 | 50 | 45 | 30 |

*(Table continues)*

**Table A-3** *(Continued)*

| | | | | *Previous Senate election* | | | *1996 Voting ratings* | | | | | |
|---|---|---|---|---|---|---|---|---|---|---|---|---|
| *State, senator* | *Party* | *Years of Service* | *Age* | Year | Primary (%) | General (%) | CC | PU | PS | ADA | ACU | ACU (Career) |
| Virginia | | | | | | | | | | | | |
| John W. Warner | R | 18 | 69 | 1996 | 65 | 52 | 89 | 93 | 42 | 5 | 95 | 95 |
| Charles S. Robb | D | 8 | 66 | 1994 | 58 | 46 | 79 | 76 | 85 | 80 | 20 | 20 |
| Washington | | | | | | | | | | | | |
| Slade Gorton | R | 14 | 66 | 1994 | 53 | 56 | 95 | 90 | 45 | 15 | 85 | 62 |
| Patty Murray | D | 4 | 46 | 1992 | 28 | 54 | 18 | 95 | 89 | 90 | 0 | 0 |
| West Virginia | | | | | | | | | | | | |
| Robert C. Byrd | D | 38 | 78 | 1994 | 85 | 69 | 32 | 82 | 81 | 70 | 15 | 28 |
| John D. Rockefeller IV | D | 12 | 59 | 1996 | 88 | 77 | 30 | 93 | 93 | 85 | 16 | 1 |
| Wisconsin | | | | | | | | | | | | |
| Herb Kohl | D | 8 | 61 | 1994 | 90 | 58 | 32 | 84 | 88 | 75 | 20 | 17 |
| Russell D. Feingold | D | 4 | 43 | 1992 | 70 | 53 | 16 | 87 | 86 | 95 | 10 | 10 |
| Wyoming | | | | | | | | | | | | |
| Craig Thomas | R | 2 | 63 | 1994 | unopp. | 59 | 95 | 98 | 29 | 5 | 100 | 89 |
| Michael B. Enzi | R | 0 | 52 | 1996 | 32 | 54 | — | — | — | — | — | — |

[a]Ben Nighthorse Campbell switched from the Democratic to the Republican Party on March 3, 1995.

**Table A-4** Senate, 104th Congress, 1995

| State, senator | Party | Years of service[a] | Age | Previous Senate election: Year | Previous Senate election: Primary (%) | Previous Senate election: General (%) | 1994 Voting ratings: CC | PU | PS | ADA | ACU | ACU (career) |
|---|---|---|---|---|---|---|---|---|---|---|---|---|
| Alabama | | | | | | | | | | | | |
| Howell Heflin | D | 16 | 73 | 1990 | 81.0 | 61.0 | 88 | 66 | 85 | 55 | 28 | 26 |
| Richard C. Shelby[b] | R | 8 | 60 | 1992 | 61.5 | 64.8 | 96 | 50 | 67 | 30 | 55 | 59 |
| Alaska | | | | | | | | | | | | |
| Ted Stevens | R | 26 | 71 | 1990 | 59.0 | 66.0 | 87 | 73 | 52 | 25 | 77 | 57 |
| Frank H. Murkowski | R | 14 | 61 | 1992 | 80.5 | 53.0 | 90 | 92 | 34 | 10 | 96 | 78 |
| Arizona | | | | | | | | | | | | |
| John McCain | R | 8 | 58 | 1992 | unopp. | 55.8 | 73 | 91 | 44 | 10 | 96 | 87 |
| Jon Kyl[c] | D | — | 52 | 1994 | unopp. | 53.7 | 94 | 96 | 44 | 5 | 90 | 95 |
| Arkansas | | | | | | | | | | | | |
| Dale Bumpers | D | 20 | 69 | 1992 | 64.5 | 60.2 | 63 | 86 | 95 | 80 | 4 | 16 |
| David Pryor | D | 16 | 60 | 1990 | unopp. | unopp. | 62 | 84 | 95 | 80 | 4 | 15 |
| California | | | | | | | | | | | | |
| Dianne Feinstein | D | 2 | 61 | 1994 | 74.0 | 46.8 | 44 | 89 | 92 | 70 | 8 | 11 |
| Barbara Boxer | D | 2 | 54 | 1992 | 43.7 | 47.9 | 19 | 92 | 87 | 95 | 0 | 4 |
| Colorado | | | | | | | | | | | | |
| Hank Brown | R | 4 | 54 | 1990 | unopp. | 56.0 | 77 | 93 | 21 | 30 | 92 | 91 |
| Ben Nighthorse Campbell[d] | R | 2 | 61 | 1992 | 45.5 | 51.8 | 48 | 78 | 83 | 55 | 25 | 24 |
| Connecticut | | | | | | | | | | | | |
| Christopher J. Dodd | D | 14 | 50 | 1992 | unopp. | 58.8 | 24 | 90 | 95 | 80 | 0 | 10 |
| Joseph I. Lieberman | D | 6 | 52 | 1994 | unopp. | 67.0 | 45 | 76 | 88 | 65 | 8 | 21 |

*(Table continues)*

**Table A-4** *(Continued)*

| | | | | *Previous Senate election* | | | *1994 Voting ratings* | | | | | |
|---|---|---|---|---|---|---|---|---|---|---|---|---|
| *State, senator* | *Party* | *Years of service*[a] | *Age* | Year | Primary (%) | General (%) | *CC* | *PU* | *PS* | *ADA* | *ACU* | *ACU* (career) |
| Delaware | | | | | | | | | | | | |
| William V. Roth Jr. | R | 24 | 73 | 1994 | unopp. | 55.8 | 66 | 77 | 56 | 35 | 68 | 68 |
| Joseph R. Biden Jr. | D | 22 | 52 | 1990 | unopp. | 63.0 | 31 | 92 | 89 | 80 | 0 | 13 |
| Florida | | | | | | | | | | | | |
| Bob Graham | D | 8 | 58 | 1992 | 84.3 | 65.4 | 53 | 85 | 92 | 75 | 8 | 25 |
| Connie Mack | R | 6 | 54 | 1994 | unopp. | 70.5 | 94 | 89 | 40 | 10 | 96 | 94 |
| Georgia | | | | | | | | | | | | |
| Sam Nunn | D | 22 | 56 | 1990 | unopp. | unopp. | 91 | 66 | 89 | 50 | 33 | 45 |
| Paul Coverdell | R | 2 | 55 | 1992 | 50.5 | 50.7 | 90 | 95 | 35 | 5 | 100 | 96 |
| Hawaii | | | | | | | | | | | | |
| Daniel K. Inouye | D | 32 | 70 | 1992 | 76.0 | 57.3 | 42 | 92 | 95 | 75 | 0 | 7 |
| Daniel K. Akaka | D | 5 | 70 | 1994 | unopp. | 71.8 | 31 | 94 | 97 | 85 | 0 | 2 |
| Idaho | | | | | | | | | | | | |
| Larry E. Craig | R | 4 | 49 | 1990 | 59.0 | 61.0 | 94 | 98 | 30 | 0 | 100 | 98 |
| Dirk Kempthorne | R | 2 | 43 | 1992 | 57.4 | 56.5 | 94 | 98 | 31 | 0 | 100 | 100 |
| Illinois | | | | | | | | | | | | |
| Paul Simon | D | 10 | 66 | 1990 | unopp. | 65.0 | 17 | 96 | 85 | 95 | 4 | 5 |
| Carol Moseley-Braun | D | 2 | 47 | 1992 | 38.3 | 53.3 | 13 | 91 | 86 | 85 | 4 | 2 |

| | | | | | | | | | | | | |
|---|---|---|---|---|---|---|---|---|---|---|---|---|
| Indiana | | | | | | | | | | | | |
| Richard G. Lugar | R | 18 | 62 | 1994 | unopp. | 67.4 | 78 | 78 | 45 | 10 | 76 | 82 |
| Daniel R. Coats | R | 6 | 51 | 1992 | unopp. | 57.3 | 91 | 89 | 42 | 5 | 92 | 92 |
| Iowa | | | | | | | | | | | | |
| Charles E. Grassley | R | 14 | 61 | 1992 | unopp. | 69.6 | 69 | 87 | 34 | 15 | 92 | 78 |
| Tom Harkin | D | 10 | 55 | 1990 | unopp. | 54.0 | 10 | 97 | 92 | 100 | 0 | 5 |
| Kansas | | | | | | | | | | | | |
| Bob Dole | R | 26 | 71 | 1992 | 80.4 | 62.7 | 97 | 96 | 35 | 0 | 100 | 82 |
| Nancy Landon Kassebaum | R | 16 | 62 | 1990 | 87.0 | 74.0 | 63 | 61 | 74 | 45 | 48 | 56 |
| Kentucky | | | | | | | | | | | | |
| Wendell H. Ford | D | 20 | 70 | 1992 | unopp. | 62.9 | 61 | 82 | 92 | 60 | 24 | 27 |
| Mitch McConnell | R | 10 | 52 | 1990 | 89.0 | 52.0 | 87 | 92 | 37 | 5 | 92 | 87 |
| Louisiana | | | | | | | | | | | | |
| J. Bennett Johnston | D | 22 | 62 | 1990 | 54.0 | e | 74 | 78 | 85 | 55 | 22 | 42 |
| John B. Breaux | D | 8 | 50 | 1992 | 73.1 | e | 78 | 78 | 85 | 55 | 17 | 32 |
| Maine | | | | | | | | | | | | |
| William S. Cohen | R | 16 | 54 | 1990 | unopp. | 61.0 | 65 | 96 | 63 | 40 | 45 | 51 |
| Olympia J. Snowe[c] | R | — | 47 | 1994 | unopp. | 60.2 | 79 | 67 | 60 | 30 | 57 | 51 |
| Maryland | | | | | | | | | | | | |
| Paul S. Sarbanes | D | 18 | 61 | 1994 | 79.0 | 59.1 | 13 | 98 | 95 | 95 | 0 | 4 |
| Barbara A. Mikulski | D | 8 | 58 | 1992 | 76.8 | 71.0 | 29 | 90 | 93 | 85 | 0 | 4 |
| Massachusetts | | | | | | | | | | | | |
| Edward M. Kennedy | D | 32 | 62 | 1994 | unopp. | 58.1 | 19 | 94 | 95 | 90 | 0 | 3 |
| John Kerry | D | 10 | 51 | 1990 | unopp. | 57.0 | 16 | 94 | 90 | 95 | 0 | 5 |
| Michigan | | | | | | | | | | | | |
| Carl Levin | D | 16 | 60 | 1990 | unopp. | 57.0 | 16 | 92 | 90 | 95 | 0 | 8 |
| Spencer Abraham | R | — | 42 | 1994 | 52.0 | 51.9 | — | — | — | — | — | — |

*(Table continues)*

**Table A-4** *(Continued)*

| | | | | *Previous Senate election* | | | *1994 Voting ratings* | | | | | |
|---|---|---|---|---|---|---|---|---|---|---|---|---|
| *State, senator* | *Party* | *Years of service*[a] | *Age* | Year | Primary (%) | General (%) | *CC* | *PU* | *PS* | *ADA* | *ACU* | *ACU* (career) |
| Minnesota | | | | | | | | | | | | |
| Paul Wellstone | D | 4 | 50 | 1990 | 60.0 | 50.0 | 3 | 94 | 82 | 100 | 4 | 4 |
| Rod Grams[c] | R | — | 46 | 1994 | 58.0 | 49.1 | 97 | 99 | 39 | 0 | 100 | 100 |
| Mississippi | | | | | | | | | | | | |
| Thad Cochran | R | 16 | 57 | 1990 | unopp. | unopp. | 94 | 82 | 45 | 10 | 92 | 79 |
| Trent Lott | R | 6 | 53 | 1994 | 95.0 | 68.8 | 100 | 97 | 40 | 5 | 100 | 95 |
| Missouri | | | | | | | | | | | | |
| Christopher S. Bond | R | 8 | 55 | 1992 | 82.7 | 51.9 | 90 | 78 | 49 | 20 | 83 | 82 |
| John Ashcroft | R | — | 52 | 1994 | 83.0 | 59.7 | — | — | — | — | — | — |
| Montana | | | | | | | | | | | | |
| Max Baucus | D | 16 | 53 | 1990 | 83.0 | 68.0 | 50 | 86 | 89 | 85 | 0 | 11 |
| Conrad Burns | R | 6 | 59 | 1994 | unopp. | 62.4 | 94 | 84 | 43 | 5 | 92 | 90 |
| Nebraska | | | | | | | | | | | | |
| Jim Exon | D | 16 | 73 | 1990 | unopp. | 59.0 | 63 | 78 | 84 | 65 | 25 | 45 |
| Bob Kerrey | D | 6 | 51 | 1994 | unopp. | 54.8 | 47 | 83 | 90 | 80 | 24 | 11 |
| Nevada | | | | | | | | | | | | |
| Harry Reid | D | 8 | 55 | 1992 | 52.8 | 51.0 | 41 | 88 | 90 | 85 | 4 | 22 |
| Richard H. Bryan | D | 6 | 57 | 1994 | unopp. | 50.9 | 48 | 85 | 85 | 75 | 12 | 26 |

| | | | | | | | | | | | | |
|---|---|---|---|---|---|---|---|---|---|---|---|---|
| New Hampshire | | | | | | | | | | | | |
| Robert C. Smith | R | 4 | 53 | 1990 | 65.0 | 65.0 | 88 | 96 | 20 | 5 | 100 | 96 |
| Judd Gregg | R | 2 | 47 | 1992 | 50.4 | 48.2 | 78 | 84 | 42 | 15 | 79 | 86 |
| New Jersey | | | | | | | | | | | | |
| Bill Bradley | D | 16 | 51 | 1990 | 92.0 | 50.0 | 7 | 84 | 80 | 85 | 4 | 11 |
| Frank R. Lautenberg | D | 12 | 70 | 1994 | 81.0 | 50.3 | 19 | 84 | 82 | 95 | 4 | 7 |
| New Mexico | | | | | | | | | | | | |
| Pete V. Domenici | R | 22 | 62 | 1990 | unopp. | 73.0 | 94 | 78 | 53 | 25 | 84 | 68 |
| Jeff Bingaman | D | 12 | 51 | 1994 | unopp. | 54.0 | 53 | 84 | 89 | 60 | 16 | 15 |
| New York | | | | | | | | | | | | |
| Daniel Patrick Moynihan | D | 18 | 67 | 1994 | 74.0 | 55.2 | 16 | 92 | 84 | 100 | 0 | 6 |
| Alfonse M. D'Amato | R | 14 | 57 | 1992 | unopp. | 49.0 | 84 | 82 | 34 | 20 | 92 | 55 |
| North Carolina | | | | | | | | | | | | |
| Jesse Helms | R | 22 | 73 | 1990 | 84.0 | 53.0 | 87 | 95 | 19 | 0 | 100 | 99 |
| Lauch Faircloth | R | 2 | 66 | 1992 | 47.7 | 50.4 | 100 | 98 | 24 | 5 | 100 | 100 |
| North Dakota | | | | | | | | | | | | |
| Kent Conrad[f] | D | 8 | 46 | 1994 | unopp. | 58.0 | 53 | 85 | 89 | 85 | 12 | 23 |
| Byron L. Dorgan | D | 2 | 52 | 1992 | unopp. | 59.0 | 44 | 86 | 81 | 85 | 8 | 19 |
| Ohio | | | | | | | | | | | | |
| John Glenn | D | 20 | 73 | 1992 | unopp. | 51.0 | 23 | 90 | 95 | 80 | 4 | 13 |
| Mike DeWine | R | — | 47 | 1994 | 52.0 | 53.4 | — | — | — | — | — | — |
| Oklahoma | | | | | | | | | | | | |
| Don Nickles | R | 14 | 46 | 1992 | unopp. | 58.5 | 88 | 94 | 25 | 5 | 100 | 95 |
| James M. Inhofe[c] | R | — | 60 | 1994 | 78.0 | 55.2 | 97 | 99 | 45 | 0 | 100 | 96 |

*(Table continues)*

**Table A-4** *(Continued)*

| | | | | *Previous Senate election* | | | *1994 Voting ratings* | | | | | |
|---|---|---|---|---|---|---|---|---|---|---|---|---|
| *State, senator* | *Party* | *Years of service*[a] | *Age* | Year | Primary (%) | General (%) | *CC* | *PU* | *PS* | *ADA* | *ACU* | *ACU* (career) |
| Oregon | | | | | | | | | | | | |
| Mark O. Hatfield | R | 28 | 72 | 1990 | 78.0 | 54.0 | 34 | 34 | 77 | 80 | 29 | 26 |
| Bob Packwood | R | 26 | 62 | 1992 | 59.1 | 52.1 | 47 | 63 | 55 | 50 | 67 | 42 |
| Pennsylvania | | | | | | | | | | | | |
| Arlen Specter | R | 14 | 64 | 1992 | 65.1 | 49.1 | 61 | 56 | 56 | 55 | 46 | 39 |
| Rick Santorum[c] | R | — | 36 | 1994 | 81.0 | 49.4 | 94 | 83 | 56 | 15 | 81 | 79 |
| Rhode Island | | | | | | | | | | | | |
| Claiborne Pell | D | 34 | 76 | 1990 | unopp. | 62.0 | 28 | 92 | 98 | 95 | 0 | 7 |
| John H. Chafee | R | 18 | 72 | 1994 | 69.0 | 64.5 | 42 | 46 | 80 | 65 | 30 | 28 |
| South Carolina | | | | | | | | | | | | |
| Strom Thurmond | R | 40 | 92 | 1990 | unopp. | 64.0 | 97 | 93 | 39 | 5 | 96 | 90 |
| Ernest F. Hollings | D | 28 | 73 | 1992 | unopp. | 50.1 | 71 | 80 | 86 | 50 | 22 | 0 |
| South Dakota | | | | | | | | | | | | |
| Larry Pressler | R | 16 | 52 | 1990 | unopp. | 52.0 | 84 | 89 | 34 | 0 | 96 | 78 |
| Tom Daschle | D | 8 | 47 | 1992 | unopp. | 64.9 | 38 | 91 | 94 | 80 | 4 | 14 |
| Tennessee | | | | | | | | | | | | |
| Fred Thompson | R | — | 52 | 1994 | 62.0 | 60.4 | — | — | — | — | — | — |
| Bill Frist | R | — | 42 | 1994 | 44.0 | 56.4 | — | — | — | — | — | — |

| | | | | | | | | | | | | |
|---|---|---|---|---|---|---|---|---|---|---|---|---|
| Texas | | | | | | | | | | | | |
| Phil Gramm | R | 10 | 52 | 1990 | unopp. | 60.0 | 93 | 94 | 36 | 5 | 100 | 96 |
| Kay Bailey Hutchison | R | 2 | 51 | 1994 | unopp. | 60.8 | 94 | 94 | 38 | 10 | 96 | 95 |
| Utah | | | | | | | | | | | | |
| Orrin G. Hatch | R | 18 | 60 | 1994 | unopp. | 68.9 | 94 | 95 | 37 | 5 | 100 | 93 |
| Robert F. Bennett | R | 2 | 61 | 1992 | 51.4 | 55.4 | 94 | 91 | 38 | 5 | 100 | 94 |
| Vermont | | | | | | | | | | | | |
| Patrick J. Leahy | D | 20 | 54 | 1992 | unopp. | 54.2 | 6 | 96 | 89 | 95 | 0 | 5 |
| James M. Jeffords | R | 6 | 60 | 1994 | unopp. | 50.3 | 25 | 32 | 79 | 85 | 12 | 25 |
| Virginia | | | | | | | | | | | | |
| John W. Warner | R | 16 | 67 | 1990 | unopp. | 81.0 | 84 | 77 | 60 | 20 | 80 | 78 |
| Charles S. Robb | D | 6 | 55 | 1994 | 58.0 | 45.6 | 45 | 82 | 85 | 60 | 12 | 25 |
| Washington | | | | | | | | | | | | |
| Slade Gorton | R | 12 | 66 | 1994 | 52.0 | 55.7 | 84 | 76 | 48 | 30 | 80 | 66 |
| Patty Murray | D | 2 | 44 | 1992 | 28.3 | 54.0 | 13 | 98 | 94 | 90 | 0 | 0 |
| West Virginia | | | | | | | | | | | | |
| Robert C. Byrd | D | 36 | 77 | 1994 | 85.0 | 69.0 | 69 | 73 | 74 | 75 | 40 | 28 |
| John D. Rockefeller IV | D | 10 | 57 | 1990 | 85.0 | 68.0 | 34 | 90 | 97 | 95 | 0 | 11 |
| Wisconsin | | | | | | | | | | | | |
| Herb Kohl | D | 6 | 59 | 1994 | 90.0 | 58.3 | 41 | 75 | 81 | 90 | 12 | 16 |
| Russell D. Feingold | D | 2 | 41 | 1992 | 69.7 | 52.6 | 9 | 84 | 65 | 100 | 4 | 8 |
| Wyoming | | | | | | | | | | | | |
| Alan K. Simpson | R | 16 | 63 | 1990 | 84.0 | 64.0 | 100 | 86 | 40 | 15 | 88 | 91 |
| Craig Thomas[c] | R | — | 61 | 1994 | unopp. | 58.9 | 97 | 92 | 42 | 5 | 89 | 87 |

*Note:* In compiling this table, the conservative coalition, party unity, and presidential support scores were calculated to eliminate the effects of absences, as follows: support = support/(support + opposition).

*(Notes continue)*

[a] Service beginning in or after November in a given year is not counted as a year of service.
[b] Richard C. Shelby switched from the Democratic to the Republican Party on November 9, 1994, the day after the election.
[c] These former House members are serving their first term in the 104th Senate. Their scores are compiled from votes in the 103d House.
[d] Ben Nighthorse Campbell switched from the Democratic to the Republican Party on March 3, 1995.
[e] Louisiana has a two-step election process in which candidates of all parties run against one another in a September primary. If no candidate wins 50 percent or more of the vote at that time, the top two candidates run against each other in November. If a clear winner emerges from the September primary, no candidates compete in the November election.
[f] Kent Conrad won a special election on December 4, 1992, to fill the seat formerly held by Quentin N. Burdick who died on September 8, 1992. Conrad had announced his retirement in April 1992, but decided to seek the open seat after Burdick's death.

*Sources: Congressional Quarterly Almanac,* various years; *Congressional Directory,* various years; *Congressional Quarterly Weekly Report,* various years; American Conservative Union; Americans for Democratic Action.

3S

# Index